"How did privacy policies become licenses to spy? And do we have any hope of effective data regulation? In vivid and accessible prose, *Industry Unbound* offers deep insight into contemporary corporate power to monitor workers, manipulate consumers, and influence governments. With a skilled attorney's understanding of contracts and statutes and a rigorous sociologist's command of empirical methods, Waldman tells a story of 'privacy professionals' who gradually accommodate themselves to surveillance capitalism. This brilliant book is a must-read for understanding the failures of contemporary privacy laws, and how they might evolve toward more robust protections."

Frank Pasquale, Professor of Law, Brooklyn Law School, and author of *The Black Box Society* and *The New Laws of Robotics*

"Ari Waldman peels back the curtain on internal privacy practices at the most powerful tech companies to reveal an alarming trend: Despite robust privacy programs, teams of employees devoted to protecting privacy, and significant laws and regulations requiring many internal measures to safeguard privacy, the reality on the ground is that these things are often failing. Waldman provocatively contends that corporate power turns compliance with even robust privacy laws into an often hollow exercise. As legislatures rush to pass privacy laws, *Industry Unbound* is a wakeup call that these efforts will not end the nightmare. This eye-opening and unsettling book is also constructive, as it offers productive recommendations for a new direction in privacy law. Lively, alarming, and insightful, *Industry Unbound* deftly unites theory, practice, and law. It is essential reading for anyone who cares about the future of privacy."

Daniel J. Solove, John Marshall Harlan Research Professor of Law, George Washington University, and author of *Understanding Privacy*

"Ari Waldman's powerful new book combines fascinating on-the-ground insights and a sharp critical eye to help us understand why, despite touted improvements in data protection, our privacy remains in jeopardy. *Industry Unbound* is clear, compelling, and essential reading for the personal data field and anyone who is concerned about privacy."

Woodrow Hartzog, Professor of Law and Computer Science, Northeastern University, and author of *Privacy's Blueprint*

Industry Unbound

In *Industry Unbound*, Ari Ezra Waldman exposes precisely how the tech industry conducts its ongoing crusade to undermine our privacy. With research based on interviews with scores of tech employees and internal documents outlining corporate strategies, Waldman reveals that companies don't just lobby against privacy law; they also manipulate how we think about privacy, how their employees approach their work, and how we use their data-extractive products. In contrast to those who claim that privacy law is getting stronger, Waldman shows why recent shifts in privacy law are precisely the kinds of changes that corporations want and how even those who think of themselves as privacy advocates often unwittingly facilitate corporate malfeasance. This powerful account should be read by anyone who wants to understand why privacy laws are not working and how corporations trap us into giving up our personal information.

Ari Ezra Waldman is Professor of Law and Computer Science at Northeastern University School of Law and Khoury College of Computer Sciences. A graduate of Harvard Law School and Harvard College, he also earned his PhD in sociology at Columbia University. He is a widely published and award-winning scholar and teacher focusing on the ways law and technology entrench traditional hierarchies of power.

Industry Unbound

The Inside Story of Privacy, Data, and Corporate Power

Ari Ezra Waldman

Northeastern University

CAMBRIDGE
UNIVERSITY PRESS

CAMBRIDGE
UNIVERSITY PRESS

University Printing House, Cambridge CB2 8BS, United Kingdom

One Liberty Plaza, 20th Floor, New York, NY 10006, USA

477 Williamstown Road, Port Melbourne, VIC 3207, Australia

314–321, 3rd Floor, Plot 3, Splendor Forum, Jasola District Centre, New Delhi – 110025, India

103 Penang Road, #05-06/07, Visioncrest Commercial, Singapore 238467

Cambridge University Press is part of the University of Cambridge.

It furthers the University's mission by disseminating knowledge in the pursuit of education, learning, and research at the highest international levels of excellence.

www.cambridge.org
Information on this title: www.cambridge.org/9781108492423
DOI: 10.1017/9781108591386

First published 2021
Reprinted 2021

Printed in the United Kingdom by TJ Books Limited, Padstow Cornwall

A catalogue record for this publication is available from the British Library.

ISBN 978-1-108-49242-3 Hardback

For GWL

CONTENTS

ONE BOOK IN ONE PAGE

This is a story about people, privacy, and power. It is based on nearly four years of interviews, surveys, field observations, and reviews of both public and confidential internal documents. Its central argument is simple: antiprivacy work is routinized throughout the information industry. The implications of this are profound: even those frontline workers who consider themselves privacy advocates are so steeped in antiprivacy discourses and so constrained by antiprivacy organizational structures that their work ends up serving corporate surveillant interests in the end.

To routinize surveillance, executives in the information industry use the weapons of coercive bureaucracies to control privacy discourse, law, and design. This works in two ways: it inculcates antiprivacy norms and practices from above and amplifies antiprivacy norms and practices from within. Tech companies inculcate corporate-friendly definitions of privacy. They undermine privacy law by recasting the laws' requirements to suit their interests. And they constrain what designers can do, making it difficult for privacy to make inroads in design. As this happens, corporate-friendly discourses and practices become normalized as ordinary and commonsense among information industry employees. This creates a system of power that is perpetuated by armies of workers who may earnestly think they're doing some good but remain blind to the ways their work serves surveillant ends.

This strategy facilitates data extraction while undermining individual, social, institutional, and legal resistance to corporate power. It can persist without buy-in from engineers and privacy professionals; it can persist even as they think they're doing their best. The results are bleak. The edifice of privacy law becomes little more than a house of cards. Resistance is necessary.

PREFACE

I get emails. Some of them are from corporations in the information industry. In the span of three months in 2018 (March through May), fifty-seven companies sent me fifty-nine different emails, almost all of which started with at least one of these statements:

We care about your privacy.
Your privacy is important to us.
We take your data privacy seriously.

Sometimes, they took my privacy "very" seriously. A few even said that my privacy was "very important" to them. One said, *Your privacy. We care.*

The flood of emails was anticipating the May 25 effective date of the European Union's new data protection law, and almost every company that had, at some point, collected data about me was making some changes to its privacy policy. But with each email, I rolled my eyes. The information industry – the ecosystem of for-profit companies that collect and derive some value from our data – has been playing fast and loose with our privacy for decades. So we can be excused a little incredulity when technology companies say they care about our privacy. Snapchat lied about the privacy features of its not-so-ephemeral ephemeral messaging service. Pokemon Go forced its users to disclose information it didn't need. Zoom's default settings gave third parties access to user information. Femtech apps extract data from their users without their knowledge. Uber designed its app so it could follow smartphone users even after they deleted the Uber app. In-home assistants like Amazon's Alexa listen when they're not supposed to. Google G-Suite is so invasive that the company had to be sued to stop it from stealing data from university

students. I could go on. No wonder studies show that few people would associate the words *very*, *important*, *seriously*, and *care* with tech companies' approach to our privacy.[1]

Why say you "care about" my privacy when you've been selling my data to third parties? Why say my privacy is "important" to you when your privacy policy allows you to do pretty much anything with almost any data you've collected about me? Why say you take my privacy "very seriously" when your data-for-profit business model shows that you don't?

And yet, these companies have been using those words for decades: in the press, in their privacy policies, in their statements before Congress, in legal arguments in front of judges, and in emails to their customers. The language persists even though many people think it's more halfhearted PR than anything else.

I read on. Thirty-three of the emails I received continued with some version of this:

> *At* [insert company name here], *you are in control.*

Another nineteen told me how:

> We want to give you the information you need so you can make the choices that are right for you.

Four sentences into a spammy email and I had the beginnings of an idea for this book. These companies and I are thinking about the words *care* and *privacy* in very different ways (and, for that matter, probably the words *very* and *important*). By *care*, they mean giving me control; by *privacy*, they mean giving me choices.

"We care deeply about privacy here," said a privacy leader at an invitation-only presentation about his company's recent technical work in artificial intelligence. When I asked him how a particular artificial intelligence (AI) product reflected the company's commitment to privacy, he said, "We are transparent about the information we collect and use to build these tools to make your life easier and help researchers do their job." A colleague of his in the audience added, "When we say we care about your privacy, we really mean that up and down the line. We're constantly thinking about ways of putting you in control of what information you want to share and what you don't, what tools you want and which you don't."[2]

I then asked an acquaintance who worked for Facebook at the time. Here's an excerpt of the exchange:

"Does Mark Zuckerberg really care about my privacy?" I asked.
He responded: "It's my job, and the jobs of a lot of hardworking people here, to make sure he cares about your privacy and to make sure we, as a company, do right by you and your privacy."
"Can you tell me what you mean by 'do right by you and your privacy' and what you do in your job to achieve that goal?"
"If you take a look at the privacy settings on Facebook, you see how much we've done to put you in control of what happens, both in what you see on Facebook and what happens to your information. We've closed those loopholes where your information is used without you knowing. Just last week, we," by which he meant privacy lawyers, "sat as a team to figure out what we could do better in a few specific areas, like with third-party apps and how we can stop the next Cambridge Analytica with better privacy protections."

He was referring to the scandal in which Facebook allowed a data analytics company working with a Republican presidential campaign to collect and analyze the personal information of more than 87 million users without them knowing, resulting in advertisements that suppressed votes, amplified scare tactics, and spread misinformation.[3]

"That's great. How are you approaching this work? What are some of the ideas you threw around?"
"It was easy for us to agree that the millions of people whose data was used without them knowing was a problem for us."
"But didn't Facebook's lawyers make the argument to the FTC that the 87 million people did consent to the use of their information when they signed up and agreed to the terms of service and privacy policy?" I asked.
After a period of silence, he responded: "Of course, we don't always live up to our standards, but who does? Do you?"

There's a lot in that short exchange, much of which we'll tease out in this book. In between a little defensiveness and a lot of well-timed deflection, there was insight. *It's my job*, he said, to get his company and his bosses to care about our privacy. Along with tens of thousands of other privacy lawyers, privacy professionals, and privacy engineers, it is his job to make privacy a priority. He

does that by thinking about ways to inform us about how Facebook is using our data, which reflects a particular value-laden approach to privacy with important implications for the rest of us. What he thinks and what he does matters when we're trying to understand the past, present, and future of privacy in an information age.

I rolled my eyes at corporations saying they cared about my privacy because I was focusing on the antiprivacy political economy in which all of these companies operate: informational capitalism. Informational capitalism refers to a system in which market actors commodify and extract profit from the personal data they gather about us, often without our knowledge. As they do so, Julie Cohen argues, they leverage legal tools to support their data-extractive business models and insulate themselves from liability, making the law complicit in the exploitation of our data for profit. Informational capitalism is a good description of the political economy of our time. It is therefore only rational to be skeptical when informational capitalists, especially those with checkered histories in the privacy space, profess to care about our privacy.[4]

A narrative of political economy frames – but does not fully explain – privacy's fate in informational capitalism. Systems of power need foot soldiers, whether they be true believers, mercenaries, or the merely complicit. What they think and how they do their work matters. And how they come to conceptualize their responsibilities requires us to study the link between law, organizational behavior, identity, performance, and science and technology. That's because the emails I received weren't written by an economic system or by the legal levers that perpetuate it. Nor were they written by faceless organizations we call Google or Facebook. They were written by people doing the jobs they were hired to do. These real people made the choice to use language that they ought to know makes us roll our eyes. Why would they do that? What's really going on here? More to the point, how does a regime of informational capitalism somehow result in fifty-nine emails that all use roughly the same hard-to-believe line?

Of course, we're not just talking about emails. We're talking about what I'll call the social practice of privacy law: the behaviors that implement privacy law on the ground. We're talking about how compliance professionals construct organizational systems and how engineers translate legal requirements into code, about the

arguments lawyers make in court and the counsel they provide in house, about the defaults on the smartphones we buy and the data collection going on in the background while we browse the internet, about the design of "smart" devices in our homes and the tools we have to protect ourselves. We're talking about how it all fits together into a system of corporate power that is taking away our privacy.[5]

This is a story about how companies *do* privacy. And it turns out that saying "We care about your privacy" or "Your privacy is important to us" is not an isolated email from a bad PR team. It is, I argue, a product of the routinization of antiprivacy norms and practices throughout the discourse, law, and design work of the information industry.

The risks to our privacy are so deeply embedded in the organizational, day-to-day practice of the information industry that even those people who say they truly care about our privacy are doing work that serves surveillant ends. Rather than pushing their companies to do better, something I have no doubt some of them hope to do, they often become unwitting accessories to a data-extractive business model they cannot escape. If you're wondering how an anodyne email that most of us deleted immediately is part of that story, read on.

Industry Unbound unearths what privacy scholarship has been missing: a portrait of the social practice of privacy in the political economy of informational capitalism. That portrait is one of corporate decisions constraining and influencing the rank and file and routinizing antiprivacy work, the performance of which normalizes it as the best and most commonsense approach to privacy. When this happens, the social practice of privacy law seems real to those performing it, but it really is just an act. Corporate surveillance is routinized and normalized. Privacy doesn't have a shot.

INTRODUCTION

We are told by companies, by lawmakers, and by civil society that privacy law is getting stronger. The European Union's General Data Protection Regulation (GDPR) has been called "comprehensive" and "one of the strictest privacy laws in the world." Between 2018 and 2020, nine proposals for comprehensive privacy legislation were introduced in the US Congress; two ballot initiatives and forty-two proposals were introduced in twenty-eight states in that same time. Several of those became law, including the California Consumer Privacy Act (CCPA). The Federal Trade Commission (FTC), the de facto privacy enforcer in the United States, is putting limits on the collection, use, and manipulation of personal information with unprecedented billion-dollar fines. The US Supreme Court has started to reclaim the Fourth Amendment's historical commitment to curtailing pervasive police surveillance. And the European Union's Court of Justice has challenged the cross-border transfer of European citizens' data, protecting the privacy of European citizens in the process.[1]

Even the information industry – the ecosystem of companies that collect, process, and use our data for profit – seems to be getting on the privacy bandwagon. Apple markets its iPhones as privacy protective. Facebook, today's dominant online social network, promises to build a future of "private, encrypted messages." Google "build[s] privacy that works" for us. These tech giants, and many far smaller ones, have spent millions of dollars and hired thousands of privacy professionals, privacy lawyers, data protection officers, and privacy vendors. Even some software engineers,

historically not known for their concern for privacy, are coming to work recognizing that they have to do better to protect our privacy.[2]

These workers are at the front line of the social practice of privacy law, by which I mean the practices, behaviors, and performances that implement or navigate privacy law and privacy design on the ground. They write policies, interpret and apply the law for their employers, translate legal requirements into technical specifications, set up internal systems, write litigation briefs, build products, consult with coders and programmers, coordinate across departments, conduct internal assessments, manage audits, answer questions about privacy, and then some. When you talk to them, read their resumes, or scan their profiles on LinkedIn, they will tell you they are "committed" to privacy. Many are eager to "work with companies who care about" making "data protection a central part" of their business. Privacy professionals are focused on helping "businesses manage privacy risks" and dedicated to "compliance done right." Privacy engineers are committed to "bringing privacy into design."

And yet, every day, our privacy is slipping away. Face surveillance, DNA-testing kits, "smart" devices, gratuitous location tracking, and manipulative "dark patterns" are increasingly commonplace. Platforms like Google, Facebook, Snapchat, Pokémon Go, and Zoom, not to mention in-home assistants like Amazon's Alexa, are designed without our privacy in mind. Other products – like Uber's mobile app – were maliciously designed to invade our privacy, while social platforms like Facebook are designed to manipulate us into disclosure. Despite repeatedly promising to do better after privacy scandals, muckraking investigations revealing invasive designs, and a growing backlash to surveillance practices, very little has changed on the ground. There are some bright spots: Mozilla's Firefox, the DuckDuckGo search engine, the Signal messaging app, and Apple's decision to notify iPhone users when geolocation tracking is on. But these are exceptions, not the rule. Our websites still track us. Our apps still follow us. Our choices are limited. Our privacy is disappearing.[3]

Microsoft may have an experienced privacy team, but Windows 10 gathers information about us when we use its apps and when we browse the web, tracking our locations, our various machines, our home, our place of work, and our travel routes. Google makes much of its integrated approach to privacy (as have scholars),

but the company's suite of products are data collection juggernauts. Google has been sued for its surveillance overreach in tracking university students but only because the company's practices violated a contract, not because they violated privacy law. And Facebook, a repeat offender in the privacy space, tracks not just our interactions on Facebook, Instagram, and WhatsApp, but almost everywhere else on the internet. The information industry is one big surveillance machine with powerful financial interests in commodifying our behavior. And it designs products to serve those interests.[4]

We have opposing interests. Some of us want to remain obscure from prying eyes and share intimate secrets with our families, our friends, and even strangers, all interests that are weakened by widespread surveillance. We want to make free and autonomous decisions and not be coerced by deceit or hidden manipulation. We have interests in equality and social justice that are undermined when our data is used to discriminate. And yes, although we also have interests in frictionless access to platforms that let us socialize or buy the products we need and we don't all think about privacy the same way, we all have individualized, collective, and dignitary interests in privacy that sometimes run counter to the data-hungry interests of the information industry.[5]

The Questions

How can privacy law and corporate commitments to privacy be on the rise without it having a significant effect on the designs of new technologies? We are supposed to be protected by privacy laws. Are they ineffectual? Are they not being enforced? Are they not even being implemented? We are supposed to have privacy advocates on the inside: armies of privacy professionals, privacy lawyers, and privacy engineers that are supposed to be changing the corporate culture. Are they all just marketing gimmicks? Are they undermining our privacy while misleading us about their privacy work? Are their employers' promises about doing better hollow? And what about laws like the GDPR that explicitly rely on in-house privacy professionals to do the ongoing work of interpretation, monitoring, and compliance? Is this approach to privacy law at all effective?

Stories about good versus evil are frequent in fiction, yet rarer in reality. It would be easy to dismiss corporate surveillance as

the product of greed. And don't get me wrong, there *is* greed. A lot of it. But far more complicated structural and subtle forces are at play. Greed, for lack of a better word, is a bad look. Data-extractive capitalists who brag about how little they care about privacy are pilloried in the press. Even more importantly, greed cannot be the only motivator when there are armies of privacy professionals working inside technology companies with the earnest goal of protecting privacy. What's more, law is supposed to rein in the excesses of capitalism. But privacy laws on the books are not being translated into privacy protection on the ground. I went inside the information industry to explain why.

This book is about how actors in the information industry *do* privacy, or more specifically, how they can earnestly say they care about our privacy while simultaneously undermining it in practice. It focuses on what companies and their employees do behind the veil, behind the marketing, and behind the puffery when they actually translate the requirements of privacy law into their legal, organizational, and discursive behavior.

My findings are based on nearly four years of fieldwork, including interviews with current and former employees of large and medium-sized technology companies, interviews with start-up entrepreneurs and their venture capital backers, surveys of privacy professionals and software engineers, inductively coded analyses of industry literatures, interviews with in-house lawyers and their colleagues in private practice, reviews of internal protocols and procedures, analyses of legal arguments and public statements to legislative bodies and the press, observations of design processes, and listening and learning from those doing the work of privacy on the ground. The book consciously attempts to understand social phenomena from the ground up. And to do so, it relies on a diverse, interrelated set of conceptual models from law and the social sciences, including Foucauldian discourse theory, actor-network theory, science and technology studies (STS), performance theory, and critical sociolegal studies. I went into this project with an open mind, conscious that the truth always lies somewhere between cartoonish villainy and false heroism.[6]

The information industry often presents itself as contrite and dedicated to doing better at taking its privacy responsibilities seriously. Privacy scandals and new statutes trigger earnest

rethinking among lawyers, privacy professionals, and technologists. Policy makers have passed new privacy laws that do more than require privacy policies that no one reads. But this work rarely has more than marginal effect on technology design. Why?

The Argument

The organizational, technological, and discursive system is stacked against privacy. Our privacy is at risk because of two related social forces operating within the information industry: coercive bureaucracy and normalizing performances. Tech companies use the tools of coercive bureaucracies to routinize antiprivacy norms and practices in privacy discourse, compliance, and design. Those bureaucracies constrain workers directly by focusing their work on corporate-friendly approaches to privacy. As information industry workers perform these antiprivacy routines and practices, those practices become habituated, inuring employees to data extraction, even as they earnestly profess to be privacy advocates. The result is a system in which the rank and file have been conscripted into serving the information industry's surveillant interests, and in which the meaning of privacy has been subtly changed, often without them even realizing what's happened.

Coercive Bureaucracy

Norms and routines inside corporations are the products of several internal and external influences. Situated within a socio-legal context, corporations are influenced by the web of laws, court decisions, rules, and real and threatened litigation and investigations that constitute the regulatory environment in which they, and their competitors, operate. They are also influenced by public opinion, market forces, and the behavior of their competitors. As a collection of individuals, corporations are also influenced by endogenous factors, including corporate structure and the embodied experiences of the real people doing the real work in the company's name. Of course, many of these influences overlap, but each works together to develop routines and embed norms throughout the corporation. Given this, some corporations inside the information industry work hard manipulate law, scholarship,

structure, and the workplace experience to embed antiprivacy norms and routines wherever they can.[7]

When privacy professionals and privacy lawyers approach their work, they do so with background assumptions and understandings about what privacy means and how to protect it. Those ideas are heavily influenced by the values of informational capitalism. Industry leaders seek to influence how we think about privacy not just to erode our interest in and capacity to enact robust privacy laws, but to entrench corporate-friendly ideas as common sense and mainstream among their workers. This is the power of *discourse.*

The dominant privacy discourse today, from Silicon Valley to Washington, DC, centers around notions of choice, consent, and control; in other words, that privacy is about making our own choices about what to disclose, when, and to whom. It is a vision of privacy so narrow that it allows companies, their employees, and their allies to honestly say they care about privacy and still do little to improve privacy protections for their customers. But when you talk to people on the ground – the privacy professionals, the privacy lawyers, and the public policy shops – their independent self-reported views on privacy, though rarely hostile to corporate interests, are far more diverse than the party lines. Yet, few of those pro-privacy voices have any impact where it matters. In legal briefs, public reports, new products, press comments, and in testimony to Congress, discourses that protect corporate interests remain dominant.[8]

That is because tech companies use subtle and, at times, invisible strategies to silence pro-privacy voices and channel their employees' work to suit their ends. Industry executives set agendas for their privacy teams, require prepublication approval of academic research, control academic discussions through external funding of research, threaten researchers with restrictions on future access to data, and perpetuate false narratives about the efficacy of data-hungry AI tools. Lead in-house counsel and partners at private firms help determine legal strategies based on myopic definitions of privacy and enlist their subordinates in the effort while systematically denying them opportunities to voice alternative viewpoints. At the same time, many employees have internalized corporate cultures that encourage, value, and reward deference to leadership. This pushes them to incorporate the views of their bosses into their own,

marginalizing their own views in the process. Together, these discursive tactics inculcate tech company workers with notions of privacy that perpetuate corporate power.

With these ideas in place, privacy law is undermined by narrow definitions of privacy that put few obligations on companies to actually protect privacy. And the privacy professionals on whom we depend to implement the law on the ground are so steeped in corporate-friendly privacy discourses and constrained by organizational structures that they end up weakening the laws we have even further. This is the power of *compliance*.

The newest privacy laws and proposals, from the GDPR to the CCPA and the roughly fifty new proposals for comprehensive privacy law in the United States, rely on internal organizational structures for implementation and ongoing monitoring. It reflects an incomplete form of collaborative or "new" governance. Reviews of these compliance structures, interviews with privacy professionals and lawyers, and observations of compliance operations in practice suggest that the largest and most entrenched companies in the information industry have built a house of cards of compliance structures. Tech companies make it look like they are following the law, but in truth, they are reframing it to achieve their own data-extractive ends. This happens in part organically. If you filter legal requirements through a corporate or managerial lens, you're going to get corporate and managerialized law. Management amplifies these effects by subtly manipulating and undercutting privacy professionals, reallocating budgets away from privacy, placing privacy advocates in stifling reporting hierarchies, siloing their departments, and leveraging workplace pressures and threats to silence pro-privacy voices.[9]

It is in this environment that the information industry designs its data-extractive products. When we share images with our friends on Instagram, buy products on Amazon, or conduct teleconferences on Zoom, we do so on their terms, not ours. Companies use this power of design to serve their data collection goals while making it difficult for us to realize our own privacy preferences. They build products that collect information without any benefit to us. They gather data from our clicks, our browsing, even where we move our cursor. They trick us into sharing information, hide opt-out buttons, make privacy navigation inordinately difficult, and trigger cognitive biases that constrain our choices.

It's fashionable to blame engineers for all of this; technologists are not trained to think about or design for privacy. That may be true, but programmers also work within corporate hierarchies that constrain and channel their work. Their work is just as much the product of manipulative social structures within organizations as it is the product of code. This is the power of *design*.

There are undoubtedly software engineers and compliance professionals and lawyers who are not only indifferent to privacy but see it as an impediment. The real story, however, is more nuanced. Corporate power over law and design processes means that companies can leverage internal organization, hierarchies, and policies to systematically devalue privacy and maximize data extraction in how they interpret the law and how they design new products, making antiprivacy designs more likely. Within this structure, even those software engineers and privacy professionals aware of their power and cognizant of privacy issues would nevertheless have a hard time pushing back against privacy-invasive corporate behavior. The result is a process that makes it difficult for privacy to establish a beachhead in design.

At the heart of this story is something more dangerous than mere bad faith: By influencing privacy discourse, undermining privacy law compliance, and constraining design processes, tech companies have not only unshackled themselves, they have created a corporate culture and environment in which all work, regardless of worker motivations and intentions, serve corporate antiprivacy goals. And the law not only allows this; it explicitly welcomes it.

Normalizing Antiprivacy Practices among Privacy Professionals

Throughout my research, I was struck by a disconnect between the stated motivations of information industry executives and those of their employees. Leaders are primarily motivated by capitalistic interests, which are almost always data extractive and, therefore, independent of or in conflict with privacy. "Too much privacy," one head of product development told me, "means our products won't be able to give people what they want: access, fast access, convenience, connection, and fun." A start-up executive in New York admitted that "privacy isn't at front of mind when you're trying to make it, like make it in this business. Data means better

targeting, which means more money, and more investments. I need that data if I'm going to succeed in this environment." "Restrictive privacy law is bad for us," another executive admitted. These comments aren't isolated. Some information industry executives are on record asserting that privacy is in conflict with their businesses' success. Even those that recognize the importance of privacy do so in the interests of profit.[10]

But those doing the work of design and privacy law on the ground profess to find motivation elsewhere. Software engineers want to solve exciting engineering problems (even privacy ones!), to think of ways to make products more efficient, and to develop exciting new technologies; privacy professionals, for the most part, want to pragmatically facilitate privacy compliance. These motivations aren't capitalistic per se. They are technical, vocational, and careerist, just like many of the reasons we all go into our careers of choice. And yet, despite these differing motivations – some of which seem at odds with one another – the information industry realizes its surveillance goals in the end: Technologies are far more likely to ignore or violate our privacy than accommodate our interest in it.

The information industry perpetuates its power through a process of normalization. Tech companies focus their privacy work on narrow privacy discourses. They create compliance mechanisms that reduce privacy law to check boxes and outsourced technologies that allow industry to escape accountability. Companies then design new surveillant technologies while silencing pro-privacy voices. At each stage, corporate data extraction and the actions that facilitate it are normalized as ordinary and routine. With every privacy assignment focused on notice or security, employees become conditioned to thinking about privacy in narrow, underinclusive ways. With compliance focused on paper trails, checkboxes, and prefilled reports from outsourced vendors, privacy professionals come to confuse mere symbols of compliance with actual adherence to privacy law. And with every small engineering team focused on a narrow engineering problem, software engineers become accustomed to thinking that privacy is someone else's responsibility. These anti-privacy practices then become common sense for information industry employees, making it difficult for them to see privacy law as anything but what they have been doing.[11]

These practices are performative. By "performative," I don't mean that they're fake, ersatz, or cynical false fronts. They can be. But performances in this context are actions and behaviors that communicate something to the self and others. Performances are performa*tive* when their repetition and iteration socially construct and define our identities, our realities, and, I argue, privacy law. The social practices of privacy law feed and perpetuate themselves, constructing a reality where discourses of control and symbolic compliance *are* privacy law. And that's why they don't work. A regulatory regime that relies on regulated entities to flesh out the details of the law in practice performatively constructs a privacy law that is not only weak, but counterproductive. Symbolic compliance legitimizes what is really a con game.[12]

Privacy professionals, privacy lawyers, and software engineers perform privacy within constraining organizational bureaucracies. As they do, as they repeat practices described in Figure 1 that end up marginalizing privacy voices, their performances become routine, their routines become habits, and their habits become part of how they conceptualize privacy law. In other words, as they repeat corporate-friendly privacy practices, they normalize them and that normalization feeds back into a bureaucratic system built to drive corporate-friendly privacy discourses, compliance, and design. Therefore, our surveillant technological landscape is less the result of corporate shills than it is the product of organizational structures where antiprivacy work is habituated and normalized by ongoing performance.

Discourse	Compliance	Design
Discursive practices normalize corporate-friendly discourses of privacy – particularly, privacy-as-control – as common sense. These discourses form the backdrop for legal and technical work.	Constrained by corporate bureaucracies, privacy offices routinize compliance practices that normalize symbolic compliance.	With weak privacy discourses and symbolic compliance, bureaucratic practices not only take advantage of designer disinterest in privacy, but also remove opportunities for privacy entrepreneurship in the design process.

Figure 1 Privacy performances.

Resistances

Escaping from this status quo will not be easy. Privacy isn't naturally in the vocabulary of a capitalistic system in which information is profit. It would be easier if surveillance had a single cartoonish villain: Luke Skywalker had Emperor Palpatine, Sherlock Holmes had Professor Moriarty; Jerry had Tom. The information industry has its villains, but the problem is structural, political, and social. Silicon Valley CEOs willing to lie to and manipulate their users would be powerless without a friendly privacy discourse, an army of foot soldiers who ironically see themselves as part of the resistance, and a sociopolitical system conducive to corporate power.

Enacting new and radically different privacy laws is only the first step at solving this problem. We also need to expand what we mean by "privacy law." More than mere data governance, privacy law should be about the regulating the power structures of informational capitalism. That means we not only have to change how companies *do* privacy, but how public authorities and corporate power operate, how we relate to industry, and how the privacy and engineering professions approach their work and obligations. We need to change the external theoretical and legal environment in which data extraction occurs and the internal organizational and social experiences of those compliance professionals and software engineers who have the power to make or break the future of privacy. We need a privacy and engineering profession focused on its responsibilities to consumers, not to industry. We need new legal frameworks and a new regulatory boldness. We need a law and political economy approach to privacy.

The law and political economy framework refers to a way of thinking about the relationship between public governance and economic systems. It asks us to focus on the ways in which law and politics create economic power by making choices about winners and losers. We should not be fooled by the myths of the information industry; even today's self-regulatory approach is choosing winners and leaving the rest of us behind. I argue that privacy should be conceptualized, privacy laws should be written, and privacy organizations should be built expressly as counterweights to information industry power. Privacy discourses should be explicitly consumer-focused, built around notions of justice, equity, human flourishing,

and democracy. Privacy *is* power. As feminist scholars have taught us, privacy has long been used as a pretext to protect traditional hierarchies of power. Privacy also has a history of being less of a right for everyone and more of a benefit for the wealthy and privileged. No more. Privacy must be understood as a democratic tool of resistance to corporate power. Practically, that means privacy law will have to change. Rather than laying out the "rules of the road" that merely legitimize corporate data extraction, as it does now, privacy law should identify structural power asymmetries that give corporations too much power over individuals and deploy legal tools to combat that power. Organizations, including privacy civil society, privacy professional organizations, and higher education, should also be counterweights to information industry power, organizing and training a future workforce that fights for privacy.[13]

Structure of the Book

Privacy's otherwise robust research agenda pays insufficient attention to the dynamics of law's social practice. And yet the future of law and technology depends on real people and real organizations subject to exogenous and endogenous pressures and constraints. This book fills a void in law, sociology, and technology scholarship by identifying some of the sociopolitical reasons why our privacy seems to be slipping away. It highlights specific strategies leveraged by information industry actors to free themselves to design technologies as they see fit, all the while resting on the efforts of a sometimes-unwitting army of workers. My goal is to show how several overlapping stories – about how we think about privacy, how we write privacy laws, and how we design new technologies – are really a single narrative of power where, far too often, we lose our privacy. Ideally, this narrative is a wake-up call to those honest and hard-working professionals within the information industry, and I hope my macro and micro proposals are considered, studied, and challenged as we pursue a more balanced and normatively fairer relationship with technology companies. I also hope this book will spark additional research inside organizations that are critical to our future. Only then might we be able to escape this vicious cycle.

This book proceeds as follows. After this Introduction, Chapter 1, "A Day at the Office," provides a stylized narrative of

a visit to a technology company. The narrative is a compilation of events from the meetings I observed, interviews I conducted, and documents I reviewed, stylized into a chronicle of a single day.

The next several chapters provide an on-the-ground account of the information industry's privacy performances, highlight the ways in which technology companies stifle privacy and routinize antiprivacy work throughout their organizations. Chapter 2 focuses on discourse and the inculcative tactics management uses on its employees and the rest of us. Chapter 3 is about compliance and the organizational strategies companies use to ensure that privacy law is interpreted and implemented in ways that do not interfere with corporate data extraction. Chapter 4 zeroes in on the design process and describes how internal company policies make it difficult for designers to make the products they create more privacy protective. These chapters draw on my surveys and interviews with privacy professionals, lawyers, software engineers, and others, as well as legal briefs in privacy lawsuits, internal and public reports and other documents, articles in trade journals, and analyses of websites and industry webinars aimed at the privacy community.[14]

The final two chapters discuss the implications of performative privacy law. Chapter 5 shows why privacy professionals, lawyers, and engineers cannot easily escape the constraints placed upon them by their bosses, offering an account of bureaucratic power that may not be unique to tech companies, but is certainly playing out in force in the information industry. In short, it's not that people become privacy professionals, privacy lawyers, or software engineers to purposely undermine privacy and then lie about it. They often study privacy in school because they care about it, and then go into privacy jobs for the same reason. Prosaic pressures – to do well, to get promoted, to maintain access to bosses, to not get fired, to do what's asked of you – pressures we all face in the workplace, combine with management's stifling control of corporate bureaucracy do more work to sustain information industry power than active, overt, and malicious approaches to user privacy. That these pressures and bureaucratic levers will always exist in for-profit companies suggests that a data governance regime that explicitly depends on industry itself being an honest regulatory partner will always be insufficient. Despite this bleak view, Chapter 6 offers several avenues of resistance to corporate power, each of which will

require far more than the kind of window-dressing and marginal tweaks to which we have all come to accept with great resignation from the law. There are specific steps we can take about how we think and talk about privacy, how we write privacy laws, and how companies do the day-to-day work of privacy on the ground all focused on a progressive approach to privacy.

We close with optimism. Power may seem entrenched, but every relation of power creates its own opposite force, which not only gives us a roadmap for resistance, but also hope that we may, one day, succeed.

1 A DAY AT THE OFFICE

"New Forms of Encryption"

I arrived at 8:30 to begin observations and interviews, and was met by Bill, the company's chief privacy officer, a man in sneakers and jeans roughly in his mid-sixties.[1]

"We are thrilled you were able to make it, and we're excited to share with you what we've been working on in privacy," he said.

"Thank you for taking the time."

"We take our customers' privacy quite seriously here. I know everyone says that, but I like to think we mean it. I mean, they hired me, so it must mean the people in charge care about privacy. I've spent my entire career doing this work."

We walked to his office after passing through a security protocol he called "overzealous, but necessary."

"Ha! Which is it?" I asked, as he looked at me blankly. "I look forward to meeting everyone. Can you a tell me a little about yourself and your background?"

"I'm an electrical engineer and a computer scientist by training, degrees in both. I started out in systems design, but moved pretty quickly to privacy work."

"What kind of privacy work?"

"At my second or third job, so I was pretty young, I was responsible for overhauling the whole way the company kept customer information secure and protected. We were really conscious, not just of international hackers, but really of anyone, any criminal, who wanted to access the data. It made me think this was really important."[2]

"How did you move from an engineering job to privacy?"

"I realized that privacy was going to be important to every new business. Boom or bust cycles, it didn't matter. Privacy was going to be essential for business. There were a few colleagues I talked with."

He listed their names, all men.

"And we thought we should market our skills in this particular area. I went from there to [a larger company] that didn't just need a privacy overhaul, but also wanted to put policies in place to make sure things worked even after we all retired and new kids came in. It was at that point that the job became less about privacy design and more administrative."

"I want to get to that, but can you tell me a little more about what you mean by 'privacy design' work, before you moved on to administration. I'm not an engineer or a computer scientist, so I just want to make sure we're on the same page, if that's cool."

"Sure. I'll give you a really clear example. I can't remember when this happened, but it was early on, probably after the early 'dot com' bubble, about the year 2000. [The company] was looking ahead and collecting more data than it had before. Things were definitely moving in the direction we see them today. . . . But we wanted to do it respectfully and properly and not run into problems. We took a page from other sectors and worked hard to find new forms of encryption that really hadn't been around before. Not saying we made up new math, but we got creative and innovated ways to encrypt all our customer data."

"So, you . . ."

"It's a perfect example of how demands for privacy can be good for business. We were ahead of the game. We knew we needed to encrypt the data so people would trust us, so we came up with new ways of doing it. My team was at the center of that."

"Could you describe your privacy work outside of encryption?"

"Oh, of course that's not all we did. We anonymized data because you can do a lot with anonymized data. No one needs the name. You don't need all this personal information to succeed. You take the data and make conclusions based on the inputs. If you anonymize the data, it protects everyone. Early on, we were one of the first, and we came up with the standard, the anonymization techniques that a lot of people used. Of course, it's all so much better now. In this business, a handful of years is enough to be made obsolete."

"You mentioned a bit ago that your job had become more administrative. Can you explain that in a little more detail?"

"Well, now I have staff, I hire people, and not just programmers and other software engineers. I also work with these teams to write policies about how privacy work should be done going forward. We've put into standard procedure things like encryption standards, we implement NIST [the National Institute of Standards and Technology] guidelines, and put in place new protocols to make sure nothing goes wrong. I'm in charge of writing all the rules and monitoring how privacy is done inside these walls."

"What's your reporting structure? Above and beneath you?"

"I report the Chief Risk Officer and also work closely with Chief Technology Officer and the General Counsel."[3]

"Do you have a direct supervisor? Are you on the same level as the CTO and GC?"

"We're a little more informal here, but technically, the Chief Risk Officer is my direct report. In terms of 'on the same

level,' if you mean on the org chart, yeah, but you may get a different answer from [the GC] and [the CTO]." He laughed.

"Why do you laugh?"

"Oh, just corporate politics. It's everywhere. I think one thing you'll learn is that nothing is as simple as an org chart. The GC makes decisions about how we work with outside counsel, how we interpret and implement new privacy laws and consent decrees. The CTO makes decisions about how we use vendors and technological tools to protect our and your information."

"What does that leave to you?"

"I'm in the middle. I make it all work. I make us work together and help those guys make sure we're thinking about privacy."

A young lawyer knocked on the open door and introduced herself. "I'm going to be your guide for part of the day. It's such a pleasure to meet you."

The "Broteam" Meeting

We walked through the halls to an enormous, floor-through open-plan workspace with different clusters of computers. This was just one floor for the company's employees. Rows of computers ringed the office at the outer edge. A walkway separated those workspaces from inner workspaces, where I found the legal department, the risk group, and others. Conference rooms, with their schedules posted on small computer screens next to each door, were at the center of the floor.

My host led me into a conference room. The scheduled meeting, called "Broteam," was about to begin. Within several minutes, six young men walked into the room. I introduced myself, showed my visitor badge, and sat in the corner. My host joined me. All six of the meeting participants were software engineers; one was also a product manager.

"This is Ari, and he's a professor," said the meeting's leader, a product manager named Anthony. "He's signed the

confidentiality agreement, so don't worry about what you say in this meeting. I'm sure someone from legal will go after him if he published something he isn't supposed to." The last line was said with a little bit of a laugh.

"Can we make this quick? I've got several thousand lines [of code] to go through," said one of the meeting attendees.

"We're here to just update everyone on where we are [on the mobile game] project. I know there's one issue we need to discuss. Joe, would you fill us in?"

"Yeah, account set up. We have options. ... How do we play this?"

Joe went through several technical approaches to how users would set up an account to play a new mobile game. They were considering using email sign up, logging in through Facebook and Google, guest log ins without a full account set up, no log in at all for anyone, and several other options. They also spoke about the advantages and disadvantages of each:

"So, the benefits of this one is it's easy. Click here and you can immediately sign in through Google and Facebook. This is also super easy to design. We could also have an option for an email. We have to decide if we want the experience to be different. We also have to decide what to do about ads based on this."

"No one is going to use this if we make it difficult to sign up and sign in. We have to make it easy, simple, and quick. Have you seen what [another company] does? Their interface is like the least intuitive. Super busy and people have to go through multiple screens to get to the game," said the most junior programmer in the group.

"What do they want?" asked one engineer of the product manager, referring to management.

"We've been given two goals: engagement is the first, sustainable growth is the second. I think we're set on the growth metric. Steven created a network of in-app purchases and a [fee-based, non–ad supported] version that

should work well. Engagement has to be in the background of everything we do."[4]

"So, we have to make this simple, then," said the young engineer. "If we have users sign up with their names, emails, have an account set up, we can gather data we need on the back end, connect with other platforms as necessary, and make it work on its own, through Facebook, whatever."

The group discussed technical matters for the next eight minutes. As for the account set up, they narrowed their options down to a "required sign in, with the option to use Facebook or Google or an email, with the key being a seamless process so there's no interruption in access anywhere." Anthony ended the meeting, and I walked with him to his computer.

"I was told you were going to ask me some questions about how we do things here. So . . . ask."

"I'm here to observe and interview some people, yes. How did you think that meeting went?"

"In and out, fine," he said. "They know what they have to do; it's a good group of guys."

"The word 'engagement' came up a few times. Can you tell me what that means in terms a layperson could understand?"

"Look, I don't have time to lay this all out for you. Engagement is use, it's the amount of time people use it, how much they use it, how often they click on what we want them to click on, how often they buy things. Engagement with the product."

"Got it. Is 'engagement' usually 'in the background,' as you said, of what you do?"

"Almost always, it has to be, or else what we build won't be successful, you know? We can't make it if people don't use our apps and if people don't use our apps, then we're all out of a job. I'm sure I could get another one, but that's not the point. Why be in business at all if we're not building things people will use?"

"You're a product manager," I said. "How do you make sure privacy issues get addressed? Let me ask that better. What have *you* done in the past to make sure the work you and your team are doing include privacy consideration?"

"What do you mean by 'privacy'?"

"I'm not normally here, so you wouldn't have had the benefit of asking someone from the outside what privacy means to them," I said.

"I mean, privacy is important around here. But I really have no idea what it means other than making sure everything we do is secure up and down the line. That's just what privacy is. Obviously, I can wrap my head around that. I trained for it. I've built things. I've done everything my team does now. But a lot of people talk about privacy and I don't always know what they mean."[5]

"So, based on what you think privacy means, what actual steps have you taken in your job here to make sure the products you and your team design have taken privacy into account?"

"Nothing goes out this door if it creates vulnerability. You probably don't want me to get into threat modeling. And we know that if a product we sell has problems – if people can steal information, if it's left unencrypted, if we store information in insecure ways or in unsecured places – we're going to hear from people about it. We take privacy very seriously."

"That's Usually Someone Else's Job"

I caught up with a team of software engineers stepping out of their own meeting in a nearby conference room. My host introduced us. "This is Ari," she said, "and he's doing some research on ... companies like ours. He's signed the confidentiality agreement. Do you have time to chat with him?" Three of us scheduled phone interviews in the future; one walked with me to his computer. His name was Gavin.

"What were you and your team working on in there?" I asked.

"We're building a photo sharing app. We have meetings constantly. I think a lot of people don't realize that. You're writing something up about this, right? Would you tell people that people like me (engineers) aren't always spending their days staring at computer screens? We spend more time in meetings that I can remember."

"I, too, have too many meetings, many of which could be emails, and many of which could be texts."

"Right? Anyway, you share photos with friends, right? We want to make that entire process better, more efficient, streamlined, super easy, like ordering food. You should be able to do everything you possibly want in one app. Now, people like you and I and celebrity PR teams use multiple apps to edit, design filters, even put text on top of pictures. What if you [could] create everything easily on your phone, like an artist? Well, that's what we were talking about."

"How do you get the app to talk to Instagram?"

"That's the easy part. Lots of apps do that." He went on for a few minutes describing how third-party mobile apps already integrate with Instagram and other platforms so you can upload edited pictures or other media. He then continued: "It's so efficient. That's the goal."

"What's the goal?"

"Apps should be efficient and not messy and give you what you want. If you want to upload touched up photos to Instagram and Facebook is not letting you do what you want, you shouldn't have to mess around with five apps or whatever. And when you do work with an app, that interface and the back end should be simple and efficient, no delays, no complex code."[6]

"When programs have to talk to each other, are there privacy issues you have to deal with?"

"That's usually someone else's job because I'm not super experienced in that area. Usually the way it works is that we

have a team working on a product. We bring different skills to the table, although when you work at [a place like this], everyone's a pretty good coder. Well, mostly everyone. Anyway, we each take a part or parts of the product and we work on it either by ourselves or in smaller teams. That depends on how many people there are. At this company, it's a mix. I used to work at [another company], and the process was different."[7]

"So you haven't done privacy work per se?"

"That's really for someone else to do. I don't know. It gets done, I'm sure. But I don't do it."

Another software engineer named Tom was sitting next to us as we spoke, and he chimed in. A young man, he couldn't be more than a few years out of college. Though he only mentioned he graduated from Stanford, he didn't say when:

"I've done some of that. I did it when I was an intern at [another big company] and then again between undergrad and grad school. It's a challenge, but a cool challenge that reminds you why you went to school for this. It's almost impossible to do what they want, though. I can't take this idea – privacy – and write code for it."

"Yeah, same," Gavin noted. "I'm not totally sure everyone means the same thing when they say 'privacy' or 'your privacy is important to us.' All I know is, as someone who's expected to write the damn code for these products to work, if you give me something that I can code for, I will do it, and I'll do it well and fast. But I don't know how to do the other stuff."

"I haven't done any privacy work here, though," Tom added. "There are definitely people whose job it is to do that."

"Could you offer a little more detail? What do you mean by 'privacy work'?" I asked.

"I think a lot of the bosses know people are big on privacy now," Tom said. "We can't do things like they used to. My generation isn't going to stand for it, in a lot of spaces. So,

the privacy people and probably some lawyers get together and write up these policies and rules about what we can and cannot do."

"What policies and rules?" Gavin asked. "I haven't seen anything like that."

"I haven't, either," Tom agreed. "But I know the privacy people write these rules and they have something called a privacy assessment or something. We've talked about them in meetings with our managers."[8]

"Did you ever have a meeting with legal?" I asked.

"Only when I got in trouble once," Gavin said.

"We're Almost Like Their Consultants"

I ate lunch in a conference room with three privacy lawyers and the chief privacy officer. They introduced themselves and shared a little about their background. The three lawyers had previously worked at private firms in three different cities in the United States. None of them thought they would go into the privacy field while they were in law school; they each became junior associates in corporate and transactional departments after law school, moving in house several years later.

"Did you take any privacy or 'law and tech' courses when you were in law school?" I asked the three lawyers.

"Nope," said Jamal.

"No," said Louis.

"No. They didn't have anything like that when I was in school," said Anita.

"I wouldn't have taken it anyway," Jamal added. "I don't really have a tech background and I think you'd need that."

"You don't," I said, "but that's another conversation. On that point though, you don't have technical backgrounds, none of you, right?" They nodded. "Yet you work at a tech company. Any concerns or issues there?"

"I don't know about the other people in the room," Louis said, "but a lawyer is a lawyer. I have expertise like the coders over there have expertise. I stay in my lane and they stay in theirs. I don't think I need a tech background to do this work."

"I agree," said Anita. "Though it's helpful when I do meet with one of my teams to be able to speak their language."

"You're right, Anita," said Jamal. "It's not always easy to do, though. They look at me like I'm from another planet, and in a way, I am sometimes. We use different words. We think about things differently. We obviously have different responsibilities."

"That raises an interesting question, though," I noted. "How does it work here? What is your relationship, when it comes to reporting, process, collaborations, whatever, with the engineering and programming teams?"

"I think each company does it differently," Louis said. "At my last job, which was at a much larger company, we were assigned to be the lawyers for specific teams working on specific projects. We called them our 'clients.' That was the culture. We were there for them, but just them. That makes sense at a big, huge company. Here, we're not as big, so there are only a handful of us. We're the only privacy lawyers, which I think is actually a lot for a company our size. So, we're basically the privacy people for all the products we make."

"What role do you folks play in the design of a product, from beginning to end?"

"Um, we don't design anything," Louis said.

"What do you mean by 'design of a product'?" Anita asked.

"From the time someone has an idea for a new product, a new app, a new device to the moment it gets launched, what's your role in getting that product out the door?"

"The tech boys do the building," Louis said. "We're almost like their consultants. They come to us when they have

questions and we do our best. Our expertise is knowing about all the privacy laws out there, and when they give us a problem or ask a question, we see how it might run up against or not those privacy laws. As you know, we're also constantly reading what the [Federal Trade Commission] says and what data protection agencies in Europe are doing."

Anita added: "That's about right. I wouldn't describe it exactly as a consultant, but more like a resource. We're here and we get stuff done, so they reach out to us when we're needed. A lot of my time, and I know it's true for you guys, too, isn't focused on the engineering teams, but also writing privacy policies, working with outside counsel, coordinating across business units when legal issues come up. We have a ton of nontech stuff on our plate even though we're privacy lawyers at a so-called 'tech' company."

"Can you talk a little about the 'privacy' side of your work?"

"Sure. One thing we do is work with outside counsel whenever there are problems, like security breaches."

"Yeah, that's right," the chief privacy officer chimed in. "I have a small team of privacy people who work with these great lawyers right here to notify people when something unfortunately has gone wrong. But of course, we're always trying to prevent that from happening in the first place."

"Yup, data breach notification statutes and working with our outside counsel is one part. We also parse FTC consent orders and European [data protection agency] reports, including everything published by the Data Protection Board, to see what the law really is out there. It's a lot of patchwork stuff, but you already know that."[9]

Anita added: "I'd say one of the biggest struggles there is getting [the CEO] to see and understand what's going on. When the law is clear – you have to notify these people within a certain number of days – it's easy. I tell [the general

counsel], he tells the CEO, we may have a meeting and we go to work. When it's a lot of this fuzzier stuff about best practices and recommendations from the FTC, it's hard to get him to embrace what we think he needs to do."

"Is that an ongoing struggle at work?" I asked.

"Yes, but that, I would say, is secondary to a bigger skill I've had to learn, which is when and how to say no."

"Saying no to your boss? About a product? To an engineer?" I asked.

"Really any of those. Here's the problem. You can't be the one saying no all the time. That's one of the reasons people hate lawyers so much. And being a Black woman who was one of the few Black women to graduate from [the law school], I know people have this attitude, especially toward people who look like me. If I say no too often, no one is going to listen to me anyway, especially when it matters most. If I'm the one who always gets in the way of what the engineers or the businesspeople or the sales guys want to do, I'm the bad bitch. And then, they ice you. They find a way to go around you, or to a colleague who undermines you. Or they start keeping things from you. This hasn't really happened here, but I've been in rooms where I'm the last one to know things because they purposely told me too late to do anything about it. I've learned I've had to figure out a way to make my voice heard when it needs to be heard. But I can't cry wolf all the time."[10]

"I certainly cannot know what it's like to be a Black woman in this space," said Bill. "But there is some truth to that for us all. I see myself as being the privacy voice, but lots of people think the privacy voice is getting the way. So, if the privacy voice keeps saying 'but what about this' or 'don't do it that way,' pretty soon the executives and the front-line engineers aren't going to listen at all. Anita used the word 'iced' and I think that's spot on. We can lose our access to the people we need to make a difference. We can lose out on budgets when we say no too much. It's a dance. And one of the skills I look for when we hire is the ability to walk that tight rope."[11]

"True," said Jamal. "We have to almost market privacy to our boss in a way that gets his attention. But it's not all that hard. We have best practices that have become standard in the industry. NIST standards are helpful. We do our best to interpret the law in a way that makes sense for our bosses and we make it doable for the business."

There was a long pause.

"What does that mean, though? 'Doable for the business'?" I asked.

"When I was at a firm, we told them what the law was and then they had to deal with it. Now, all the risk is on us. We have to not just identify the law, but we also have to get other people on board, and we have to, at the end of the day, make a profit for our shareholders. If we think the law says we have to change some tech practices, I need to get the CTO on board. He controls the budget and he ultimately decides what we do on that front, so I need to sell it to him that action is necessary. If I think I have a better argument we can make in an ongoing litigation, then I have to get my boss on board and maybe go against what outside counsel said. If we need to change technical specifications, wow, I have to get the engineers, the managers, their product managers all on board. I've learned that being in house is like translating a language we all know for people who have no idea what I'm talking about and don't want to know."[12]

"There's another piece to that," said Louis. "Our boss, [the general counsel], is really the main person responsible for deciding what we tell [the CEO] and others about what the law says we have to do. We are part of that process, but it's not like reading a case and saying what the law is like we did in law school."

"Oh, thank god it's not like law school!" said Jamal.

"It's about taking what we think the law states and translating that into terms our nonlegal colleagues can understand and terms that make sense for us as a business."

"You Have No Idea How Hard It Is"

My next meeting was with three privacy professionals: Bill, the CPO; Janice, whose title was Director of Privacy, and Lacy, a privacy analyst who had just been hired after two years working for Mozilla.

When I met her, Janice had been a privacy professional for "at least 20 years." I joked that she could be a CPO herself, which elicited a few awkward giggles from Bill. Though she is not a lawyer by training, Janice noted that she has "worked so many of them, [she] might as well be." She graduated from the University of California system and worked in compliance at a bank before "moving into the modern world and working for a tech company." She started as a "risk analyst and learned about privacy." She added: "For all I know, I was one of the first people to take the Certified Information Privacy Professionals exam. I mean, I don't think I really was. But I've been in this business a long time, and I love it."[13]

Lacy graduated from the University of California, Los Angeles, where they didn't offer a privacy course at the time, at least not to her knowledge. "I was interested in privacy because I got hacked as an undergrad. That was not fun. And literally no one was ever held responsible." She learned what it meant to be a "privacy professional" – she used air quotes four times – on the job.

> "Can you describe how your privacy office fits within this company's organizational structure?"
>
> "We're under [the company's] Risk Management team," Bill said, reminding me that he noted that when we first met.
>
> "Don't they have a new name for it now?" asked Lacy. "Something 'Risk Experts.'"
>
> "That was a rumor," Janice said curtly. They wanted to be more like those startups that call everyone 'ninjas,' which, I don't know about you, I think is really racist."
>
> "Anyway, yes, we're under the risk team. I report to the Chief Risk Officer, and these members of my team report to me," Bill continued. "It can be a little more complicated when we need to do certain things, though. Our compliance responsibilities are why we're in the risk group, but

sometimes, we need to do other things besides privacy impact assessments, which we can get to. Have you seen ours? Are you familiar with them? Anyhow, our budget is under risk, but our budget for legal is under the GC and our budget for tech is under the CTO."[14]

"Your budgets are split between three departments?" I asked.

"Not really. Almost everything, uh, we need to do is risk related so that's where our budget is. That's where our salaries are and such. But privacy technology vendors, that comes out of the IT budget. Legal counsel we might need comes out of the GC budget, obviously."

"Sometimes that's a struggle," Janice added. "It always has been. I remember a couple of jobs ago, we had a similar situation where I had to work with the IT guy, and it's a guy, yeah, to pay for a few things we needed to do, and he wasn't budging. It's part of the job to learn how to sell what you need to do to people who either always say no or just like to speak a different language than you."

"Things work pretty well here, though," Bill said. "We have a good working relationship."

"I agree," said Lacy. "It's our job to be the privacy voices inside the company and I was told early on that the best way to do that is to get everyone else on board, too. Use their language, use their needs."

"What are some of the struggles you face being the quote 'privacy voices' here?" I asked.

"I have the most experience, so I'll take that," Janice noted, with a laugh. "The biggest problem I have, and I have always had, it's not unique to [this company], is walking that line of being a privacy person and also being a counselor to the business. We really spend a lot of time trying to persuade our bosses that they should take this seriously, but we do it in a way that is attractive. It's tough."

"I'll agree with that," said Bill. "But there are definitely differences between companies. You can see how some take it seriously and some don't."

"What are some indications, in your experience, of companies that quote 'take it seriously'?" I asked.

"At [my last company], it was always a lot of reasons why not. And a lot of times, I wouldn't have a lot to do because they wouldn't give us work. Their approach was elsewhere. Here, I am so busy. The law has changed, too. The GDPR is a really strict and robust privacy law. You can tell: we're always working on things to do this better, always working with this amazing team. We churn out work product all the time. It's a big deal. It gives us a job! The CCPA, too. Every time the FTC gets involved, we have more work to do. It's great."[15]

"I'd like to add something." Lacy had been mostly listening and nodding up to this point. "I haven't been here that long. And I haven't been doing this precise work for that long, either. But I've had one big adjustment. It's how to know when to say no. You have no idea how hard it is being a privacy person when your business is data. It's almost weird. I never know if I'm stepping out too far or doing the right thing. I always ask Janice for advice and you, Janice, have been great."

"Thank you."

"But it's definitely not always clear what the right approach is. When a law says you have to notify users within ninety days, that seems clear. But even that requires us to negotiate with our colleagues. The CTO might want to word the notice one way; the GC another. That's not really a big deal, we have boilerplate. But think about risk assessments, which the GDPR is all about. We developed these risk assessment templates, and we talk often about whether something we do is going to open us up to litigation. There's a real pull against being cautious. And when do we put our collective foot down?"

"Have you ever done that? Have you ever stopped a product from going out?" I asked.

"I haven't," said Lacy.

"Me either," said Janice.

"But we could," said Bill.

"How would that work, practically?" Lacy asked.

"The key is making sure we don't have to stop a product from going out the door because we were involved from the beginning and guided it in the right way," said Bill.

"But have you ever done it? I repeated.

"No, not me. I personally haven't had a reason to. Everyone's been great," Bill said.

"Can you describe how you get involved early?" I asked.

"There are so many examples!"

"Can you share one? Without any proprietary information?"

"I was involved in the development of [a product]. One of the features they were discussing was how third parties would be able to access user profiles and information and app functionality. I'm no tech expert, but it was about the API. Anyway, I happened to be passing by the engineering team working on that stuff and we chatted for a little bit. They brought me up to speed on what they were working on. I told them, 'We need to make sure that people have a choice, right? Could you make it so they have the option to allow or not allow third-party access?' There was some hesitation among the group, so we pressed on and I asked about giving users' the option to log in differently, to decide for themselves if they wanted to grant Facebook access or if they wanted to keep that separate. We made progress there. That's what it's about, right? We worked to make sure people had a choice and some control over what information they were giving up. I was proud of that."[16]

"Not Having to Deal with That Was Totally Fine with Me"

Matthew, an engineering manager who was leading an artificial intelligence project, joined me in a conference room with

four of his team members: Alex, Max, Peter, and Spencer, all software engineers, all Stanford graduates.

"Did you know each other in school?" I asked.

"Alex and Peter did, but I was three years behind them, and I don't really like to socialize," Spencer said.

"Bro, we were just out at a bar last night until three," Peter reminded us.

"My name is Ari, and I'm here to learn a little bit about how you do your work. I'm interested in privacy-related things, and I'm not here for anything confidential or even the substance ..."

"Unless it's about privacy," Peter interrupted.

"I'll let you know if I'd like to go further based on your answer, but don't feel like you have to answer because ..."

"Good because that isn't really what I spend my time on," Peter again interrupted.

"What do you mean?"

"Privacy isn't my job. That's someone else's job. It's just not how it works. We focus on what we know, and I have a lot of expertise [designing games]. Our manager, Matt in this meeting, would give us an assignment to focus on. Usually, we need to design a piece of a larger project, or solve some particular cool problem, or go through lines of code looking for something, or fix some awful mess someone wrote years ago. I focus on that, it's what I'm told to focus on. And other people do other stuff."[17]

"We try to make everyone understand that privacy is part of everyone's job," Matthew added.

"Can I go now?" Peter asked Matthew.

There was silence. "I don't mind," I said. "Thanks for taking time out of your day.

"Later, bro."

I turned to Alex, Max, and Spencer. "Thanks for participating. I promise I won't take too much of your time. As I was saying before, I'm interested somewhat in what you do, but very interested in how things work around. What I mean is, could you tell me a little about what you're working on and how you go about it."

"I'm working on natural language processing," Max said.

"And me, I'm working with Matt," said Spencer.

"I'm building a new retail platform for customers," added Alex.

"We can't say much about our project," Matt added, "because we're trying to keep it under wraps, but it's pretty cool and we think it will be a game changer. It has to do with AI and photos."

"During any of your work on these projects, or since you arrived here, have you had much interaction with the privacy lawyers?"

"Legal gets involved when something goes wrong. Or when we do something wrong, right?" Spencer laughed. "Seriously, though, I know them. They sit on the other side of the floor, but we haven't been in meetings together. They're there as a resource for us if we have questions."

"What kind of questions?"

"Like if we're concerned about what data we're using," said Alex, "or if we're doing something that we think may be a problem for privacy, we ask."

"I've actually had more interaction with them, but maybe that's because I've been here a little longer. There's obviously onboarding, but that was like maybe an hour with someone, and a training. Oh god, the training. That was such a waste of time, but that's another story."[18]

"We can get back to that," I said.

"Right. What I was saying was that I've sent questions up the chain, from me to my manager, like Matt, and then it

gets to the privacy folks, I guess. Sometimes, I'll get one of them coming by my desk to answer a question I had or can just track them down. Helpful."

"I've had more meetings with them, probably because I'm a manager now," Matt added. "When you move up, a lot of your work becomes administrative, and it's kind of annoying sometimes, but that's how it works. But when I was sitting where these guys are now," as he pointed in Spencer and Alex, "it was pretty rare, and that's not just here. I was at two ... big Silicon Valley companies before this and even the big places, where there are tons of lawyers, we don't really see them. At both places, they were literally in a different building. Here, we're just smaller. I'm actually kind of surprised they're not on another floor!"[19]

"You're working on data-heavy projects. How do you integrate privacy into your work? Or do you?" I asked.

Alex responded first. "What do you mean by 'privacy in our work'?"

"I'll let you interpret privacy the way you see it," I said.

"I guess it can be a lot of things. I don't want to be using anyone's email address. And I'm sure people don't want their credit card passing by everyone's eyes."

"How does any of that get to be part of the work you do here?"

"We make decisions all the time about privacy," said Max. "We're the ones building these things, so we have to make decisions as they come up. Do we use this or that? What kind of encryption do we use? When do we use it? Is it enough that this data was anonymized? Will this be secure? We usually make those decisions in teams or with our manager. I'd rather it be people like me making those decisions than politicians. I hear all this stuff about regulating quote 'Big Tech' and forcing us to do certain things. But they don't have the expertise. They're going to tell us to do something that won't make sense. Privacy can stop stuff that could be useful. What if the law banned the technology we needed to detect breast cancer?"

"Sometimes we don't even get to making decisions. I can speak from experience at my first job," Alex added. "Bigger company, so we had teams of guys working on projects, but we got lists of things to get done, each of us. It was like we were each working on a part of a larger project, and we had a shit ton to do, all the time. My manager used to say, every time I would ask a question that wasn't squarely in my project, 'that's not your job.' I never took much interest in privacy until we were designing stuff for [a photo sharing app] and then it kind of just struck me. But it's not as if I could have done anything about it. It wasn't my job. I had my things to work on, people left me alone, I did the work, and I liked it. A lot of my colleagues didn't want to be bothered with this other stuff that isn't squarely in their wheelhouse, you know what I mean?"

"I think that's definitely a problem, generally," Matt added. "Which is one of the reasons why we have meetings with everyone. That's a lot easier to do at a smaller company."

"When I was at [another company]," Spencer said, "privacy was a department separate from us. We had to get privacy's approval for stuff, just like you had to run things by legal, by whatever. They were the experts on privacy, not us. So, we would run stuff by them and they would approve."[20]

"When in the design process did you quote 'run it by' privacy?" I asked.

"Tough to say, but I will say they never made me change anything too substantial. We were definitely later on in the process and I'm sure they didn't want to be the ones to stop [innovation]. Plus, it would be like forcing me to go back and do another thousand hours of work on something that was totally fine the way it was. I didn't mind. Them checking the box is something I needed them to do, and not having to deal with that was totally fine with me."

"What, if anything, would make it easier for you to address privacy issues as you're doing your work?"

"I think a better understanding of what they mean by privacy would be helpful," Spencer said.

"Some policies," Alex added.

"I'd love for people to stop giving me these pie in the sky ideas of what they want. I'm a software engineer here, right? I'm not a privacy expert. I'm a coding expert. Give me something I can code. If there is a rule that says we can't do this or that, tell me straight up and I will make it happen if the technology allows. But I watch *Law and Order*, when someone says, 'expectation of privacy,' which is probably how a lot of us hear about privacy, certainly not in school, I'm like, there's no way to code for someone's expectations. So, what am I supposed to do?"[21]

"You could . . ."

"There's no way to code ambiguity. Computers are shit at ambiguity. They're stupid. I have to tell it every single thing I need it to do."

"Transparency Is Important"

My last meeting was with four individuals in different departments. Natasha, a director of public affairs; Lester, the general counsel; Seth, Chief Risk Officer; and Elliot, the head of engineering who declined to give me his exact title.

"How has you day been so far?" asked Seth.

"Productive and really informative, thank you. It's great that we're ending the day here because there a few things only you folks could speak to."

"That's great," Natasha said. "We're really proud of work we're doing here. We know we have a lot of work still to do, but we're making progress in a lot of areas."

"What's the role of the public affairs office, here?" I asked.

"We work with people like you, with government officials, the media, and the public. We try to contribute to public debate about important issues. Issues that we care about and issues that are important to our customers."

"Can you give me an example?"

"We have an academics council, a fellowship program, and we like to invest in people who are going to help us, and yes, challenge us. We also have to do our best to make sure people like you and others in academia and in the media know the work we're doing here. We get a bad name sometimes, but that's to score political points. What's really going on here is different, I mean, real hard-working people are making things better, and it's my job to amplify their work."[22]

"Can you give me some examples of that in the privacy space?"

"Sure, we have some great experts here in privacy law and compliance. Lester and Seth can talk more about that. But it's my job to push out that work, to make sure we advise policymakers on how we welcome their input and the kinds of regulations that are going to make sense. We've done that at [congressional hearings]. And we work with regulators all the time. We are constantly being asked to help write and provide input for their reports. I help organize some of that, but a lot of it goes through legal."

"Is there one view here about what 'privacy law and compliance' looks like? By which I mean, do you fight it out in meetings about what this or that policy should be?"

"All the time," said Seth. "But we take our cues from the top. Lester and [our CEO] set the tone for our work. And we make sure we channel that into the work we do."

"OK, then, Lester. Can you describe how you set the tone for privacy work here?"

"Privacy is important to us. If our customers don't feel we're protecting their privacy, no one is going to do business with us. I think that's true up and down [the industry]. I make sure everyone understands that."

"Could you be more specific? I'm trying to understand what's behind the word 'privacy' when you take it seriously. If there's one thing I've learned from my work and even interviews today, it's that there are lots of different things people mean."

"Well, there isn't one definition of privacy, but we try to do what the law says we have to do. We're committed to protecting your privacy."

"When you say you're committed to protecting our privacy, how do you do that?" I asked.

"I'll give you an example."

"Yes, thank you."

"The customer is always in control of his data. To do that, we make sure we are up front about what we're doing and give them the opportunity to craft their relationship with us in a way that reflects their choices. I recently worked with [our outside counsel] to figure out how we do that in concert with the FTC's recent consent decrees."[23]

"Do you believe that people have a privacy interest in the information they disclose while using [your app]?"

"Of course. You share information with us, not with the government. And you share that information under certain conditions that we lay out in our terms of service. If we violate those terms, we are responsible. I am responsible, even. It's my job to make sure we stay with our commitments."

"But then could you explain why you, in a brief in [a privacy case in federal court], argued explicitly that users don't have privacy rights once they disclose information on [the app]?" I handed Lester a copy of a brief he signed.[24]

"We have a responsibility to zealously advocate for the company, and our outside counsel, who really wrote this brief, is hired to do just that. It's a reasonable argument to make as a matter of law, but we obviously go above and beyond the minimum we have to in order to protect the trust of our consumers."

"You make the argument a few times in several cases, though. It doesn't seem like you think people do have an expectation of privacy, which is fine if that's your position. I'm not challenging you. I'm trying to understand what you mean by privacy when you say people don't have it on [your app]."

"Wow, I didn't realize this was going to be an interrogation."

"It isn't, sir. I'm just trying to understand what you mean by privacy," I said.

"Privacy is about building trust with our customers by giving them control over what information they share."

"If I could just jump in here," Seth said.

"Yes, thank you," I said as I turned to Seth. Lester walked out.

"There is much more to our work here in privacy than the arguments we have to make in a brief. The GDPR, as I'm sure you know, gives companies like ours clear guidelines about what we have to do when we collect and process information. The requirements, from giving people access rights to privacy impact assessments, really push privacy into every corner of our business, and it keeps privacy front and center in our minds as we're doing our work. Legal briefs aren't the entirety of the work when it comes to privacy."

"Undoubtedly true. What's been the effect of the GDPR on the work you do?"

"The GDPR has certainly changed the way we do our risk assessments and our compliance work, to be sure," Seth noted. "For one thing, we're doing more and we're spending more. The GDPR has made privacy a requirement here, and I think, elsewhere. So we're now clearer on how we can assess the risk for any given product."

"How do you do that?"

"We have several ways of assessing risk. We consider what our liability would be if we design things in a certain way. If we have a way of designing something in way that would expose us to less privacy risk, we go ahead."[25]

"Thank you. I'm sorry, I interrupted you before. You said 'for one thing' and then were going to continue."

"Yes, thanks," said Seth. "We now work with a lot more vendors, these companies who have come in to help us meet our compliance obligations. Third, we have the ammunition, if you will, to go to other parts of the company to make them take privacy seriously. And we've created a lot of programs within the company to make sure people know what they have to do. We have a designated data protection officer, we have a standard impact assessment that people use. We worked with Elliot to help engineers consider privacy issues during their work, too."[26]

"Yeah, it was a really interesting project to work on this," Elliot added. "We were trying to translate privacy into some clear guidelines for those guys doing the coding work. They're the ones who are going to see these issues first, so we might as well make it easier for them. That's what privacy by design is all about, right?"

"I'll second that," said Seth. "If we could get our engineers to make the right privacy choices at the front end, we have nothing to worry about."

"How do they know what you guys mean when you say 'make the right privacy choices'?"

"There's an ethos here. There's a corporate culture," said Seth. "We aren't trying to be villains. We're the good guys, and I think everyone we hire reflects that. When engineers have questions, they can rely on our culture or just ask anyone. And we do a lot of work to push out to every employee our commitment to privacy and to protecting our customers' power to control what happens with their data. But that doesn't mean we don't also have policies."

"Can we return to the impact assessment or risk assessment? Privacy impact assessments are now required by the GDPR. What does a PIA look like here?" I asked.

"I'm not sure if we're allowed to show you, probably are, but, in short, we assess the risks of the data-related things we're doing," Seth said.

"What else do you do?"

"We do what the law requires of us. Impact assessments, designating privacy officers, keeping records, and so on. I mean, that's what the law is. It's what we do," Seth added.

"When I spoke to Bill earlier, he mentioned that there is a division of responsibility between the Risk department and the general counsel's office and the CTO when it came to privacy. Since Lester isn't here, could you describe that division, Seth?"

"Well, we do that because privacy is important up and down the line, so everyone has to think about it and get involved."

"Who is responsible for working with outside counsel?"

"The GC, of course."

"What about technology vendors who help with privacy compliance?"

"Bill does a lot of that through [the CTO's office]."

"What about litigation strategy when it comes to cases involving privacy?"

"I'm sure Lester consults Bill on that."

"Who handles compliance?"

"Bill's team."

"Who handles testimony and other communications with elected officials on privacy?"

"Usually it's an executive called in or we work with our partners in [a trade organization], a group we helped to found. We make sure we distribute our talking points to everyone working in privacy so the company is on the same page."

"I have here a redacted budget that Bill gave me, showing expenses and planned increases in all of these areas over the next few years."

"That's exactly right. Without getting into too much detail or into too many weeds, so to speak, we know this is going

to be important and increasingly important, so we're spending the money we need now and have been spending the money to prepare."

"But it looks like the budget is divided between four different departments. Why is that?"

"That's just how we do things, I guess."

"How Bad Can That Really Be?"

As I was leaving the meeting, and saying goodbye to my hosts, I found Lester, the company's general counsel, waiting for me at the elevator.

"I wonder if I could have a word with you," he asked.

"Sure thing. It's been a long day."

"I know we all appreciate you coming and hearing from us. I'm sorry I left the meeting so quickly. I had a few other meetings to go to."

"It's fine. I understand and appreciate the time you offered."

"I also wanted to add something."

"Sure, go ahead," as I took out my notes.

"Companies like ours, much less so than companies like Facebook, but still, the media makes us out to look like the bad guys in this space, privacy, that is. I just wanted you to know that we're doing our best. We know we're not perfect. But sometimes people hold us up to a standard that's just not obtainable in any real world and they're just trying to make us look bad. I hope you won't do that."

"I'm here listening to you. I'm not trying to do anything other than learn what really goes on when companies say they quote 'care about our privacy.'"

"I'll tell you what happens. These people come to work every day just trying to do a job. It can be high profile, but also really pretty mundane. You're a lawyer. You know

what being a junior associate is like, do you? Did you ever do any real work?"

"I think what I do now is real work, but if you mean was I an associate at a firm, yes, I was, for a total of four years."

"Well, yeah. People are just coming to the office to do their jobs. There's nothing wrong with that. Everyone deserves counsel, whether you're rich or poor, and I don't have to apologize for representing a tech company. It's not like I'm representing Big Tobacco or the NRA. All we do is build these really exciting and fun digital tools for people to use. How bad can that really be?"

2 PRIVACY'S DISCOURSES

Privacy's performances begin with discourse. This is an important step. By influencing how we think about privacy, by inculcating definitions of privacy that are so narrow, outdated, and corporate-friendly, tech companies can ensure that even those employees who consider themselves privacy advocates will nevertheless end up serving data-extractive business models in the end.

As we saw in the last chapter, many people I spoke to talked about the importance of privacy. The discourse of importance did not surprise me, nor should it surprise anyone who has received an email from a company letting us know that they've updated their privacy policies. "Your privacy is important to us," and, "We care about your privacy" are likely the single most commonly used corporate privacy talking point. But the discourse's uniformity and frequency were striking. Everyone used the exact same words, and most of them used those words toward the beginning of our conversations or in response to a difficult question. Even more important, though, was that privacy's importance was independent of privacy's meaning.

Bill talked about encryption when I asked him about his privacy work. Anthony, the product manager and former engineer, wasn't sure what privacy meant, but when pressed, he spoke about cybersecurity. Tom spoke about how he "did some of that" privacy work, but noted that it was difficult to "code for" something like privacy. Several of Anthony's engineers, some of whom missed privacy issues as they discussed account set up, may not have had a conception of privacy in their minds at all. But those that did slipped between privacy and security. That slippage was common,

though certainly not universal, among professionals with technical backgrounds. They would use the word "privacy," but it was clear from their discussion that they were talking about keeping data secure, preventing leaks and hacks, and the other aspects of systems security that they were taught in school.

Others thought privacy was about making choices to disclose information to others. Lester spoke of transparency. This too was common among many of the privacy professionals I interviewed for this project. Some interviewees suggested that privacy was about gaining people's trust. There were other definitions as well. The word "privacy" was also accompanied by other empty vessel terms and phrases like "doing it properly" and not wanting to "run into problems." But, at least in Bill's case, he may have been using the language of privacy, but he was talking about how he "innovated ways to encrypt" the data he held.

Privacy, of course, is not the same as encryption or security. Nor should privacy be limited to choice or control or transparency. But these narratives of privacy are relevant because what these people think about privacy matters. If they think their privacy responsibilities end at encryption, technology designs will look different than if they were concerned about data processing. It is no accident that privacy-as-security and privacy-as-choice were common privacy definitions among information industry employees. Conceptualizing privacy in these ways is both a direct result of corporate inculcative behavior and an important factor in surveillant designs.

Tech companies inculcate definitions of privacy that are so narrow and corporate-friendly that they end up serving as facades for data extraction. There are, undoubtedly, numerous discourses at play in informational capitalism; these discourses valorize innovation as a normative good and decry regulation as stifling and strangling, elevate the importance of free speech while ignoring its effects on equity and justice, and laud freedom and autonomy while triggering xenophobia and hate. Julie Cohen has described how these discourses come together to immunize the information industry from public and legal accountability. This chapter focuses squarely on how discourses of privacy – specifically privacy-as-choice or control, or that privacy as the ability to make fully informed decisions for ourselves about how, when, and to whom we will share our information – are inculcated all the way down the

ranks of information industry employees. Industry may say that it wants to "do better" when it comes to privacy, but only if "privacy" means what industry wants it means. Therefore, management relies on a variety of tactics, both inside and outside the organization, to routinize industry-friendly discourses of privacy among the rank and file as ordinary, common sense, and true.[1]

This chapter is about the information industry's coercive control of privacy discourse. We start by defining discourse and explaining why controlling discourse is a source of power. Then, we define and trace the broad reach of privacy-as-control and show that, despite its superficial empowering rhetoric, its chief beneficiaries are companies that want to extract and profit from our data. The bulk of this chapter describes a series of manipulative tactics tech companies use to embed privacy-as-control in the ethos, practice, and routines of their employees, particularly privacy professionals and privacy lawyers, and within the legal consciousness of the public at large.

Discourse as Power

Foucault described "discourse" as the "bodies of knowledge," ideologies, assumptions, and modes of thought behind what we mean when we think and talk about a concept. So, when we think and talk about privacy – or any topic, for that matter – we are doing so within society's collective understanding of the field. We are all steeped in society's discourses. The foundations on which we think about, advocate for, and seek liberation from oppression and structural change are set by institutional discourses about what is open for discussion, what society thinks is true, and what is acceptable, normal, and appropriate. Such foundations, Foucault says, are difficult to escape.[2]

Discourse is a tool of power. A given discourse on a topic decides what is up for discussion and what is not, empowering or disempowering those fighting to get themselves and their issues heard. Think about the power of agenda-setting, Questions Presented on legal briefs, and a parent's ban on political debates at Thanksgiving dinner. They all can help predetermine how a meeting, an appeal, or a social interaction will play out and can empower the status quo by silencing dissent or erasing new ideas.[3]

Discourse also serves a normative normalizing function, defining what is acceptable and valued in society. For example,

Foucault showed how same-sex sexual activity came to be understood as "abnormal" and stigmatized, burdened with medical discourses of disease, religious discourses of immorality, and institutional discourses of distrust, to keep queer people marginalized and disempowered. Feminist scholars have made similar arguments about the way medical, religious, and political discourses have constructed gender norms to keep women out of power. Discourses imbued with historically contingent conceptions of knowledge can, therefore, choose who has access to power.[4]

Discourse also helps define what people think is true. For example, racist, sexist, and homophobic discourses construct persons of color, women, immigrants, and queer people as "others" in the collective imagination of society. These discourses then exert power through what the French philosopher Louis Althusser called interpellation, or the discursive power through which people encounter their culture's values and internalize them. Discourses in psychology and criminology also developed certain historically contingent so-called truths about human behavior, deviance, and recidivism to help the state coerce, imprison, and pacify populations. And, as Kathleen Jones has argued, the discursive "truth" of political action – namely, that political authority is associated with strength and rational decision-making – automatically excludes women, whom society associates with nurturing, emotion, and the home. This makes discourse a weapon of exclusionary power.[5]

Finally, discourses can also determine who has access to justice, what triggers legal accountability, and when the law gets involved. Consider this simple fact pattern that I share with law students: A mobile dating app, which, among other things, permits users to post their HIV status, disclosed that it "may share some" user information with third parties. Pursuant to that policy, the app disclosed users' HIV status with a digital marketing platform for the purposes of facilitating both public health announcements and targeted advertisements.[6]

Where, if at all, did an invasion of privacy take place? Users voluntarily disclosed the information and clicked "I Agree" to the privacy policy when they signed up, downloaded, or used the app. The information was disclosed to third parties, but the disclosure caused no monetary harm other than the distress that attended learning about the disclosure. My students' thoughts vary

widely; this is their first day of a privacy law class, so their answers are based on their intuitions. Some find no privacy issues because users chose to share the information under the terms of the privacy policy. For others, the disclosure gives them pause because HIV status is sensitive, but wonder why it matters if nothing went wrong. Others take a *per se* approach: a person's HIV status is so deeply personal that it should never be shared by anyone other than the individual herself. Some suggest that sharing personal information with marketers and advertisers is dehumanizing and commodifying, while others remind the class that "that's how the internet works."[7]

How we think about privacy, then, necessarily impacts how we understand the lawfulness or propriety of data collection in any given situation. If we think privacy means the right to choose for ourselves what will happen with our data, we could argue that the original disclosure was a choice that eroded our privacy rights. However, if we think privacy is bound up with trust or that privacy means only sharing information where it is appropriate in context or with those in our social networks, we might be more inclined to see an invasion of privacy at the moment users' HIV status jumps from the confined community of app users to a third-party advertiser.[8]

If privacy professionals and privacy lawyers think about privacy in terms of the right to choose for oneself what information to disclose, to whom, and when, then they would write privacy policies that detail their company's data use practices. They would focus on the benefits of transparency, as Lester and his colleagues did in Chapter 1. Software engineers who conceptualize privacy in the same way would design consent toggles, checkboxes, notifications, and "Agree" buttons and consider their privacy responsibilities fulfilled. However, if designers thought about privacy in terms of trust or networks of information, they would create different designs – inaccessible APIs, coding to prevent scraping, automatic deletion of data, and blocking of cookies, just to name a few. Putting the promise to delete old data in a privacy policy reflects an understanding of privacy bound up with notice-and-consent. A design that automatically deletes data after a certain period of time may reflect a different approach, one in which maintaining trust or obscurity mattered more than consent.[9]

Notions of privacy in the popular imagination also affect design. Several engineers I interviewed talked about how "everyone already knows that free websites operate on data" and saw their jobs as developing new ways to collect and use that data "to make the service better." A product manager working on a photo-sharing app wanted to "meet our customers' expectations about their data. We want to be where they are, not ahead or behind. That's what's going to make [the product] successful." Popular understanding of privacy, then, could influence design choices.

Control over privacy discourse, therefore, amplifies power. Those who can establish, disseminate, and inculcate discourses can do so to maintain their power. Similarly, if one social group, with its own agenda, perspective, assumptions, biases, and language, takes control over the discourses of privacy, that group will have the power to define both the law of privacy and the designs of new technologies to suit their interests.[10]

Privacy-as-Control and Corporate Power

It's difficult to study privacy without encountering the discourse of control. Academics may lament that privacy is "vague" or in "disarray," but privacy scholarship began with the discourse of choice and control. Samuel Warren's and Louis Brandeis's canonical article, "The Right to Privacy," argued that individuals "retain [the] power" and are "entitled to decide" whether, when, and to whom information will be disclosed. Granted, Warren and Brandeis spoke of a right to be let alone as a way of preserving "solitude" and a "retreat" from others, but their primary focus was choice. The law, they argued, "secures to each individual the right of determining, ordinarily, to what extent his thoughts, sentiments, and emotions shall be communicated to others." Alan Westin defined privacy as the "claim of individuals ... to determine for themselves when, how, and to what extent" they will disclose information to others.[11]

Other scholars have followed their lead. Jean Cohen described privacy as the power to determine "whether, when, and with whom" to disclose intimate information. Julie Inness talked about privacy in the context of "having control" over information and making personal "decisions about ... access" to oneself. Fred Cate argued that the entire purpose of privacy is to "facilitate ... free

choice," while Charles Fried argued that we have different groups of friends because we actively choose to share more with intimates and less with acquaintances. Fried noted that "even between friends the restraints of privacy apply; since friendship implies a *voluntary* relinquishment of private information, one will not wish to know what his friend or lover has not chosen to share with him." And for the philosopher Steve Matthews, privacy is making the choice to "control" and "manage" the boundary between ourselves and others. Many other scholars have based their understanding of privacy on autonomy and freedom to choose as well.[12]

Undoubtedly, privacy scholarship is far more diverse than privacy-as-control. Sisella Bok spoke about privacy in terms of "being protected" from surveillance, while Edward Shils described privacy as being "secluded" and "separated" from others. Jeffrey Rosen used the language of "shields" or protected "spheres" to conceptualize privacy. Danielle Citron has recognized that "sexual privacy" is more than just making choices about what we do and don't do with our bodies. Neil Richards teased out the concept of intellectual privacy as an opportunity to develop new ideas "separate and apart from" the normalizing effects of public pressure. Woodrow Hartzog has written extensively about privacy in terms of "obscurity," an overt attack on those who think privacy in public is impossible. Helen Nissenbaum has thought about privacy in terms of "obfuscation," or "the deliberate addition of ambiguous, confusing, or misleading information to interfere with surveillance and data collection." In various writings, Richards, Hartzog, and I have independently conceptualized privacy in terms of trust; that is, privacy is a facet of social life that gives people the confidence and moral space to share information with others. Indeed, over time, academics have offered many robust privacy discourses, from intimacy to separation from the world, and, like Daniel Solove and Nissenbaum, even eschewing definitions that reduce privacy to a single common denominator. Feminist scholars, social theorists, and a long list of legal scholars have certainly challenged the individualist paradigm of privacy-as-control. But despite their alternatives, the discourse of control has become entrenched.[13]

That is no accident. The discourse may have started with academics, but its stickiness today is far more a product of corporate strategy than widespread and lasting scholarly acceptance.

Privacy-as-control remains dominant because those with power over our data – the information industry – have a strong interest in defining privacy-as-control. This may seem counterintuitive. How could giving us control over our data help industry extract it from us? Easily. The discourse of control is the discourse of self-governance. And self-governance is a sham.

The Flaws of Privacy of Self-Governance

At least on the surface, having control over our data means the freedom to make our own decisions about what happens with our information. If those who collect our data explain their data use practices in detail, we could make informed disclosure choices and retain control over our data, how it's used, and when it's shared. If we had the right to access, correct, and have companies delete our information, we could be in control of what happens with our data. Privacy-as-control, then, is privacy self-governance. The privacy law scholar Daniel Solove has argued that privacy self-governance "involves the various decisions people must make about their privacy and the tasks people are given the choice to do regarding their privacy, such as reading privacy policies, opting out, changing privacy settings, and so on." Leveraging feminist and queer literature, Alice Marwick calls it "privacy work," the privacy self-help in which people have to engage because their privacy is not protected by default. This system, however, is built on shaky ground. Its efficacy and legitimacy are based on three faulty assumptions: (1) that we can adequately process corporate privacy notices, (2) that our decision-making is rational, and (3) that consent is the same as making a real choice.[14]

Though at the foundation of "notice-and-consent" and still prominent today, privacy notices are exceedingly difficult to parse, written in language even experts cannot always understand. Notices are supposed to give us the information we need to make informed decisions. But scholars have shown that it would take us nearly 244 hours per year to read the privacy policies of the websites we visit just once. Even experts have trouble understanding them. Even if we could find some way to make privacy notices perfectly comprehensible to nonexperts, structural asymmetries between the information industry and users would remain. As two privacy researchers have noted, despite "lengthy and growing terms of service and

privacy, consumers enter into trade with online firms with practically no information meaningful enough to provide ... either ex ante or ex post bargaining power."[15]

Notice may be effective in discrete decision-making – when we have to make one decision about one choice. But it doesn't scale. A doctor tells us the medical risks associated with one procedure. She can sit in front of us, give us the space to ask questions, discuss alternatives, and engage in a holistic approach to care. Notice in the privacy context asks us to get up to speed on how hundreds of websites, mobile apps, in-home assistants, and other digital platforms collect and use our data en masse. And if it weren't difficult enough to read, analyze, and integrate the notices of, say, the fifty websites we visit in a day, there is another problem besides decision fatigue. There are hundreds of websites we never see that track us, monitor our browsing behavior, and share our information with others. Those platforms may have posted privacy policies somewhere, but we can't look for something we don't know is there. Functional notice, therefore, is illusory.[16]

The second faulty assumption of privacy-as-control is rationality. Rationality was a foundational principle in the classic privacy literature, from Westin's three categories of consumers as privacy "fundamentalists," "unconcerned," and "pragmatists" to Richard Posner's economic analysis of weighing pros and cons prior to disclosure. It remains a bedrock assumption among policy makers as well.[17]

And yet, we do not act rationally when we click an "agree" button. Our choices, whether to disclose personal information or buy a product, are not made in vacuums. Psychologists Daniel Kahneman and Amos Tversky demonstrate that mental shortcuts and cognitive biases dominate our decision-making processes. That is, instead of rationally weighing risks and benefits when making a decision, we are more likely to use heuristics and fall back on first impressions, even if they lead us astray. In a series of works, Richard Thaler and Cass Sunstein also showed how "choice architecture," or the context in which people make decisions, can "alter people's behavior in a predictable way without forbidding any options," like how grouping expensive cereals at eye-level and relegating the cheaper ones below encourages a more expensive purchase. Leslie John and several colleagues have found that we

often rely on comparative judgments when making disclosure decisions: if we perceive that others are willing to disclose, we are more likely to disclose. John has also found that we are more willing to disclose bad behavior on websites that have an unprofessional aesthetic. Other researchers have found that our subjective assessment of privacy's importance is not the primary mover of our willingness to disclose personal information. As Will Oremus has noted, "study after study has found that people's valuations of data privacy are driven less by rational assessments of the risks they face than by factors like the wording of the questions they're asked, the information they're given beforehand, and the range of choices they're presented."[18]

Sharing is contingent on both our mental capacity and constraints placed on us by designers. By making the process of navigating our privacy choices easier or harder, platform designers can tinker with our propensity to disclose. Our disclosures, then, are not manifestations of our autonomous decisions about our privacy. Rather, they reflect predetermined responses to platform manipulation by design. The media scholar Siva Vaidhyanathan has made this precise point before, noting that people's privacy choices online "mean very little" because "the design of the system rigs it in favor of the interests of the company and against the interests of users."[19]

The steps we do have to take in order to manage our own privacy are more burdensome that empowering. We have to make our privacy choices, website by website, app by app, sometimes many choices per platform. We are responsible for reading privacy policies. We are tasked with finding alternative platforms – if they even exist – when we object to data collection practices. We have to navigate a platform's opt-out process. Rights of access, correction, and deletion require additional privacy work, not to mention the ability to navigate a company's approval, verification, and appeals process if they reject our requests. And we have to do this within an environment designed to extract our information. Indeed, the onus of protecting our privacy is almost entirely on our shoulders.

That burden is too heavy to bear. Eszter Hargittai and Alice Marwick showed that social media users to navigate platform settings to match their privacy preferences, but feel resigned to failure because of a perception that privacy violations are unavoidable. Other scholars have found that users feel powerless and helpless.

This leads to what scholars have called "digital resignation." Digital resignation describes how we give up when we see how hard it is to protect our privacy or navigate opt outs, consents, and cookie requests online. We don't just stop trying to protect our privacy; we also give up the expectation that it's even possible. Along similar lines, one legal scholar has noted that "managing one's privacy is a vast, complex, and never-ending project. … The best people can do is manage their privacy haphazardly. People can't learn enough about privacy risks to make informed decisions about their privacy. People will never gain sufficient knowledge of the ways in which personal data will be combined, aggregated, and analyzed over the years by thousands of organizations." There are too many organizations collecting our data and too many websites and app that require our attention. We cannot adequately estimate the risk of future harm. Nor can we comprehend how the aggregation of seemingly innocuous data can come back to haunt us and undermine our safety, security, and future. As a result, privacy self-governance turns us into nihilists. The discourse of privacy-as-control, then, isn't as liberational as it seems. It transforms us into passive users, accepting information industry power because there doesn't seem to be anything we can do about it.[20]

The third foundational error of privacy-as-control is its conflation of consent with real choice. The right to give consent can be a source of great power. In other areas of law, we consent to medical procedures only after full disclosure of risks and benefits. The law of sexual assault gives us the power to consent to intimate touching and sexual encounters, and gives us important tools to protect that power.[21]

But consent in the privacy context bears few similarities to consent in these other areas of law. When a doctor explains a procedure's risks, we can ask questions, listen to answers, and consider alternatives from a voice we trust. We can become active participants in our own health care. Privacy consents, on the other hand, are based on ignorance and a lack of options. We don't have the cognitive ability to process and understand privacy policies. It should come as no surprise, then, that we have no idea what we're doing when companies ask us to consent to something. Studies by Joe Turow and several colleagues demonstrate that only 30 percent of nonexpert respondents correctly understand the privacy (or lack

thereof) associated with their online transactions. Nearly two-thirds of people do not realize that a supermarket is allowed to sell information about purchasing habits to other companies. And, remarkably, almost 75 percent of people falsely believe that when "a website has a privacy policy, it means the site will not share [their] ... information with other websites and companies."[22]

What's more, there are downstream uses of data that are simply unknowable to us at the time of consent. For example, do internet users know how their information is translated into advertisements? Did Facebook users consent to participate in the company's emotional manipulation studies in 2014, in which the company subjected its users to negatively or positively framed information in order to see its effects on engagement? In one sense, yes, by agreeing to Facebook's broad data use policy in its terms of service that could be read to incorporate the entire future universe of data uses. But in the most proximate sense, of course not, because no one consented to be part of this particular study. Similarly, although Facebook users may consent to share their "likes" with Facebook, they cannot seriously be permitting Facebook to learn everything it does from that "like," especially since that generated information can be deeply personal. Researchers found that Facebook could tell that "users who liked the 'Hello Kitty' brand tended to high on Openness and low on 'Conscientiousness,' 'Agreeableness,' and 'Emotional Stability.' They were also more likely to have Democratic political views and to be of African-American origin [and] predominantly Christian." This is just one of myriad correlations Facebook can make from its trove of data about us. But someone's willingness to disclose that they enjoy Hello Kitty cannot imply a similar willingness to disclose emotional, political, and racial information. In this context, then, consent is uninformed and informed consent is impossible.[23]

Consent is also easy to manipulate and manufacture. Platforms can use dark patterns to make it seem like accepting cookies, geotracking, or surveillance is the only option. And they can frame opting out as tantamount to lack of functionality. We see this throughout the digital ecosystem: The social practices of consent are "Accept" buttons that have no "Reject" buttons, "Click I AGREE to continue," consent by continued use, take-it-or-leave-it privacy terms, and manipulative consent interfaces. And if consent

is easy to manufacture, then consent isn't our own. Nor does it serve our interests. Rather, it is the product of manipulation in service of someone else's (usually) contradictory goals.

In the end, then, operationalizing consent in the privacy space achieves the exact opposite of individual control and empowerment. As one leading privacy scholar put it, the information industry "take[s] refuge in consent" to absolve them of their data protection responsibilities because "consent legitimizes nearly every form of collection, use, or disclosure of personal data." Like notice, consent doesn't scale. Woodrow Hartzog thinks that we "can feel so overwhelmed by the thousands of requests for access, permission, and consent to use our data that we say yes just because we are so worn down." That's not control; that's beating us down until we give up and sign away our rights like an innocent arrestee under intense interrogation. Our consent isn't free. Twenty years ago, Joel Reidenberg noted that notice-and-consent and privacy-as-control were being sold to us as "predicated on the philosophy that self-regulation will accomplish the most meaningful protection of privacy without intrusive government interference, and with the greatest flexibility for dynamically developing technologies." We were sold a lemon.[24]

Amplifying Corporate Power

Privacy-as-control is not just bad for privacy, it affirmatively amplifies information industry power. What is sold to us as control is weaponized a way of saddling us with the responsibility for whatever tech companies want to do with our data. What is sold as rationality is weaponized against regulation as evidence of consumer demand. What is sold as self-governance is weaponized against regulation and legal accountability, a tactic Julie Cohen calls the "surveillance-innovation complex." Privacy-as-control, then, is less a discourse about privacy than it is a discourse about corporate power and immunity from law.[25]

"There Is No Privacy Interest"

Privacy lawyers in the information industry have been making this argument for years, hiding their most explicit and egregious weaponization of consent in legal filings few people read.

In 2019, while Facebook was trying to dismiss a lawsuit for the company's failure to stop Cambridge Analytica from unlawfully mining user data, Orin Snyder, a partner at Gibson Dunn & Crutcher LLP, told Judge Vince Chhabria that "there is no privacy interest" in any information Facebook has. Users "consent[ed]" to the terms of service and engaged in "an affirmative social act to publish," which "under centuries of common law, ... negated any reasonable expectation of privacy." Snyder said that "users were told" that Facebook "can't control what third parties do with your information" and that Congress "expressly authorizes the recipient of information with consent," that is, Facebook, "to share it with the world." When the judge asked if it would be an invasion of privacy for Facebook to break a promise not to share your information with third parties, Snyder claimed that "Facebook does not consider that to be actionable," citing both user behavior and consent to Facebook's privacy policy. In its briefing, the company went even further, arguing that because users "can control how" their content is shared, anything they then share is ripe for Facebook's and third parties' use.[26]

In *Campbell v. St. John*, a case about Facebook's practice of scanning users' private messages to collect data for behavioral advertising, Facebook argued that the plaintiff users lacked standing to challenge any Facebook data practice because they "consented to the uses of ... data." In *Smith v. Facebook*, the company made the same argument, noting that Facebook should be allowed to track users wherever they go on the internet because users "are bound by their consent to those policies." And in *In re Google, Inc. Cookie Placement Consumer Privacy Litigation*, Google moved to dismiss all claims around the unauthorized use of cookie tracking and the unlawful interception of user data by arguing that "both Plaintiffs and the websites they communicated with provided their consent to Google ... when they sent a GET request ... so they could browse websites containing Google ads." In other words, the mere use of Google is tantamount to consent to all of Google's data use practices, putting on our shoulders all the responsibility for any consequences.[27]

Similarly, in *Patel v. Facebook*, which challenged the company's collection and use of biometric information, Facebook argued that no one could ever bring a lawsuit against the company for use of

any kind of information, let alone biometric data, because "plaintiffs knew exactly what data Facebook was collecting, for what purpose, and how to opt out of Tag Suggestions." This immunity was so broad, Facebook suggested, that it held up even if the company's notices were not sufficiently specific. Facebook users consented to all data collection practices when they signed up for accounts, and since privacy law only requires choice, consent, and control, users who signed up but never opted out had given up their rights to their data. And in another case Facebook argued that the only way users could expect privacy on the internet was if users themselves "take steps to keep their browsing histories private." Otherwise, mere internet use implies no privacy.[28]

Facebook has even argued that its own privacy promises are meaningless because notice-and-consent empowers only Facebook to define the privacy rights of its users. For example, in several ongoing lawsuits about Facebook's practice of tracking both users and nonusers across the internet, Facebook argued that its promise to remove cookies that identify a particular user's account was not a "promise[] to not record the communication" and that promises of anonymity do not create expectations of privacy. In the same case, Facebook argued that all user information available to Facebook – including every website we visit – is "voluntarily disclosed."[29]

These are just a few examples. Big tech companies like Microsoft, Apple, Facebook, Google, and Amazon have submitted hundreds of motions to dismiss and motions for summary judgment on privacy-related claims against them based, at least in part, on user consent manifested through acknowledging terms of services and privacy policies. In many of these cases, the self-governing regime based on privacy-as-control does not empower users to make choices. Rather, it protects the information industry, allowing tech companies to do almost anything they want with our data after we use their platforms.[30]

It's worth noting that at all times during the five years in which Facebook's and Google's lawyers were making these arguments, both companies had privacy-focused internal organizational structures in place in accordance with the GDPR. Both companies had long been operating under FTC consent decrees that required, among other things, comprehensive privacy programs. Both companies also claimed to be compliant with the

GDPR as of 2018, a year before *Patel* and two years before arguing that the only way Facebook users could expect privacy on the internet was if they used a virtual private network, or VPN. Therefore, having compliance systems in place did not stop the companies from engaging in legal practices that eroded privacy rights for users. We will return to the mismatch between privacy law and corporate practice in the next chapter. For now, it is clear that even with this new round of privacy laws, data-extractive companies are going to "take refuge" in consent.[31]

This Is "What People Want"

Assumptions of our rationality also allow the information industry to look at our disclosure behavior, our eagerness to click "Agree," and our acceptance of cookies to argue that our actions suggest that we want more tailored advertisements, recommendation algorithms, third-party sharing, and the data collection and processing that those things require. In other words, they rely on the so-called privacy paradox – people respond to surveys saying they want more privacy but behave in ways that suggest the opposite – to argue that their customers don't really want privacy. If we did really want more privacy, the argument goes, we wouldn't be sharing and clicking and disclosing so much information. It's easy to fib on a survey – social scientists call it a social desirability bias when people answer the way they think the surveyor wants them to answer – but our actions speak louder than words. "At the end of the day," said a privacy manager at a large e-commerce platform, "people don't have a problem with what we're doing, especially if you look at how we've only grown." This argument presumes that our behavior is rationally related to our privacy preferences. It isn't.[32]

Relying on the privacy paradox to argue that we don't actually care about privacy ignores the fact that, as we discussed earlier, online disclosures are contextual, influenced by others' behavior. Our disclosure behavior is also manipulated by design: design has signaling functions that encourage us to make certain choices, it provides us with only a certain defined set of options, and it manipulates us by triggering the many cognitive limitations that make perfect autonomy impossible. But although technologies' surveillant designs presume and take advantage of our irrationality, the

law of privacy-as-control presumes our rationality. Notice-and-consent presumes we can read privacy policies and make privacy decisions as a result. The GDPR's rights of control, including rights of access, correction, deletion, and portability, make the same assumptions about our ability to overcome platform manipulation. This leaves us unprotected against the power of design and unfairly saddles us with the responsibility of our manipulated choices.

In my interviews, I noticed a baffling cognitive dissonance about this: many privacy professionals refused to see this mismatch as a flaw in privacy law. Instead, some of them relied on presumptions of rationality to prop up current privacy law based on notice-and-consent. Among many of the software engineered I interviewed, the manipulative power of design was a fact, an ordinary, commonsense part of life. "That's what advertisements in newspapers have been doing for centuries," one said. he idea that internet users want a faster, efficient, tailored experience is dogma for many software engineers as well. Clive Thompson found this among the technologists he interviewed for his book *Coders*. Surveys of software engineers say the same. Many with experience building several different social platforms and mobile apps point to our disclosure behavior as well. A former Facebook engineer now working as a product manager at another company noted "how massively popular any tailored experience is. You do a little research about the most popular news, the most popular games, the most popular social, the most popular anything, and they're those that allow you to get you want out of it, to tailor it to your experience. That tells me where people are at, not a survey." When I noted that he and his colleagues routinely manipulate user behavior through design, dark patterns, and various subtle and obvious tactics, I was rebuffed: "That's just normal. There's nothing wrong with that, and it's certainly not manipulative and evil. It's just how it works."

Among privacy professionals and lawyers, assumptions of rationality manifest in rhetoric about variable privacy preferences among different users. A privacy leader at a health care company who used to work in Silicon Valley responded to a question about whether there should be a nationwide comprehensive privacy law by saying that "a one-size fits all approach to privacy doesn't make sense. Different people want different things at different times from different platforms, so a single set of rules would look okay for

some people, but get in the way at other times." A sales professional at Uber noted that "we need to be nimble because what people want from social isn't want people want from us which isn't what people want from dating apps. It's all different, and we look to our customers to see what the demand is." This view of our variable privacy preferences has made its way into industry-backed policy recommendations that would erode robust privacy regulations. It is also what allowed Facebook's privacy professionals to sign off on a project where the company paid teenagers to install a VPN that spied on them.[33]

When I suggested that online behavior may not be an accurate reflection of people's preferences, I received a mix of resistance and resignation. "You're taking away too much agency from people," said a privacy leader who had recently left Google and calls themselves a "privacy advocate." "No one is a robot, they have free will, so you're minimizing people's freedom." Another privacy manager said, "That's just academic speak. We make decisions in the real world here, and in the real world, people can decide for themselves. No one is forcing them to click on this or that. That's why it's so important for us to transparent about our data use practices. This way, we know that decisions people make are really truly informed." This is a discursive trick: By using the word "forcing" to describe the opposite of people "deciding for themselves," this privacy professional conveniently transformed manipulation from a question of degree to an either/or. We are either "free" or "forced." In that world, there are no gray areas of manipulation, dark patterns, and coercive designs.

Others were more resigned to the inadequacy of looking to disclosures manipulated by design, suggesting that "what else are we supposed to do" or "we can't divine the demand, we have to look for it." "It's not my job," said one privacy professional who used to work at Facebook, "to be the consumer's mommy or daddy. We work really hard and have improved the ways we give them notice and then let them make their own decisions."

Many of the privacy professionals I interviewed stated plainly that "notice and choice is not enough." But, at the same time, most refused to acknowledge that a privacy law regime based on transparency, notice, and choice inadequately protected individuals in a world of manipulated disclosure. This group argued either

that our disclosures are not really that manipulated or dismissed the reality of manipulative design, suggesting that our clicks really do reflect our privacy preferences. In so doing, these privacy professionals were perpetuating corporate-friendly discourses about privacy, one that allows industry to extract as much data as it wants as long as it can manipulate our actions online.

A Free Market without Law

The logical endpoint of the rationality discourse is the valorization of a free market for data and a demonization of privacy regulation. That is, if privacy is about making rational choices about disclosure, then our sharing-heavy behavior on digital platforms must be evidence of great demand. Data, as MasterCard CEO Ajay Banga said, is the "new oil," with consumers preferring "convenience over security" because data exchange can offer us all sorts of benefits. Kiran Bhageshpur, CEO at Igneous and a member of the Forbes Technology Council, a fee-based organization of chief information and technology officers and other technology executives, said that like oil, data "can improve our lives." By this logic, the market for data is a normative good. And I don't just mean a market in which data is exchange for money, like when Facebook paid teenagers twenty dollars for extensive access to their phone's data. Rather, the market for data is a market of exchange: data in exchange for access or social interaction or search, sex, love, or a job. This is what the people want, companies say, and all they're doing is giving it to them.[34]

Many privacy professionals believe that we should retain the current sectoral approach to privacy, where health care companies are regulated differently from internet service providers, and where social media is regulated differently from platforms dedicated to children. Faced with the prospect of new state and federal privacy laws in the United States, however, the information industry has started playing both sides. It has opposed state privacy laws on the grounds that uniformity at the federal level is the better approach. At the federal level, industry has called for any new federal law to preempt state and local laws even with a federal law that boils down to more transparency, more notice, more consent, and not much else. In other words, they want some minimal baseline of privacy

law – perhaps notice-and-consent "with bite" – but with sectoral differences in place. In oral and written testimony before the US Senate, industry representatives and industry-funded advocacy groups have called for control rights, but no enforcement. They've called privacy a fundamental right, but have proposed transparency as the way to protect it. The cable industry has said it's different from other industries, but wants to be governed by the same notice-and-consent regime the FTC uses for everyone else.[35]

These arguments are part of a larger discourse demonizing privacy law. If our disclosure behavior depicts a robust market for data and evidences our consent to corporate data use practices that create our tailored experiences, then law is a hindrance, not a boon. Put another way, the logics of power embedded in discourses of privacy-as-control do not just inculcate the idea that privacy self-governance is the norm, they also imply that robust legal interventions that challenge self-governance are bad ideas. As Julie Cohen has argued, market-based approaches to privacy discourse begin with freedom and end with law as antithetical to that freedom. They do this through discourse of innovation.[36]

Innovation, industry says, is always a normative good. Innovation means new products, new opportunities for connection, new apps that automate and speed up old services, new consumer welfare, and new efficiencies. Set aside for the moment that something isn't better just because it's new and shiny; a faith in newness is the least of the information industry's disingenuousness. Tech company discourses turn almost extortionate when they focus on the law. That is, the information industry argues that if we want a world where entrepreneurs are building the next TikTok, the next Amazon, or whatever the next "big thing" will be, then law not only has to facilitate innovation, it has to stand aside. For example, Matt Perault, Facebook's former Director of Public Policy, told the House Judiciary Committee that "acquisitions directly facilitate innovation," "accelerate innovation," and help create "new products and technologies . . . [that] yield improvements in features and services of users." But that will only happen if anticompetition and antitrust law lets Facebook do whatever it wants.[37]

The information industry argues consistently that law stifles innovation. Leading information industry players, from Facebook to Salesforce, have recently joined the bandwagon for federal privacy

regulation in the United States. But they are quick to say that they would welcome the "right regulation." They want a law that "still allow[s] companies to innovate and develop." Ajit Pai, Chairman of the Federal Communications Commission and a former lawyer for Verizon, has stated that telecommunications over the internet is the "greatest free-market success story in history." Best we leave it that way, he said, calling for a "return to light-touch regulatory framework." Industry representatives have testified before Congress to argue that privacy law will stifle progress, make it difficult for companies to comply with the law, and place a particular burden on small business that lack the resources of their larger competitors. For example, the Interactive Advertising Bureau, an industry trade group, told the Senate Commerce Committee that privacy regulation will "impose significant burdens on consumers ... [and] also fail to recognize the ways in which digital advertising subsidizes the plentiful, varied, and rich digital content and services consumers use." The Advertising Bureau's preferred legal response was more transparency, better notice, and more choice.[38]

In addition to these arguments, the information industry argues that privacy regulation will harm small business. Experian's Senior Vice President for Regulatory and Government Affairs told the Senate that "information-sharing significantly enhances economic productivity" and benefits "nonprofit organizations" and "small businesses." The industry-funded Direct Marketing Association also told the Senate Commerce Committee that the data economy contributes "675,000 jobs" and "helps small business" so they "can come in and compete with the big boys." And, with no trace of irony, Facebook has argued that stronger and more robust enforcement of anticompetition law would actually harm small businesses because it would interfere with Facebook's and other large companies' ability to acquire those small businesses and bring new "efficiencies" and "resources" to improve their products.[39]

Notably, only Big Tech makes these arguments. All the witnesses to argue that law stifles innovation and that regulation will harm small businesses – leaders of trade organizations, lawyers at leading law firms, and industry executives themselves – were all funded by or worked for the largest technology companies in the United States. The argument's framing is also suspect: It sets up a binary choice where no such choice actually exists. Nor did it matter

to them that there is no evidence that privacy law actually stifles innovation, or that the internet was by no means a success of the free market. These arguments from leading executives, industry representatives, and government officials with strong ties to business are, if not outright lies, at least disingenuous. And yet, they are pervasive, even all the way down throughout the rank and file.[40]

Discourses of Control Are Pervasive in the Information Industry

It is one of the singular triumphs of the information industry that policy makers and regulators talk about privacy using discourses of control, consent, transparency, and choice. In a 2013 Senate Commerce Committee hearing on data brokers, for example, then-Chairman Jay Rockefeller of West Virginia recognized the "thousands of data points" in "intimate profiles of American consumers" collected by unregulated data brokers, but lamented only that the information is collected without public awareness and without the "right to see these pictures of ourselves." Senator John Thune of South Dakota, the ranking member, framed the "privacy implications" of the data broker industry as "whether consumers are aware of the instances in which their personal information may be collected, bought, and sold, resulting in calls for more transparency." During a later hearing a federal data privacy law, Senator Thune repeated this view, boiling down privacy to "transparency," which "allows consumers to make informed decisions about the products and the services that the use." At the same hearing, Jessica Rich, Director of the FTC's Bureau of Consumer Protection described the FTC's work on data brokers as working to bring "transparency" and "access" to data and protecting "sensitive consumer report information" from getting into the hands of identity thieves. During his questioning, Senator Ron Johnson focused entirely on transparency and potential improvements to privacy and data use notices.[41]

To their credit, many policy makers have criticized the governing notice-and-consent framework. Senator Brian Schatz of Hawaii recognizes that privacy law should include some "affirmative obligation ... not to harm you." Senator Ed Markey of Massachusetts, a long-time privacy advocate, has asked about rights

of access, correction, and deletion. Senator Maria Cantwell of Washington has noted that inappropriate data transfers and use can also constitute privacy violations. But when other policy makers associate privacy, or lack thereof, with "tracking devices" and raised concerns that smartphones "monitor our movements, our health, and even our family affairs," they nevertheless frame the solution around consumers "simply want[ing] to choose how that information is used or shared." Senator Markey has spoken about privacy issues in terms of the "intimate secrets" in "digital dossiers" collected by data brokers and the potential for discrimination. But when suggesting a framework for a federal privacy law, he starts with "knowledge, notice, and 'no': . . . knowledge that their data is being used or shared, notice when their data is compromised, and the ability to say 'no' to entities that want their personal information." And even as he noted his concern about Google's data collection, Michigan senator Gary Peters questioned the company's CPO about whether "Google's dashboard disclose[s] information to your users about how you're tracking them across the internet."[42]

These views, and the persistence of privacy-as-control even among policy makers who recognized the need for more robust approaches to privacy, stems, at least in part, from industry, its representatives, and its privacy professionals testifying before Congress and advising policy makers and their staffs on privacy legislation. For example, at a 2019 hearing before the Senate Commerce Committee, Jon Leibowitz, a former chairman of the FTC, a partner at the elite law firm Davis, Polk, & Wardwell LLP, and the co-chair of the telecommunications industry–funded 21st Century Privacy Coalition, testified that the "framework" for a federal privacy law should give "consumers more control over their data" and provide "greater transparency." His proposals for that new privacy law boiled down to "transparency," giving consumers "statutory rights to control how their personal information is used and shared," and "promot[ing] consumer control and choice by imposing requirements for obtaining meaningful consent." Michael Beckerman, the president & CEO of the Big Tech-funded Internet Association, said that "people should have access and control of their data." He suggested that legislation should "empower people to better understand and control how personal information they share is collected, used" and should

include "the development of tools to give users more control over their personal information." In 2018, Bud Tribble, then vice president for Software Technology at Apple, and Rachel Welch, senior vice president for Policy and External Affairs at Charter Communications made similar comments.[43]

Sundar Pinchai, the CEO of Alphabet, Google's parent company, said that YouTube protects people's privacy by giving "users a choice of either consuming [content] as a subscription service or using it with ads." He doubled down on this conception of privacy nine times throughout his testimony, adding that he "always believed that privacy is a universal right and Google is committed to keeping your information safe ... [and] putting you in control." Mark Zuckerberg, Facebook's CEO, said the company has made changes to its platform "to protect user privacy and give people more control." A lobbying group funded by Google but claiming to be a voice for entrepreneurs told Congress to pass a "robust" federal privacy law that "provide[s] transparency and user choice." The National Association of Realtors also wants legislation to focus on "transparency and consumer choice." Keith Enright, then Google's Chief Privacy Officer, told a Senate committee in 2018 that Google's "key elements" for any privacy discussion are "transparency, control, portability, and security." Executives at Twitter repeated the privacy-as-control discourse, noting that "privacy" means the company "should be transparent about, and provide meaningful control over what data is being collected, how it is used, and when it is shared." All in all, in more than fifteen hearings between 2015 and 2020 before the Senate Commerce Committee alone, information industry executives have pushed the discourse of privacy-as-control every time.[44]

The International Association of Privacy Professionals (IAPP), the largest professional organization for those working in privacy, routinely and consistently pushes the privacy-as-control discourse. In a random sample of 120 articles published between 2014 and 2020 in the IAPP's blog, "Privacy Perspectives," a widely read blog among privacy professionals and privacy lawyers, 61 percent addressed the need for adequate notice, consent for data collection, or the need for more individual control. A closer read of these sources shows just how pervasive the choice discourse really is; it dominates even those articles that nod to other privacy discourses,

including intimacy, sexuality, trust, and obscurity. An article primarily about how privacy protects celebrities' intimate photos defined privacy as "personal control." Another article about surveillant technology designs suggested that the way to solve the privacy problems associated with the Internet of Things was to "give users more choice about what is collected at all and offer better transparency about how data is collected, used and shared."[45]

A discussion of connected toys aptly noted the intimacy of collected information, but framed recommendations around greater choice. In another article, the privacy problems accompanying a WiFi-enabled pacemaker were framed as a lack of choice. And a post about building trust with consumers defined privacy as providing better notice and choice. Elsewhere, leaders among the privacy professional class have spoken about their companies' privacy challenges in earnest; they talk about trust and power and limitations on data use. But when they start talking about the practical steps their companies are taking, they focus on giving us "all the information required" and the "choice" to use tools like location tracking, cookies, and ad targeting. One "Privacy Perspectives" piece went even further, stating clearly that "enabling broad participation in privacy self-management ... can ultimately enrich business and the marketing industry." The path to that was "radical transparency," "opt ins versus opt outs," and "consent." These privacy professionals are content with "augment[ing] privacy policies or data subject access requests with infographics" that tell customers how they "are benefited" by data extraction.[46]

The organization also facilitates privacy-as-control's dominance by pushing transparency and consent-based solutions and by perpetuating other industry-friendly ideas about privacy. Consider, for example, the articles the IAPP published about the *Schrems II* decision by the European Union Court of Justice. *Schrems II* invalidated the Privacy Shield, which was a regime permitting US companies to process data about European Union citizens. The Court invalidated the Privacy Shield because US law inadequately protected the privacy of EU citizen data, allowing the US government to easily access information about EU citizens, insufficiently protecting European data from misuse, and failing to provide appropriate remedies. And yet, rather than suggesting that companies should stop collecting the kinds of user data that troubled the EU Court of

Justice, the IAPP's articles focused on "presenting to customers updated terms" and sticking to its Privacy Shield obligations to avoid an FTC investigation. Another article called for "due diligence" on the part of companies collecting European data, but never mentioned that no level of due diligence will be enough to adequately protect EU citizen data if US privacy laws remain the way they are. A final article focused on how the end of the Privacy Shield should encourage more companies to transparent about the kinds of data requests they get from the US government. The point is not that the IAPP does not also publish dissident views. It does, albeit rarely. Rather, the IAPP's insistence on pushing the idea that transparency is an appropriate response to privacy problems perpetuates industry-friendly discourses about privacy.[47]

To see if the institutional discourse at the IAPP level reached down through the rank and file, I interviewed thirty-eight privacy professionals at privacy conferences or over the phone. This was by no means a random sample. But these interviews hinted at the privacy discourses running through the profession. Seven associated privacy with European "data protection," by which they meant management of the processing of data. Four suggested that privacy involves companies taking on fiduciary (or trust-based) responsibilities toward their users, explicitly referencing some of the scholarly work on privacy and trust. A group six privacy leads, all of whom were women, spoke about the need to explicitly protect intimate data. But again, almost everyone – thirty-two of thirty-eight – and even some who thought about privacy also in terms of trust, intimacy, and restrictions on companies – included some notion of choice, consent, and transparency. "I get nervous," one said, "when people start talking about taking away user choice, but at the end of the day, we all have the right to make our own privacy choices." A chief privacy officer in Washington, DC, suggested that "privacy is about choice, right? It reflects our reasonable decisions about what we want and when we want it, especially when it comes to tech that gives us amazing things, like the ability to talk to our grandparents from far away." Another said, "If I could put myself in my customers' shoes, I would want control over what happens to my data, to say I want this but I don't want that." And speaking for four privacy leaders whose companies deal regularly with data analytics vendors, one CPO thought privacy was about "making sure the people we

hire to learn from the data we collect respect what our users want." The privacy professionals I interviewed may not have believed that more notice-and-consent was enough to solve today's privacy problems (only three said so), but almost all of them conceptualized privacy in terms of choice and consent.

Similarly, many lawyers, both in-house and in private practice, think about privacy predominantly in terms of choice. Seventeen of the twenty-four lawyers I interviewed for this project included at least one reference to privacy-as-control. A partner at an AmLaw 100 law firm saw privacy "as the notion that you should have some control over your data." A colleague suggested that "privacy is about companies giving you the tools you need to control dissemination of your data. We can help our clients do that by clearly and adequately laying out data use practices." A senior associate at a small firm specializing in internet and privacy matters agreed, stating that "privacy is about giving ... users notice about what will happen to their data. This allows them to go to another website if they want to." An experienced partner at a New York law firm stated that her team "spend[s] a lot of time reviewing statutes, FTC actions, and anything we can get our hands on. The law is clear. Our clients have to provide users with notice and choice. It's repeated over and over. And we help them do that." When I followed up with these interviewees in 2019 – after passage of the CCPA and more than one year after the effective date of the GDPR – they recognized that "things are changing rapidly." The law firm partner, who, by 2019, assumed a leadership role in her firm's privacy practice, stated that "obviously the new laws put additional requirements on our clients, and we parse that for them, but the foundation really hasn't changed. We still want to give everyone more control over their data."

"Consent" is the watchword among privacy professionals and privacy lawyers. Everyone I interviewed spoke about consent in empowering ways, using words and phrases like "you decide," "only with your consent," "up to you what happens," and "without consent, there's no trust." But what happens after consent? A privacy lawyer with both firm and in-house experience in the information industry said, "well, hopefully, you know what you're consenting to and it's what you want." We then had the following exchange:

"But you have to know that most people don't read privacy policies," I said.

"Yes, that's a problem, but there's not much we can do about it."

"Would you consider consent valid if the user didn't know what she was agreeing to?"

"Consent should be informed, that's why we have notices, and we really want to make sure people make the choices they want."

"But if that isn't the case, what then?"

"By consent, we all mean voluntary and informed consent. Like the common law."

"Right, so doesn't the common law vitiate consent when it's not truly voluntary or informed?"

"We put all the information out there, so it's informed."

"Once people consent without reading a privacy policy, for example, do you think there's any issue with that consent?"

"Consent is under your power, consent is up to you. We learn that in Torts 101, right?"

"OK, you've got my consent, but then a company uses my data in ways that offend my expectation of privacy, and I didn't know you were going to use it in that way. Is there a privacy problem?"

"Once you consent, you can't then say you didn't consent when you don't like what happens. At some point it has to mean something. We're responsible for getting your consent and we try to make it fully informed. Consent is what makes this your experience. You consent to what you play, what you click, what you do online. That's powerful."

Among privacy professionals I interviewed, many recognized that consent should be updated and routinely obtained over time. As one said, "just because you consent once doesn't mean you consent all the time. Like sex." Many recognized that individuals need more than the right to choose. But when I asked those same

privacy professionals about the legal impact of consent, and how including consent as a means of permitting data extraction could be a license for data misuse, one theme emerged: denial. "We can't read people's minds. We take getting consent very seriously. Consent is important." An experienced chief privacy officer said that "your consent means everything. I get there are issues with overstepping consent, but you have the consenting power." A privacy attorney at an AmLaw 100 firm said that "consent is the most important thing we do for our clients because it's only with consent that they can do what they need to grow." A CPO in San Francisco said that although "consent is not the only method we have, but it is the biggest and the most common, and it's so important for us to get consent." None of those answers were responsive. Along with these denials came some acknowledgment of that problem. In one interview, an associate general counsel at a Silicon Valley company said that "consent protects us. I mean, it protects all of us, you too." Our conversation ended immediately after. Therefore, among the privacy professionals and lawyers who considered themselves privacy "advocates" while doing their jobs, consent's failures did not diminish their belief in its potential.

Many interviewees also spoke about innovation and the "right" privacy regulation out of vague (mis)understandings about both. A sales representative at Uber spoke of the need for "privacy to strike the right balance between what we need to do and what people want" because "I try every day to make people's lives better and easier, and I wouldn't be able to do that if we didn't have flexibility." When I asked why she thought privacy would get in the way of achieving her goals, she offered only hyperbole: "Well, some people want to use privacy law to stop us from collecting any data on our customers, no?" A former software engineer at Facebook running his own start-up in New York said that "privacy is going to be great for business, but law has to take its foot of the gas to let tech thrive, which is a real engine of productivity today." I asked if there are any particular parts of privacy law that were stifling his ability to innovate. "I can't think of anything in particular, but too much regulation is a bad thing."

Thirty-six out of thirty-eight privacy professionals put privacy and innovation in conflict with each other during our interviews, either by speaking of the need to "balance" the two or by insisting that "small companies will bear the burden" of privacy law. I asked

each of them why they framed privacy and innovation in conflict, here are some of the responses:

> "They aren't," but this was after the interviewee had said "we need to balance the need for privacy with our need for data."
>
> "Too much red tape bogs you down."
>
> "Our engineering department is moving too fast for the slow gears of the law. We need to be flexible so we can act proactively."
>
> "That's what law does when it goes overboard."
>
> "I recognize the need for regulation. It's important and we want it."
>
> "Like what's happening in Europe, with the GDPR."

When I asked what evidence they had that the GDPR was stifling innovation in Europe or that law generally stifles innovation, I received more incredulous looks than actual evidence, as if the law-and-innovation discourse is axiomatic and commonsensical that it needn't be proved. There was recognition that some regulation is necessary and even a good idea, but every such acknowledgment was cabined by concerns that privacy law will go too far.

The way this group thinks about privacy and the assumptions and background knowledge they bring to their work is particularly important. Privacy professionals and lawyers play important sociolinguistic functions inside the information industry, translating the law into real corporate procedures that affect how companies approach the collection and processing of user data. Some scholars have suggested that privacy professionals are actively filling the gaps left open by inadequate privacy laws on the books, creating a so-called company law of privacy. If that is the case, these privacy professionals are not just interpreters or translators; they are on-the-ground policy makers developing the social practice of privacy law.[48]

How Did This Happen?

Investigations by major media outlets have uncovered the industry's robust lobbying campaigns, threats to withhold

investment, crusades to weaken privacy laws, and the distribution of company funds to academic centers as key components of a multifaceted approach to push this privacy discourse throughout the population. Furthermore, as Gordon Hull has argued, the practices of privacy-as-control – the "click-to-agree" buttons, cookie self-management, and acceptance of terms of service – also normalize privacy self-governance among users who have known nothing else. These are important drivers in the viral spread of privacy-as-control among the public. And all of us are undoubtedly influenced by them.[49]

Corporate rhetoric also plays a role. Privacy policies and emails about changes to data use practices remind us that the information industry "cares about" our privacy. "Your privacy is important to us," they say. "We take your privacy seriously," they remind us. Amazon's privacy policy starts this way: "We know that you care how information about you is used and shared, and we appreciate your trust that we will do so carefully and sensibly." These are performances, banging us over the head with frequent (albeit dubious) assurances that we can trust tech companies with our data. But industry's goals are far more modest; tech companies know we don't trust them. The discourse of privacy's importance is "a marketing tool, a type of quality representation that consumers find meaning in and rely upon." It is a clear "top-level assertion[]" that we see first and often, and one that is separate from the laundry list of data-extractive practices that are in fine print of the privacy policy itself. Assurances of privacy's importance, therefore, create an empty vessel into which both individuals and industry employees can pour their own expectations about what a company *should* do with their data. This is already happening in a way that serves industry's interests in our data. Research shows that most individuals think that merely having a privacy policy means that companies have to keep their information confidential. Statements of privacy's importance mask the backstage of data policy – namely, rampant collection, processing, and commodification of our data for profit. For Google, Facebook, and Amazon, for example, their privacy policies permit vast data collection, even from those individuals who do not have Google accounts, Facebook profiles, or Amazon memberships. But those details, and the vague language that permits it, are hidden behind assurances of trust, loyalty, and care.[50]

But how does an industry embed these discourses among its rank and file, among people who are trained to know better, and among people who say they care about privacy? It uses subtle, yet powerful tools of coercive bureaucracies and coercive corporate cultures. More specifically, the information industry emphasizes privacy's importance while adopting narrow definitions of privacy, sets the privacy agenda for its workers, forces lawyers staffing privacy litigation to adopt disingenuous arguments under the guise of zealous advocacy, engages friendly academics and encourages employees to cite scholarship of dubious validity, and uses magicians' misdirection to give the impression of honest pro-privacy action. Privacy-as-control's reach among privacy professionals is, therefore, a triumph of the inculcative aspects of the information industry's coercive bureaucracies.

"Privacy Is Important"

Tech companies tell us that privacy is important all the time. We're never told what privacy is, but we're told that the information industry takes it very seriously. Industry workers are fed the same vague discourse every time there is a well-publicized data breach and when they receive privacy training. This has an inculcative effect. Repetition influences our beliefs; we come to believe the things we hear often. Some communications offices inside the information industry take this a step further, creating talking points for their employees not just for those rare occasions when they talk to researchers or the press, but also for when they work with each other.[51]

"We take our customers' privacy quite seriously here," said a CPO at an app development company who was an early hire in Silicon Valley. "I know everyone says that, but I like to think we mean it. I mean, they hired me, so it must mean the people in charge care about privacy. I've spent my entire career doing this work." Notably, almost every CPO and privacy leader I interviewed said the exact same thing: "Everybody says that privacy is important, but we really mean it."

I asked several people who work in public policy for large tech companies if the line was a talking point. One stated that "we absolutely remind our team to think about privacy's importance.

Every time we say it, that privacy is important here, it puts privacy front and center." A human resources professional showed me several job announcements for security engineers, and all of them included the following line: "Privacy and security are important" at the company. She noted that this is "part of the onboarding process now. Every new employee here is reminded how important we consider your privacy throughout our work. We have a privacy training and we encourage people to highlight privacy's importance during their work." When I asked what that meant in practice, she said, "We want our team members to remind each other that privacy is important." A colleague who had worked as a software engineer at seven companies over seventeen years added that "the privacy people want us to talk about privacy, so they sent everyone a memo about how to talk about it. 'Privacy is important.' 'We take privacy very seriously here.' Those were all in here, plus some others I can't remember.

In practice, repeating the mantra that privacy is important – without following up with any detail about what privacy means – has two effects. It normalizes the idea that privacy actually *is* important to the company, even if the company's actions are contradictory. It also allows information industry employees to attach their own definition to the word "privacy" and then cite their and their companies' work in that sphere as evidence that they do, in fact, care.

Those software engineers that did not immediately say that privacy wasn't their job cited their and their companies' work on security fixes, encryption, and cryptography to prove that there was substance behind the "privacy is important to us" line. For example, a group of engineers working on cloud computing at a large technology company insisted that "privacy is central to everything we do" and only listed "our state-of-the-art encryption techniques, authentication requirements, unprecedented security measures to prevent attacks, [and] anonymization" as examples of what they did to protect privacy. At smaller companies, the lists are shorter, but the pivot to security and encryption was nearly universal, including among engineers designing the mobile game and photo-sharing app, both of which implicated significant privacy issues.

For their part, privacy lawyers and privacy professionals spoke of their work improving transparency, notice, and control while giving people more choice and control over their data. One

in-house lawyer at company that filters out spam emails said, "It isn't a line here, that we care about your privacy. It's pretty clear that we go above and beyond: we've created a page that tells you precisely how we interact with your email provider so you know exactly what's happening. I'd say that shows that privacy *is* really important here." A privacy lawyer at a company in the email space said that her company "absolutely cares and I know that because we've spent so much time building tools and internal systems to give people access and control rights and to adjudicate those requests. Why would a company do that if it didn't care about privacy?" Therefore, statements like "we care about your privacy" can mean whatever people want it to mean, allowing workers to construct for themselves any ex post explanation.

When privacy means whatever you want it to mean, it's relatively easy to find evidence of it. But consistent attention to privacy was lacking. I asked each of these interviewees about their products' privacy-unfriendly defaults. Products designed by the cloud computing team gave their employer access to personal information about users. The photo-sharing app was defaulted to the least privacy-protective settings, allowing third parties to access user information and permitting all cookies and behavioral advertisements. The mobile game was designed with the same defaults. "We're allowed to do that," I was told by the cloud computing team. "I don't see that as a problem," said the team's privacy lawyer. "Anyone can opt out." A lawyer at the company designing the photo-sharing app echoed this view, stating, "I don't think that changes things. We are letting people opt out." When I noted that the opt-out process is difficult, requiring users to navigate a multilevel and nonintuitive privacy center, the respond was terse: "You find it nonintuitive. I find it easy. And besides, we're not obligated to do more." Most remarkably, several privacy lawyers joined the chorus from the engineers noting that surveillant defaults are "not . . . privacy issue[s], that's a matter of functionality."

Conceptualizing privacy in terms of consent and control allows information industry workers to disaggregate their work on privacy from actual privacy protections. They can think they are doing a lot of substantive work on behalf of privacy, but they may not realize that they're building a vision of privacy that enriches their bosses at the expense of meaningful privacy protections for the rest of us.

"Privacy Is Hard"

After assuring me of privacy's importance, leaders and rank-and-file workers reminded me that privacy is "hard." But what precisely was hard about it varied depending on the job. A common refrain among software engineers was that privacy "is just hard because I have no idea how to reduce that to code." According to one privacy professional in Silicon Valley, privacy was "really hard to do right because there are vague standards and so many different laws to comply with at once and constant threats." To one CPO, privacy was hard because he was "trying to understand what our customers want and we have millions of customers." An entrepreneur starting an app development company in New York said that "privacy is really hard because we have a ton of competing demands and I don't know how to meet those and do what they're saying we have to do on privacy."

As this suggests, the discourse of difficulty is malleable. Some software engineers see privacy's lack of codability as making it difficult. For an entrepreneur, privacy is hard because he thinks it's standing in the way of him making money. The people interpreting privacy law think privacy is hard because it can be vague or because, as we discussed above, they think that different people having different privacy preferences means that they have to cater to all of them. But for all of them, difficulty was an excuse for inaction. Whenever I proposed additional privacy strategies beyond greater transparency and notice, my interviewees relied on the discourse of difficulty.

What about changing defaults to the most privacy protective rather than the most surveillant? "Well, that's really hard to do because not everyone wants that," said one CPO in San Francisco. "Also because then we have to determine what is 'privacy-protective.'" Why is that any harder than leaving the defaults as is? "Well, that's what our users have come to expect, to be able to easily connect and share."

Could you start with data minimization rather than collecting information you don't need? "Nice idea in theory, but what does that actually mean in practice? There are always needs for our data, so we can make a better product," said one software engineer at one of the largest tech companies in the United States.

What about creating a product that doesn't track users? One VP of design said that he would "rather give people a choice

about what they want. Making a one-size fits all decision seems like a really troubling thing to do, no? Besides, it would be so much harder to meet demand if we did that."

Why are you suggesting that a privacy impact assessment can be completed by this simple checklist? "Privacy law is really complicated, and we have to do our best to make sure our team members and engineers are doing what they're supposed to."

The discourse of difficulty is not unique to privacy. Scholars researching content moderation regularly acknowledge, as evelyn douek has noted, that "it is not *hard* to get content moderation right at ... scale; it is impossible." Tarlton Gillespie said that "moderation at the major platforms is as much a problem of logistics as a problem of values." But among the rank and file, the acknowledged difficulty of designing for privacy, implementing privacy law, and creating robust privacy structures is, at least for some, an excuse for inaction.[52]

The discourse of difficulty is received wisdom among many in the privacy professional class, perpetuated, at least in part, by professional organizations, colleagues in the field, and information industry executives. Every conference I attended included at least one panel on "getting the law right," usually referring to the GDPR or the CCPA, and in each of those panels, at least one speaker noted how difficult complying with privacy law has become. One privacy lawyer in New York noted that "there are a ton of local, state, national, and international laws on privacy. This is a lot for us to keep track of for our clients and a lot of work has go into compliance." The information industry perpetuates this idea as well. At one company, a presentation for one of its privacy trainings includes three slides on "Getting the Hard Parts Right: Privacy." An internal memo from the general counsel's office at a large financial company in New York states that "privacy done right is hard work, but if you follow these steps, you will be doing it right." And in testimony before Congress, Mark Zuckerberg referred to how "hard" it was to respect the privacy of Facebook users. He said it's "hard for [the company] to have a full understanding of what's happening" to data it shares with third parties, adding that although Facebook will "have more than 20,000 people working on security" by the end of 2018, "some of this stuff is just hard."[53]

The information industry has a vested interest in the discourse of difficulty: if privacy is hard, then privacy lapses are errors,

not intentional or negligent invasions of privacy; if privacy is hard, then we should expect mistakes, giving companies leeway; if privacy is hard, then invasions of privacy lead to shrugs, not resistance. This discourse allows the information industry to profess it's "doing better" when it comes to privacy without any material improvements for user privacy on the ground. It's a refrain we hear often from Big Tech, particularly Facebook and Google: We made a mistake, we promise to do better, but it's hard, so be patient. After seventeen years of this discourse, both companies are collecting more information on their users than they ever did before.[54]

A Privacy Agenda Focused on Control

The coercive effects of discursive repetition are subtle. Setting the discursive agenda is both less subtle and more coercive. Agenda-setting determines what is up for discussion and what isn't. And, over time, coercive agenda-setting inside organizations normalizes a shrunken range of discursive options, thereby inculcating only certain ideas among participants. With that in mind, information industry executives set their companies' privacy agendas to focus their work on transparency, notice, and consent – all the pieces of privacy-as-control – while squeezing out other options.[55]

There are many public examples of this. In his testimony before Congress in 2018, Mark Zuckerberg focused almost exclusively on notice-and-consent when answering questions about what kind of new privacy regulation he would like to see. Erin Egan, Vice President and Chief Privacy Officer of Facebook, worked with her team of privacy professionals and privacy lawyers to publish a report on transparency. Echoing privacy-as-control's misleading discourse of self-governance, the report begins by stating that "people have to be meaningfully informed in a way that empowers them to make choices about how they participate online and share their data." The report talks about how hard Facebook has worked "to make privacy notices more user-friendly," ignoring the fact that platform's privacy center is rife with dark patterns that manipulate users into making antiprivacy selections. Facebook, the report continues, "embrace[s its] responsibility to help people become informed ... about how and when their data is collected, shared, and used." At Microsoft, the company's research on privacy is under

the same umbrella as its research into encryption and cryptography, indicating a norm that privacy can be bundled together with security. Of all the privacy issues with apps on Apple's App Store – the spyware involved in intimate partner violence, the manipulated disclosures, the lack of built-in privacy safeguards, for example – Apple chooses to focus on app developers' privacy notices and disclosure requirements. And when TikTok hired Google's David Lieber to be its new Privacy Policy Counsel, his first public announcement related to his role noted that "transparency is a core value at TikTok, and I'm looking forward to the opportunity to help tell that story." This type of agenda-setting is commonplace.[56]

One of my interviewees cited Acxiom's "About the Data" program as evidence that privacy professionals and the information industry are prioritizing privacy. But when an investigative reporter reviewed that initiative, he concluded it showed nothing of the sort. "About the Data" was supposed to make the company's data use practices more transparent, but it actually gave users very little insight into what Acxiom collected and what it did with that data. Instead, it gave users the illusion of control by providing a few buttons here and a few options there, but never enabled users to make the kind of choices that privacy-as-control promises. Therefore, this program doesn't just double down on the transparency rhetoric, it actually is barely transparent, suggesting that some companies leverage the "political expediency of transparency … to continue or expand their surveillance practices."[57]

This is not to say that these companies or these privacy leaders do not also do work outside of notice and transparency. But their choice to publicize and define their privacy work through the lens of privacy-as-control has both an inculcative effect through the ranks of the information industry and a practical effect on privacy professionals' work. Interviews with ten former privacy professionals at large technology companies on the West Coast suggest that much of their time both before and after the enactment of the GDPR was spent exclusively on work product related to control and transparency. "The GDPR has revolutionized what we do in a lot of ways," one told me. "It definitely has given us more work to do with more specific requirements, and we've come with a system to answer access requests. But we're still

focused on giving notice to our customers. My work on that hasn't really changed. It's gotten more substantial, but hasn't changed in that regard because we were already caring about this for a while." Another said that his "work was about the lack of or problems with our notices. That's what the FTC investigates and looks at, so that's how our leadership focused our work." Young professionals felt the focus on notice, choice, and control explicitly. "We were told at the beginning that we will pay attention to privacy policies." Even when new people joined the team, their "work would also focus on privacy policies." These interviews suggest that the practice of privacy law, at least for some in the information industry, is being reduced to work on notice, consent, and control. That restriction comes from the top, but it also inculcates a corporate-friendly approach to privacy in the ethos, practice, and routine of company workers.

Confusing Privacy and Security

When a company experiences a data breach or a hack, incident response teams, which include engineers, lawyers, executives, and other stakeholders, get to work. Technology vendors also specialize in security incident response. Among other tasks, engineers patch security holes and design new security protocols. Communications teams issue press releases and inform customers. Lawyers report breaches to authorities, prepare legal defenses, and provide necessary documentation to regulators. Executives speak to the press and may shuffle personnel to deal with the fallout. Several AmLaw 100 firms specialize in cybersecurity incident response and provide their clients with step-by-step post–data breach counseling. There are plans in place.

Privacy issues – things like third-party access to data, using intimate information for behavioral targeting, or failing to police uses of application programming interfaces, or APIs, to name just a few – should sometimes merit different responses. And yet, we know both from interviews with those involved and public statements to the press that some companies respond to *privacy* issues with *security* fixes. This is not a universal tactic; many companies will stop the offending practice, like no longer sharing information with Facebook even before consenting to data use practices, or

claim that their data practices are lawful as a "legitimate interest" under the GDPR. But those that do turn to cybersecurity when lax security wasn't the problem are taking action without actually solving the problem. They are, in short, performatively constructing *privacy*-as-*security*.

Ten software engineers I interviewed had been involved in their current or former employers' response to press, civil society, or other investigations into their data use practices. Seven of those engineers said that their job was to update security and introduce new encryption tools. "We had an emergency meeting after [the] report came out," one said, "and my team was told to come up with new strategies for securing and encrypting data over and above what we've done before because, and I'm paraphrasing here, 'we need to show the press we're doing something.'" Four were involved in making changes to developers' API access. One worked with a team to redesign the app from the ground up, but retained almost all data sharing with Facebook in the new version. As for the other three engineers, they said they didn't do much. "It was a lot of hurry up and wait, and then wait and then wait, and then we didn't end up doing anything. It kind of blew over." None of these ten engineers reported making any material change in the data collection practices of their platforms.

Lawyers and privacy professionals also play roles here. A lawyer in New York with ten years' experience working in cyber incident response told me that he would "work with companies going into crisis mode when there was a data breach, and there would be a ton of things we needed to do." When I asked him about the advice he gives clients if, say, a product is found to be sharing personal and identifiable information with third parties in violation of the platform's privacy policy, he said, "Well, the first thing is either stop it or change the privacy policy. I would notify the FTC out of an abundance of caution, but we don't always have to. And I would recommend new encryption and better security so people can have peace of mind that nothing will happen with their data." Better security may calm fears of harm from future data breaches, but it seems orthogonal to a data misuse problem. It's performance: it doesn't hurt, but while it's not actually solving the problem, it is socially constructing *privacy* work as *security* work.

Of course, privacy and encryption are not the same; the latter is a necessary, but small, part of the former. Privacy is, at its

core, about the social relationships governing disclosure between and among individuals and between users and the platforms that collect, analyze, and manipulate their information for some purpose (often for profit). But even for those who think privacy is and always will be about choice and control, it is clear that privacy is not the same as security or encryption.

Security is far more about preventing, assessing, and addressing unauthorized access to systems and attacks on data safety and integrity. President Obama's Cyberspace Policy Review, for example, defined cyber security as "strategy ... regarding the security of and operations in cyberspace, and encompasses the full range of threat reduction, vulnerability reduction, deterrence, international engagement, incident response, resiliency, and recovery policies and activities ... as they relate to the security and stability of the global information and communications infrastructure." Legal scholars have offered similar definitions, focused on "criminality" and "espionage" or "using computer technology to engage in activity that undermines a society's ability to maintain internal or external order." Conflating the two often means that consumer privacy gets short shrift. When Mark Zuckerberg, Facebook's CEO, announced a new "privacy-focused" vision for the social network, his proposed changes focused almost entirely on encrypted messaging and ignored privacy issues like access to data, third-party sharing, and secondary uses. Software engineers understand that a lack of security is a threat to their products. As several of them explained, the full breadth of their privacy-related work was to prevent their products from getting hacked. The nonsecurity aspects of data privacy and consumer expectations got short shrift. That was no accident. Indeed, it's a clever trick: The information industry gets to engage in a lot of window dressing without making any material changes to their data-extractive business model while at the same time, strategically nudging their employees to think that the misdirection is, in fact, no misdirection at all. [58]

Strategic Punishment for Employees with Pro-Privacy Views

Investigative reports suggest that some tech companies routinely punish whistleblowers. In August 2020, for example, BuzzFeed reported that Facebook punished a senior engineer for

collecting evidence showing the company was giving preferential treatment to conservative accounts and helping them remove fact-checks from their content. The engineer's access to internal data was revoked and he was fired days later. Other Facebook employees who gathered evidence that Breitbart, the right-wing conspiracy theory website, was being protected from the company's policies on misinformation had their internal access revoked as well. Google took the same approach to its employees who blew the whistle on the company's efforts to suppress unionization, its cozy relationship with outside advisers with long histories of homophobic and racist comments, and its entanglement with Customs and Border Protection. Google even fired the prominent AI researcher Timnit Gebru for trying to publish a paper on language algorithms that threatened the company's bottom line. This type of job insecurity has a chilling effect on managers, dissuading them from speaking privacy truths to data-extractive power.[59]

The information industry's attack on internal privacy advocates may be less draconian, but no less powerful. Rather than firing privacy professionals and software engineers who want to decelerate the development of a particular product with significant privacy risks, some tech companies just stop listening to them and consign them to less attractive work assignments. This happened to several privacy professionals and software engineers I interviewed. In one case, the CPO at a cloud computing company wrote memos and spoke to her bosses and colleagues about significant privacy risks in a product that could result in liability under the GDPR. The company's general counsel "conducted an internal review that took all of one day and got back to me that they were willing to go ahead given, and I quote, the 'low likelihood that a [data protection agency, the privacy regulators in Europe] would overreact like' I overreacted." After this incident, she said, "I was left out of meetings and when I was there, they wouldn't let me speak, or let me speak and ignore me." Importantly, she added: "I knew after this that I had to change my tone and sort of finesse or modify what I said or I would be pushed to the side the whole time. I would probably have been fired had I kept that up." Of course, not all privacy professionals are subject to such overt and obvious marginalization, but my research indicates that is one strategy among many for limiting the impact of those who try to affect real pro-privacy changes in design.

Privacy engineers were also silenced in the design process. Over the last five years, many companies in the information industry have hired "privacy engineers" to, supposedly, integrate privacy into design. "That's what I was hired to do," said one of these engineers. "But the job immediately became much more about reviewing someone else's work. They would ask me to review new features for what they called 'privacy risk.' But they wouldn't ask me to do anything until something was basically done. They said I would be doing design work, but all I was doing was reading other people's code for security vulnerabilities." Facebook's Privacy Engineer job postings are now up front about this, stating explicitly that the job involves "conduct[ing] technical reviews" and providing product teams with "guidance and best practices." That could be helpful, but only if anyone actually listened to them. Only one company I visited and only a handful of those represented among my interviewees had privacy engineers. None of them did any design work themselves, and none of them had successfully changed the privacy-related design features of a product they had been asked to review. This anecdotal evidence cannot speak for the entire information industry as a whole. Rather, the point is that companies can hire privacy engineers and silence them within their bureaucracies.[60]

Zealous Advocacy and Privacy Legal Arguments

The information industry also takes advantage of lawyers' training and commitment to "zealous advocacy" to conscript rank-and-file privacy lawyers into making unabashedly antiprivacy arguments in litigation. We discussed some of those arguments above; they include asserting that internet users have no expectation of privacy, defining privacy as secrecy, and denying liability based on a single "click-to-agree" button. A constellation of workplace pressures makes it difficult for lawyers, especially young lawyers, to push back when their bosses give them research and litigation assignments. But tech companies also encourage their lawyers to see arguments that are harmful to privacy as not only an ordinary part of their job, but as actually good things for customers: tough arguments in court, the argument goes, free the company to do right by customers on the market.

Many lawyers are taught that zealous advocacy for their client is a canonical ethical duty. Henry Brougham, an early evangelist

of zealous advocacy, described it as the command to do what is necessary to "save that client" even if it might cause "the alarm, the torments, [or] the destruction" of others. Others see it as the obligation to bracket away personal moral, political, or partisan beliefs in favor of pursuing the client's agenda, whatever that may be. Today, many litigators and transactional attorneys see zealous advocacy as a central component of a client-centered service even though scholars who have studied the zealous advocacy mantra argue that it harms clients and operates as a license for incivility, ethically dubious behavior, and harassing tactics that teeter on the edge of legality.[61]

At a minimum, though, lawyers are trained not to push back when their bosses require them to make legal arguments that may be contrary to their own beliefs. This role separation allows privacy lawyers to claim to be privacy advocates within the industry while making antiprivacy arguments that serve their employers' interests in litigation. As one privacy attorney at an AmLaw 100 firm told me, "I have no problem making these arguments in court because that's my job. I can support policy changes in my own personal capacity, but I'm not going to fail my client just because my personal opinions are different." Lester, the general counsel we met in Chapter 1, used the zealous advocacy ideal to explain how his company could both say it cares about its customers' privacy and argue in court that its customers had no privacy whatsoever. As Seth, the company's risk officer explained, "There is much more to our work here in privacy than the arguments we have to make in a brief."

That may be true, but many information industry executives argue that making unabashedly antiprivacy arguments in litigation is a normal and normatively good way of enhancing privacy protections for consumers. "These cases we're talking about," one general counsel in Silicon Valley told me, "are seeking billions of dollars and want to just undermine the entire business model. How could that be a good thing? It would be better for everyone if we had the freedom to do what we know best, respond to what people need and want." The CEO of a dating app in New York agreed, noting that "there is no world in which things are better if we have to pay a multi-million-dollar fine. We can't provide a service when we're constantly at risk of a lawsuit. We're already doing a lot of great work doing better at privacy. We just can't do it via a punitive attack from the privacy

bar." These sentiments were echoed down the line. An associate general counsel at a mid-size company in the email space told me that "it may sound weird, but punishing us isn't the answer. Our team is far more nimble when we don't work under a strict consent decree." A partner at an AmLaw 100 firm also said that "some of our clients have already instituted brand new privacy changes on their own, and we encourage them to do that. I'd rather protect them from billions in dollars in a settlement so they can continue the good work they've done by hiring privacy leaders and experts."

The selective use of canons of legal ethics to persuade rank-and-file lawyers that making antiprivacy arguments in litigation is both a good thing and entirely in line with privacy advocacy is a practical means of immunizing the information industry from legal accountability. As Julie Cohen explains, tech companies deploy overlapping and sometimes conflicting tools of the law – from intellectual property to the First Amendment – to create "zones of legal privilege," where no one can object to corporate conduct. By cloaking antiprivacy arguments in the trappings of legal ethics and by arguing that the best way to protect consumer privacy is through best practices, innovation, and other market-based strategies, information industry executives conscript privacy lawyers into their own fights. Put another way, leadership disingenuously creates space for lawyers to separate their work from their personal beliefs and fall in line with industry advocacy. Those lawyers then perform in court (or wherever they advance antiprivacy arguments) and construct the practical reality of privacy law that they come to believe is accurate and true.[62]

Management also hides the ball from its more junior attorneys. This happens both in-house and at private firms that represent tech companies in court. Many junior attorneys at large law firms are introduced to litigation practices with research assignments on discrete legal questions and they rarely, if ever, have the chance to see how their work fits into a larger legal argument. They rarely, if ever, can affect the theory of the case with their own, perhaps contrary, views. Several attorneys acknowledged this problem during our interviews, with one senior associate justifying the practice as "a necessary form of training." A partner at a leading law firm with a well-known privacy practice said that "our young attorneys are amazing, and I absolutely want to hear from them if they

have ideas, but we do need them to focus on the project at hand, especially as we staff our matters so lean[ly]." We see the same results in-house. "When I first moved in-house," one New York lawyer who has been in-house at a tech company for two years told me, "I knew intellectually that in-house lawyers were generalists. We did everything. But I didn't really realize it, you know?" This meant he had to prioritize where he put his efforts. "I don't always have the time to think broadly about every case I'm working on, let alone others.' I just make the best arguments I can for the company."

Friendly Academics

The information industry also launders its arguments through seemingly independent academic research. The best example of this is in the field of AI and automated decision-making systems. AI is an umbrella term often imprecisely used to refer to set of technologies "best understood as a set of techniques aimed at approximating some aspect of human or animal cognition using machines." For AI systems to work as promised (which they rarely do), their developers require enormous tranches of data for the purposes of training and improving accuracy. AI policy, therefore, is inextricably linked to privacy: the less regulation around the collection and use of personal data, the easier it will be to design, market, and deploy AI; the fewer guardrails around the use of AI, the more companies will extract our data. Scholars in law and the social sciences are interrogating AI and its use in social policy decisions. They have highlighted problems of bias, lack of accountability, structural injustice, and invasions of privacy. Other researchers, however, have become apologists for industry's AI-related data grabs.[63]

The MIT Media Lab, for example, not only cozied up to Silicon Valley billionaires to build potential funding streams, but also allegedly aligned some of its policy recommendations on data collection and AI with Big Tech's antiregulatory posture. In the AI space, the information industry prefers a light (or no) touch approach to tweaking AI's bias problem; they have co-opted the notion of "AI ethics" as a means of replacing public governance with their own internal structures. Industry also invests millions to create a narrative about bias, data privacy, and the role of government. They funded MIT Media Lab research that was

eventually cited in reports published by Microsoft, Google, IBM, Facebook, and Amazon calling for self-regulation. In response to industry pressure, Media Lab executives allegedly "water[ed] down" AI law and policy recommendations to the California legislature that were at odds with the research done by its own experts on the ground.[64]

Amazon paid scholars at Antonin Scalia Law School at George Mason University to push their favored discourses. After the antitrust scholar Lina Khan wrote an article targeting Amazon as anticompetitive and calling for reinvigorating antitrust law to take on the internet giant, Amazon paid pro-corporate scholars to write an article lauding Amazon's monopolistic practices as good for consumers. It's hard to know how often this happens. But even when scholars acknowledge their corporate funding streams in footnotes, the discursive damage remains.[65]

There is more to this story than a few grants, even if those grants add up to a several millions of dollars. Many scholars who receive Google, Facebook, or other Big Tech funds insist that the money doesn't influence their writing. And for many, that is true. Merely receiving money from a target of research does not necessarily prove bias. But we also have evidence that the nonprofits that receive those funds make personnel and substantive decisions that accord with the views of their biggest tech donors. In 2017, for example, the entire competition team at a Google-funded think tank was fired after its leader pushed for more rigorous antitrust enforcement against Google.[66]

The information industry is also far more subtle as it seeks influence over academic discourse about privacy, law, and technology. For instance, company representatives will often only speak with independent researchers about already public documents and reports and then only on "deep background," thus limiting what academics can learn. This happened to me during research for another project, where a Google attorney and several colleagues were only willing to discuss Google Play's published guidelines and only without attribution. I ended the call. Five academic colleagues experienced the same tactic, including one who was interested in Facebook content moderation who was told "only on the condition that you can't quote anything we say." This tactic may sound counterproductive to building friendly discourses in academia; *not*

talking is a bad inculcative strategy. According to a former member of Google's policy shop, the deep background strategy "gives us an opportunity to share our side of the story without pinning a quote on one person because quotes can always be misleading and edited to make us look bad."[67]

Several companies incentivize friendly coverage by dangling research funds in front of junior scholars. Young researchers and PhD students are particularly susceptible to corporate influence because of the need to pay for their fellowships, publish to get tenure, the possibility that access will translate into undiscovered research, and the small stipends they receive from their institutions. The Facebook Fellowship, for example, includes full tuition and a $42,000 annual stipend, paid visits to Facebook, and all expenses paid participation in the annual Fellowship summit. Undoubtedly, merely participating in this program does mean that these junior scholars are unduly influenced by Facebook. But much of the Fellows' already published research fits neatly within privacy-as-control's logic of power. Among thirty-six Facebook Fellows in 2020, six classify their work in some way related to privacy. Along with several co-authors, these fellows have published academic articles arguing that the tool Mark Zuckerberg plans to use to create a "privacy-focused" Facebook – end-to-end encryption – is the "best way to protect" privacy on social media. In another article, researchers used studies to buttress the feasibility of privacy self-governance and argued users of messaging services are willing to trade security for convenience. Other Fellows researching AI and fairness issues have published articles proposing changes that companies can make themselves, perpetuating, even inadvertently, the self-regulatory ethos. I am not suggesting that all of these promising young scholars are part of a cabal of researchers plotting to spread pro-Facebook messages throughout academia. Switch it around: Facebook is choosing to provide ample support for research that perpetuates privacy-as-control's logic and using its soft power to create friendly relationships among promising future academics.[68]

To my knowledge and based on the experience of several academics in law, surveillance studies, and sociology, Facebook and Google often, though not always, require preapproval of all quotes and related text before an academic publishes scholarship based on interviews with company representatives, a grant from the company,

or pursuant to officially sanctioned field work. This is a particularly pernicious tactic. One colleague I interviewed for this project has saved email conversations with Facebook in which company representatives required articles to be embargoed and precleared before submission. I did not get that far with Facebook, which refused to participate in this research. Another colleague reported that some Facebook and Google grants they received had "no strings attached, it was money for a conference or a project or whatever, but they just gave it," but "research money always came with questions and invitations and, ultimately, they wanted to know what my conclusions would be. I gave back the remaining funds much to [my university's] chagrin."

Corporate-friendly academic research makes its way back into the information industry, inculcating the rank and file along the way, because corporate researchers, public policy teams, and other lawyers and privacy professionals are encouraged to cite and refer to it in their work. Several privacy professionals and lawyers outside Silicon Valley showed me internal documents focusing both on the benefits of privacy notice, choice, and control and how to improve it, and they all rely on research from Facebook Fellows, Google-funded research projects, and encryption-centered work at Microsoft Research. Of course, independent academics are cited as well. But, often, those academics are cited for background; their pro-regulatory proposals are ignored. For example, Facebook cited work from Lorrie Cranor, Aleecia McDonald, Helen Nissenbaum, and me, among others, in its public report on improving notice and transparency. But when it came time to thinking about solutions, Facebook touted its own solutions, as if to suggest that the problem can be solved without the law getting involved.[69]

Performing Accountability

Another common tactic I observed during my interviews is what Julie Cohen has called performing accountability, or doing something "designed to express a generic commitment to accountability without … meaningful scrutiny of the underlying process." Magicians use the word "misdirection" to describe a related phenomenon: while we're distracted by some of the information industry's cynical trappings of accountability, tech companies are busy undermining our privacy.[70]

A paradigmatic example of this strategy comes from the related context of content moderation. Content moderation refers to how platforms regulate the material available on their sites. Sarah Roberts has called content moderation "a powerful mechanism of control" that has "grown up alongside, and in service to" private companies in the information industry. Platforms moderate content in order to achieve optimal engagement. Platforms develop their own rules for what is and what is not allowed to be posted and they apply those rules using both humans and algorithms.[71]

Content moderation at Facebook has garnered outsized attention in the media, among policy makers, and among academics. Many high-profile content moderation controversies at Facebook have caused such a crisis of confidence that the company announced, with significant fanfare, that it was creating an oversight board to hear appeals of moderation decisions from the front lines. The idea is that an independent board would routinize, rationalize, and publicize content moderation decisions, generating trust and confidence.[72]

Per a search on Lexis Nexis, 2,210 newspaper and magazine articles have been written about the Oversight Board between November 2018, when the board was announced, and May 18, 2020. Over 565 days, that's an average of nearly four articles per day! Facebook pitched many of these stories to both leading outlets like the *New York Times* and the *Wall Street Journal*, as well as to general interest blogs and tech-focused news outlets. During this time, 189 law review and journal articles at least mentioning the board have been published. And that doesn't even include the many hundreds that are being written, under submission, and soon-to-be published at this book went to press. A May 18, 2020, Google search for any content with the exact phrase "Facebook Oversight Board" yielded 236,000 results; millions more have all of those terms. Facebook has pushed out several reports and issued press releases dutifully picked up by news outlets and commentators. The company's representatives have given countless talks at universities, as well as public and private fora, from Princeton University to the Aspen Institute.[73]

This onslaught was evidently intentional, but the attention paid to the board is disproportionate to its power. The board says it will focus on "the most challenging content issues for Facebook, including ... hate speech, harassment, and protecting people's

privacy." But, as the media scholar Siva Vaidhyanathan notes, "only in the narrowest and most trivial of ways does this board have any such power. The new Facebook review board will have no influence over anything that really matters in the world." A quick look at the board's Charter proves he's correct.[74]

The board can only hear appeals for content that has been removed, not the misleading and harmful content that remains. Nor can the board make binding decisions about the fate of specific pieces of content on a case-by-case basis. It is supposed to make its decisions within ninety days of a filed appeal, but can expedite certain decisions within thirty days. Its decisions have zero precedential value. It has no binding impact on policy, even on policies about content moderation! It cannot change the way Facebook is run or materially change how Facebook makes decisions about content. It won't be able to address the fact that Facebook's failure to remove misleading "deep fake" videos or "fake news" can sway an election. It can't do much about the rampant hate speech and human rights violations that persist. It has absolutely no voice in Facebook's continued misuse of user data. And it will play no role in corralling misinformation and harmful conspiracies rampant throughout the platform. The last two points are rather ironic: the board's announcement came in reaction to a *New York Times* report about how Facebook publicly lied, deflected blame, and tried to cover up both its failure to recognize and police Russia's use of the platform to interfere in the 2016 US presidential election and its flagrant misuse of user data in the Cambridge Analytica scandal.[75]

Why, then, has the board received so much media and scholarly attention? The strategy is intentional, meant to distract us from everything Facebook isn't doing. Joan Donovan, the research director of Harvard's Shorenstein Center and an expert on media manipulation, called the board a distraction from "what really needs to happen, which is to design technology that doesn't allow for the expansive amplification of disinformation and health misinformation." Facebook isn't changing its business. It isn't taking down fake videos or limiting the lies from right-wing politicians. Nor is it changing the very financial model that makes it in the company's interest to extract our data, leave up conspiracy theories, fake news, deep fakes, and other sensationalized content. Dipayan Ghosh, a fellow at Harvard and former Facebook

executive, wrote that the board is "a commercial thing of convenience for the company both in its name and its function; it gives the impression that the board will provide true oversight by graduating the responsibility of determining what should constitute hate speech to an external party with public credibility, allowing the company to skate over the threat of a more rigorous regulatory policy that might emerge from relatively aggressive legislatures that might wish to target the firm's business model itself." The board's impotence, then, is real, but its discursive effect is not. Facebook engaged in an aggressive strategy involving earned media and friendly academics to make a lot of noise about something that will barely be a blip on the screen of Facebook's vast problems. Its full court press is nothing short of a concerted strategy to redirect us from its other failures.[76]

The same strategy has been deployed to inculcate the values of privacy-as-control as obvious, common sense, and normatively good. Privacy self-regulation, notice-and-consent, and privacy policies are "commercial things of convenience," as well: privacy policies give the impression that the information industry is doing something to protect our data and small, marginal changes after privacy scandals facilitate an escape from greater regulatory oversight. This misdirection has been so successful at inculcating a perception of accountability among members of the public that many people think a company with a privacy policy is promising to keep our data private! Whenever I questioned the privacy-invasive designs of several companies' products, the usual response was to redirect my attention to the company's cybersecurity work. We saw this in Chapter 1, where both privacy professionals and software engineers touted their encryption and state-of-the-art security techniques as proof that they cared about privacy. The privacy lawyers I interviewed highlighted their work improving transparency. In several instances, these lawyers would note that "no one is perfect" and that "we're doing better" by showing how they have redesigned their notices to be more readable. These are, at their core, misdirections. Improving notice and strengthening cybersecurity are not bad ideas. But they don't speak to design. Nor do they serve any purpose outside the privacy-as-control framework. Asking us to focus on notice not only perpetuates its legitimacy as a privacy practice, but it also keeps the rank and file focused on performances of privacy

rather than pulling back the curtain on the industry's legal and discursive crusades against it.[77]

Privacy Disempowerment

Coercive bureaucracies in the information industry are inculcating corporate-friendly privacy discourses throughout their organizations. They are strategically setting agendas, allocating assignments, punishing dissent, redirecting attention, and leveraging professional ethics and prosaic workplace pressures. One of the goals of this unprecedented effort is, in part, to enlist an army of foot soldiers for tech company executives to implement their antiprivacy plans.[78]

The endgame, however, is bigger. Tech companies are trying to undermine the development of privacy law as well. By defining privacy in terms of control and self-governance, both of which are already reflected in today's notice-and-consent regime, the information industry is fighting against change. It would be better, tech companies argue, to empower individuals to make their own privacy choices than let the government decide what's best. If privacy-as-control is what we have and if what we have is empowering, liberating, and good for privacy, then any change, if it's needed at all, should be marginal. And if we do need to make some changes, they should adhere to the basic assumption that privacy means giving individuals control over when, how, and with whom they share their information.

Even within this discursive context, privacy law has undergone some significant change, at least on the surface. In 2018, the European Union enacted a comprehensive new data protection law that puts unprecedented new requirements on business that collect data on European Union citizens. A year later, after more than a decade of issuing consent decrees to hundreds of companies, the FTC issued a record-breaking $5 billion fine against Facebook for its privacy failures. In 2020, California enacted a comprehensive privacy law that applies across the board rather than only to specific sectors. Other progressive states, including New York and Washington, are considering similar proposals.

The information industry, having successfully weakened the ground on which their employees think and talk about privacy, has also influenced not just the drafting of privacy laws and FTC rules, but

also their implementation. In many respects, this new page in privacy law reflects privacy-as-control's reach. But it also reflects another facet of the information industry's coercive bureaucracies. After making it more likely that new privacy rules will reflect corporate-friendly privacy discourses, the information industry turned next to undermining the implementation of those rules, putting another barrier between the laws on the books and our privacy on the ground.

3 PRIVACY COMPLIANCE

The information industry's discursive performances have influenced everyone, including policy makers, privacy professionals, and ordinary users of technology. The campaign has seen its greatest success in the United States, where tech companies and their allies are actively undermining the push for a comprehensive national information privacy law, where studies show many people have given up on the hope that they can adequately protect their privacy online, and where many privacy professionals see corporate-friendly privacy discourses as ordinary, routine, and common sense.[1]

The current system for regulating data use, processing, and distribution in the United States reflects discourses about the neutrality of technology, valorization of markets, critique of regulation, and privacy-as-control. Federal privacy law is sector specific. Laws like the Children's Online Privacy Protection Act (covering some children's data), the Health Insurance Portability and Accountability Act (some health data), and Gramm-Leach-Bliley (some financial data), among others, operate alongside broad notice-and-consent enforced by the FTC. Many of these sectoral laws are paradigmatic manifestations of the discourse of privacy-as-control. The laws are primarily notice-and-consent regimes. And the FTC's approach to date has been a veritable clinic on the influence of privacy-as-control: throughout its privacy regulatory history, it has primarily pursued companies that break their promises in privacy notices and terms of service and, as several scholars have already demonstrated, almost universally focuses on information industry behaviors that deceive individuals and create information asymmetries that undermine markets. That means that

the FTC is focusing on threats to self-governance, rational decision-making, and control. This regime is littered with holes and zones of immunity for the information industry to do what it wants.[2]

But scholars and commentators have also said that privacy law is changing, becoming more robust over time. The FTC went from telling Congress it didn't want privacy regulatory authority and that companies should regulate themselves to what the legal scholars Daniel Solove and Woodrow Hartzog have called a broad "common law" focusing on deceptive practices, unfair treatment of users, lack of security, and more. State attorneys-general have grown into their roles as privacy enforcers, and Danielle Citron has shown how they may be more effective than federal regulators at bringing technology companies to heel. And Kenneth Bamberger and Deirdre Mulligan have argued that privacy professionals are going above and beyond these laws, filling in gaps left open by current privacy law and creating new standards and protocols for integrating privacy into design.[3]

Jurisdictions have also enacted and proposed new privacy laws. In 2018, the European Union's GDPR took effect. The CCPA took effect in 2020. From 2018 through the end of 2020, twenty-eight US states proposed more than forty new comprehensive privacy bills; members of the US Congress introduced ten. Lilian Edwards has called the GDPR "the most significant data privacy reform process in history." Others call it "the most consequential regulatory development in information policy in a generation . . . [and] brings personal data into a complex and protective regulatory regime." The GDPR enacts "protections that follow the data" and placed "duties on companies regardless of whether individuals invoke their individual rights." For its part, the CCPA has been called "strict" and the most "far-reaching" privacy law in US history.[4]

Maybe, but compared to what? These new developments in privacy law sound remarkably robust, but it's only telling part of the story. Law isn't an ontological institution. Nor does a chronicle of laws on the books capture the full breadth of the law. Laws are tools, not rules, implemented and deployed by people operating in organizational structures, whether that's the Environmental Protection Agency interpreting and implementing the Clean Air Act or a corporation interpreting and implementing privacy law. Law is also a social practice. In other words, what the law says matters, but who

interprets it, how it's implemented, and the social dynamics in which it is interpreted and implemented matter a whole lot more. In the privacy space, the European Union, the US Congress, and various states can pass all the privacy laws they want, but those laws are going to be mobilized by the information industry to achieve its profit-making goals. One way companies do that is by creating an organizational environment where the people responsible for implementing the laws we pass – lawyers and privacy professionals – create structures, systems, protocols, policies, and procedures that look like they comply with the law, but actually serve to undermine the law's effectiveness. This is the power of compliance.[5]

Think back to what we learned in Chapter 1. Bill noted early on that his job as a privacy professional was almost entirely administrative; it included instituting polices and routinizing work. That means he played an important gateway and interpretive function, translating the law into something his company could do implement. As lawyers, Anita and Jamal interacted with coders, answering their privacy questions as they came up. But the organizational rules of their company determined how they worked with engineering teams, forcing them to act as "consultants" or "resources." Internal rules, which include reporting hierarchies and budget allocations, also determined how Bill, the company's chief privacy officer, did his job. He had to negotiate with the chief technology officer to hire outside vendors and had to get approval from the general counsel for any privacy legal work. His direct boss, the chief risk officer, was responsible for all privacy compliance matters. This makes privacy advocacy precarious and difficult.

Janice spoke about how splitting the privacy budget between different departments could be detrimental to privacy work. The "IT guy" who controlled her budget just "wasn't budging," which prevented her from having the kind of imprint on design that she wanted. Anita and Jamal said that they had to work hard to get their bosses on board with taking privacy law seriously. Ensuring that executives listened to their advice was even more difficult. As Anita noted, "you can't be the one saying no all the time." Bill also admitted that he would moderate his advice in order to maintain access and guard against being largely sidelined within the company. These fears were structural; they were based on the fact that

companies have a history of hiring privacy professionals, giving them an office, and never giving them power to make change. Those very real threats caused privacy lawyers to moderate their advice, with none of the interviewees ever going so far as to decelerate or stop a product that posed privacy risks. They recognized that it may have been possible for them to do that; Bill suggested he was technically empowered to do so. And I have no doubt privacy leaders at some companies have similar powers. What matters for our privacy, however, is not so much whether the privacy department *can* exercise that power, but rather whether any of them actually do.

Privacy law was also foregrounded as a tool of corporate power over design. Bill thought the GDPR and the CCPA were "strict" and "robust" based on how much work he and his team had on their plates and the amount of work product they were churning out. But he never went into detail about how that work translated into better protections for consumers. As a metric, effort and worker hours are orthogonal to substantive changes in privacy protections. When pressed on how product designs were actually different, he had no answer.

Although he left early, Lester spoke pointedly about how arguing that individuals do not have privacy rights on the company's platform is an example of the aggressive advocacy he brings to his client's defense. Jamal and Anita acknowledged that part of the role of the in-house privacy lawyers is to translate legal requirements for their CEO so he could make decisions about how to implement those requirements throughout the company. That was an ongoing struggle, one made more difficult by privacy law's sometimes vague provisions, but it's end point – the need to make privacy "doable" the company – means that privacy's law on the books is being transformed, moderated, or even undermined in corporate-friendly ways on the ground.

In this chapter, I will argue that the privacy laws we have enacted will not succeed at materially altering the data-extractive behavior of the information industry because those laws still reflect corporate-friendly privacy discourses and, most notably, the companies that those laws are supposed to regulate use their power over compliance infrastructure to create symbols of compliance that

stand in for real privacy protection. The sociolegal scholar Lauren Edelman calls this a problem of *legal endogeneity*.[6]

Edelman describes how the law, rather than constraining or guiding the behavior of regulated entities, is actually shaped by ideas emerging from the space the law seeks to regulate. It occurs when compliance professionals on the ground have significant power to define what the law means in practice. When given that opportunity, some compliance professionals frame the law in accordance with managerial values like efficiency and reducing corporate risk rather than the substantive goals the law is meant to achieve, like consumer protection or equality. This opens the door for companies to create structures, policies, and protocols that comply with the law in name only. As these symbolic structures become more common, judges and policy makers defer to them as paradigms of best practices, mistaking mere symbols of compliance with adherence to legal mandates. And the rest of us start to think of these symbolic structures as what the law actually requires. When this happens, law fails to achieve substantive goals because the compliance metric – the adoption of symbols, processes, and procedures within a corporate environment – may be completely independent of or even detrimental to actual progress. Put another way, privacy law becomes a house of cards.[7]

But it doesn't stop there. Influenced and inculcated with antiprivacy discourses, privacy professionals and privacy lawyers create and implement these symbolic structures. Over time, after they are routinized in daily practices, and as they are performed over and over again, privacy professionals normalize mere symbols as what the law actually requires. As a result, even those privacy professionals who see themselves as privacy advocates may think they're faithfully executing the law and protecting their customers' privacy, but are, in fact, entrenching corporate power.

This chapter explores the ways in which corporate power over compliance can undermine privacy law. It begins by defining compliance and reviewing how privacy law has recently evolved from the notice-and-consent regime we discussed in the previous chapter to a compliance-based system of individual rights and corporate procedural responsibilities. Although this represents a shift in the social practice of privacy law, even these new privacy laws remain weak on their face. On top of that, they have been

undermined by corporate managerialism and two complementary forces: the intentional tactics of information industry organizations to weaken privacy structures and the normalization of corporate-friendly symbols of compliance. In the end, the information industry has reduced privacy professionals' ability to have any impact on privacy in design even as it boasts of its robust privacy practices. This means that in addition to inculcating their privacy professionals and privacy lawyers with corporate-friendly privacy discourses, which dampens the rank and file's interest in and capacity to push their employers to better protect our privacy, the information industry takes the desire for change and cuts it off at the knees. Privacy professionals' best efforts will, at best, lead to marginal results.

Compliance as Power

Compliance is sociolegal, sociotechnical, and sociolinguistic. I define it as the translation of law into internal procedures and the evolving use and reification of the resulting procedures. For example, the law may say that private employers may not engage in gender stereotyping. But the tools of compliance that develop in the wake of that law, including policies, reporting procedures, appeals processes, trainings, and the company's posture toward complaints, often matter more for individuals on the ground. They develop out of negotiations between compliance officers and other executives, between market pressures and legal interpretations, between different definitions legally relevant words, and between earnest advocates and conservative elements who like things the way they are, among other dynamics.[8]

In the privacy space, compliance also involves technological tools that translate legal requirements into code. For example, if a privacy law mandates that individuals must be able to request access and make corrections to their data, a company holding that data must know what data it has, where it is, how to grant access, and how to fix errors. That will require a technical system, but one that incorporates social and legal decisions, including about the extent of access and correction, the degree to which individuals will be able to understand correction procedures on their own, how to adjudicate requests, and how easy or difficult it is to fulfill a request. Someone has to make those decisions, someone has to write the code for it,

and someone has to manage and use it. Many companies in the information industry outsource some of their compliance requirements to third-party vendors that design compliance software tied to their interpretations of specific legal requirements. Indeed, in the last three years alone, the IAPP has identified more than 300 companies in the privacy technology vendor market, many of which apply technological answers to compliance problems and instantiate their interpretations of legal rules into their technology designs.[9]

And just as design translates policy into the language of code, compliance translates exogenous law into the language of process, procedure, and paper trails. For example, a substantive rule prohibiting workplace discrimination becomes policies, trainings, forms, reporting procedures, review boards, and appeals processes, among other structures. In so doing, compliance transforms the law on the books into a particular corporate vision of what the law requires on the ground.

Compliance, then, is another tool of corporate power. Compliance professionals filter and interpret the law for their corporate employers. They engage with and respond to parallel or conflicting interests among different social groups within their companies and develop procedures that reflect internal political decisions about how to manage the law's requirements in the context of an overarching profit-driven mission. Scholars have recognized the ways compliance can filter and recast the law to suit the interests of corporate actors. In this chapter, we will go deeper inside the information industry, identifying the ways in which tech companies actually develop and deploy compliance systems in coercive bureaucracies to frustrate the goals of privacy law.[10]

Privacy Law Today

In the last chapter, we discussed some of the ways in which traditional privacy law reflects a legal regime focused primarily on notice-and-consent. We also discussed the inadequacies of that approach. Let's now discuss what's new in privacy law. Some scholars and commentators see the FTC levying unprecedented fines against Facebook and insist that the agency is taking a more aggressive posture toward the information industry. They see the FTC's requirement of "comprehensive privacy program[s]" as bringing

privacy voices to the board rooms. They see the GDPR and its authorization of large fines as having so great a substantive effect on companies and individuals that Europe will lead the world in protecting privacy. And they foresee the CCPA making it difficult for both large and small companies to take cavalier approaches to their customers' data. These conclusions miss the mark. The CCPA may be more specific about the rights we have to our data, but it is almost entirely a product of discourse of privacy-as-control. Nor have recent FTC actions and the GDPR made privacy law stricter, stronger, or more robust. They have just changed privacy law's tactics from inadequate self-regulation to a public-private partnership in the development and enforcement of law that collapses into self-regulation under internal consistencies and corporate capture. Compliance-based privacy law imagines a regulatory environment where the law on the books states rules of the road and regulated entities are responsible for creating organizational procedures that demonstrate compliance with those rules. That was a gift to the information industry and it is taking full advantage.[11]

A Shift in Privacy Law's Tactics?

Both the CCPA and the GDPR guarantee certain rights to individuals, including the rights of access, portability, and deletion. The right of access means that European citizens and California residents have a right to request that a company disclose all the personal information the company has about them. This right includes disclosure about what the company does with that data, including whether and to which third parties the information is shared. That sounds a lot like notice, albeit a little more specific. The right of data portability means that individuals can have their information transferred from one company to another. Although only the GDPR includes a specific right to request that a company does the transferring itself, the rights are substantially similar in both statutes. And deletion gives an individual a right to have a company delete the personal information it has already collected. Both statutes require companies to respond to these requests with specific steps. They also impose notice requirements on companies that collect our data and have roughly similar (though not identical) definitions for "personal information."[12]

The CCPA is an opt-out regime, permitting data collection and processing unless an individual makes an affirmative choice to say "no." The GDPR says that a company cannot collect or process any data unless it has demonstrated one of six "lawful" bases for doing so. The CCPA only includes rights to access, portability, and deletion; the GDPR guarantees individuals a handful of other rights. These include a right to correct inaccurate data, a right to restrict data processing, a right to object to data processing, and a right to an explanation of the "logic" behind how an automated decision-making system affected their rights and opportunities. The GDPR's penalty ceiling is higher than the CCPA's, and the CCPA carves out a broader exemption for small businesses.[13]

Despite all the rhetoric surrounding the GDPR and CCPA, the rights guaranteed in each perpetuate a self-governing privacy regime and fall into some of the same traps as notice-as-consent. Granted, Californians have more rights of control than the rest of us and their privacy notices have to be more detailed than they used to, but those notices will still be long, unreadable, and, as we discussed in the last chapter, utterly inadequate at actually protecting privacy. Rights of control still require individuals to overcome every trick designed into platforms that encourage inertia or inaction or disclosure. The CCPA, then, represents more of the same. Indeed, the law itself, together with attendant rhetoric about its robustness, may weaken the drive for further regulation: it continues notice-and-consent's performance of privacy, inculcating the discourse of control with each click, and creates the misleading impression that our privacy problems have been solved. European data subjects may have even more affirmative rights to their data, but both laws ignore the cognitive limitations that constrain our autonomy. Both laws require us to overcome our inertia, figure out how to exercise the few rights we have, and take affirmative steps to take back some control over our data. The history of privacy self-governance suggests that more opportunities to make privacy choices won't actually help us protect our privacy.[14]

Neither the GDPR nor the myriad recent proposals for comprehensive privacy laws in the United States end with additional rights for data subjects. The other half of those laws impose obligations on technology companies that collect and process our data. This part of the law and recent FTC jurisprudence do represent

something of a second wave in privacy law – namely, a change in tactics from notice-and-consent to compliance.

Privacy's compliance-based regime is part of the model of collaborative governance. Margot Kaminski describes collaborative governance as governance that relies on a partnership between public authorities and private actors to achieve regulatory goals. More flexible than the blunt axe of command-and-control regulation and stronger than mere private ordering, collaborative governance is "a highly tailored, site-calibrated regulatory system that aims to pull inputs from, obtain buy-in from, and affect the internal institutional structures and decision-making heuristics of the private sector" while maintaining popular legitimacy and achieving better social welfare outcomes. It purports to operate as a true partnership. The government plays the role of a "back drop threat" that encourages private sector engagement, convenes regulated entities and civil society together, certifies compliance protocols, and, if necessary, an enforcer when things go awry. Alongside regulators, private actors develop the systems of compliance on their own, seek certification, share ideas with their industry, create standards, and maintain sufficient accountability on their own to ensure adherence to regulatory aims. And there is a broad toolkit for doing so, ranging from legal rules, negotiated settlements, safe harbors, codes of conduct, audits, informal delegation of interpretation authority to private actors, and incentives for private ordering in the public interest. The goal of collaborative governance, Kaminski continues, is to keep sufficient flexibility in the legal system so regulated entities will want to participate and enough strength in regulation so companies will do so in the public good.[15]

Accountability is central to collaborative governance, lest it fall back into unsupervised, self-serving "self-regulation." Kaminski acknowledges this, noting that accountability has to take the form of legitimacy-enhancing checks on corporate decision-making, or regulatory insurance against corporate mischief that will prove to members of the public that the system is working in their – rather than in corporate – interests. Ideally, this system of self-monitoring or third-party assessment, whose reports would be published for everyone to see, would allow individuals to choose which companies adhere to their values, pressure private actors to do better, and influence lawmakers to pass laws needed to fill gaps in the regime.

And because this governance regime is iterative, creating a repeated feedback loop as compliance protocols and audits are turned into public knowledge that spurs market-based and legal responses, it allows for flexibility, innovation, and tailored approaches that work for one industry but not another.[16]

The GDPR represents a weak and incomplete form of collaborative governance. It lacks a robust way for individuals and civil society to keep authorities and regulated entities honest. And, as Bill McGeveran has argued, European regulators have insufficient enforcement power. But the GDPR nevertheless creates a system in which rules are interpreted and implemented by regulators and industry working together. Kaminski notes that the GDPR includes several "deliberately vague" provisions that become less vague once the language is interpreted in context, using the law's preambles (or recitals), guidelines published by national data protection authorities and the European Data Protection Board, and industry best practices and norms. The law calls for the information industry to develop codes of conduct "for the purpose of specifying the application of" the law. These codes, once approved by a data protection regulator, act as safe harbors: companies can follow certified codes of conduct and know they won't be held liable for violating the GDPR. The law even states that these codes may be implemented as requirements across the EU. And several provisions in the GDPR envision integrating industry-developed technical standards into law and encourage companies to get together to develop self-certification rules that can help consumers distinguish between those companies that meet certain objective standards and those that don't.[17]

The GDPR also affects corporate structure and internal behavior. Companies have to hire data protection officers (DPOs) to oversee and ensure corporate compliance with the law. Companies also have to keep rather extensive data processing records, which can be requisitioned by regulators during an investigation. And, in certain circumstances, the GDPR requires regulated organizations to conduct impact assessments about data processing and collection and platform design. Impact assessments are mostly internal documents that are supposed to give companies a standard protocol for assessing privacy risks, but Kaminski suggests that over time, these assessments may affect general compliance by standardizing expectations and behaviors across the information industry.[18]

The FTC's regulatory approach also reflects elements of compliance-based regulation. Its "common law" of privacy is based almost entirely on negotiated settlements with regulated entities in the form of consent decrees. Consent decrees differ from court orders or injunctions; the latter are mandates handed down by a court or agency usually without input from their targets, while the former are compromises or agreements between government regulators and private actors intended to avoid unpredictable and costly litigation. Those consent decrees implement a collaborative governance regime. They create an ongoing regulatory partnership between government and industry by, among other things, requiring companies to meet industry standard best practices, develop a "comprehensive privacy program" that includes hiring privacy professionals, meeting reporting requirements, opening up to inspections, and conduct privacy assessments. The decrees also lay out broad legal rules – reasonableness, for example – that the FTC defines with reference to standards developed by the National Institute of Standards and Technology (NIST) that reflect aggregated industry best practices. The FTC's reports and guidance documents also frequently defer to and incorporate industry best practices as possible approaches to meeting FTC standards.[19]

A New Social Practice of Privacy Law

Some scholars have criticized new privacy laws, arguing that they lack essential elements of effective governance. Kaminski notes that the GDPR makes it difficult for civil society to participate and provide oversight, especially since many of the assessments and records required by the GDPR will never be made public. In the United States, civil society organizations like the Electronic Privacy Information Center routinely write amicus briefs in support of effective privacy enforcement, but lack standing to bring cases on behalf of ordinary citizens. Nor can individuals keep the information industry honest. Most privacy laws in the United States lack private rights of action and even where members of the public are permitted to bring cases, restrictive rules on standing, courts' long-standing unwillingness to recognize the gravity of privacy-related intangible harms, and the federal judiciary's notorious pro-corporate biases make it difficult to hold corporations accountable to the public.[20]

Privacy's take on collaborative governance means that the point at which law is developed, interpreted, and translated is inside the offices of armies of privacy professionals and lawyers on the ground inside the information industry, mostly out of reach of advocates and users. Compliance and legal professionals already play important gatekeeping and filtering functions inside corporations, translating exogenous law into practice. But collaborative governance regimes imbue these professionals with unique and explicit power to define what the law means for their employers and for us. Compliance leaders integrate their interpretations into governance through their work product: best practices, codes of conduct, paper trails, management reform, and so on. In the privacy space, privacy lawyers and privacy professionals play this role and they are integral to the social practice of privacy law.

Today, most large companies have a CPO who leads a staff of privacy and compliance professionals, and CPOs are becoming more prevalent throughout all industries. The IAPP reports that most privacy leaders are housed within "legal and compliance departments" with a smaller number in information security and IT departments. In 2018, 37 percent of CPOs said they reported directly to the board of directors. In the information industry, legal departments often have in-house lawyers focused exclusively on privacy; this is not only true at large companies like Facebook, Google, Apple, and Microsoft, but at mid-sized companies as well: a company I visited with approximately 800 employees had 15 attorneys, three of whom focused exclusively on privacy. Ninety-six of the AmLaw 100 law firms have separate privacy and cybersecurity practices. The IAPP, the industry's primary trade organization, reached 50,000 members in May 2019 and its conferences usually attract thousands. Bamberger and Mulligan have called this a "sea change" in how privacy is practiced "on the ground." They note that "corporate structures [now] frequently include direct privacy leadership, in many instances by C-level executives. The individuals managing corporate privacy have an applicant pool of trained professionals to draw from. There is ongoing training, certification, and networking. A community of corporate privacy managers has emerged. Ready evidence suggests that substantial effort is made to manage privacy."[21]

Bamberger and Mulligan suggested that many lawyers and privacy professionals are eager privacy advocates and "allies

already," working hard to fill in the gaps left by privacy law with a "company law" of privacy. Through a series of interviews with privacy professionals recognized as leaders in their fields, the researchers found that privacy leads were "innovating," getting creative, and using their best judgment to advance the privacy cause. They found that CPOs understood privacy to be more than just giving users notice and saw their companies' responsibilities as more than just compliance. To these CPOs, legal rules provided a floor. And privacy was a constantly evolving user-focused concept about which they had to think proactively and strategically. Many of Bamberger's and Mulligan's interviewees felt that corporate privacy strategy was about maintaining user trust and being sufficiently flexible, adaptive, and forward-looking to meet consumer expectations whatever they might be. It was not about doing merely the least they could do to forestall being sued. Rather, they had to engage in ongoing management of risk and keep up with consumers' changing expectations. Several CPOs talked about their jobs in fiduciary terms: they were "steward[s]" of data and "responsibl[e]" to consumers. They saw their primary objective as creating and maintaining "the company's trusted relationship" with customers, employees, and society itself. Other privacy professionals have called compliance-based system "a potential cure-all" for industry privacy woes.[22]

Privacy lawyers, CPOs, consultants, and their staffs are responsible for putting (and keeping) their companies in compliance with the GDPR and FTC orders. To do that, they deploy many tools. They help write privacy notices, design and conduct privacy trainings, work with outside consultants to conduct audits, develop privacy protocols explaining what employees can and cannot do with customer data, answer privacy questions from business units and work with executives to apply privacy rules to their projects, have input on corporate reports for investors and regulators, create privacy impact assessments, hire statutorily required employees or third-party assessors, contract with vendors to automate compliance, integrate recommendations from NIST, and work with colleagues in other companies to develop codes of conduct and industry best practices, among the myriad compliance responsibilities involving record keeping, internal assessments, and document collection. This work happens in a field with a growing and

organized civil society community, with the IAPP running certification programs and hosting examinations and other industry organizations creating privacy seals to verify compliance with certain industry standards. As such, privacy professionals, in-house counsel, and lawyers at private firms play critical roles in privacy's collaborative governance regimes.

Few privacy scholars have recognized this; Bamberger and Mulligan are the exception. That scholars have praised the GDPR's "substantial" or "very large" fines – up to 4 percent of worldwide revenue – as triggering a "worldwide rush of companies to create internal compliance regimes to comply with the GDPR" without actually looking under the hood at those compliance regimes suggests that much of the literature neglects the social process by which real people translate law into practice. Similarly, scholars have praised the FTC for moving beyond broken promises litigation without looking at the detritus that its broader jurisprudence has created on the ground.[23]

To their credit, Bamberger and Mulligan did recognize the importance of the privacy professional class, demonstrating that the people in the trenches were building tools that both reflected and went beyond the laws on the books. Bamberger called this process of corporate compliance professionals filling in law's gaps for their companies' contexts "regulation as delegation," arguing that it offered flexibility, buy-in, and greater efficacy. But there is the grave and perhaps inevitable risk of capture. For it to work well, a compliance-based regulatory regime requires resources and political will to enforce the laws on the books and should include public interest civil society organizations to help oversight and accountability. But given that the GDPR and FTC consent decrees rely on public-private partnerships to have any hope of effective implementation, the value of collaborative governance in privacy cannot be assessed without exploring the role, work, motivations, constraints, and contexts of privacy professionals. Recognizing that the GDPR's future also depends "on companies themselves," Kaminski asks the right questions: "As industries come together to determine codes of conduct and certification criteria and relatedly the content of appropriate technological design, will they (voluntarily) engage external stakeholders, including members of impacted communities? Will they use these systems to try to constrain rogue bad actors within

industry?" I'll add a few more: Will the information industry use its role in privacy's collaborative governance regime to achieve the social goals of the law, or will it reshape the law to achieve its own goals? Unfortunately, we're already seeing evidence of the latter.[24]

Undermining Privacy Law

Interpretations of the GDPR and FTC actions neither emerge in a vacuum nor necessarily take on the color that statutory drafters or the FTC intend. The people writing, interpreting, and implementing privacy law are affected by biases, social influences, and institutional pressures. But who are the people interpreting privacy law? By the FTC's own count, the agency averages only ten privacy-related cases per year, limiting the sources lawyers have from which to glean lessons and find clarity. Even if clarity is to come in the future, the FTC and data protection authorities will only have the opportunity to issue official judgments after protracted investigations and litigation. Until then, corporate actors on the ground are the first to move and they can entrench their interpretations of the law before any court has its say, interpreting vague terms in light of corporate, rather than consumer, values. They take advantage of their size and resources to shape the law in ways that benefit them and their interests. This is where the real work of the social practice of privacy law happens; somewhere between lawmaking and adjudication, the information industry has the chance to frame the debate. And as the responsibilities for legal interpretations increasingly shift to compliance professionals with interests not necessarily aligned with their customers, privacy becomes harder to achieve.[25]

I surveyed and interviewed privacy professionals and privacy lawyers to understand their motivations, their work, and their constraints. I reviewed unredacted internal policies and redacted memos written by interviewees and their colleagues. I also researched how, if at all, policies developed by privacy professionals affected how other business units did their work. My research suggests that far from constituting a flexible, practical, and effective middle ground between too much and too little regulation, compliance-based regulation in practice can neither adequately protect privacy nor put any meaningful constraints around data

processing. That is because the information industry uses its organizational power to undermine the law.

Privacy law is a victim of symbolic compliance – companies are creating systems that may have the look and feel of actual compliance but are, in reality, mere window-dressing. Rather than collaborating with public authorities to achieve social goals, the information industry is recasting privacy laws to suit its interests in data collection and use. Privacy professionals are part of this process, sometimes eagerly and sometimes as unwitting accomplices, steeped as they are in pro-industry privacy discourses even as they see themselves as privacy advocates. Often, they are constrained both by their own conceptions of their role, by the political and social contexts imposed upon them by corporate structures, and by the normalizing effects of routinized practices. The result is the collapse of privacy governance, such that it is, and the erosion of the privacy laws we manage to enact.

Legal Endogeneity

In her book, *Working Law*, the sociolegal scholar Lauren Edelman showed how form over substance in corporate compliance with civil rights law was having a deleterious effect on real progress on workplace equality. Edelman wanted to understand why, fifty years after the passage of the Civil Rights Act and the establishment of the Equal Employment Opportunity Commission (EEOC), "substantial workplace inequality on the basis of race, sex, and other protected categories persist[ed]." Although there could be many reasons for failure, her research suggested that rather than enforcing the substance of civil rights laws, courts and the EEOC were deferring to the in-house structures – trainings, antidiscrimination policies, complaint procedures, and diversity officers, just to name a few – that companies had developed in the wake of the Civil Rights Act as evidence that they were actually complying with the law, even when those companies still failed to hire or promote minorities.[26]

Sometimes, these structures have important expressive effects: a policy of nondiscrimination is a first step toward embedding nondiscrimination in the ethos of a company. But they can also be a glossy veneer for noncompliance. For example, a company can have a nondiscrimination policy, but never enforce it; it can hire a

diversity officer, but give her office no power; it can have a board focused on ethics in AI, but use it as a form of performance; it can develop extensive internal hearing procedures to deal with alleged bias, but use review boards to deny all claims; it can have a supposedly independent third party make important decisions, but give that board little power to solve the company's systemic problems. And yet, despite the use of these structures to create the aura of legitimacy without any of the substance, these symbols were nevertheless accepted by the courts as evidence that companies were complying civil rights laws. Indeed, when an alleged victim of discrimination sues her employer, both the lawyers and judges turn to these systems and sometimes confuse the existence of formal compliance structures with actual substantive compliance.[27]

Edelman also found that legal deference to mere symbols of compliance with civil rights laws was not accidental. Rather, it was part of the endogenous development of law, a process in which compliance professionals played a starring, yet frustrating, role. Sociologists of law argue that law is a product of social relations: lobbying, social movements, bureaucracies, arguments in adversarial proceedings, and the organized legal profession, to name just a few. Indeed, it is even the product of the environment it seeks to regulate; judges and legislators often come from industry or have experience representing industry players. This, combined with a professional tendency among compliance officers to fully document their work, lends itself to reliance on shorthand heuristics to prove compliance with the law. The result can be a perverse practice of law: instead of looking for evidence of substantive progress or adherence to legal principles, courts end up deferring to the veneer of compliance that companies create.[28]

In particular, Edelman identified six stages of legal endogeneity that ultimately undermined workplace antidiscrimination law. The process started with ambiguous or vague legal requirements. Title VII and the other statutes that constitute employment discrimination law do not specify the meaning of discrimination, "on the basis of . . . sex," or "equal employment opportunity." Nor do they specify how courts should determine if an employer is engaging in discrimination. These ambiguities may be intentional or the by-product of compromise or the limits of language, but regardless of their origin, they leave the door open to wildly

different interpretations from those responsible for compliance on the ground.[29]

But vagueness is not the only problem. Edelman also noted that Title VII cases like *Meritor Savings Bank v. Vinson*, which suggested that a functional antiharassment policy and grievance procedure could shield a corporate defendant from sexual harassment liability, and *Faragher v. City of Boca Raton*, which solidified *Meritor*'s suggestion as an official affirmative defense, formalized a safe harbor: it gave employers a process-oriented escape hatch from substantive adherence to a law that prohibits sexual harassment. *Meritor* and *Faragher* legitimized protocols, policies, and paper trails, independent of those structures' connections to achieving Title VII's goal of gender equality. This suggests that vagueness and procedural safe harbors are the real culprits.[30]

Legislative ambiguity and process-oriented rules give corporate professionals – lawyers, consultants, and compliance experts, for example – the chance to define what the law means and protect their employers. This, after all, is their job: they act as the filter between the law and the company. In the civil rights context, human resource professionals and in-house counsel play central roles in this process because they design, monitor, and administer personnel policy. And Edelman found that because of inculcative corporate discourses about risk, these professionals used the leeway they were given by ambiguous law to conclude that their goal was to minimize the risk of litigation for their employer, not actually eliminate bias, discrimination, and inequality.[31]

These professionals then used the process-oriented parts of the law to develop compliance solutions in response to legal requirements as they saw them. Ambiguity in the law allowed these professionals to get creative, to do their best to comply with their framing of the law without substantially interfering with an overarching goal – the continued productivity and profiting of the company. To comply with Title VII in the wake of *Meritor* and *Faragher*, for example, companies drafted policies, created new offices and positions, developed dispute resolution mechanisms and reporting structures, hired consultants to craft new approaches, and kept detailed paper trails, to name just a few steps. And these systems spread rapidly through industry as professionals shared their plans with their colleagues.[32]

With these systems in place, the law became managerialized. Julie Cohen has described the managerialization of law as the implementation of legal rules through the guiding prisms of efficiency and innovation, i.e., managerial values, rather than legal or social values. The process helps companies avoid the costs of litigation and outsources what they see as cumbersome and analogue procedures to in-house representatives and even technologies with corporate interests in mind. Put another way, as corporate compliance structures become the sites at which the law is actually applied on a regular basis, the law is applied with an eye toward corporate rather than social goals. For example, when an employee has a discrimination claim, she does not immediately go to a judge or even a lawyer. She tells her diversity officer (another corporate employee) who may ask for proof, at which point the allegation may be transferred to an in-house review team. In-house lawyers will get involved and companies will use processes that look very much like adversarial proceedings or dispute resolution, yet with few of a court's protections and rights for aggrieved plaintiffs. Instead, at each point, the professionals determining what the law means and how to apply it in any given circumstance are the in-house lawyers and compliance professionals who developed the structures in the first place and are guided, in the first instance, by management and productivity goals rather than the goals of the law they are ostensibly applying.[33]

Corporations then use structures to immunize themselves from accountability. In the Title VII context, research showed that companies erect procedural barriers for discrimination victims. Management lawyers also discouraged victims them from going through internal processes even as those same lawyers used those structures to quash employee attempts to use the courts. Edelman found that this had three negative effects on the law's capacity to create real change: it discouraged individuals from taking action in response to rights violations, allowed compliance structures to enter into the legal consciousness as evidence of real progress, and transformed the few workplace discrimination proceedings into debates over corporate structures rather than the substance of civil rights.[34]

The final stage of this process is deference to symbolic structures, or when corporate compliance systems become embedded in institutional interpretations of law. This happens in three steps. In workplace discrimination cases, judges started by

mentioning that corporate defendants had systems in place, including diversity officers and internal dispute resolution processes. Over time, these mentions became evidence in the factual question of whether discrimination actually occurred. Finally, some compliance structures became so closely associated with the legal consciousness that judges simply took their mere presence as sufficient evidence that a company did not engage in discrimination. There are many reasons why this happened in Title VII cases: judicial preference for heuristics in decision-making, specific decisions in which federal courts noted that compliance structures would have helped a defendant's case, the increasingly common tendency for lawyers on both sides of discrimination cases to refer to these structures in their briefs, judicial politics, and the persistent power of neoliberal ideas and discourses in law and policy, among other factors.[35]

All this had the effect of conflating tools of compliance with actual adherence to the substantive requirements of nondiscrimination law. And the more that happened, the more these structures of compliance entered into our collective consciousness about what the law requires. But symbols of compliance and actual compliance are two different things. Employers and their compliance professionals equated the two, frustrating Title VII's goal of a more equal workplace and contributing to the collective impression that the law is ineffective as an institution intended to protect people.

Legal Endogeneity in Privacy Law

Edelman is unsure whether nondiscrimination law can ever recover from its erosion at the hands of merely symbolic compliance. That a similar narrative is playing out in privacy law today, then, is particularly worrisome. Compliance-based approaches to privacy law, from the GDPR to FTC consent decrees, with their process-oriented regulatory levers, safe harbors, and explicit partnerships with regulated entities open the door for companies to frame the law in ways that serve corporate, rather than consumer, interests. The compliance ecosystem dominates the social practice of privacy law because these compliance professionals, and not legislators or regulators, embed their vision into corporate practice and technology design. These groups are most often limited by both the sociopolitical context in which they work and their own

conceptions of their role. As a result, they create structures that managerialize privacy law, focusing more on implementation that preserves corporate efficiency than on substantive privacy protections. These structures proliferate throughout the privacy compliance market, thus affecting the legal consciousness; judges, regulators, lawyers, and even consumers are starting to assume that the mere presence of compliance structures is evidence of substantive adherence with the law. Whether this narrative is as indelible in privacy as Edelman fears it is for Title VII and workplace equality depends on several legal and social factors. But the problem of endogeneity in privacy law is unmistakable.[36]

Ambiguity and Procedural Escape Hatches in Privacy Law

Privacy law's flexible definitions and standards, sometimes challenging even in the hands of lawyers, are particularly vulnerable to being weakened and undermined by symbolic structures. We usually think about judges as arbiters of statutory meaning, interpretation, and construction; that is, after all, how we teach law to students. But in the social practice of law, courts are often the last group to interpret a law. To do their job, courts need cases, and cases need allegations of legal noncompliance, and those allegations depend on individuals and organizations operating (or, more accurately, failing to operate) under the law. So, whenever a new law comes into effect, decision makers within regulated entities are the ones first empowered to consider new regulations, adapt them to their circumstances, and put themselves in compliance. Enforcement agents, administrative agencies, state attorneys-general, or other regulators may publish opinion statements or detailed rules, but those take time and even after they're in the mix, regulated entities have been already thinking about what the law means for them for some time. In the privacy context, the information industry gets the first say on the meaning of law, and much of that law is "staggeringly complex" and "ambiguous."[37]

Consider just three examples. Pursuant to Article 6(1)(f) of GDPR, collecting or processing data is presumed unlawful unless companies have a "lawful basis" for doing so. There are only six such bases: consent, performance of a contract to which an individual is a party, a vital life-or-death interest of the individual,

a legal requirement imposed on the company, the public interest, and the company's legitimate interests. The last option – processing data is permitted when it is in the "legitimate interests" of the company – could swallow up the entire GDPR if interpreted broadly. But there is precious little clarity in the law itself about how far legitimate interests go. Recital 47 says that the legitimacy of a corporate interest should be based on individuals' expectations about what kind of processing is reasonable, which is itself undefined. The same recital also states that marketing can constitute a legitimate interest, but stops there. The European Data Protection Board was similarly vague when it stated: "In the view of the Working Party, the notion of legitimate interest could include a broad range of interests, whether trivial or very compelling, straightforward or more controversial." The shibboleth of "legitimate interests" under Article 6(f), then, is balancing the company's legitimate interest, which is subject to few boundaries, against the rights of individuals. Balancing tests are not new to the law. Nor are they new to privacy. But they are flexible, and the GDPR and the Working Party's opinions explicitly envision corporate representatives conducting that balancing test themselves.[38]

Moreover, although it is one of the first attempts to regulate purely automated decision-making, the GDPR leaves the details up to regulated companies themselves. Several provisions of the GDPR require that organizations provide "meaningful information about the logic behind" any automated or algorithmic system – like a credit rating or a decision on a loan application, among others – that makes social decisions about European citizens. But neither the statute nor its recitals explain what "the logic behind" actually means. The Data Protection Board doesn't go into much detail either, other than calling for companies to "find simple ways to tell" individuals the "rationale behind" the decision or the "criteria relied on" when the computer spit out a number that impact their rights, opportunities, or entitlements. Rationale, criteria, and logic can take many forms. Companies could release the underlying code, which requires specialized knowledge to understand. They could release a list of the algorithm's independent variables, or factors included in the model; but that might mean very little without additional information about exactly how those factors fit into that model. Companies could release a privacy policy-like legalese explanation

that no one would read. These explanations could also be written in ways that discourage resistance, taking advantage of framing biases by explaining why using an automated system to determine credit risk or prison sentencing was a good idea. The lack of clear guardrails in the statute and interpretive documents means that those leveraging algorithmic decision-making systems are the ones bringing substance to an otherwise bare bones law.[39]

A third example is Article 25 of the GDPR, which calls for privacy "by design and by default." Beyond a general understanding that privacy-by-design refers to making privacy part of the design process for new technologies, what privacy-by-design means in practice is far from clear. Ira Rubinstein and Nathan Goode argue that privacy-by-design requires translating privacy principles into code, both in the back-end infrastructure of data collection and front-end user interfaces. I've suggested that the only way to give real meaning to privacy-by-design is to take lessons from the common law of products liability for design defects. This would, in short, require companies to not only balance privacy risks with product benefits, but also to prove that they designed a product with the most privacy protective means possible without sacrificing substantial functionality and to update programs regularly with privacy improvements. Other scholars have suggested a variety of other definitions, ranging from vague privacy principles and privacy-enhancing technologies to sets of values or "boundaries and goals" for design to norms based on products liability for design defects. Even guidance documents add little clarity, noting only that companies that "place privacy and data protection at the forefront of product development will be well placed to ensure that their goods and services respect the principles of privacy by design." While this ambiguity persists, privacy-by-design is still the law, and as such, it requires the information industry to develop its own understanding and its own tools for compliance, if any.[40]

Alongside the GDPR, privacy professionals in the United States must incorporate the many privacy-related FTC consent decrees and, perhaps, new state and federal privacy rules into the legal context in which their companies operate. Over time, even those orders that don't directly apply to a given company have become a sort of "common law" of privacy that gives companies a general guide to the FTC's perspectives on privacy. But those

consent decrees often include vague requirements, giving professionals on the ground wide latitude to determine what the law means in practice.[41]

For example, the FTC ostensibly requires companies to provide "adequate" notice to consumers. In *FTC v. Frostwire, LLC*, for example, the agency alleged that the company failed to "adequately inform[] consumers that [an Android file sharing] application" required several steps to protect the privacy of some files. In *FTC v. Echometrix*, the FTC found that broad statements in a privacy policy were too vague and "failed to disclose adequately" the company's data collection regime. And in *In re Sears Holdings Management Corp.*, the FTC concluded that Sears's long, legalese licensing agreement "failed to disclose adequately that the software application, when installed" would monitor a long list of consumer behavior. The FTC has never clarified the meaning of adequacy, instead choosing a step-by-step common law approach. Indeed, arguably the only piece of the FTC's privacy jurisprudence that is not left open to interpretation on the ground is the FTC's baseline and clearest rule: do not lie.[42]

FTC consent decrees also often require companies to develop a "comprehensive privacy program," but details are scarce. For example, in a consent order about Google Buzz, Google agreed to establish a "comprehensive privacy program that is reasonably designed to: (1) address privacy risks related to the development and management of new and existing products and services for consumers and (2) protect the privacy and confidentiality of covered information." It doesn't say what that entails. Solove and Hartzog have suggested that these privacy programs would be similar to corporate best practices with respect to security, which include steps to "identify risk, train employees, appoint a responsible coordinator of the program, and engage in regular evaluations of the program." But those details were developed by the companies themselves and not laid out by the FTC. Indeed, the FTC's annually updated Privacy and Data Security report has never explained what a comprehensive privacy program really is, even while it boasts that the requirement is one of several it uses to vigorously "protect consumers' privacy and personnel information." This empowers privacy compliance personal to develop these programs on their own, thus creating a public-private partnership in a form of collaborative governance.[43]

Some scholars argue that seemingly vague terms in the GDPR become clear when we combine the GDPR with interpretive tools, including reports from the Data Protection Board. Others argue that lawyers and privacy professionals may be able to piece together what does and does not constitute compliance from the sum total of FTC consent decrees. These and other vague provisions in privacy law are not just susceptible to transformative interpretations by corporate actors on the ground. Collaborative governance explicitly invites them. And the information industry is already developing best practices that can serve as safe harbors for noncompliance, much like companies created networks of nondiscrimination procedures so they would fall into the *Meritor* and *Faragher* safe harbors. Under the GDPR, data-processing records are required, and data-protection impact assessments can protect companies from liability even when engaging in data processing that carries a "high risk to the rights" of data subjects. Scholars have proposed that companies that hire "algorithmic decision-making officers" or data protection officers could take advantage of a safe harbor from liability under the GDPR. Others have proposed safe harbors in the form of codes of conduct and industry best practices, as well as industry-wide certification programs that indicate compliance with certain objective standards laid out by industry representatives themselves.[44]

Researchers have identified the "importance of the increasingly professionalized privacy officer community in filling in the details of" ambiguous privacy laws on the books. But not all privacy professionals approach this task the same way. The privacy professionals I interviewed conceptualized this role in three ways: as a responsibility, a benefit to their employer, or a place where they were uniquely suited to add value. Half of the privacy professionals and in-house privacy lawyers I interviewed used the words "my job," "our responsibility," or derivations thereof to describe bringing detail to vague terms. Seven were sanguine about that responsibility, noting they "have an opportunity to do some good" or were "happy to do what [they] can when it's impossible to get anything done in Washington." Others in the responsibility camp were less optimistic, with two calling it a "burden" and three noting the difficulty they have in doing their jobs. One of those interviewees noted specifically that she was working "without any real guidance.

We have to rely on our peers. It's a lot of work to do this without much of an idea of what's ok and what isn't."

Twelve interviewees saw their active role in putting "meat on the bones" of privacy law as a way to help their employers achieve their goals. "If I can take this complex law and boil it down so it's manageable for us," one said, "then I will have helped make my colleagues' job easier. That's a good day." Eight of these interviewees explicitly noted that their job was to build out privacy compliance in ways that facilitated productivity, with one noting that he has "to come up with ways to get it (privacy) without grinding us to a halt" and a CPO stating that when her team do its job, it "helps our bosses and our engineers to their jobs effectively, efficiently, and correctly."

The last group of interviewees described how "vague rules" not just required but actively invited their "unique expertise" to make them work. "My colleagues and I," a former CPO at a New York finance company noted, "are trained for this. It's not just about school; we're not all lawyers, nor do we have to be. We are trained in compliance and systems and privacy law wants our expertise." A veteran privacy professional with nineteen years' experience as a consultant jokingly stated that he "loved reading the early draft of the GDPR because of what it meant for people like" him – someone who "advises companies and what to do when these new standards come down without much specificity on what they have to do to comply."

Although these categories may not describe the way all privacy professionals and privacy lawyers conceptualize their work, they all stem from a feature, not a bug, of privacy law's incomplete version of collaborative governance: relatively vague standards on the books are meant to be interpreted by regulated entities on the ground. Where legal requirements are specific, privacy professionals and privacy lawyers have an easier time. During a meeting I observed at a mid-size tech company in the Bay Area, a product manager stated, "We can't leave this box checked. I have a memo from legal saying that it's not allowed in Europe." He was referring to a European Court of Justice ruling holding that "pre-ticked boxes or inactivity should not therefore constitute consent" under GDPR. Another team leader said that "people aren't going to accept" the way "we used to do things, and that's fine. Your job is to come up

with another way," suggesting that designers have to get creative to find ways to achieve their goals under new constraints.[45]

But specific legal requirements are both rare and underinclusive. The limitations of language and the legislative drafting process often result in statutes and rules that leave their meaning and details to those interpreting them. And the debate over standards and rules is as old as the common law. Specific rules about specific instances of corporate behavior are usually the result of case law, which takes years to develop and only adjusts design after the fact. Otherwise, privacy law leaves the information industry relatively unconstrained when privacy professionals sit down to do their work. Therefore, how they think about privacy, their role, and the law matters a lot.[46]

Framing Corporate Obligations Narrowly in Terms of Risk Avoidance

Recognizing both the ambiguity and potential for industry-developed safe harbors in privacy law, privacy professionals on the ground have the opportunity (and responsibility) to translate the law's requirements for their employers in a way that makes compliance possible. As Edelman describes, these professionals "make certain laws or norms visible or invisible to employers and frame those laws' relevance to organizational life." In so doing, they shape the "aesthetic of the law," determining not just what laws make it through the filter, but what those legal obligations look like. In Edelman's work on the implementation (or lack thereof) of civil rights laws, they frame compliance with Title VII in terms of minimizing the risk of a lawsuit from an employee rather than actually eradicating sex discrimination in the workplace. In the privacy space, lawyers, CPOs, consultants, and their staffs could and should assume the principal legal filter role and should ideally frame corporate legal obligations in terms of the laws' underlying purposes – namely, to create more robust privacy protections, to protect consumers from predatory data collection practices, and to minimize privacy risks to consumers.[47]

But that is not always what happens. As we saw in Chapter 1, some companies in the information industry structure their privacy teams within their risk management departments, following a decades-long trend in other industries. This structure means that

companies will bring risk management mindsets and incentives to privacy problems. That, on its face, is neither neutral nor good for privacy. Thinking about privacy in terms of the cost-benefit analyses that have come to characterize risk management endorses and operationalizes the notion that the only things that matter about privacy are those things that can be quantified. Not only have scholars shown that risk management cost-benefit analyses gloss over the differences among types of risk and often function as barriers to change, a numbers-only approach also undervalues intangible harms that can't be reduced to dollars and overestimates the present value of compliance. But privacy harms are overwhelmingly intangible: Privacy harms are about risk, anxiety, lost opportunity, and surveillance-induced behavioral change. Privacy also involves questions of power and justice, most of which are elided by a simple reduction of law to plusses and minuses. This means that organizations that situate privacy in corporate risk management are structurally biased against a robust approach to privacy.[48]

Structure, however, is not the only problem. As a matter of social practice, a risk-based approach to privacy often frames privacy law compliance as a means of minimizing the risk to the *company*, not protecting consumers from data use harms. This risk framing pervades the privacy compliance landscape. When the NIST published its *Privacy Risk Management Framework*, it focused on developing standards for an organization-wide "program that involves the *management of organizational risk* – that is, the risk to the organization or to individuals associated with the operation of a system." In the *Journal of Data Protection and Privacy*, an industry journal offering analysis of international privacy developments, several articles in the journal's first five volumes focus on minimizing corporate risk. In "The Risk-Based Approach to Privacy: Risk or Protection for Business," for example, the authors recognize the GDPR's requirement that privacy protection mechanisms be proportional to the risk data processing poses to users. But the lion's share of the article focuses on how privacy impact assessments (PIAs) can be used to mitigate corporate exposure to GDPR penalties. Two do the same. But although PIAs are supposed to help companies "identif[y] and evaluate potential threats to individual privacy, discuss alternatives and identif[y] the appropriate risk-mitigation measures for each," a company merely looking to avoid risk to itself could see

a PIA as a convenient paper trail documenting a check-the-box approach to privacy.[49]

In the last five years, more than 300 privacy technology vendors are marketing themselves as capable of helping companies comply with the GDPR and new FTC consent decrees. Many of them also frame their value-add in terms of reducing corporate risk rather than privacy risks to individuals. ZLTech, for example, markets its "GDPR-Ready Solutions" as ways to avoid "the risk of unprecedented sanctions." And Clarip, a software-as-service provider, bills itself as "the next generation … data privacy platform that helps brands minimize privacy risks." Ethyca puts "data privacy" and "risk management" together and wants to automate privacy "with no loss of efficiency." And he compliance assistance company, 2BAdvice, wants to show its clients how "to save time and money and minimize risk through automating processes." These are just a few examples. Risk avoidance is a trope in the privacy technology vendor market: of the companies profiled in the IAPP's 2020 Privacy Technology Vendor Report, nearly 100 of them describe their risk-mitigation work in terms of reducing corporate risk; only four talk about minimizing privacy risks to customers.[50]

Law firms run risk minimization Continuing Legal Education programs that focus entirely on risks to the company. Privacy trade groups also frame compliance as a means of minimizing corporate risk. For example, the IAPP and TrustArc published a study focusing on prioritizing different parts of GDPR based on the risks of noncompliance to the company. The IAPP has also framed data minimization as a way of reducing corporate risk and hosted webinars in which experts have said that the "heart" of data protection compliance is doing what "you can to manage the risk to the company" posed by new privacy laws. And it has published articles on its *Privacy Perspectives* blog that argue that "legal teams might measure success [in privacy] in terms of regulatory risk reduction." This focus ultimately encourages many companies to house their privacy officers within their risk management departments, an example of which we saw in Chapter 1. It also puts a decidedly corporate spin on privacy law itself. In other words, only collecting as much data as is necessary for a particular purpose does reduce the risk of litigation or investigation because data minimization is required by the GDPR. But the purpose of the requirement is to

reduce privacy risks *to consumers* associated with the collection and processing of personal data. The GDPR is explicit about this. Recital 75 states that the "risk to the rights and freedoms of natural persons, of varying likelihood and severity, may result from personal data processing which could lead to physical, material or nonmaterial damage." Skilled privacy lawyers recognize this. Framed narrowly, however, data minimization means doing the least possible to shield a company from liability. It turns the social practice of privacy law into a project about what a company can get away with as opposed to how to actually protect people's privacy.[51]

I spoke with a small group of privacy professionals and corporate privacy lawyers about this at the IAPP's "Privacy. Security. Risk." conference in 2017 and the Privacy+Security Forum in 2018. To their credit, each interviewee recognized that the GDPR and other risk-based approaches to privacy defined "risk" in terms of privacy risks to the individual consumer. But two additional themes came through. A deputy general counsel who had previously worked at an AmLaw Top 100 firm noted that "many of the privacy risk programs [he has] seen are more based on organizational risks, like the risk of a fine or lawsuits or the kind of reputational harm that comes with a data breach or having to testify before Congress." A lawyer at a large international law firm agreed, noting that "for better or for worse, that's what risk programs often turn into: the company is obviously interested in keeping itself out of the papers, and of course out of court." A privacy consultant told me that companies assess risk based on "how big a footprint the company has and how big a target they are." These and other professionals suggest that risk framing creates incentives to orient compliance programs around corporate risk avoidance rather than substantive adherence to the law much in the same way standardized testing can encourage "teaching to the test" rather than holistic learning.

Framing the data privacy landscape as one based on corporate risk is not surprising. Some argue that risk framing can actually encourage compliance with the law by persuading executives to treat it as a high priority, especially when some executives still see privacy as inconsistent with corporate profit goals. The risk of a fine of 4 percent of global revenue under the GDPR could also go a long way to making privacy compliance a central corporate

mission. Risk framing also makes sense from an endogenous political perspective. By emphasizing the dangers of noncompliance, privacy professionals stake out important territory at the highest levels of corporate decision-making, giving them seats at the table and the capacity to influence policy. This can also encourage third-party vendors seeking corporate contracts to follow suit because it allows them to market themselves as sharing the same values as their corporate clients.[52]

But risk framing is problematic if the goal is adherence to the substantive goals of privacy law. First, it is incomplete. There is more to privacy than managing risks of a lawsuit. Privacy also involves managing users' expectations, their desire for obscurity, their need for trust, and their consistent distaste for transfers of data to third parties. Operating along narrow risk-mitigation paths distracts corporate attention from more important, substantive mandates and focuses employees' squarely on their employers' interests. Second, and perhaps more importantly, framing privacy obligations in terms of corporate risk focuses only on the avoidance of a corporate problem rather than the achievement of an affirmative social goal – namely, greater user privacy and safety and limits on the collection and processing of personal data. In a regulatory context where lawsuits are nearly impossible and regulatory oversight is spotty at best, recasting the GDPR's attention to risk undermines the law's ability to effectuate real change in corporate behavior and technology design. So, although some scholars have suggested that some privacy professionals see the law's requirements as a floor for their work, evidence on the ground suggests otherwise.[53]

Symbols of Compliance

Having interpreted privacy law for their corporate employers and framed corporate privacy obligations in terms of risk rather than substantive privacy protections for users, compliance professionals create internal structures to comply with their version of the law. Edelman defines a compliance "structure" as any corporate office, program, policy, or practice that exists independently of a particular person. A privacy office is a structure, as are internal data access rules, mission statements, privacy policies, dashboards, organizational structures, privacy teams, in-house training systems,

compliance protocols, and so forth. Some of these structures are tied to specific provisions of privacy law. For example, because the FTC often requires regulated companies to implement a "comprehensive privacy program" and because the GDPR requires the designation of a DPO, many companies have to hire new professionals. Similarly, because the GDPR gives consumers a right to access their information and erase any irrelevant, incorrect, and outdated information, companies have to develop systems to find and categorize user data. And laws like the CCPA require privacy notices that describe data use practices. But where legal requirements are flexible – What is a CPO/DPO supposed to do? How do companies have to present their data use practices to users? What is a code of conduct supposed to include? How are companies supposed to design products with privacy in mind? – and the mere existence of structures can serve as a safe harbor from liability, compliance structures often become *merely symbolic*.[54]

Symbolic structures are those that carry with them the aura of legitimacy because they resemble preexisting forms already having the imprimatur of the law. Think of a show trial where the defendant's fate is a foregone conclusion, but a trial – with judges, attorneys, juries, and witnesses – is performed nonetheless. A human resources board that hears appeals of claims of discrimination and harassment may give an employee the opportunity to represented by an advocate, admit evidence, and plead their case, but those trial-like procedures are symbolic if the board rubber stamps pro-employer results and bases its decisions on sexist stereotypes. These structures are sometimes little more than cynical performances, but we don't always realize it. For example, privacy policies are so effective at using legalese language and take advantage of the trappings of legal jargon that many Americans think that they are binding, contractual commitments to protect our privacy.[55]

A nondiscrimination policy, with legal-sounding terms of art, or internal dispute resolution systems are examples of symbolic structures that resemble legal processes. Notably, symbolic structures can be helpful. An equal opportunity employment policy can have both expressive and substantive effects when companies take it seriously, and a fair dispute resolution system can give victims of discrimination an opportunity to make their voices heard and seek equal treatment. But when these structures become *merely* symbolic,

when they offer just the veneer or the trappings of compliance with no substance, then they can frustrate the goals of the law. This is what is happening in privacy law right now.[56]

Over the last ten years, many companies have developed increasingly complex privacy structures, hired CPOs and downstream privacy professionals, and created protocols to manage access to personal data, among many other steps. In many companies, these structures are taken seriously. But these structures can also ossify into symbols. One of the best examples of this from traditional privacy law may be corporate privacy policies. Though privacy policies developed first as industry's way to stave off regulation, they are now required by many state and federal laws. Many of those laws require that privacy policies be sufficiently "conspicuous" to users, and yet privacy policies today are confusing messes of legalese jargon and vague marketing platitudes that, as we have discussed, don't actually provide notice. They do, however, make us think of them as legally binding commitments, and they are designed and presented to us to intentionally manipulate our behavior. As such, they are merely symbolic structures: they technically comply with the law in that they are lists of data use practices, but they do not fulfill the law's purpose of actually providing sufficient transparent notice to users to inform privacy decision-making.[57]

Privacy compliance programs can also become merely symbolic when they are reduced to flow charts, check lists, and templates that create the illusion of compliance but really just facilitate avoiding as much responsibility as possible. I reviewed internal privacy memos and other compliance documents at three different companies, all of which say they are compliant with the GDPR's impact assessment requirements. Per the FTC, PIAs are used to analyze "how personally identifiable information is collected, used, shared, and maintained." They are supposed to be deployed at the beginning of the design phase of a data collection or processing tool to identify risks, errors, and privacy issues before it's too late. But it doesn't always work like that. Several companies' PIAs were lists of questions tracking several GDPR rights and the six lawful bases in Article 6, each with three possible answers: "Risk Mitigated," "Risk Not Mitigated but Accepted," and "No Risk" (or language to that effect). An app that required a log in through Facebook or Google had "No Risk" checked next to the lawful basis questions. A PIA for

a game that mined users' entire contacts list as a prerequisite for playing against friends was considered "Low but Acceptable Risk." When I asked how designers and other stakeholders made these determinations, one said that his "boss just wants to see that we do this. I've never been asked by anyone to go into depth on this." Another remarked that "the specific check mark doesn't matter as much as going through this process." Interviews with in-house lawyers and privacy professionals echoed that sentiment: "I don't know," one said, "how effective these will be, but going through the motions keep privacy at the front of people's minds." Performing the impact assessment process could have that effect, but some of those on the ground see it as more theater than anything else.[58]

Step-by-step checklists were also common in my research. One in-house counsel suggested that checklists are frequent compliance tools because they "help people in their jobs simplify responsibilities and make sure they're following the rules set down for them by the GC [general counsel] office, [the CPO], or their manager." Other scholars have found similar internal tools at work at other companies. It's Weberian bureaucracy come to life![59]

But checklists can also become merely symbolic while amplifying the power of local decision makers on the ground. For example, since the GDPR requires a lawful basis for data collection and processing, one large Silicon Valley company opted to send a "Lawful Basis Under the GDPR" memo to all product managers to distribute and discuss with their engineering teams. The memo recommended that managers have their teams use a checklist of lawful bases for data privacy issues in design. I reviewed redacted versions of these checklists, which were little more than two columns titled "Basis for Data" and "Choose One," with "legitimate interests: marketing, engagement, advertising" checked for each. According to the product manager, the engineers are tasked with checking the appropriate boxes, but none of the engineers I interviewed could explain why they chose the "legitimate interests" box. One said: "It sounded legitimate to me, and they don't want us to bother with opt-in consent." Another said that "it seemed weird checking that because, I mean, what do we really know, right?" When I took these anonymous comments to one of the company's privacy lawyers, she lamented that "this is the best we're doing right now."

Such structures are not problematic, at least in isolation. But extensive qualitative research suggests that many of these policies are policies in name only. As one former engineer put it, "we would need to run our design by privacy, legal, and marketing." But the process was "compliance-style. I remember being told by my manager that 'privacy checked the boxes, so we can go ahead.'" And there was a sense among three interviewees that even though it was a privacy professional's job to audit new designs, the privacy team did not really want to get in the way. "Nobody wants to stop creativity," one former engineer at Google said. "I can't say for sure, but I'm sure privacy didn't want to, either. They didn't stop us from doing our work." This narrow, compliance focus reduced internal compliance rules into a merely symbolic structure.

FTC-required assessments have also become merely symbolic structures that can impede the substantive implementation of privacy law. The FTC requires companies operating under consent decrees to submit assessments roughly every two years for the life of the order. Assessments have to be completed by a "qualified, objective, independent third-party" auditor with sufficient experience. And they must describe specific privacy controls, evaluate their adequacy given the size and scope of the company, explain how they meet FTC requirements, and certify they are operating effectively. That seems specific enough, without much opportunity for error. Assessments, like those required of Google and Facebook, are often the only real weapons in the FTC's arsenal because they ostensibly require a qualified, independent third party to verify corporate compliance. And they have been heralded as game changers.[60]

In reality, assessments have failed to achieve that goal because some of them have become mere symbols of compliance. The FTC requires *assessments*, and assessments are not the intense, independent, under-the-hood investigations we think of when we think of audits. They leave wiggle room for regulated companies. Audits are independent third-party analyses, where the auditor herself reviews evidence and makes conclusions independent of the audit subject. Assessments are based on assertions from management rather than wholly independent analyses from auditors, and are usually framed by goals set by management. That means that the company that is supposed to be the subject of the assessment is, in fact, determining the bases upon which it gets

evaluated, thus giving companies some power to predetermine the results. For example, the FTC wanted an assessment to ensure that Google, for example, had a privacy team, an ongoing and flexible privacy assessment process, relationships with vendors capable of protecting data, and a few other related requirements. But based on a redacted version of the report, the assessment used conclusory language that was based almost entirely on Google proffers. For example, the report states that "Google has implemented a privacy risk assessment process in order to identify reasonably foreseeable, material risks, both internal and external," tracking the language of the FTC order explicitly. As evidence for this conclusory statement, the report refers the reader to Google's responses to the auditor's questions, not any actual evidence. Later, the report concludes that "Google's privacy controls were operating with sufficient effectiveness to provide reasonable assurance to protect the privacy of covered information," based only on "the Google Privacy Program set forth in Attachment A of Management's Assertion in Exhibit I." In other words, the only evidence showing that Google met FTC requirements was Google's statements to that effect. The fact that these assessments can be fulfilled through rough conclusory statements without independent investigation shows how assessments can become mere symbols of compliance.[61]

The Managerialization of Privacy Law

Checklists, compliance templates, assessments, and other symbolic tools have diffused through the privacy ecosystem. Professionals share their experiences and recommendations with each other through both formal and serendipitous interactions at workshops and conferences. I witnessed this first-hand at the IAPP's national conference and at smaller professional gatherings of privacy professionals, including the Privacy+Security Forum. This can be helpful; professionals can learn from each other, offer suggestions based on experiences, and improve their own protocols. The spread of these programs through social networks can also contribute to what organizational sociologists Paul DiMaggio and Walter Powell have called "isomorphism," or the tendency of companies in the same market to function, hire, and structure themselves in similar ways.

That is why we see similar privacy compliance checklists and similar privacy organizational structures in many companies.[62]

Another consequence is that these structures – and their designers – become the loci at which privacy law is negotiated, addressed, and implemented on a regular basis. As the center of power shifts to corporate actors, corporate values shape implementation. When Edelman discussed the managerialization of antidiscrimination law, she noted that compliance professionals interpreting policies and running internal review processes imbued their processes with managerial values like efficiency, productivity, and stability rather than the social values embedded in Title VII. What is happening in privacy law is similar. Even where in-house privacy professionals see themselves as working hard on behalf of privacy, the tendency to managerialize compliance can shift the decision-making vector from *How can we reduce privacy risks to our customers?*, to *How can we best address this efficiently and with minimal interference with corporate goals*? This shifts the goal of compliance from substantive adherence to procedural box-checking.[63]

Compliance professionals inside companies contribute to the managerialization of privacy law by talking about privacy in managerial terms. In the employment discrimination context, Edelman noticed that despite the fact that the Civil Rights Act specifically spoke in terms of race and sex discrimination, compliance professionals on the ground tended to couch their work in terms of diversity, generally, and offered managerial (i.e., profit), rather than social, justifications for increased diversity. This has the effect of encouraging even those executives who care about racial and gender equality to think about diversity in more nebulous terms and through a corporate profit lens. Some privacy professionals are doing the same thing to privacy. Six lawyers at private firms and twelve privacy professionals I interviewed saw privacy as one part of a compliance ecosystem focused on enhancing efficiency, speed, and productivity, while reducing the risk of debilitating fines. A partner at a firm in the top twenty of the AmLaw100 stated that "the best we can do is make sure our clients handle compliance efficiently, and with as little disruption to their business as possible." A CPO in New York stated that she has "to build a privacy infrastructure that is efficient and lean because that's the best way to achieve do our jobs while they (the rest of the company) does theirs." These professionals are also likely to see

privacy structures in marketing terms: Users are more likely to continue to share information with data collectors if users feel their privacy is protected. A privacy consultant in San Francisco stated that "the goal of a privacy program should be to enhance the productivity of the company as a whole, while telling customers that this company can be trusted." This also tracks the industry literature. Granted, consumers can benefit when companies start thinking about privacy as good for business, but the value proposition is nevertheless shifted from what helps consumers to what helps corporations.[64]

The increasing tendency to outsource privacy compliance is paradigmatic of the managerialization of privacy law. In the economics literature, outsourcing is a cost-saving corporate strategy meant to enhance efficiency, reduce waste, and allow the company to focus on value creation. Therefore, even though outsourcing carries with it significant social costs, its proponents see it as an effective way to achieve management goals. AuraPortal, for example, offers a GDPR compliance tool actually called "GDPR Accelerator" and markets the product as a way to "accelerate compliance in record time." DataFleets, which offers anonymization tools, wants to "make data sharing, access, and innovation faster and more efficient, while helping manage controls and meet compliance requirements." MinerEye "enables companies to efficiently discover, analyze, and act on data for data privacy and security." Nice, a small company in Hoboken, New Jersey, wants "to efficiently manage interactions and policies." And Poslovna Inteligencija, based on Zagreb, Croatia, markets a "a state-of-the-art software platform designed to help companies perform efficient management of personal data and processes for the EU General Data Protection Regulation." OneTrust, one of the largest privacy technology vendors, claims to have "pre-built templates to assess the validity" of using contractual agreements to transfer data between the United States and Europe that "reduc[e] the burden" of privacy compliance. OneTrust announced the availability of these templates in an email on September 1, 2020, only a few weeks after the European Court of Justice invalidated the primary mechanism for cross-border data flows. Making compliance easier is not a bad thing, but it is difficult to ignore the extent to which managerial values of efficiency are affecting how companies comply with privacy law and the ease with which a company can just pay a vendor to have its compliance forms already mostly filled out.[65]

Many privacy professionals are eager to automate compliance without regard for what that says about their work, their employers' commitment to privacy, and actual privacy protections for people on the ground. And the IAPP, the largest professional organization for privacy professionals, pushes this drive to outsource privacy law. In one of its reports, organization stated that the growth of privacy technology vendors was a positive development: privacy professionals "can now shop among dozens of vendors to find solutions to challenges created" by the GDPR and other laws. The organization has a financial interest in saying that. Many of the IAPP's conferences are sponsored by privacy tech vendors: the IAPP's 2020 Summit Sessions, for example, were principally sponsored by OneTrust Data Discovery, TrustArc, Cisco, BigID, OneTrust Vendorpedia, and WireWheel, all privacy technology vendors on the market. Not one of the panels criticized the automation of privacy compliance.[66]

This is not to say that all automation is bad. Automated systems that help companies identify the data they have so they can comply with rights of access, correction, deletion, and portability make sense. But outsourcing compliance carries far more risk when it means engineers are instantiating legal rules into code to make privacy compliance a fill-in-the-blank process. It characterizes the skills of legal interpretation and implementation as routinizable, irrational, imperfect, or just too human. As Frank Pasquale has argued, the notion that any engineer, entrepreneur, or businessperson can neatly code privacy law, and the human judgments and negotiations it demands, into a machine loses the "qualitative evaluation and . . . humble willingness to recalibrate and risk-adjust quantitative data" that come with human experts. It also only covers codable parts of privacy law. Some privacy compliance technologies, therefore, embody an epistemic error: they assume that privacy law is reducible to factors that AI and code can identify, which, of course, is wrong. In addition, a world where technology vendors determine what the law requires and design those requirements into compliance tools is a world where the discourse of law becomes the discourse of engineering. Put another way: "Compliance: There's an App for That." This disempowers consumers, who have little access to the black box of technology, and serves to undermine the promise of privacy law as consumer protection.[67]

Translating law through code also undermines due process. Privacy technologies embody particular visions of what privacy laws require. But the design process where that instantiation occurs is almost entirely hidden to us. Law, however, is traditionally interpreted out in the open, with explanations: legislative hearings are public records, legislative histories are integral to legal understanding, judicial opinions have explanations designed in, and every state and the federal government have open records laws that make the practice of policy open to the public. Moreover, law is normally characterized by procedural and substantive due process that safeguard its legitimacy. As Danielle Citron has argued, the tendency to shift legal decisions to automated technologies erases these safeguards, leaving consumers unprotected. The more we ask "black box" algorithms to implement the law, the more we undermine the project of public governance.[68]

Routinizing automated privacy compliance is precisely what management wants. It removes the rank and file from the work of privacy on the ground, replacing them with engineers and algorithms. Computers don't talk back or protest or blow the whistle on a company's complicity in systemic harm. And yet, many privacy professionals see automated privacy compliance as the future of privacy law. I spoke to privacy leaders whose work included significant vendor management who said that "vendor management may be another thing on my list, but if I can work with a vendor to handle the complexity of state-by-state compliance and GDPR compliance and everything I have to do, I will have achieved efficiencies that I otherwise couldn't." This focus on efficiency in privacy compliance managerializes the practice of privacy. Outsourcing is efficient – a company can pay a vendor far less than the annual salaries of human workers. Outsourcing is also a slippery slope: when a profit-making company realizes efficiencies in one area by automating data discovery, it is far more likely to automate another area of privacy compliance even though tricky legal questions are glossed over, ignored, or answered by engineering fiat.

I spoke to privacy professionals who understood the risks of checkbox privacy. I spoke to leaders who recognized that vendor management was a full-time job to "make sure, even before you hire a vendor, that the relationship is right. It's also going to be a constant thing on your plate. It's management, with regular check-

ins and questions and answers." But none recognized that automating privacy is likely to result in narrower privacy protections for individuals. Nor is acknowledgment of this risk anywhere in the industry literature. Much that literature is about effective vendor management, accountability, and efficiency. The consumer is nowhere to be found.

When managerial values become too powerful, compliance structures may frustrate privacy law's social goals. Corporate goals like efficiency, productivity, and profit are often thought to be in tension with the substantive goals of regulatory legislation, like equality, nondiscrimination, or, in this case, privacy. Even though scholars have shown that no such conflict exists, corporate interests and their vendors on the ground are contributing to a narrative that regulation is antithetical to innovation and, more specifically, that consumer privacy rights have to take a back seat to corporate goals.[69]

Managerialization and the Perception of Compliance

This happens because the use of managerial rhetoric around privacy and the proliferation of compliance structures influences the perception of adherence. That is, if we understand privacy law in managerial terms – as focused on managing corporate risk, balancing regulation and profit, and enhancing innovation – instead of protecting individuals, we tend to see merely symbolic structures developed in line with those terms as constituting compliance with the law. They get so engrained in our legal consciousness that, over time, no one notices that they are hollow shells. The effect is the frustration of consumer privacy rights because users assume the law cannot help them, thus reinforcing an antiregulatory discourse.[70]

The focus on documentation as an end in itself elevates a merely symbolic structure to evidence of actual compliance with the law, obscuring the substance of consumer privacy law and discouraging both users and policy makers from taking more robust actions. Paul Butler made a similar argument about the effect of *Gideon v. Wainwright* on the incarceration of poor persons of color. By focusing on a process right – the right the counsel – *Gideon*, Butler argues, obscured the "real crisis of indigent defense" that prison is designed for poor people and not rich ones. Ensuring some adequate representation "invests the criminal

justice system with a veneer" of legitimacy, impartiality, and protection for ordinary persons, discouraging anyone from digging any deeper. Butler concluded that "on its face, the grant that *Gideon* provides poor people seems more than symbolic: it requires states to pay for poor people to have lawyers. But the implementation of *Gideon* suggests that the difference between symbolic and material rights might be more apparent than real."[71]

The same thing is happening in privacy law. Joe Turow has shown that we assume websites with privacy policies actually protect our privacy, even though a privacy policy is merely a statement of data use practices rather than a promise of confidentiality. Internet users are likely to give up on privacy navigation as soon as it gets too hard. And many report feeling nihilistic about their ability to protect their information online. We also live in a legal environment in which privacy rights mobilization is already difficult. Standing requirements and other hurdles hamper privacy plaintiffs' use of tort law, contract law, and federal privacy statutes to vindicate their privacy rights. Even the FTC's power to force a company to overhaul its approach to privacy and security is under attack. And most users are dissuaded from even learning about their privacy rights because so many corporate executives and self-styled experts say that privacy is dead.[72]

By focusing on compliance paper trails, managerialization of privacy law makes vindicating privacy rights even harder. Eleven of thirteen privacy compliance professionals I interviewed agreed with the assessment from a risk and compliance executive in New York that "we document everything so we have a log when someone comes after us." Even the Information Commissioner's Office (ICO) of the United Kingdom fell into this line of thinking. In its *Guide to the General Data Protection Regulation*, the ICO counseled companies to document processing activities to "help [them] demonstrate [their] compliance with other aspects of the GDPR."[73]

When a company can claim that it should not be held responsible for data misuse because, despite privacy problems in a final product, they completed a private impact assessment and documented internal approaches to privacy issues, individuals and regulators are both immediately put on the defensive and may be dissuaded from mobilizing their rights and investigative powers in the first place. Granted, the GDPR includes documentation requirements; companies

need reports to prove they took "reasonable and appropriate" steps to protect consumer privacy under FTC consent decrees. But the way some market players conflate the structure of compliance (the records) with actual compliance (following the GDPR) is striking. Privacy professionals' and third-party vendors' focus on records and documentation offers a convenient veneer of legitimacy to a process of technology design, data use, and information flow that remains unaltered and harmful to consumers.[74]

Deference to Symbols in Privacy Law

The legal endogeneity narrative reaches its climax when, after becoming part of our collective legal consciousness, merely symbolic structures are leveraged by lawyers, judges, and regulators as actual evidence of adherence to the law. There are three steps in this process: "reference, relevance, and deference." Reference occurs where judges merely refer to symbolic structures in their decisions. Relevance involves a judge noting or ruling that having a structure, like an internal dispute resolution process, is relevant to whether a company complied with a law like Title VII even though Title VII doesn't require structures, only nondiscrimination. And deference, the final stage, occurs when judges see the mere presence of a compliance structure as dispositive. In the employment discrimination context, Edelman found evidence of deference to merely symbolic structures littered throughout the law. Management attorneys listed them in their defense briefs, judges referred to them and pointed to them as evidence of compliance, and even plaintiffs' lawyers adopted them as goals for injunctive relief. In the privacy space, it remains difficult to assess legal endogeneity just yet because a new privacy law landscape is still unfolding. But the process is indeed ongoing.[75]

Almost all of what Solove and Hartzog have called the "common law of privacy" – the decades of FTC consent decrees – are actually settlement agreements with regulated entities. That means that the law regulating technology companies is, in part, dictated by the companies themselves and by the many corporate-friendly deals they can strike during secret negotiations with managerialized regulators who are more concerned about facilitating corporate innovation than doing their jobs. Indeed, not "burdening" business is a central part of the FTC's mission.[76]

The FTC also defers to industry practices in the area of data security. Companies will often promise that customer information is encrypted, secured, or adequately protected. But when there is a data breach, the FTC relies on the customary practices of industry to set a baseline for what a company should have done in the first place. In *United States v. ValueClick*, for example, the FTC alleged that ValueClick "did not encrypt sensitive information consistent with industry standards." And in *In re Eli Lilly & Co.*, the FTC alleged that the company failed to use the "industry standard secure socket layer encryption." Industry custom has long been a yardstick by which the common law measured reasonable care. But even customs have to be reasonable, suggesting a two-step reasonable care analysis. By starting with a heuristic set by industry, the analysis becomes endogenous, giving companies the opportunity to set a presumption that needs to be refuted, rather than the other way around. And even if we accept the relevance of industry custom in the FTC's privacy "common law," the prevalence of industry standards still speaks to the way regulated entities set the baseline on which they will be judged.[77]

The FTC also defers to other industry structures of symbolic compliance. After the organization TRUSTe, now rebranded as TrustArc, started issuing privacy "seals" certifying that a website's privacy policy met certain standards and norms, the FTC incorporated those seals as evidence of compliance. In *FTC v. Toysmart.com*, for example, the FTC noted that Toysmart had become "a licensee of . . . an organization that certifies the privacy policies of online businesses and allows such businesses to display a . . . trustmark or seal." In so doing, the FTC was referring to a structure a third party had developed on its own, thus pushing TRUSTe's seals into the legal consciousness.[78]

And despite their hype, the FTC's privacy assessments defer to corporate compliance structures all the time. Because assessments are based on attestations from corporate officers rather than independent investigation, Facebook was able to lie routinely to the FTC during its initial and biennial assessment reports required under the 2011 Consent Decree. And the FTC's latest settlement with the company offers more of the same in this respect. Rather than empowering a strong independent public regulator, the settlement permits assessments to be based entirely on documents Facebook

provides to the assessor. That means that Facebook will set the terms for its own evaluation, with assessors never looking under the hood.[79]

The GDPR also incorporates industry structures. Recognizing the importance of an internal advocate for privacy, the GDPR requires companies to hire a DPO and involve her "in all issues which relate to the protection of personal data." Article 35 also requires companies to complete impact assessments before processing data. Both of these elements are undoubtedly important. But a data protection office is a structure that could become merely symbolic if, as research has shown, the office is marginalized, unsupported, and disconnected from the process of technology design. And impact assessments can become simple paper trails when seen as ends in themselves rather than as a substantive guide for helping a company determine if it should go ahead with or abort its planned data use. Companies can, therefore, take advantage of the delays and complexities in judicial decision-making to decide for themselves what the GDPR requires in practice.[80]

In the end, these seemingly small beachheads of symbolic structures in the law are nevertheless worrisome because they may have an anchoring effect on judges and regulators. In this context, a symbolic structure like a seal or a CPO office could anchor an impression, later made official in a judicial decision or regulatory order, that a company is compliant with the law, even if the seal is meaningless or the CPO's office cannot influence design or data use.

The Organizational and Social Forces Driving Endogeneity in Privacy Law

One of the recurring themes in almost all of my interviews and observations of privacy professionals and privacy lawyers was that they were doing their best, but not achieving the best results. Many privacy professionals knew that the GDPR's risk-based framework focused on privacy risks to individuals and yet, they all seemed resigned to the existence of programs – programs for which they are responsible – that focus on corporate risks. Several recognized that their coworkers were cynically performing privacy – "going through the motions" – and knew such performances wouldn't be successful even as they justified it as bringing privacy

to the table. Some lamented that software engineers were making privacy decisions ad hoc, knew it was happening, and said they were doing their best in a "tough situation." It is, of course, possible that privacy professionals aren't doing their best, that some have become shills for the data-extractive interests of their employers. There are undoubtedly privacy professionals and privacy lawyers who see their jobs primarily through managerial lenses, conceptualizing themselves not as privacy advocates but as the foot soldiers best suited to get privacy law out of their employers' way. This was particularly true for lawyers at private firms for whom "doing whatever our client asks us to do" is dogma. For one AmLaw 100 partner with fourteen years' experience in privacy and security, "going through the motions required by the GDPR, the records, the DPO hires, and other things, that's what's ultimately going to protect our clients from investigation." That said, most in-house privacy lawyers and privacy professionals I interviewed were disheartened that their structures weren't always working, and they expressed a desire to do better. As a chief privacy officer at a data analytics company told me, "you don't understand the constraints we're under." But they're only noticing a select few of those constraints; they are unwitting accomplices as well.

Hobbling the Privacy Office

Those constraints became obvious during interviews, reviews of corporate hierarchies, and surveys of privacy professionals. Most of the tactics hobbling privacy offices were the creations of management, which used internal rules and corporate structures to both limit pro-privacy voices and trigger ordinary worker concerns about how to do their jobs well and how to build their careers. The end result was a privacy professional community that may have far less substantive impact than scholars have so far presumed.[81]

Undoubtedly, privacy law's compliance-based governance scheme, which explicitly calls for a public-private partnership, opened the door for the information industry to take control of the compliance process. And, as noted above, many privacy professionals are steeped in the same neoliberal privacy-as-control discourses as we are, further entrenching a discourse that fosters

corporate, rather than individual, power. More practically, companies have taken one or more of four aggressive steps to quiet dissident privacy voices.

The easiest thing a company can do to weaken a privacy office even further is push the CPO lower down the corporate hierarchy. Many companies put privacy alongside general compliance teams in Risk Management or Compliance and Risk departments. That alone may not be problematic, but it does mean that a privacy leader would report to an executive imbued with managerial values or focused on matters other than privacy. I spoke to seven privacy professionals who worked in this kind of corporate structure and four of them called it a "problem." A privacy manager at a San Francisco-based technology company said that he has

> "a boss who is an old school compliance guy from a bank. He's great at what he does. But he channels everything I say through that lens, which was probably built over years working on Wall Street. So, when I take him something that I think appreciates context-specific privacy issues, something that isn't necessarily boiled down into a checklist, it goes into his office and almost always comes out as some bastardized version of what I gave him. And it's always thinner, weaker, and just not what I want."

Taking these professionals at their word, many of them are trying to help, but are hampered by their managerial bosses.

Even at those companies where the chief privacy officer is a C-Suite level position that reports directly to a board of directors, the privacy budget may be partially controlled by another department. Budgets are moral statements of priorities and whether we're analyzing a government's fiscal policies or revenue allocations by a profit-making corporation, budgets hint at what executives think are important. Of the thirty-eight privacy professionals interviewed for this project, fourteen reported that their budget was controlled by their companies' legal and regulatory affairs department. Fewer – eleven and nine – said their budgets were part of compliance or information technology (IT). Sometimes, privacy professionals work well within these departments. However, many reported that trusting the privacy budget to a department with interests often independent of privacy causes tension. "If I want money for

something," a Silicon Valley privacy professional told me, "I have to ask IT. I have to get lines in his budget for almost everything my team does. And even when I do, sometimes things happen and budgets get shifted. The first thing in the IT budget to go in a crisis is the privacy budget." More than half of the privacy professionals I interviewed agreed with this statement about their own budgetary issues. One added that at her former employer, "the GC got it and understood what I was trying to do. Now it's a fight. And he wins too often."[82]

Where a privacy department has a significant budget on its own or within another department, management can squelch privacy's influence by shifting significant responsibilities elsewhere. For example, at a New York financial company, the CPO reported that she is in charge of policies, standards, trainings, and hiring outside counsel. Her office has no control over privacy audits. When asked why this was the case, especially given the importance of audits in privacy law's collaborative governance regime, she said, "it's just one of those things companies do because of expertise. There are lots of audits, so we have a separate department that's in charge." This tracks the results from several surveys of the privacy industry in which privacy leaders reported the greatest control over trainings, drafting policies, publications, communications, and travel, but far less responsibility for things that really matter to the law: audits, data inventory, and technology.[83]

And then there are companies that silo privacy departments, even where those departments are led by C-Suite executives and have substantial budgets. A siloed privacy department may be robust on its own; I observed substantial work product that included detailed protocols, advice on addressing privacy and security questions, and standards to follow. Its weakness is in its inability to have much of an impact on the rest of the company, particularly the software engineers designing new products. Bamberger and Mulligan recognized the limitations of siloed departments; they recommended integrating privacy professionals into business units. But I noticed both siloed departments and smaller silos within those units. Siloed privacy departments may be located in offices or areas far away from engineering. They may never speak to designers other than when they lead intermittent trainings. And they may take on check-the-box-style relationships with design teams whereby product

managers ask privacy professionals to sign off on designs rather than engage them in the design process. Even when privacy professionals are assigned to particular products or projects, they don't sit near their engineers. Not one of the privacy professionals I spoke to had their desk near designers, and none of them knew of any colleagues in other companies who did. Nor do they actively engage their engineers in privacy discussions during design, as we will discuss in more detail in Chapter 4. Rather, they wait for designers to come to them, a process enforced by corporate hierarchies and reporting structures laid down by management. In the end, some privacy professionals may have the titles and assignments that evoke an integrated privacy team, but that integration can be a sham.[84]

Any one of these constraints, not to mention combinations thereof, contribute to the endogeneity of privacy law. Privacy departments that are siloed, starved for cash, or organizationally subservient to business units with independent or contrary interests have weaker voices in making policy. As a result, corporate obligations are framed in terms dictated by more powerful organizational actors, whether that's the general counsel, whose job it is to minimize legal risks to the company, or the vice president for IT, whose job it is to define the technical aspects of corporate practice. Neither of them is necessarily an active and overt antiprivacy voice. But their perspectives, goals, and metrics on which they are judged are orthogonal to privacy, which makes it more likely that privacy laws would be framed in terms of corporate risk and privacy would be defined in narrow, technical terms.

Social Forces Amplified by Management-Imposed Constraints

The ease with which many executives can ignore, dismiss, or undermine their privacy offices puts privacy teams in an uncertain and unstable position within the corporate hierarchy. With her budget controlled by the general counsel, one CPO stated that her "entire career felt like I was walking on eggshells because I never had the power I needed to do the job right." An in-house lawyer assigned to three product teams at a large technology company lamented that he had to "wait around for the engineers to come, and when they did come, I always had to keep in mind that if I keep saying no to something, my boss is going to have a meeting with the CEO and

that won't be pretty." Put another way, hemmed in by management-imposed routines, privacy professionals felt the more prosaic pressures of corporate work more acutely, which further diminished their privacy advocacy. Four of those pressures – the need to maintain access to executives, the desire to be seen as a team player, the perceived lack of expertise, and the need to perform – had a direct and negative effect on privacy professionals' ability to affect pro-privacy changes inside their companies. Let's call these the access trap, the career trap, the expertise trap, and the work trap.

The Access Trap

The access trap is the softening or outright silencing of advice in order to maintain access to superiors. Victims of the access trap keep a good distance from design because of a difficult double bind – namely, the choice between being an aggressive privacy advocate and "being a 'no' broken record," on the one hand, and focusing only on the absolute worst privacy risks and "keeping a seat at the table to do" the job, on the other. These concerns are real and difficult to navigate on the ground, but the net effect of the access trap that some privacy issues are not raised.

Law and society scholars have long argued that some in-house counsel are structurally incapable of constraining corporate actions. They either lack sufficient independence or take advantage of their legal interpretation and filtering responsibilities to frame the law in ways most attractive to their employers. This orientation is, at least in part, a product of an ongoing ambiguity and confusion about what in-house counsel's role should be: an "adviser" that facilitates or a "police" person who stops bad behavior. Which way lawyers conceptualize their jobs dictates how they perform and affects how successful they are achieving compliance with public law. According to one formulation, approaches to in-house counsel jobs exist on a spectrum: On one side of the spectrum are "advocates" who pursue the substance of the law vigorously and adopt adversarial approaches to management. On the opposite end are "team players" who try to resolve issues with the least disruption to the company as possible and see their employers, not the law, as their client. In between are detached "professionals," who insist on neutral, yet engaged application of

the letter of the law, and "technicians," who focus on paper-pushing, collecting compliance data, filling out forms, and exhibit disengagement from the substance of the laws they are supposedly implementing.[85]

Robert Nelson and Laura Beth Nielsen offer a related conceptualization of the in-house adviser role. These scholars suggest that in-house counsel generally fall into three ideal types: cops, counsel and entrepreneurs. A lawyer functions as a cop when she almost exclusively polices her employer's behavior through her legal expertise; she functions as a counsel when she provides both legal and ongoing, sometimes extralegal advice on business, ethics, and social responsibility; and lawyers act as entrepreneurs when they leverage their legal background to help pursue the profit-making goals of the company for which they work.[86]

Nelson and Nielsen interviewed forty-two attorneys for their study of how in-house counsel construct their roles. Many of them admitted that "in order to ensure that business professionals will continue to consult them, lawyers try to make their advice more palatable to businesspeople." One attorney reported that "when individuals in the organization come to me[,] ... if I come across to them ... as cops, they are not going to come to us. They are ... either going to go elsewhere or operate in the dark without lawyers." Another said that attorney autonomy is constrained by the need to maintain access to and the goodwill of executives: "Every business manager says they want honesty. They don't mean it, none of them mean it.' ... It's a no-no to say no." Lawyers, therefore, have to use their powers "judiciously" to not seem "obstructionist."[87]

Some in-house lawyers take this approach because it is the only way to achieve even modest or limited success in an environment downright hostile to privacy. Just as Nelson and Nielsen found among in-house counsel, I also found many privacy professionals felt that they were constantly pushing back against businesspeople who thought they were just "in the way." The business side "didn't really want me around," noted a privacy professional and lawyer working for a content creation company in New York. A colleague of hers agreed, stating that "people think privacy is just a cost center. We have no revenue, and the engineers and business guys who want the newest product see us as barriers. I have to make the job work somehow in that."

If they wanted to have some influence, many moderated their advice, stayed silent, and, as two privacy professionals put it, "pick[] your battles." A chief privacy officer at a New York data analytics company said that he "make[s] strategic decisions all the time about whether to make an issue about this or that because I can't be the guy that cries foul every single day. If I do, no one's every going to listen to me and I could be fired. Better to get involved when it's *really* necessary than every time I see something." An attorney working for one of the largest Silicon Valley technology companies echoed this point, noting that she "has to balance law and the realities of life: I can't always say 'don't' even when I think I should for lots of reasons, not the least of which is they will probably do it anyway and then I get sidelined." Marginalization was indeed a significant concern among privacy professionals. Seven interviewees suggested their silence on some issues is good for privacy; one asked rhetorically, "Would I rather be ignored all the time or be on their good side to have some influence when it really matters some of the time?"

As a result, many privacy professionals silenced themselves or took creative approaches to their work. The most common response was to transform their role from privacy advocacy to "stopping the biggest things that carried the most risk." When asked if that meant there were privacy issues that should have been addressed but were not, the attorney noted, "ideally, yes. But that rarely happens. They're usually good about those things." That was a curious response, especially given the fact that this attorney had listed almost all of the above pressures as reasons he stayed silent altogether. Therefore, when attorneys and privacy professionals fall into the access trap, it could mean a lack of attention to privacy matters during design.

Those who fall into the access trap trade privacy advocacy for getting things done. The irony of this behavior is that studies show that compliance professionals who are "allies already" and internal advocates for the communities protected by the laws they interpret and execute are the ones most likely to persuade their employers to take the law seriously. The sociologist Elizabeth Hoffman showed the efficacy of internal advocacy in the context of the Lactation at Work law, which amended the Fair Labor Standards Act to mandate basic provisions for employees to express

breast milk at work. Those who shared the values underlying the Lactation at Work law and knew breastfeeding mothers were better at mobilizing their workplaces, organizing stakeholders, and getting their buy-ins than those who did not see themselves as advocates for the laws on the books.[88]

Instead, many privacy professionals I interviewed had become so used to moderating their advice that they normalized and routinized both their rationales and their practices. The vast majority perceived that they would lose their seat at the table if they were louder privacy advocates, although none had any evidence of their counterfactual. And several privacy leaders reacted to questions about why they declined to call out antiprivacy designs in platforms designed by their employers by saying that "this is how it's done." One suggested that "you don't understand how it really works. Our work is about the groundwork. It's about the policies and the training and the procedures in place. You don't blow up at a meeting. That's not how it's done." But what about when your company is about to release a product that you really feel is a huge privacy risk? "We don't do that, of course. But it's not how it works; the CPO doesn't stop the presses when I'm pissed off at something."

The Career Trap

The career trap is related to the access trap. It manifests in some of the same social behaviors – namely, silencing and moderation of robust advocacy voices – but for distinct purposes – namely, in the name of image management, career advancement, and promotion. The career trap operates in parallel, amplifying rather than overlapping the drive to maintain access.

Almost everyone feels the pressure to take the next step in their careers. And for many of us, seeking a promotion causes behavioral modification. The sociologist Erving Goffman long ago recognized that people behave differently in professional contexts than they do in purely social contexts. Those behavioral changes are intentional: they reflect a concerted attempt by workers to present themselves in accordance with contextual norms. In the organizational context, image management can manifest in many behaviors, including performing agreeability and staying silent when the norm is that only senior voices should speak, because employers looking to

hire professionals into team environments – in-house lawyers and privacy professionals all work in teams – will seek out candidates who exhibit, among other characteristics, agreeability, cooperative capacity, and modesty. Therefore, employees at all stages of their career engage in image management to project these qualities. Employees also stay silent or acquiesce to practices they may dislike for careerist interests. One scholar called this "pragmatic silence," or a strategic decision not to speak up that sometimes reflects a lack of opportunity to make one's voice heard or the need to protect oneself from others. Women, persons of color, queer people, and members of other marginalized groups feel this acutely, as do junior-level employees, all of whom, studies have shown, don't speak up at one time or another because they think no one will listen or because they worry it will damage their prospects for employment in a structured workplace. Who among us hasn't felt a similar pressure, whether during our first job out of college, prior to tenure on a university faculty, or as a minority in a hostile environment.[89]

These are natural, rather than maliciously selfish, behaviors. Although there is substantial evidence that many people loathe the games they have to play to succeed, they recognize the need for image management. I found this in my interviews as well. Some privacy professionals feel can't be too aggressive in their privacy advocacy because "if I say no all the time, I mean, I'll get fired." An in-house lawyer in Silicon Valley said, "Everyone wants to work here. The environment is good, the salary is good. People who stand against their managers a lot aren't going to be around too much longer, whether they're fired or pushed out or iced out."[90]

The most common response to these pressures is to behave like a team player and moderate their advocacy. Team players are, after all, flexible and harmonious, not barriers to innovation. Team players aren't "advocates" or "cops." Nor are they shills on the opposite end of the spectrum. The privacy professionals and lawyers I interviewed seemed to have carved out a middle ground, focusing on preventing only the worst excesses. They don't jump in to address every or even most incidents of technology designs that invade users' privacy. They will mostly leave software engineers to their own devices, save for the policies they write and trainings they lead. That is, until something really bad is about to happen; only when a project clearly violates a legal rule will the privacy

professional take the initiative and prevent a worst-case scenario. It is, they say, the best they can do without angering their bosses and risking their jobs.

Privacy professionals shared several stories paradigmatic of this approach. A CPO with two decades of experience said that much of her career was "about making tough choices because there was no way someone like me was going to turn a big corporation ... into one that suddenly was a privacy defender." One such choice came after a meeting in which her boss, a senior executive, criticized her for recommending against moving forward with a software product because its data processing scheme was going to violate several European privacy rules:

> "It was after this meeting, where I was told to "stop saying no to profit or else we can't work together," that a manager on one of our largest products came to me with several data and security questions. I told him that there is a difference between what we should do and what we can do. He asked me what we can do and I gave him advice that mostly had to do with data security. We left the data use issues because I knew stopping him and his team was not going to end well, for me and for the future of privacy at [the company]."

An in-house privacy lawyer lamented that he "wasn't involved until the end" on an online gaming platform designed while he was at a former employer, so he "had to stop the worst leak. The water was already coming in so to speak, but maybe I could buy us more time. At that stage, no one is stopping anything, I don't care what anyone tells you, and if they try to, they may get fired." And a director of privacy with experience in both Canada and the United States told me of a

> "meeting we had with the entire engineering team working on [a well-known app] where I got up to list 7 – yes, 7 – privacy issues that I thought needed to be addressed and was shouted down at the end when the VP asked, 'so what are we supposed to do, shut down, go home, and not make money any more? Come on!' So, I told them they should at least do 1 and 2. They ended up fixing only one, and that was the best I could do."

Those seven privacy issues, as best as this interviewee could remember, involved transfers of data between the app and third parties, default options, and the collection of information for no purpose other than for future monetization. The only issue on her list they addressed was the gratuitous data collection, which was minimized to data that could be used to improve the service and create targeted advertisements.

The Expertise Trap

Some privacy lawyers embrace a corporate structure that requires them to wait for engineers and product managers to come to them for advice as a valid division of labor. Many of them thought it wasn't their job to assert themselves in design at all, suggesting that it would cause friction on their team and would be overstepping their bounds. Many of the attorneys I interviewed saw themselves as passive participants in the design process not because they didn't care, but because of professional timidity with technology. This is the expertise trap.

Legal education is well known for its lack of technology education. Only about one-quarter of law schools, for example, offer a class in information privacy. Alongside internet law or cyberlaw, information privacy courses expose students to some technologies that implicate privacy issues. Privacy casebooks includes cases on networked technologies, heat sensors, GPS, wiretaps, email, computers, encryption, video surveillance, AI, face surveillance, online searches, and much more. Criminal procedure classes may spend many class hours on federal and state surveillance under the Fourth Amendment and federal statutes, but few of those courses dedicate time to the technological aspects of GPS, algorithmic systems, and data collection. But outside of occasionally providing general summaries of how relevant technologies work, court opinions can only take law students so far. Most law students major in nontechnical fields in college. They may now come to law school with facility in using technology, but many lack a willingness to understand how they work.[91]

I found some evidence of this in my interviews with privacy lawyers in private firms. "Thank god I don't have to be an engineer to draft changes to a privacy policy," a junior attorney at a large,

highly regarded law firm in New York City. Another young lawyer at a different firm stated that "no technical background required" could be the slogan for his technology law education. Partners at these firms are quick to point out that they are eagerly searching for tech talent, even outside the narrow confines of patent practice groups, which often hire law students with technical degrees. They recognize that technological expertise can help: "I would love an engineer on my cases. They look at problems differently, sure, which helps, but sometimes a client has a new device or a problem that started online and my 12-year-old daughter is more equipped to understand it than I am. No joke." This kind of self-deprecation and admission to a lack of technical skills was quite common.

Granted, lawyers do not need to be lawyers and engineers at the same time. But lawyers' lack of technical skill limits their ability to help integrate privacy into design in several ways. First, a limited knowledge base can erode confidence in one's ability to affect positive change. Several in-house lawyers suggested that they were disinclined to take the initiative and reach out to engineers during design because they "couldn't contribute. I'm not a coder. I don't want to get in the way." As a result, lawyers don't get involved even when they might be the ones most able to spot privacy. Second, an inability to speak with or relate to engineers on their level erodes trust. Trust is important among members of teams. Without some level of trust – in a worker' technical skill, dedication to the work, and commitment to others – team members do not have the confidence to reflect, ask challenging questions, and solve problems. Indeed, trust allows workers to share experiences and provides "psychological safety" for team members to challenge each other's assumptions. To gain that level of trust with engineers, lawyers need to "speak their language." A senior lawyer at large technology company who serves as the legal point person for several design teams told me that it is "important to learn about the product, be passionate about it, do research on it so I can talk intelligently about what my [engineers] are doing. Otherwise, my [engineers] would see me as an impediment, not a teammate, and I am a member of the team." When the lawyers I interviewed did not have even a modicum of facility with technology, they responded by becoming bystanders in design.[92]

This organizational arrangement was also normalized and routinized throughout much of the information industry.

The privacy lawyers I interviewed spoke about how "this is how we do it" and how "it would be very unusual to have it any other way." Several were even surprised when I suggested that they could sit in design meetings, with one asking, "You mean actually be with the engineers?" Siloing lawyers from the technical aspects of design had become so routine that it had been engrained as commonsense and obvious. The alternative was hard to imagine.

The Work Trap

A significant minority of the privacy professionals and privacy lawyers I interviewed for this project felt that privacy law was already robust. One said that the "sectoral approach is really what we need because every industry is different, and anything more strict would be bad for consumers who want innovation in apps and in detecting breast cancer." Most thought privacy law was *becoming* more robust, and almost all cited the GDPR, the CCPA, and other privacy laws and regulations in the United States and Europe. But when I asked for evidence showing precisely how these laws enhanced privacy protection, most interviewees pointed to their work, how much work product is coming out of their offices, how much they're spending on privacy, and how many new people and vendors they're hiring to accommodate all the increases in work. This is the work trap: thinking the law is substantively effective because you have a lot of work to do.

Three CPOs captured this sentiment in their comments. A CPO in Berlin said privacy law "was making my office a centerpiece. We have to do things now we didn't do before and my team is growing to meet the work demands." A colleague in New York was even more explicit: "We went from one person to 15 people in a year, and each of them are overworked. The GDPR is requiring a lot of us. It's not like it was before." And another CPO based in San Francisco said that the CCPA in particular was "making business as usual a thing of the past. We have records requirements, access requirements, new policies, and so forth, and my team is working hard to catch up."

Suggesting that privacy law is robust because privacy teams are busy, growing, and doing a lot of work in response to those laws evaluates privacy law's efficacy on two metrics – effort and process – both of which are detrimental to realizing privacy protections for

individuals. Many privacy professionals confused the amount of work they do with privacy law's efficacy. But effort is not always related to substance. This is like confusing riding and sweating on a stationary exercise bicycle with biking long distances: If you're goal is to get somewhere, you didn't, but you did work really hard. Or like a student who studies the wrong topic and answers the wrong question on an exam: she did a lot of work, but that doesn't mean she will get a good grade. When pressed further, the only examples privacy professionals and privacy lawyers could give of more robust privacy protections for their customers in their companies' products were more transparency, more notice, and more consent, again suggesting the extent to which privacy-as-control remains entrenched in people who profess to care about privacy. A few nodded toward products like Firefox or changes in defaults, but the vast majority of supposedly privacy-enhancing changes in the products most of use have been superficial at best.

The second metric is process. Almost every privacy professional and privacy lawyer I interviewed acknowledged that their industry did not always have a great track record with respect to privacy. And although some of them insisted without evidence that their company was somehow different, they all fell back on some variation of "doing [their] best." "We're doing better here," said a privacy manager at a large technology company, "and we weren't always this focused." Another said that "my team doing its best" when it came to privacy. But the examples they gave about their "best" were all about procedure. They spoke of new assessments and PIAs, new record keeping and consent tracking, documentation that they were "painstakingly filling out to make sure we do right by our customers," according to one DPO. When I asked several interviewees how filling out forms protects individuals or enhances their privacy in the final product, the DPO said, "Well, not directly, but that's not how it works. I do this to make sure my company is doing this stuff up and down the line, and then it trickles down." A CPO in New York said their work "was getting the job done and elevating privacy inside the company." Two privacy lawyers at a Los Angeles technology company said that "our work is dedicated to making things better for the consumer, and that's why we have all of this work," as they pointed to several check lists and PIAs on their desks. Lawyers like process; lawyers

are trained in process. But that doesn't excuse the conflation of process with real substantive results for individuals.

Legal Disempowerment

Privacy law and the privacy profession are having minimal effects on design. The law is being undermined by symbolic compliance, and even those privacy professionals who think of themselves as privacy advocates are embracing those symbols as the real social practice of privacy law for a variety of reasons. They don't want to be the ones that say "no" all the time, and they want to maintain access to their bosses. They don't want to get fired or they perceive that they don't have the expertise to get involved. They also tend to confuse work and process with actual improvement in substantive privacy protections for individuals.

The privacy professional has helped to transform corporate policies into mere symbols of compliance as lawyers and privacy professionals either resign themselves to an immovable superstructure or settle for "stopping the most stupid stuff" as the best they can do. Management wants it that way. Some executives have structured privacy offices to have a lot of impact for marketing purposes, but very little impact when it really matters. These companies issue press releases when they hire new CPOs and their communications departments seek laudatory exposés for their companies' privacy-focused innovations. Executives go before Congress to talk about returning "control" over data to individuals and start emails, testimonies, and statements by acknowledging how "important" privacy really is.

Behind the veil, privacy departments at some companies are mere symbols. But the privacy professionals I studied were active in interpreting, implementing, and realizing privacy law on the ground. They just weren't having the kind of impact that would improve privacy for individuals on the ground. Privacy offices were often sequestered from the rest of the business by corporate reporting structures and hobbled from having any significant impact by corporate power grabs, intentional organizational design, and budget fights. This created instability in privacy offices that made ordinary workplace pressures feel more acute, resulting in privacy professionals and lawyers moderating their advice so as to maintain access, keep their jobs, or stay in the lane of their expertise. So, although the

ecosystem of privacy professionals churned out reports, policies, trainings, assessments, public statements, standards, and checklists, those structures were sometimes reduced to check-the-box compliance or limited to trainings and guides that failed to influence how software engineers made privacy decisions in the moment.

As symbols replace actual compliance, the social practice of privacy law becomes a performance. And as people go through the motions of performing privacy law, they may soon lose track of the difference, conflating their performance with what the law actually requires. Edelman was concerned about this happening in the judiciary, as courts increasingly turn to symbols of compliance as evidence for its adjudication of legal questions. But the problem of legal endogeneity, symbolic compliance, and performance is far broader. Legal performance is a Foucauldian "technique of power," inculcating the perception among performers and their audience that something is happening, that the law is working, and that surveillance will be reined in. When it isn't, when structures of power remain intact because the performance was all a sham from the start, nihilism takes hold. We give up. We think protecting our privacy or maintaining control of our data is too difficult to be worth the effort. We cede what little remaining power we had. To anyone who has tried to opt out of cookies without success or turn of tracking on 300 smartphone apps before giving up on the fifteenth or find a way to use a website without agreeing to the platform's data extraction, this should feel eerily familiar.[93]

The forces hobbling privacy governance inside the information industry are, for the most part, creatures of management. And that makes sense. Having worked hard and spent billions of dollars to weaken the ground on which we think, debate, and write about privacy, the information industry could take advantage of another tool of power – compliance – to undermine the effectiveness of the privacy laws even that friendly discursive terrain managed to create. In doing so, they created a sociopolitical context that was tilted against privacy and was able to trigger and rely on common workplace pressures to soften or silence internal privacy voices. These strategies disempowered privacy law from the start. Hard working professionals on the ground never had a chance. And, over time, even those who considered themselves to be privacy advocates came to accept and normalize process over substance, falling in line with the information industry's plans to marginalize privacy every step of the way.

4 DESIGNING DATA-EXTRACTIVE TECHNOLOGIES

Through a long campaign to inculcate corporate-friendly discourses about privacy, the information industry tilted our legal consciousness away from privacy and enlisted even those employees who see themselves as privacy advocates in their data-extractive missions. This softened the discursive ground on which we think and talk about privacy and weakened the privacy laws we manage to pass. Technology companies then took advantage of public-private partnerships explicitly built into those privacy laws to undermine their effectiveness. They used coercive bureaucracies and took advantage of power asymmetries to develop compliance programs that reoriented and recast privacy laws in ways that served their surveillant interests. As a result, the information industry undermined the institutions that are supposed to protect our privacy.

Having weakened those exogenous constraints on their data-extractive behavior, tech companies turned their attention inward, to endogenous sources of dissent. In Chapter 2, we saw how they used the weapons of coercive bureaucracies, including strategic allocation of assignments and tactical punishments for whistleblowers, to indirectly influence employee conduct. In Chapter 3, some of those weapons were deployed to hobble the privacy office directly. In this chapter, we will see a similar strategy applied to the design process itself, resulting in the silencing of privacy voices and the elimination of opportunities to integrate privacy into design.

Recall how some of the designers we met in Chapter 1 described how they did their work. Gavin and Peter described engineering and design teams suggests that some companies divide coding

responsibilities among different teams and keep each team focused on its own narrow agendas. These internal organizational rules and norms allowed Gavin and Peter to focus squarely on the work in front of him. Gavin admitted that he wasn't "super experienced in that area," referring to privacy, but it was the company's organizational practice of dividing tasks among small steams that allowed him to assume that privacy work was being done elsewhere. For Peter, small teams amplified his sense of territoriality; he noted several times that privacy wasn't his "job." He also noted that he "hadn't seen anything" like formal policies about how to integrate privacy into design, suggesting a breakdown in how the privacy department communicated its interests to those doing design work on the ground.

Gavin and Tom, both engineers, had only met with lawyers once between them, and that was only because Gavin "got in trouble" for something he didn't explain. Janice, the experienced privacy professional, and Anita and Jamal, the privacy lawyers, also didn't always realize that there were formal and informal barriers between them and technology design. Neither of them had the power to go directly to engineers and affirmatively spot privacy issues or help the software teams do their privacy-related work. But although they had to wait for engineers or product managers to come to them with questions, neither of them saw this as a problem. Sometimes, the privacy lawyers and professionals suggested that they lacked the expertise to get more involved in design. Elsewhere, they suggested that a passive role better suited designer productivity; they assumed a lawyer would be seen as "in the way." Others, as we shall see throughout this book, accepted that "this is how it works," as if these processes were habituated and other options were simply not possible.

At the "Broteam" meeting, a group of engineers were actively engaged in making privacy-related design decisions without acknowledging the privacy issues at play. Nor did they speak with anyone to tease out the privacy issues even though their employer had an in-house legal team that staffed each of the company's products with teams of generalist lawyers. The same was true for engineers like Alex and Max, both of whom admitted that they "make decisions all the time about privacy." They did the work on their own, approaching a multifaceted design question based solely on ease of use, the extent to which a given design would enhance or

undermine engagement, or to achieve whatever engineering goal they wanted to achieve. Those goals came from the top, from the design management team, and they always affected how engineers did their work. For almost all of them, though, they were making privacy-related decisions ad hoc, without practical input from people designated as privacy experts.

Through interviews, reviews of reporting hierarchies, and observations of design meetings at several companies, the role of coercive bureaucracy became clear: Some technology companies structure their design processes to stifle privacy by siloing designers from each other and from other corporate departments, defining the mission of design purely in terms of engagement, and amplifying privacy apathy among engineers. The result of these strategies, either alone or in concert, was the creation of an organizational environment in which the ordinary work of design, work that engineers do often without intentionally or maliciously undermining privacy, resulted in technology designs that fed the information industry's quest for data. In other words, technology companies used coercive bureaucracies to silence privacy during design and did it so effectively that their own workers didn't even realize that they were unwitting foot soldiers in a data-extractive ecosystem. The repeated performance of their tasks normalized them, social constructing design work in ways that erase privacy.

In this chapter, I discuss what I mean by design, highlight some of the ways in which technology designers are biased to be apathetic or indifferent to privacy, and then see how specific elements of corporate bureaucracy can amplify those biases and disempower privacy in the design process. Just like undermining privacy law was the result of the regular work done by compliance professionals within a biased organizational structure, so too is undermining privacy design the product of ordinary activities and pressures in a corporate environment specifically orchestrated to achieve data-extractive goals. This is the final stage of the information industry's performances against privacy: controlling design.

Design as Power

Design is the sociotechnical process by which technologies are instantiated with functionality, meaning, and values. More

specifically, design involves the technical process by which a set of specifications are translated into code. That takes specialized knowledge, which means that software engineers, computer scientists, and other technologists are usually at the center of design. However, that translation also requires judgment and a normative framework; someone has to develop the specifications in the first place and because there rarely, if ever, is one way to code for a particular function, designers have to make judgments as to how best to do their work. This means that design is not only technical. Design refers both to the code-based architecture of a technological system and the social process by which corporate interests, legal requirements, and other mandates are translated into that code. It captures both the technical and organizational elements that impact how technologies are made and what they do for (and to) their users. It also involves a group of people working together, learning from each other, making judgments, interacting through teams, and solving problems on the way to building a cohesive product.[1]

In addition to being sociotechnical, design is also sociolinguistic. Design translates exogenous requirements written and conceived by humans into language that a computer can understand – namely, code. For example, if a company's sale's team wants to target its holiday discount announcements to customers walking by the company's brick-and-mortar stores, the company's mobile app needs to track users' geolocation in real time. That rule has to be designed in and coded in some way. If a resort has a three-night-minimum-stay policy, that rule could be designed into the hotel's website by making it impossible for customers to select one- or two-night stays. And if the Fair Housing Act prohibits race-based housing discrimination, that rule has to be designed in as well: designers of digital platforms engaged in the sale or rent of homes should not even provide an option for filtering or targeting applicants on the basis of race. Design, therefore, instantiates technology with limitations, opportunities, and social values that come from a variety of exogenous sources – the law and corporate headquarters, for example – and can include the translation of values, ethics, and human rights in addition to functional limitations.[2]

That's why it's important to study design. Like discourse and compliance, design is also a tool of power. If companies want to ensure that their platforms' code tells the stories they want, or what

Mary Flanagan and Helen Nissenbaum called the platforms' "semantic architecture," they have to control design. Design expresses values. Design triggers, manipulates, and coerces our propensity to share personal information with others. When design makes things easier to do (like disclosing personal information), we do more of it; when design makes things harder to do (like protect our privacy), we do less of it. This makes design especially important for myriad values, including privacy.[3]

Indeed, as Langdon Winner argued, it's hard to understand design independent of its coercive capacities and political dynamics. Nissenbaum and Batya Friedman, as well as the legal scholars Julie Cohen, Joel Reidenberg, Woodrow Hartzog, and others, have already ably demonstrated the substantial and influential power that comes with design. Their outstanding work need not be repeated here. Suffice it to say, as Hartzog notes, that "the realities of technology at scale mean that the services we use must necessarily be built in a way that constrains our choices." We can only click on the buttons or select the options presented to us; we can only opt out of the options from which a website allows us to opt out. Design is the context in which the social world is "made to happen" and is, therefore, a weapon of power.[4]

Tristan Harris, a former design ethicist at Google and the director and a co-founder of the Center for Humane Technology, has likened the power of design to a magician's misdirection:

> "We ignore how ... [our] choices are manipulated upstream by menus we didn't choose in the first place. ... This is exactly what magicians do. They give people the illusion of free choice while architecting the menu so that they win, no matter what you choose. ... By shaping the menus we pick from, technology hijacks the way we perceive our choices and replaces them with new ones."

Sometimes, then, design can manipulate us into making choices that serve corporate interests rather than our own. We see this throughout the digital ecosystem. Facebook tells us when our friends have 'liked' a page, encouraging us to do the same; so-called dark patterns, or design tricks that manipulate us into taking certain actions online, trigger our preference for shiny colorful buttons over gray ones; platforms nudge us to buy products others have bought

before us; and apps gamify sharing by encouraging us to continue a 'streak' with our friends. Designers' power inspired the journalist Clive Thompson to call software engineers "among the most quietly influential people on the planet." Because we live in a world governed by software, and they are the architects of that software, "the decisions they make guide our behavior."[5]

Designing without Privacy in Mind

Like all of us, designers bring their priors into work. And many of those biases, developed from their education, from each other, and from their profession as a whole, suggest that they may neglect privacy in design not out of malice, but simply because privacy is not traditionally part of their worldview. This is why technologists can respond to privacy experts pointing our surveillant designs by saying that they "did not design the product with … foresight" or "never considered" privacy in design and actually speak the truth.[6]

There is, however, more to this story than just our failure to train software engineers about privacy. Structural, professional, and economic pressures amplify software engineers' ambivalence about privacy, and then corporate structures normalize that ambivalence across the board. In particular, many of the designers I interviewed fall into some combination of eight different traps that had the effect of marginalizing privacy in design. Designers can escape these traps, and many either put in the extra effort needed to do so or don't fall into them in the first place. But, as we will discuss later in this chapter, the companies in the information industry leverage coercive bureaucracies to amplify these biases and further push privacy off the table.

The Codability Trap

The codability trap, or the idea that privacy must be codable and anything not codable is impossible, is particularly pernicious for the future of privacy in design. Software engineers and product managers are particular susceptible to this trap. And its chief effect is to empower software engineers over other groups.

Many of the engineers I interviewed did indeed use diverse language to talk about privacy. But among thirty-two software

engineers asked to describe how privacy integrated into their work, twenty-two cabined references to privacy barriers with code. Privacy is about "shield[ing] what someone doesn't want to share through the code itself," one said. When I noted that many nonexperts think about privacy in terms of intimate information, another coder said, "I can code a process to exclude all references to 'sex' if I wanted to, but that will also exclude 'sex discrimination' and even the town of 'Middlesex.' What I can't code are different people's perceptions of what they think is private and what they think isn't." A privacy engineer at Google said, "The great thing about privacy-by-design is that it listened to the engineers: give us something we can code, not ambiguous terms that defy it."

This trap puts software engineers at the center of design, amplifying their power. Because design is, in part, sociolinguistic and because the only people who can translate values and policies into code are programmers and software engineers, they have unique power in the design process. Importantly, engineers also play gatekeeping roles during design meetings by telling other stakeholders what's possible and what isn't. For example, when members of a sales and marketing team wanted to integrate certain behavioral tracking tools into the design of a website, they met with engineers, their manager, and a product manager, many of whom took notes on the requests. The engineering manager ended the meeting by stating, "I'll have my team identify the things we can do and the things we can't do just yet. Right now I'm seeing a few things that will be a little more difficult to program than others, but we'll get back to you." Elsewhere, when a privacy professional cautioned about collecting user data, an engineering team lead responded: "That's fine, we want to be sensitive to these concerns, but please come to us with some specific thing that we can do. I understand values are important, but I can't ask my team to write code for good intentions. Some things just won't work." The ability to determine what's codable and what's not is a powerful gatekeeping function; it gives engineers the power to say what goes from idea to practice. That power also filters the power of others; if what is codable is possible and what is uncodable is not possible, then only those with codable proposals can ever have their ideas realized.

Some product managers, many of whom are software engineers by training who were promoted to manager positions, held

similar views. During a meeting with a privacy lawyer – requested, per organization rules, by the product manager, not the lawyer – an experienced product manager responded to several recommendations with an eagerness to implement the lawyer's ideas, but only if they could be "reduced to code." The product manager told me afterward that "there is this tension between legal and my teams. Not a personal tension mind you, they're lovely guys and women. But they give me things to do and they don't realize that building a better [platform] ... is only going to happen through programming. My engineers can't program privacy expectations."

That engineering discourses around privacy emphasize technology and code is unsurprising. Because of their training, engineers have more complex mental models of how computers, digital technologies, and the internet work. This rush to code for privacy is part of a larger technocentric movement to shift our institutions in general into the language of code. The law professor Aziz Huq has argued that government decisions by "well-calibrated" machines will improve social welfare. Anthony Casey and Anthony Niblett believe that the problems of rules and standards in the law can be entirely avoided by turning to technology, machine learning, and AI and their ability to erase the fuzziness of "reasonableness" with simple "microdirectives" for people to follow in any given instance.[7]

There are, however, important aspects of designing for privacy that do not involve code. Corporate missions and organizational structures could prioritize privacy in the ethos of a company, in reporting hierarchies, and in decision-making processes. Code cannot address the ethical responsibilities companies have with respect to our data. Nor can it ensure that third parties live up to their affirmative contractual obligations. Code can't stop discrimination; it can sometimes perpetuate it. The prolific information scholar Frank Pasquale has demonstrated the limits of using computational strategies to protect health care privacy. Boiling down notices to constituent elements that computers can understand, for example, fails to address readability, presentation, and even content. And the law professor Rebecca Crootof has ably demonstrated that despite the hype, AI is still incapable of "rule application and value balancing" necessary in law, in general, and in privacy law, in particular. What's more, the idea that computational thinking and computational language are the only weapons at privacy's disposal

is to undermine privacy from the outset: the codability trap serves to empower only one group (engineers) and preemptively and unnecessarily shrinks the world of privacy-protective tools to one that may not be the best weapon for the cause.[8]

The Encryption Trap

Many software engineers also fall into the encryption trap, or the conflation of privacy with security. The designers think that once data is encrypted it is private and their privacy responsibilities are complete. This trap allows its victims to earnestly believe they are working hard to protect our privacy when, in fact, their myopia is knee-capping efforts to engage in comprehensive privacy efforts.

For example, the programmer Steve Phillips created LeapChat.org to give individuals "a small island of privacy" in online communications. He "encrypted [it] at every point" to allow individuals to talk "privately." Engineers like Phillips working to keep law enforcement out of activist online circles may consider themselves "pro-privacy" "cypherpunk" hackers, but their "privacy hackathons" focus exclusively on encryption and security. Phillips noted that he could "write world-changing software – protect people's civil liberties, specifically the right to privacy" and "literally protect a billion people's privacy" by "encrypting" communications. And when Phil Zimmerman leveraged the work of the well-known computer scientist Whit Diffie to encrypt email, Zimmerman called it "Pretty Good Privacy." Scholars have found that when asked about whether various digital tools are protected their privacy, engineers answered by referring to the level of the tools' security. And in my own interviews, many software engineers echoed this same encryption-as-privacy discourse: several interviewees explicitly defined privacy as encrypting data, whereas others used phrases like "de-identify," "add noise," "security," or "mak[e] data impossible to hack."[9]

Responding to questions about their privacy-related work, a programmer at a publishing company said that he "was taught that part of my job was going to be to encrypt the data we collected." Another engineer stated plainly that many of his colleagues believed that "if I encrypt the data, it's private." An engineer formerly at LinkedIn engineer stated: "My job was to prevent us from getting

hacked." An entrepreneur in New York said he and his company were "taking privacy seriously" and excitedly stated that his job was to "tell my engineers, my programmers, my data guys that the shit would hit the fan if we ever got hacked. Security had to be an important priority. Sure, we all need to make money and we all want to make money. But we're not going to do that if we don't secure the data." These views had real effects on design: when they finished designing security protocols, many engineers saw their privacy obligations completed as well.

The Choice Trap

Throughout my research, I found that engineers, engineering team leaders, privacy professionals, and lawyers thought privacy was about giving us choices and control over our data. This is the choice trap. Even though choice remains an important element of our contextual understanding of privacy, privacy-as-control is a trap because it is a fox in sheep's clothing.

One engineer thought that privacy was about "giving users notice about what was happening with their data." A former product manager at Google now running his own start-up agreed: "Privacy is definitely important. We have to give users the information they need to make decisions." A senior engineer who used to work for Uber said that "we have to make sure you know what's going on. I think that's what we think about when privacy comes up: your ability to make the right decisions [about information] for you." This is why behavioral targeting is more accepted among engineers than privacy advocates. "People love [ad targeting], one engineer noted. . . . Privacy to me means giving people the choice to get the best ads possible or to see things irrelevant to their lives." A former engineer at Google and Microsoft referred to this as a "dogma" that most engineers "actually believe."

As we discussed in Chapter 2, choice seems like an empowering way to talk about privacy. But as countless privacy scholars have already demonstrated, choice is disempowering and narrow. Courts often misinterpret our choice to disclose something as the choice to give up our privacy rights entirely. Choice is also illusory. We cannot possibly exercise real choice when our only opportunity to exercise that choice is when we click on a box to

"accept" the terms and conditions of use. Nor can we effectively manifest our choices when designers use dark patterns to make it difficult to opt out of data collection or protect our information in other ways. That is, our choices are subject to manipulation. Rather than a weapon of privacy, privacy-as-control is a license for surveillance. It lays the entire burden of protecting our privacy on us and gives designers a convenient way of avoiding designing with privacy in mind. The working poor, single parents, and other members of marginalized groups do not have the luxury of sitting back and analyzing how design is affecting them when trying to find the products and connection they need. The privacy burdens of hidden surveillance are not borne equally, and some populations never have the option of pushing back. Nor does it seem fair to place the entire burden of resistance on us, especially since we lack the time, resources, and specialized knowledge to effectively counter what has become a feature, not a bug, of informational capitalism.[10]

The Efficiency Trap

Many software engineers in particular fall into the efficiency trap, or the valorization and prioritization of efficiency over other values. As Paul Ohm and Jonathan Frankle have noted, "from the first moment of undergraduate instruction in universities around the globe, computer scientists-to-be are taught always to optimize for efficiency." Harry Lewis, the computer scientist and former Dean of Harvard College, called efficiency one of the most important values in computer science and engineering. And when you talk to engineers and coders, they evaluate programming as "good" or "best" based the codes' efficiency, not on the programs' actual effects or outputs.[11]

Some have argued that the prioritization of efficiency among software designers is innate. In his book, *The Passionate Programmer*, Chad Fowler called it a "complete waste of time" trying to get software engineers into meetings to think about anything other than making efficient code. Several researchers have argued that an innate dislike for inefficiency can draw individuals to engineering in the first place; it certainly characterized the feelings of early leaders of the "hacker culture" and is evident when engineers speak about their work. And while spending several years interviewing, profiling, and observing how coders approach their

work, Clive Thompson observed that a common engineering worldview, often from early on in their education, is to "speed everything up, remove friction everywhere."[12]

Engineers were not the only ones in awe of efficiency. Sales and marketing representatives in design meetings were eager to make both the data collection process and the user interface as efficient as possible. As one vice president of sales told me, "the easier, faster, simpler we make it to buy [the product], the more [product] they are going to buy." A sales manager in San Francisco said her team has "goals to meet, and the only way we're going to do that is if we know and understand what our customers want. That's really my job." Many who work in sales departments see efficiency in the purchasing process as a boon to consumers: "Look at how easy we've made it," one exclaimed. At the same time, not only did these interviewees fail to recognize the privacy risks associated with efficient data collection, they actively downplayed it. "We can't show you what products you want without leveraging what we know about you. Would you want to see ads [that aren't relevant to you]? I don't think so. So we really need that information, as easy as possible, so we can do our jobs and earn our customers' trust."

Though far subtler, the efficiency narrative ran through conversations with lawyers as well. Generalist lawyers who worked with product teams helped achieve efficiency in design and product development through professional modesty. Not a single lawyer I interviewed felt it was their job to be inside design meetings when software engineers are developing engineering solutions to privacy-related designs. "Unless someone raises the issue to me, there's nothing I can do," noted a partner with several years of privacy counseling experience. In-house lawyers who are naturally closer to the design process than outside counsel admitted this as well. "We would let them come to us," several attorneys employed in the information industry said. Another attorney stated, "It's not my job to challenge the design process. My job is to make sure what they tell me they're doing is compliant with the law." Although the attorney's "door was always open, and I'm there to help," many in-house attorneys tasked with advising design teams waited for the designers themselves to take the first step. Indeed, a designer who worked at Google until 2014 said that "nobody at Google wants to stop creativity. I can't say for sure, but I'm sure privacy didn't want

to, either. They didn't stop us from doing our work." Therefore, the efficiency trap weakens lawyers' and privacy professionals' power in design by keeping them steps away from design work.

Efficiency can be a great thing. Consumers seem to want it. There's economic value to it: efficiency allows us to do more with less and in less time. But, as a primary value, efficiency squeezes out privacy. Allowing a user to access site functionality as soon as she visits is efficient; putting a cookie consent box in her way is inefficient. Collecting data without consent is efficient; reminding us that we have to visit our browser settings to manage ad targeting is inefficient. Remaining willfully ignorant to third-party uses of data is efficient; having to keep tabs on every company that buys your data is inefficient. Privacy can sometimes be inefficient. It sometimes requires software engineers to introduce inefficiency into their systems. And, undoubtedly, there are engineers eager to do so. But as long as efficiency remains a cardinal virtue of system design, privacy has another hurdle to overcome.

The Growth Trap

The growth trap is the persistent view that privacy is incompatible with profit. Software engineers at start-ups as well as sales and marketing teams at all the companies I researched fell into this trap. Its effect is the amplification of venture capitalist and sales team power even when those groups do not sit in design meetings.

The interests of venture capital investors loomed large in start-ups. This makes sense, especially since the fates of most start-ups depend on continued cash flow from funders. During my interviews with five start-up founders and entrepreneurs, all of whom were software engineer by background, four talked about their funders in the same way: cognizant of them, but they're not in control. A New York entrepreneur whose company completed its Series A round of financing the previous year, summarized this view when he said he was "fielding calls from some investors often. I know they want to see us succeed, but sometimes I have to remind them that I'm in charge and I'll make the decisions." This independence was oft-repeated, but limited. The fourth and fifth employees, both software engineers, at a San Francisco direct-to-consumer start-up noted that investor interests actually changed their website's

design. "We built the platform one way, to allow visitors to purchase as guest while we would only temporarily retain credit card, billing, and delivery information. One investor said no. We were told that 'the investor wants us to monetize the data we collect,' so we had to rewrite the code to store purchasing data, track cursor movements, and things like that." I never saw an investor participate in a design meeting; indeed, the entrepreneurs I interviewed said that never happened in their experience. Nevertheless, funders' financial interests could loom large in early stage designs.

Some sales and marketing teams also think privacy and profit cannot co-exist. One sales manager, for example, stated that "privacy is not my job. It definitely isn't my job when doing something for privacy makes it harder to do my job or meet our targets." A marketing manager at a large Silicon Valley-based technology company said that "when a company wants to advertise with us, they are betting that our targeting algorithm will connect them with their likely customers. We can't do that if privacy ... gets too out of control." During a meeting I observed among engineers, a sales manager, and a product manager, the sales manager asked: "How can we maximize this for in-app purchases? Are we able to find out the kinds of people who are likely to add, upgrade, and so forth?" After the meeting, I asked him how user privacy interests came into play. His response was that he "cares about privacy greatly. I have a daughter and these kids share a lot, so I understand our responsibility. But I also have a job to do, and that job is to help generate revenue, and you need data to do that today."

Law and economics scholars have long argued that robust privacy regimes undermine efficient markets. We also hear a constant barrage of criticisms from industry and conservative and neoliberal policy makers that protecting privacy can stifle innovation and growth. And an economic model premised on surveillance seems anathematic to privacy in general. Many of those arguments ring hollow. There is precious little evidence that privacy stifles innovation and entanglement between privacy and innovation doesn't mean the two are incompatible. What's more, informational capitalism's thirst for data stems from a fundamentally dubious idea: that more data means better predictions about consumer behavior. That is, industry assumes – or is persuaded to believe – that new artificial intelligence-trained algorithms can take thousands of inputs and

identify correlations among customer characteristics that neither humans nor traditional statistics software ever could. But, as Matt Salganik and others have shown, many of those algorithms are no better and predicting outcomes than traditional statistical modeling based on three or four inputs. That means that marketing and sales teams need not sacrifice customer privacy in order to their jobs. The growth trap just makes them think they do.[13]

The Bystander Trap

Also blocking privacy's way is the bystander trap, or the sense among some designers that privacy is someone else's job. This trap is based on the phenomenon, well known in social psychology, of the bystander effect, which suggests that the likelihood of individual intervention is inversely proportional to the size of the crowd of witnesses. A version of the bystander effect may also trap certain groups involved in design, particularly software engineers and sales and marketing professionals. When they do fall into this trap, they say that privacy is not their job. They rely on their job descriptions, mandates from their supervisors, and their background expertise to bracket out not only privacy, but also the myriad exogenous forces – law, public opinion, and the press – that could impact privacy's place in design.[14]

I noticed this trap while observing design meetings and interviewing designers about how they were addressing particular privacy-related issues that came up. On tracking third-party uses of data, one engineer said that "that's for some other team." On data minimization, or collecting only so much as data as is necessary for a particular purpose, another engineer said, "it's my job to make it functional; it's someone else's to actually use the thing I build." What if users don't want to be tracked? "I was asked to make it possible to [collect search history], that's all." Another software engineer stated, "I'm a coder, I was trained to write code, so I write code. We're given instructions and we sit down and solve problems together. That's what engineers do. That other stuff is not my job. Someone else does that." I asked about the steps he and his team would take if someone raised concerns about a mobile app that allowed constant GPS tracking even when the app was closed, and did not offer a chance for the user to change settings: "It depends. Another team might be working on those issues.

I could easily see how you code for fixing that, if that's really a problem." What happens if user expectations or preferences change? "I'm not sure that's my job." Fifteen of the designers I interviewed expressed this sentiment. An experienced engineer who became a senior product manager in Silicon Valley summed up these interviews: "[The company] really cared about customers trusting us. But that wasn't my job. My job was to make unhackable infrastructure." A product manager who started as a coder for a large technology company voiced the more general sentiment that although "I didn't realize this when I started, but I've found it to be true and was probably true of me: programmers don't want to be bothered by other people at their job."

Sales and marketing professionals often considered themselves ill equipped to even mention privacy issues, preferring to rely on others. For example, a director of sales who had been involved in user interface design admitted that she didn't "know anything about privacy, so it's not really for me to say." There is, however, a difference between a real lack of expertise and using niche expertise as an excuse for standing idle. Every interviewee in sales was able to construct a vision of privacy in their own lives; they recognized the creepiness of invasive behaviors like surveillance, following someone on public streets, or reading someone's diary. They were even able to understand how information collection is integrated into their work. As soon as the questions concerned privacy in design, they not only demurred on the meaning of privacy but also suggested it was someone else's job: "I have specific mandates about growth. I don't have anything to do with privacy. The privacy team handles that." A vice president of sales said he "relies on privacy people, I don't get involved." But when everyone relies on someone else, privacy is neglected.

I witnessed privacy's omission several times during design meetings. During a meeting in which a group of engineers discussed account set up for a mobile game, one engineer asked if the app should require users to enter their names, emails, and other identifying information. No one recognized this as a privacy issue; they saw it as an engineering one. For nine minutes of a thirty-two-minute meeting, the team discussed how to create "a seamless" account setup process "so there's no interruption" between user and game. Three options were narrowed down to one, an engineer took the

lead on code, and the meeting ended shortly thereafter. Like the mobile game, the photo-sharing app shared user information with third parties. Some of that sharing was for the purposes of digital advertising, but the software engineers involved in the design of the apps did not consider third-party access a privacy issue. Most notably, a small group of engineers working on the photo-sharing app reflexively set the app's default settings to the most open, which allowed for maximum data collection, permissionless access by third parties for various uses, and no privacy protection. This, one engineer noted, was "a functionality issue" because "this way, everything works better, seamlessly." It didn't occur to anyone, even though it is well known in the psychological literature, that defaults have both direct and indirect effects that make disclosure more likely. They directly set privacy terms that individuals can only change if they overcome their inertia and indirectly set the norm as what the "average" user does, thus pressuring users to keep defaults as is.[15]

The Turf Trap

On the other side of the bystander trap is the turf trap, or the jealous guarding of roles inside the company or the erection of barriers to cooperation based on a perceived encroachment on another's territory. Where bystanders stand back because they think privacy is someone else's job, those who guard their turf actively engage in behaviors that keep privacy out of their list of responsibilities. Designers who fall into the turf trap are territorialists who care less about whether privacy will get done than they do about announcing to the world that privacy isn't their job. In my research, I found that it was primarily software engineers who fell into the turf trap.

Research in organizational science suggests that territoriality is closely related to the notion of psychological ownership: "feelings of possessiveness and attachment toward an object," idea, or position. As Graham Brown, Thomas Lawrence, and Sandra Robinson note, territoriality captures the real, observable social behaviors that emanate from psychological ownership. Office environments are particularly susceptible to territoriality. Workers are in close proximity to others – in cubicles, offices, or on factory floors – and job descriptions define roles in ways that can amplify feelings of "mine, not yours." Territoriality is also a way to exert power inside

an organization. If power stems from controlling scarce resources, whether that control is over who gets paid time off or the allocation of appointments to hair stylists or personal trainers – territoriality involves "valued organizational objects over which members make proprietary claims." And although territoriality can have positive benefits – clear communication of responsibility and the fostering of a sense of ownership – territoriality also stifles organizational work. Falling headfirst in the turf trap interrupts collaboration and teamwork by making workers more self-centered and noncooperative. Erecting turf boundaries also isolates employees. Territorialists often give off the impression that they can't be trusted, which fosters the creation of cliques and exclusion. And it creates an overall perception that colleagues don't care about their workplace, which reduces overall employee satisfaction.[16]

Engineers engaged in two types of territorial behaviors during my research, one of which had the effect of marginalizing privacy in design. One example of the turf trap is what organizational sociologists call "marking," or actions that communicate to others one's territory. Marking can set helpful boundaries that ensure two people sharing the same trading desk do not annoy each other. Marking can also help workers express their identities in corporate environments that tend to quash individualism, like when we put children's pictures or nameplates on our desks. But marking can also push people apart. Engineers I observed chafed at nonengineers visiting their workplaces to speak to them about things like diversity and privacy. A group of nine engineers at a midsize company nicknamed the legal team "the no's" because, as one engineer said, "they say no a lot, like a lot." A design team working on cloud-based sharing technology reminded their coworkers that a particular conference room "is our meeting room for the foreseeable future," and then laughed that they needed it "because we're doing important shit here, and you aren't." Outside of the related bystander trap, I did not observe specific incidents of antiprivacy marking.[17]

But I did observe a significant amount of antiprivacy "defending." Where marking sets boundaries, defending responds to perceived encroachments from others. Defending results from conflict about boundaries, and conflicts happen often in organizations. Participatory governance sometimes means that two committees aren't sure which is responsible for a particular task. Vague job

descriptions can suggest similar responsibilities to two very different employees. Ambitious middle managers can encroach on others' fields to try to get ahead. In response, defenders stand their ground, sometimes to reassert effective division of labor, other times to resist change. In my research, engineers frequently communicated that design was their job, and defended their territory when a lawyer or privacy professional tried to step in. Although some senior engineers noted that, upon reflection, they would have welcomed input from privacy professionals, many technologists pushed back on working with lawyers on design. Several noted that they "are the experts here." Several junior and senior engineers felt that "lawyers do not belong in design" beyond "telling us what to do so we don't go to jail." One engineer noted that "the more other people, whether they be lawyers or marketing people or a budget guy, are at every step along the way during the design process, the more it's going to get off the rails, and then my team is going to get blamed for not meeting our goals." This is a common struggle in large organizations. As Renato Orsato, a sustainability scholar, has argued, employee resistance to input and change can create an "arena in which an indeterminate struggle unfolds," hampering innovation and productivity. In this case, by asserting that design should not involve those very people tasked with integrating privacy into design, engineers were making it harder for privacy advocates to gain a foothold.[18]

The Gender Bias Trap

The gender bias trap includes both the presence of a gender imbalance among designers and the effects of that imbalance on designer impressions of or stereotypes about women in technology. The gender bias trap contributes to discriminatory design, undermines privacy considerations, and erodes the power of women while amplifying the power of men in design. And it affects software engineers, product managers, and lawyers.

Many scholars have suggested that the lack of diverse representation of women, persons of color, members of the LGBTQ and disabled communities, and others results in discrimination. Kate Crawford, the founder of the nonprofit artificial intelligence research institute AI Now, notes that "technologies ... will reflect the values of [their] creators. So inclusivity matters – from who designs it to

who sits on the company boards and which ethical perspectives are included." The lack of diverse representation in design also means that technologies will be tested or trained on incomplete data sets. This has real effects on the ground. Gender imbalances among editors are reflected in Wikipedia, where articles about women (written by men) use language that marginalize contributions and often have significant omissions. Apple developed a so-called comprehensive health app that lets us track, of all things, our copper and magnesium intake, but doesn't allow a woman to track her period. Mobile assistants do better at understanding male voices than women's voices. It may not always be intentional, but gender imbalances set the discourse and embed discriminatory values in the design of technologies.[19]

When marginalized groups are underrepresented in design, privacy may get short shrift as well. Women, members of the LGBTQ community, persons of color, poor women, those living with HIV, those living with disabilities, and others with stigmatized and marginalized identities have different lived experiences with data, privacy breaches, and online harassment that heighten their awareness of privacy issues. Their exclusion from design means losing that keen issue spotting and outside-the-box thinking. We know that women are more concerned than men about being watched. Poor pregnant women are sapped of their privacy rights and forced into intimate, uncomfortable disclosures merely by seeking health care, visiting a hospital, and applying for benefits to which they are entitled. The privacy implications of these institutions often go unnoticed by men.[20]

A group of researchers at Cornell University has also demonstrated that mobile devices that deploy constant location tracking can facilitate ad targeting or other conveniences, but their mostly male designers lose sight of how their apps are leveraged by other men to stalk, harass, and harm women. The preeminent law, information, and speech scholar Danielle Citron has shown that social media are designed with men in mind, not women; platforms often ensure the anonymity of their users under the guise of protecting free speech, ignoring how anonymity amplifies rampant gendered cyberharassment of women. The law professor Mary Anne Franks has made similar arguments about the gendered nature of online platforms' obsession with free speech. These scholars argue that

platform idleness when men harass or share intimate images of women without their consent not only perpetuates the subjugation of women under the guise of protecting free expression, but also represents a substantive choice to privilege the free speech of men while silencing women and other marginalized groups.[21]

But gender bias goes deeper than just the negative effects of an observable gender imbalance. Gender bias may also be rooted in engineering culture and education. Meredith Broussard has argued that the centrality of math in engineering disciplines institutionalizes a particular kind of rationality that excludes women from the profession. That is, engineers don't just make assumptions about women coders as more nurturing than serious, more emotional than rational, and more caring than decisive. They see characteristics stereotypically associated with women as fundamentally incongruous with the stark rationality of the logic of math and coding. Broussard argues that this devaluation of women constitutes erasure: women and their contributions are dismissed out of hand. That may also mean that certain privacy issues will be missed.[22]

Many software engineers fall into the gender bias trap. Of the 121 people I interviewed, 49 identified themselves as engineers, software engineers, web designers, coders, programmers, or other technologists. My field observations included another forty-one individuals in these categories, though none of them were interviewed. That's ninety people in technology fields. Only seventeen of them were women, which constitutes 18.9 percent of the sample. Over nine days of observations, I observed fourteen design meetings without a single woman. Another five included one woman each, with three of those meetings including the same one woman in the company's engineering team. This gender imbalance is similar to the latest statistics for the industry as a whole. According to the National Center for Women and Information Technology, only one-quarter of computing occupations were held by women in 2015. That number has declined significantly over time. Data collected on GitHub shows that women make up only 5.5 percent of Qualcomm's development center in Austin, 6.3 percent at Dropbox, 8.3 percent at Yelp, 13.2 percent at Airbnb, and a comparatively robust 14.4 percent at Pinterest. There isn't a lack of talent out there; the talented among traditionally marginalized populations just aren't getting hired and where they are getting hired, they don't stay

around very long. The turnover rate in tech jobs is more than twice as high for women as it is for men. And according to data last updated in 2018, only 12 percent of engineers at Silicon Valley start-ups are women, and only 10 percent of Silicon Valley executives are women.[23]

In 2016, 93 percent of the partners at the leading venture capital funds were men, and an astonishing 98 percent of the start-ups they funded were founded by men. In 2015, a survey of 200 women in tech found that 84 percent of the participants had been told they were "too aggressive" in the office, 66 percent said they had been excluded from team-building and other work events because of their gender, and 60 percent reported unwanted sexual advances from their peers and superiors. Women also have more work to do to prove their worth as programmers. In a study of GitHub users, for example, code written by women was accepted 78.6 percent of the time, a higher rate than code written by men, when the genders of code-writers were kept confidential. When those genders were revealed, the acceptance rate fell for women and rose for men. That means that women are better coders than men, but gender discrimination undermines meritocracy. Even though my sample of interviewees is not random, it is clear that women are underrepresented in design.[24]

The lack of gender balance in design contributed to gender-based discrimination. Misogynistic speech among male designers was common during my visits, with seven coders chatting with each other about their female coworkers in graphic sexual terms. When women were involved in design meetings, their ideas were either ignored and repeated by men (seven times) or told their design ideas had no merit (thirteen times). In one case, a Stanford-educated woman suggested that the company's games should be gender neutral, noting that "we've released games where male characters are rescuing girls, so I'd like to work on an update with empowered women in the traditionally male roles." One of her teammates said, "Uh, you can try, but we're not doing that. Guys play [our game], so that's not going to work." I also twice observed a group of male designers shouting over a woman trying to speak during a meeting. None of these women reported these incidents or expressed any interest in reporting them. The woman who was shouted down during the design team meeting told me, "That?

It sucks, but I'm used to it. Chicks put up with a lot of shit in this business, really every business. I'm not reporting every single one, I guess because I know nothing's going to change and it could get worse if they see me as a whiner."

I asked women designers about their experiences in this space to give color to these statistics. One engineer who used to work at a large Silicon Valley technology company and is now working in game design in San Francisco told me that she was the lone woman on her design team for four years. She "came into that job knowing what it can be like for a woman both online and in one of these companies. My experience may have been better than some – I've heard some terrible, nasty, assault-type stories – but I still had to fight to be heard where if I was a man, it would be have been easier." When asked if being a woman gave her perspectives on privacy that her male designers didn't share, she said the following:

> "Absolutely. I know women who have been stalked online. And you can't imagine how much worse it is in gaming. So I cared about protecting privacy. I remember sitting in a meeting where some guy I won't name was talking about the virtues of using GPS to know where our users were at all times. I said, 'that's not something a lot of millennial women are going to like.'" I didn't get shouted down or laughed at. They stared at me as if I was speaking another freakin' language. It never occurred to them. Being a woman in this job means a lot, but one in particular is, um, *knowing* things that guys just don't."

She emphasized the word "knowing," not referring to being more knowledgeable than men, but being aware of how women and men may interact with technology differently. Another interviewee, a woman who used to work in Microsoft's Xbox division, spoke about how her gender influenced her thinking on flagging accounts. Many social platforms allow users to identify, or "flag," accounts for violations, harassment, or harm. Flagging is important to help eliminate bad actors from a digital space, but the tactic can also be misused: homophobic conservatives often flag LGBTQ accounts on Instagram to shut them down, Nazis have been shown to flag Black Lives Matter accounts, and men flag the accounts of women as part of a pattern of harassment. The Xbox designer reported that her

> "team wanted to set up a simple reporting system, and one guy argued that it was impossible for flagging to be accurate when we have so many users. He wanted an AI (artificial intelligence) to handle it. I said that that view was a cop out. Taking down accounts without intention or nuance can harm women because it's a tactic [that] attackers use. They do it on Twitter and Insta[gram] all the time. I suggested we needed a better system and proposed some changes. Honestly I don't know what would have happened had we not had another woman as my boss's boss."

The last part of this quote is particularly important because it highlights the importance of both the power of representation and the power of impact. It is one thing to have a woman (or a member of any marginalized population) in the room where it happens to spot issues, bring different views, and offer new options. It is quite another for that perspective to be taken seriously and integrated into product design. That a woman sat in an executive, decision-making position was integral to translating a woman's idea into action.

Several of the in-house lawyers I interviewed suggested that they had to put in more effort than men to be trusted by their engineering teams. A lawyer working at a large television streaming company said that she "went into meetings with some of our tech guys knowing that they'll at first dismiss what I have to say, I'll then get my male colleague to say the same thing, and they'll listen to him. It's like some shitty game I have to play." Another attorney working in-house at a major technology company on the West Coast said that "as a front-line lawyer for a team, I sometimes have to deal with the [engineering] guys a lot, but it took at least six months of them barely acknowledging I exist for them to listen. None of my male colleagues have said they had the same problem, even with the same team."

Among product managers, the gender imbalance is even more striking. Only one of the ten product managers I interviewed was a woman. Of the seven of those ten who also identified as engineers or technologists, none were women. Beyond this small sample, the evidence of gender imbalance in product management is clear. For example, Nancy Wang, a former product manager at Google and the co-founder of Advancing Women in Product

(AWIP), was the only woman on her network infrastructure team at Google and was Rubrik's first female product manager. Fidji Somo and Deborah Liu, Facebook product managers who founded Women in Product (WiP) to support career advancement for women product managers, were also the only two women in their roles for some time. In the run up to WiP's 2018 conference, Somo and Liu noted that women in product management often "feel stuck and [do] not see[] a path to the top jobs" because of gender bias. And according to AWIP, only 5 percent of women in product management feel their career mobility is equal to that of men.[25]

Assessing the impact of gender imbalances and biases in product management was difficult given my small sample set. None of the nonprofits helping women in product discuss privacy specifically. And while there is research on the impact of gender bias in engineering on privacy, no broad-based research has been done at the product management level. Therefore, ethnography can be a useful research tool to identify a narrative meriting further study. A former product manager at Google explained that "product managers are decision-makers. Because we're in charge, in the mid-level, we can make a real difference." She said she was "more cautious than some of [her] male colleagues about what we did" when it came to "using people's data." She explained that "some of the higher ups thought using that data for other purposes in the ad network was fine just as long as we didn't show ... ads, which I thought would have violated our agreement. I like to think I had an effect on policy change there." It is worth investigating whether women in product management roles have a systematic effect on privacy-related design and policies.

Overall, the legal and privacy professions may be the most gender balanced of the social groups involved in design. According to the IAPP, there is gender parity among privacy professionals, albeit alongside a legacy gender pay gap. Attendance at privacy professional conferences is also roughly equal by gender. Among lawyers, published data is scarce. There are far more men than women in senior positions in the law, in general. And based on a review of their websites, 97 of the AmLaw 100 law firms have privacy and cybersecurity practices. Fourteen of the twenty-four privacy lawyers interviewed for this project were women, but it was not clear from our interviews how, if at all, their lived experiences as women directly impacted privacy in design. Given the

overall gender imbalance among designers, however, the gender bias trap can be a significant impediment to integrating the kinds of privacy issues marginalized populations are uniquely suited to spot.

Power over Design

Although these antiprivacy traps exist among the designers I interviewed, they are not universal. Many designers can – and do – overcome these traps. Many software engineers recognize their power and are just as creeped out by corporate surveillance as we are. Some leverage their expertise to enhance privacy, long the goal of the field of privacy engineering. But even the best efforts of those who escape design's privacy traps have another hurdle to overcome: a corporation that uses its control of design's process to make it impossible to design for privacy.

The information industry uses the tools of coercive bureaucracies to amplify these traps by routinizing processes and procedures that marginalize privacy while governing design work. By design process, I mean the internal rules and practices that govern how design happens, including reporting structures, departmental organization, team size and assignments, executive mandates, and the pace of work. In the course of my research, I identified seven elements of the design process that had the effect of marginalizing privacy in design. Each of them triggers or deepens the effects of one or more of the traps discussed above. Collectively, these and other strategies can put up a wall against privacy, making it difficult for designers who want to change the status quo, minimize data collection, or make the final product more sensitive to user privacy concerns. And although I am not suggesting that every company that adopts any of these procedures does so with the nefarious intent to marginalize privacy, I will show how some combination of these tactics can be used to ensure that privacy never gets a real chance in design.

Enforced Ignorance

The end result of design – a new smartphone, a new e-commerce website, or a new mobile app – is the sum of many constituent parts. Each part is divisible into many subparts.

Each subpart involves some engineering choices, from basic functionality to privacy. Each engineering choice is made by a team of engineers. And the size of those teams, their members, and their responsibilities are controlled by someone up the organizational chart, like a product manager, or by corporate norm or institutionalized rule. This means that constructing and constraining the engineering team is an opening for stakeholders inside the company to manage the design process and guide design's outcomes.[26]

Engineering team size varies from project to project, from company to company, and from industry to industry, but they are usually small. Among the engineers I interviewed, the largest reported team was seven ("It was a mess, but we were trying to figure out how to do something that hadn't been done before."). The smallest was one. The most common size was three. But even though small teams come with a series of advantages, it is also easier for management to keep small teams siloed and uninformed about how their work fits into a larger picture. This strategy of enforced ignorance took away opportunities for engineers to impact a product's design outside of their narrow assignments.

Team size has been inversely linked to team cohesion; that is, as teams grow, their ability to work together plummets. Members of large teams report their teams are "competitive" and "more argumentative." As anyone who has sat in – or stood in front of – a large classroom knows, individual members speak up less often in larger teams than they do in smaller ones. Communication is more direct and efficient in small teams. And several studies have shown that smaller teams are more productive, able to get more done in less time, and easier to manage.[27]

The efficiency of small teams can be a great boon, but small teams both reflect and amplify engineers' efficiency trap. A mindset that valorizes efficiency welcomes membership in a small team: "When we started out at Facebook, even those teams were small," said one engineer speaking for a group of four. "But here it's such a relief to be able to work with one or two other people you can trust and just do what you have to do. Everything else is just noise." The proliferation of small teams also solidifies efficiency as a normative good, which embeds a reminder for designers to value efficiency whenever they can. A start-up executive who previously worked as a software engineer at several large West Coast technology

companies told me that he has "seen how a lot of different companies operate, and how they do their engineering work says a lot about the company as a whole, their mission, their take. Is this company going to value what I do? Is this company going to get in my way as an engineer? Are they going to stop me from getting things done? I always asked myself those questions."

Smallness comes with other risks. Small teams are more likely to be homogenous. Indeed, the design teams and meetings I observed had very few women and not one person of color. Members of small teams look the same and have similar experience, which means the skills, information, and resources they bring may be redundant. In an environment of very few women, persons of color, and those who identify as LGBTQ, limits on team size make all male teams more likely. This amplifies the gender bias trap.[28]

More significantly, though, small team size can enhance the effects of the bystander and turf traps. Like any good product off an assembly line, a new device requires several teams working at once on different engineering issues. Small teams divided among those issues suggest to their team members that the scope of their work is narrow. "You have another engineer working on this, and a different team working on that. So, you have your specific assignment and you get it done." Indeed, the smaller the team, the harder it becomes to give the team multiple responsibilities: "There's only 3 of us, we can't do everything," one Google engineer told me. Small teams also allow supervisors to reprimand employees who step out of their assigned role. For someone who wants to impact a product's privacy features but is assigned elsewhere, management can easily step in and say that privacy is not their job.[29]

The bystander and turf traps are enhanced even more when communication between teams breaks down or is intentionally shut off. Teams will sometimes take the initiative to brush up on what other teams are doing, but at mid-sized and large companies, product managers are supposed to glue these teams together; "it's my job to make sure the web team knows what we're talking about in this meeting, and that the text team knows what work is being done elsewhere that impacts their job." During my research, that communication broke down when it came to privacy because, as one team leader said in a meeting, "that stuff doesn't impact your assignment." While designing a mobile game, one team was tasked with

creating the account sign-up process. The team eventually decided on giving users options to sign up with Facebook or via email, "just like my Words with Friends app." They chose that option because "it is relatively easy to do, really no issues or big problems, and it gives us access to an entire universe through Facebook." Without mentioning "privacy," another team member asked, "Will that piss people off that they have to go through Facebook and link their accounts?" In response, the product manager said, "another team thinks about that." While looking at the product manager, the design team leader said, "that's not really our job because we were told to do the sign up, right?"

An important effect of the siloization of responsibilities among many small teams is the inability of any one team to affect the overall design of the product. Narrow assignments enhance efficiency, but they also keep engineers in the dark. Therefore, even if an engineer wanted to address what he considered a privacy issue, it would be difficult for him to do so – or even find out how the issue was being approached and addressed – if his team was not responsible for that particular issue. Product managers recognize this problem, but their job is "to get this done on time and in accordance with our mandate." As such, their leadership strategies focus on interteam communication to enhance efficiency and productivity, not to facilitate cross-team learning and adaptation to privacy concerns.

Silos and the Facades That Cover Them

If small teams, narrow assignments, and weak communication make it difficult for engineers to impact privacy in design, siloed departments and hierarchical reporting structures keep privacy lawyers and privacy professionals from having significant impact on design. This happens even when companies assign lawyers and privacy experts to specific products, as is the practice at many midsized and large technology companies. Many of those lawyers call their product teams their clients, but they wait until their clients come to them rather than actively seeking out design teams and helping them spot privacy issues. For their part, many privacy professionals are forced by the structures of their departments to be content with drafting and distributing guidelines for design and working with executives rather than engineers on the ground.

Therefore, these aspects of the design process primarily amplify the bystander and codability traps.

Others researching the privacy profession have suggested that there is extensive interaction down the corporate hierarchy between full- or part-time privacy professionals and other designers. These scholars found that CPOs and their direct subordinates would often work with business-line executives, in-house counsel, risk management teams, and others throughout the company. This teamwork allowed privacy advocate to get a "buy-in" from key stakeholders across the company. Privacy professionals were also embedded within business units, with each having subject matter and privacy expertise, so they could interact with the businesses more directly and provide decision-making guidance and training on the ground. Therefore, some CPOs deployed privacy officers across departments, from marketing and sales to finance and operations, that reported directly to their unit executives and to the CPO. The researchers suggested that this diffuse structure was critical to "positioning privacy as a design requirement rather than a legal matter."[30]

Ostensibly, the goal of this embedded network of privacy employees is to keep privacy decision-making as close as possible to the trenches of day-to-day work. That requires ongoing interaction and cooperation, but not just among privacy professionals, lawyers, and other managers. It also requires their deep involvement in design. At least with respect to the designers I interviewed, the design meetings I observed, and the corporate reporting structures at each company, however, that cooperation did not always exist. Several engineers recalled "never once" meeting with "a privacy person the entire time [they were] there." Another acknowledged that "there was a person or a team who was supposed to be our privacy and security contact, but I never heard from him." A senior technologist in Silicon Valley recalled that he "made all the decisions when they came up. I'm sure there was someone, on paper, that I was supposed to talk to, but no one ever said anything, no one made a push for it, and it just never came up." Lawyers, too, were alien to technologists. "If you hadn't mentioned that there were lawyers there, or if I didn't know independently, I could easily assume that [the company] employed zero attorneys," said one engineer. Outside counsel, one interviewee noted flatly, "doesn't have the ability to [talk to] engineers." This lack of interaction is not necessarily a meaningful thing; one interviewee

suggested that "having to take a meeting with a lawyer was a bad thing because it probably meant you did something wrong."

But it does mean that privacy issues may be missed. This possibility was made more likely by corporate reporting structures, which required engineers to report to other engineers and kept lawyers and privacy professionals in a passive position waiting for teams to come to them. Any "decision we ever had to make about privacy, when it did come up, was made according to our best intuition," one engineer noted. And these engineers rarely, if ever, could turn to a privacy expert or even a lawyer for advice. Rather, as many technologists reported in their interviews, they do their work in teams, many of which included only other designers, an artist and, perhaps, a business-oriented liaison. The team leader was also a coder; his supervisor was also a coder, promoted because he was particularly good at his job, not because he had any leadership skills or strategic planning perspective. This meant that engineers were constrained by their reporting structure. One Apple whistleblower told the Guardian newspaper that Apple provides no means for reporting privacy lapses during reviews of Siri recordings: "We're encouraged to hit targets, and get through work as fast as possible. The only function for reporting what you're listening to seems to be for technical problems. There's nothing about reporting the content." Plus, many engineers repeatedly noted the high degree of turnover within their teams. In this environment, privacy decisions were made ad hoc, without any clear guidance, and by technologists not necessarily in the best position to make them.[31]

During my talks with in-house attorneys, many of them ably recognized even subtle privacy issues associated with new technologies, including geotracking, consents, prechecked boxes, secondary uses, and predictive analytics. But the organization charts and reporting rules kept them away from design. "We would let them come to us," several attorneys employed by the information industry said. And although the attorney's "door was always open, and I'm there to help," many in-house attorneys tasked with advising design teams waited for the designers themselves to take the first step. But if the technologists are not equipped to do so, then privacy issues never get to a privacy professional's desk. Another attorney stated, "It's not my job to challenge the design process. My job is to make sure what they tell me they're doing is compliant with the law."

And outside lawyers rarely talk to engineers to get that information. That same attorney noted that he spends most of his time "talking to the CPO and the general counsel. No one wants me talking to an engineer. I need the CPO filter to translate what the engineer does into language I can understand."

Even when privacy issues did find their way to a lawyer, the lawyer could alter design only when exogenous legal requirements were specific and clear, but had little power when law was vague and flexible. During a meeting with a lawyer initiated by an engineering manager, the engineer wanted to know if the company could use the uploaded images "for our own purposes." The lawyer stated that "our Terms of Use will lay out the terms, but basically anyone who uses our app wouldn't be giving us ownership over the photos, but what we call a nonexclusive license, which is really just as good. We can use the images for many reasons, subject to some limits, as long as we say something about it in our TOS." When a team was determining the interface of the mobile game, a lawyer reported to me that she was "successful at getting my engineers and my boss to understand that Europe will not accept pre-checked boxes for consent anymore," reflecting the latest interpretation of Europe's GDPR. "But I couldn't get them to do the same thing for California residents because it's not clear that's what the [California Consumer Privacy Act] requires."

Many of the privacy professionals I interviewed suggested that much of their work focused on compliance. But several reported deep frustrations about their inability to impact the actual design of new technology products. "One of my biggest challenges is getting our work into the engineers' heads, or getting what we do into the functionality of the things we create. We have to because it's the law, but it's hard to do that when you're not in the trench." Why aren't you in the trench, I asked. "Because that's not how it works. Our jobs are to create the procedures and guidelines for them to use, and we make sure what we all do as a company complies with privacy law and respects the privacy expectations of our customers. But we don't go over to the engineering building and sit down over someone's shoulder." A privacy professional with nearly 30 years' experience reflected on her career in a similar way, noting that "we set the standards, in consultation with others and in reliance on outside organizations like NIST. Even when I was chief of privacy, I still didn't have the power to force engineers to report to my team."

Therefore, the siloization of privacy can happen even when companies adopt an integrated approach in which privacy professionals are embedded in business units and privacy lawyers are assigned to product development teams. Corporate executives can reorganize their departments all they want, but if they maintain reporting rules that keep privacy experts away from the design process until issues percolate up to the top, they are effectively creating silos under the façade of integration.

Lax Privacy Training

Cognizant that their engineers may not come to their first days on the job committed to or even trained in privacy and sensitive to outside criticism from policy makers, advocates, and the media, the information industry has turned to privacy trainings to integrate privacy into the fabric of its engineers' work. Unfortunately, many of these trainings are established with a cavalier attitude toward efficacy; they are trainings for training's sake. And many have the exact same features that make diversity trainings so unsuccessful in modern workplaces. As such, lax privacy trainings amplify the codability, choice, and efficiency traps while they give the impression of corporate action on privacy.

There is a long literature on the ineffectiveness of using corporate trainings to change behavior, particularly in the context of bias and discrimination. This research, which has been going on since the early 1900s, shows that trainings can help people respond correctly on a questionnaire about bias, but they fail to create any real change over the long term. People either forget what they learned or, more likely, the trainings simply fail to overcome embedded prejudice. Nor do diversity trainings actually create more diverse workplaces, as scholars like Frank Dobbin, Alexandra Kalev, Lauren Edelman, Stephen Petterson, and others have shown. Antibias trainings simply do not reduce bias, change corporate or individual behavior, or change the overall look and diversity of the workplace.[32]

And yet, employers turn to trainings to address implicit bias among their employees and an increasing number of technology companies say they use extensive training modules to bring their engineers up to speed on their privacy responsibilities. For the

engineers I interviewed and in the workplaces I observed, those trainings did not work. Some engineers were simply not aware of ways to help them integrate privacy concerns into their work. Eleven interviewees recalled that their only privacy training was during onboarding. "I remember being told at some point that we should think about privacy issues, but I think that was limited to the first week," one said. A web designer said that she "was told to think about privacy during a five-minute talk during onboarding. I don't think the word, or anything like it, was ever mentioned again." Another "watched a 5-minute video about handling sensitive information"; yet another recalled that her entire privacy orientation boiled down to "a warning: don't carelessly leave sensitive stuff at the gym, even in our gym." Other interviewees reported similar problems at other companies. Interviewees used words and phrases like "hands off," "absent," "uninvolved," and "not really a factor," to describe their employers' approach to privacy. And, according to media reports, privacy is not even part of Facebook's famous bimonthly "bootcamp" for new engineers.[33]

A few large companies hired privacy professionals and even university academics to teach their engineers about privacy. During my fieldwork, I observed two types of privacy education programs. One integrated privacy into onboarding and an ongoing monthly "lunch talks" series, that also included a wide variety of subjects. Another company developed a more extensive training module that required engineers to sign up for regular trainings that could be completed remotely. Both prompted disinterest or frustration from engineers. The lunch talks were "really interesting, but I go because I want to, and because I think they're cool. None of my teammates go." One engineer at a large technology company clicked through his remote training, completing a 30-minute session in a little over seven minutes, at which point he turned to his nearest colleague and said, "another pointless waste." Although my sample was not large enough to conduct a robust survey, nineteen engineer interviewees expressed similar frustration when asked about their in-house privacy trainings.

While inspiring eye rolls among engineers, the training modules I reviewed also reinforced the codability trap. One privacy presentation for new employees only addressed security issues, reifying the conflation of privacy and security. Another module focused

on security and data minimization, using Europe's GDPR as a jumping off point. The noncodable parts of privacy – understanding user expectations, integrating diverse populations' privacy concerns into design, and third-party uses of data – were missing. And the issues covered by trainings didn't always make their way into design. I had the remarkable opportunity to see this in person. A company designing a tool to make it easier to share media across platforms trained their new engineers on the importance of privacy through a presentation on, among other things, data minimization. One slide of that presentation stated, "Data minimization is the law." The week after one new employee completed his onboarding, he attended a meeting I observed where he asked if the company "wanted to collect behavioral data for future use even though we don't need it now." That is the exact opposite of data minimization. It's possible he didn't understand what data minimization meant. Or he didn't care. Or the training simply wasn't effective at getting this engineer to think differently.

The Antiprivacy Ethos of Venture Capitalists

The failure of privacy trainings mirrors a larger phenomenon in the organizational literature on diversity: real substantive change with respect to corporate diversity, bias, and organizational learning does not happen in response to exogenous forces pressuring firms to change; rather, real change happens when the values underlying those changes are already part of the firm's culture. It stands to reason then, that privacy trainings and programs would work best in companies where privacy is already part of the ethos and culture of the corporation. But that is rarely, if ever, the case. Most companies today that develop technological products that collect our data begin as start-ups funded by venture capital investors who deprioritize privacy and push a growth-at-all-costs mentality that either never includes or marginalizes privacy from the outset.

Management is responsible for what Martha Feldman and Brian Pentland have called the "ostensive" aspect of corporate routines. Management sets the tone for action, lays out a mission, and creates policies that form best practice guides. Then, routines are "performed" by workers on the ground: real people doing real work translating the mission into action, products, and widgets. In many

cases, tech companies talk about their concern for privacy disingenuously. Inside the information industry, mantras like "move fast and break things" have real meaning for work on the ground.[34]

Privacy is simply not part of the agenda for many venture capitalists. Engineers and executives at start-ups were up front about this and the pressures they face. "We just finished our Series A [round of funding], and our biggest investors want to see growth. You can't imagine the pressure I'm under to deliver that, so some things slip through the cracks." Start-ups don't hire privacy professionals or full-time lawyers to help instill an ethos of respecting privacy, just like start-ups don't hire human resources professionals to help make diversity and equality a chief goal. They "don't have the resources," one start-up executive reminded me. And most venture capitalists have no objections. For example, at the start-up Voatz, which says it has developed an app to help anyone vote from anywhere on the planet, researchers at MIT have found the app "so riddled with security issues that no one should be using it." The venture capitalist backing Voatz didn't seem to mind: "It's not that cybersecurity people are bad people per se," he told the Harvard Business Review in 2019. "It's that they are solving for one situation, and I am solving for another." Suggesting that a voting app's ability to help people vote and the app's security and privacy gaps are two different and unrelated issues suggests, at a minimum, that privacy is not getting a seat at Voatz's table.

When you ask venture capitalists today if privacy is important to them, they will jump at the chance to say "yes." Ursheet Parikh, a partner at Mayfield, a $2.6 billion early investment firm, told the IAPP that when Mayfield gets "on the board [of a new company], we do ask a lot of these privacy questions. Privacy is entering the conversation much earlier." Similarly, Steve Herrod, a partner at General Catalyst, which has funded Snapchat and Kayak, said that privacy has "really become a board-level issue for the first time." But when they say privacy, they mostly mean security. Parikh added that "data privacy is very strongly tied to the overall information security. These are discussions at a very high level" and Herrod noted that privacy is important "obviously, in light of well-publicized breaches. In many cases, IT has never been a board-level discussion. That's changed." The start-up executives I interviewed echoed this. When I differentiated between things like

data minimization and data security, one noted that the former "was diametrically opposed to what [his investor] wants; security is just good business for everyone."[35]

Interviews with several former and current venture capitalists suggested that privacy was ignored behind the curtain. One investor who had started several tech companies on his own and now uses wealth from selling those companies to invest in start-ups in the "smart" economy said that "privacy is definitely an important thing I look at when evaluating a company. When pitch decks don't come to me with something about privacy, I send them back." When I asked what he wants to see in those pitches about privacy, he said, "Encryption. Solid encryption. And making sure we're never going to have to deal with the fall out of a leak." A venture capitalist in New York who has invested in Warby Parker, among others, told me that "my partners and I have to put a primary focus on our ROI," or return on investment. "Otherwise, we're not going to be around very long in this business. If I can make money off of data we've collected from users with their consent, I'm going to do it."

With these kinds of pressures and influences, it is difficult for privacy to become embedded in the corporate ethos from the outset. Instead, venture capitalists' focus on growth and security amplify the codability and growth traps among engineers and make it hard to build a technology company from the ground up with a commitment to anything other than surveillance. It isn't impossible; there are companies in the privacy space with significant investment. But, as with all of the traps we discussed above, it does make it harder.

A/B Testing Goals Focus on Engagement

Beta testing has always been part of design. But its great power comes not only from being able to adapt technological artifacts to the people who use them, but from the ex ante decision on the metric tested in the first place. A manager or executive tells an engineer what to test for, and that decision can predetermine privacy's fate in design. If the goal of A/B testing is almost always more, more engagement, more clicks, more purchase, and more data, privacy gets shunted to the side. This amplifies the growth and efficiency traps.

A/B testing is about showing different options of, say, a design, a color, or an advertisement, to different groups to see which is best at achieving some goal – generating more clicks or buying a product. Although the term "A/B" implies two options – alpha and beta – there are many permutations of options. Google has A/B tested the color and aesthetic of its logo to see which was better at encouraging engagement. Facebook has A/B tested different approaches to its News Feed to see which produced more click-throughs. Political campaigns A/B test language to encourage people to store their credit card information, making it easier for donors to keep donating. It's an effective strategy that's been around for years, but has been made immeasurably easier, cheaper, faster, and bigger with digital technology.[36]

All of these examples have one thing in common: they all want us to do more, to share more, to disclosure more personal information. The information industry has an incentive to increase engagement: more clicks means more information about us, which (ostensibly) means more knowledge about our behavior, which means more expensive ad targeting, which means more revenue. A/B testing doesn't have to be about nudging us to disclose; schools, hospitals, and elderly homes have famously A/B tested different paint colors on their walls to achieve positive emotional responses among their populations. But when the order comes down that a website or platform has to be "optimized for engagement," a team of engineers gets to work finding new ways to push us to disclosure, often without us even knowing what's going on.

Product managers and software engineers almost universally told me that the goal of A/B testing, which appears to be common practice at technology companies of all sizes, was more disclosure from users. Sometimes that was couched in terms of making "the sign-up process easier" or "getting rid of things that slow customers down" or "trying to find out what's the best way for us to build [something] so people will click on it and enjoy it." A product manager working with a group of engineers to "make it easier" to share photos said her team tested "about 67 different elements, from where we put the ["Share"] button to how many options we give to the type of haptic feedback," on how our sense of touch responds to device interaction. By the end of the testing, "sharing had increased by 32 percent, so I'd call that a win."

An engineer at a start-up in San Francisco and formerly at Facebook thought A/B testing was "probably the best tool we have . . . . Little changes in [aesthetics and positioning], even what's bold and what isn't can be huge changes in engagement."

Greater engagement was the goal even when design work was supposed to be focusing on other things. For example, an engineering team manager told me that he was responsible for bringing a website into compliance with the Americans with Disabilities Act (ADA), which has been interpreted to require accessibility to websites for those living with disabilities. So he "worked with [his] boss and we read the [Web Content Accessibility] Guidelines," or WCAG (a baseline to which federal courts and the Department of Justice have referred when determining whether websites are "accessible") "to see how we can make this the same for the disabled." But that's not the whole story. His goal, he acknowledged, was to "design the interface so disabled people can have the same rates of engagement as" those without disabilities. That is, he defined "equal access" as "equal engagement" and A/B tested various designs on disabled populations to see which designs nudged them to click as much as those living without disabilities, not which designs satisfied the ADA's accessibility requirement. After I pointed out the difference, the team manager said: "Why wouldn't disabled [persons] want the same treatment, the same information? If we have the same kind of information from them, then they can enjoy the same experiences, advertisements, and opportunities. Isn't that equality?"[37]

This laser-like focus on engagement is one of the reasons why the information industry creates products that intentionally invade our privacy and frustrate our expectations. In designing their platforms, companies trigger our "bounded rationality" with dark patterns, or design tricks that take advantage of cognitive biases to limit our autonomy and, in this case, to navigate our privacy. Indeed, these subtle, yet powerful nudges are among the most pervasive examples of platforms' hostile approach to privacy. They are almost always oriented toward more engagement and disclosure and less data protection.[38]

Research conducted by the Norwegian Consumer Council (NCC) and a group of scholars at Princeton University offer some of the best examples of antiprivacy dark patterns to date, helping to

prove that the information industry is making specific design choices to entice and coerce disclosure. The NCC investigated updates and prompts on Facebook, Google, and Microsoft's Windows 10 during May and June 2018. The Princeton study was based on a massive web crawl of 11,000 e-commerce websites. Another study from several European scholars focused primarily on consent dark patterns. Together, the groups identified more than a dozen dark patterns, five of which manipulate us into giving up our privacy and our information.[39]

For example, some dark patterns make it difficult for us to stop data tracking. This tactic usually has two elements: an anti-privacy default option and a labyrinthine process to opt out. The NCC found that Facebook and Google defaulted to the least privacy friendly options. If you were fine with that, you could click "Accept and Continue." Pretty easy. For those users who wanted to change their defaults, Facebook required them to click a box labeled "Manage Data Settings," which took them to a page where they had to turn off "Ads based on data from partners" individually. A lot harder. Google's design was even darker. To change its privacy-unfriendly defaults, users had to find their Privacy Dashboard to opt out. The dialog box did not provide a link. These kinds of dark patterns take advantage of our inertia and our rush to use an online service without judgment. By making privacy management difficult, they trigger some of us to give up and resign ourselves to corporate surveillance.[40]

Other dark patterns use color, style, and the prominence of notifications to steer us toward data tracking and away from more privacy-protective choices. We've all seen this: Buttons to "Accept" or "Agree" to the default options are almost always bolder and easier to see, with white lettering on dark backgrounds rather than grays. Sometimes, other options are hidden entirely. The words "privacy policy" are often hidden away in small print at either the bottom left or bottom right corners of a webpage. Social networks share our friends' disclosures – liking websites, clicking on advertisements, or buying products – in bold letters above posts to make us think that disclosure is the norm. They don't share our friends' privacy-protective strategies. We tend to see the bolder options first; we're also drawn to them because their color and positioning frame them as the preferred, obvious choice.[41]

These and other examples take advantage of what psychologists call the anchoring and bandwagon effects. Anchoring is the disproportionate reliance on the information first available when we make decisions. Dan Ariely, George Loewenstein, and Drazen Prelec, for example, asked participants to provide the last two digits of their Social Security numbers and then estimate the price of a consumer good. Participants' estimates were close to the two digits they first provided, even though there should be no rational connection between random identity numbers and consumer prices. Daphne Chang and several colleagues demonstrated anchoring effects when they showed that individuals were more likely to disclose personal information after seeing examples of increasingly salacious selfie images. The pictures anchored the participants' perception of what is appropriate to disclose. Anchoring, therefore, can skew individuals' disclosure behavior based on what they see others have shared. The bandwagon effect captures our tendency to do something because others are doing it too.[42]

Designers also use language to shame us into giving up our privacy. This dark pattern focuses on the positive aspects of a privacy-invasive choice, while ignoring the negatives, thus painting protecting our privacy as somehow the wrong choice or a bad idea. The Princeton study found 169 instances of this on 164 websites, making it the fourth most popular dark pattern in their study. The NCC found many examples of manipulative language on Facebook and Google. Google couched its broad-based data tracking as a way to "make ads more relevant to you." Opting out was both somehow both a bad idea and functionally ineffective: "You'll still see ads, but they'll be less useful to you." Facebook tried to get users to use facial recognition by saying "if you keep face recognition turned off, we won't be able to use this technology if a stranger uses your photo to impersonate you. If someone uses a screen reader, they won't be told when you're in a photo unless you're tagged." At the same time, Facebook never shared any of the risks associated with joining its face recognition pool. It didn't say how else user biometric information would be used, like for targeted advertisements based on emotional state or to identify individuals who would rather remain anonymous.[43]

This tactic takes advantage of the framing effect and the problem of hyperbolic discounting. Framing concerns the way in

which an opportunity is presented to us – namely, either as a good thing or a bad thing. Positively framing a privacy policy or a product as more protective of privacy than a competitor's results in a higher propensity to disclose personal information. This is why companies explain their data use practices with leading language: "if you don't allow cookies, website functionality will be diminished" or "opting in to data collection will enable new and easier functionality." This has the effect of establishing the positives of data collection while glossing over or ignoring the negatives, thus framing disclosure as a good thing. Hyperbolic discounting is the tendency to overweight the immediate consequences of a decision and to underweight those that will occur in the future. A team of researchers led by the economists Nicola Jentzsch found that people preferred barely less expensive movie tickets even though the cheaper ticket required more extensive personal information. Yet, consumer choices changed when tickets were offered at the same price – the privacy-protective movie company won more customers. The authors concluded that consumers were heavily discounting the risks associated with disclosing personal information, even far below small differences in price. When choice toward privacy is framed in a negative light, we tend to underweight the future problems of surveillance even more.[44]

Another dark pattern requires users to go through an unrelated process, like signing up for an account or accepting marketing emails, in order to complete a task or use a website. As a matter of mere functionality, we do not need to set up accounts and provide associated information in order to make a purchase. But websites can be designed to make it seem like signing up is necessary. The NCC also found that Facebook designed dialog boxes to make it seem like users had to provide certain information to continue to use the service. In reality, users could close the box and avoid the process entirely. The Princeton researchers identified several cases where users had to accept terms of service and accept marketing emails and advertisements in order to move forward. Even CPO Magazine, a website that provides "news, insights and resources to help data privacy, protection and cyber security leaders make sense of the evolving landscape to better protect their organizations and customers" leverages this dark pattern: after scrolling most of the way through an article, the background is obscured and a pop up asks

you to sign up. It provides no "x" or "close" button, making you think you have to enter in your email address to finish reading. You don't. You just have to click outside the box and it disappears.[45]

Perhaps the most effective way designers manipulate us into disclosing information against our wishes is by leveraging the problems of scale and overchoice. Scholars have shown that when we try to navigate our privacy, we are often overwhelmed not with the choices we have, but with the number of choices we have to make. We have hundreds of mobile apps on our smartphones and we might visit hundreds of different websites in a given month. Navigating every consent – for cookies, data collection, targeted advertisements, and marketing emails, among others – on every website and on every app is impossible and exhausting. Indeed, the mobile apps we use ask for more than 200 permissions in total, with the average app asking for about five. It is hard to see how most of us can navigate it all. And when we can't, we give up, clicking buttons just to make the box go away. The information industry is counting on that; they want us to give up and accept widespread data collection without restriction.[46]

Platforms leverage dark patterns within privacy management modules to make it difficult to disclose less. These designs take advantage of framing effects and our tendency toward inertia by setting defaults to limitless sharing. One study found that nearly one-third of Facebook users kept their privacy settings at their pro-disclosure, zero-privacy defaults. Almost two-thirds were unable to accurately describe the privacy settings they did have; most of that group thought they were disclosing less than their settings indicated. Another study found that 93.8 percent of respondents shared some information they really did not want to disclosure. That was, in part, due to the designed-in hurdles to stricter privacy navigation.[47]

I observed antiprivacy dark patterns throughout my research. All three products designed user interfaces to make it difficult or impossible for users to opt out of cookies, geolocation tracking, or behavioral advertising. The photo-sharing app shamed users into not opting out of data collection by claiming that doing so meant their photos could not be shared on Facebook, which simply wasn't true. Individuals did not have to set up an account to use the rental listing platform, but the "Results" page gave that strong impression. After creating a search for Manhattan

apartments, a white log-in box appeared over a blurred and grayed "Results" page. The box stated "Log In To See Your Next Apartment," with the option of logging in via Facebook (by clocking on the blue Facebook logo) or Google (by clicking on the multicolored Google logo). It relegated "Continue to search results" to small light gray words on a white background at the bottom. Nor did the platform provide users with an opt-out button. Instead, after a four minute and thirty-four second search, I found the words "if you would like to change your settings" hyperlinked in the final paragraph of a long privacy policy. The words were underlined, but otherwise indistinguishable in color and size from the rest of the policy. Clicking on that link took me to a list of twenty-eight third-party websites, only twelve of which I could click on to visit their privacy policies to opt out of tracking. The other sixteen had the word "required" next to them.

These kinds of designs are also par for the course in the e-commerce space. A software engineer for a retail company based in New York stated that "our goal was to maximize the likelihood that you would buy our products, so we tested different designs of our interfaces and different back-end functionality. ... A/B testing is subtle, but really effective. We get to see how a very specific change affects real people. If it works, great. If not, we try again. And we don't have any of the problems associated with only testing your product out on the 30 people or so who work with you." To illustrate how this works, the same engineer showed me four different interfaces on his screen. Each had the same article of clothing and its specifications, sizes, and reviews. The first interface had a royal blue "checkout" button on the left and a darker blue "keep shopping" button on the right.

> "Let's say I want to try to vary the color and the positioning [of the buttons]. That's a matrix of four possibilities. So I roll out each one and see the effects. I can also vary where I put the reviews or, in the back end, how easy it is to access negative reviews or positive reviews. There are maybe eight variables in this one box, which is a sizeable matrix of combinations. I can write a [program to] test all of them on real people in real time and report back the results with sample sets of tens of thousands if not more."

The first time the engineer performed these tests, they produced sales analytics over a one-week period. The team's engineering manager took the data to the company's director of sales, who asked for data over a month, given that the one week studied included a holiday. After a month, these tests resulted in a specific design change to the "keep shopping" button color and position to meet the sales team's stated desire to optimize the website for buying multiple related products.

Overworking Engineers

If you ask engineers themselves, one of the primary reasons why privacy was marginalized during design was time, or a lack thereof. Admittedly, I never saw this during my observations of design meetings, but that fieldwork was not conducted during a time in which teams were rushing to meet deadlines. But almost two-thirds of the engineers interviewed for this project either overtly or obliquely suggested that they just didn't have time for privacy.

Prioritization and exhaustion are well-known issues in organizations operating in fast-moving markets, particularly in companies that develop new software and the hardware that runs them. Projects and assignments with high priority receive greater resources and attention from both management (middle and upper) and on-the-ground workers. At the same time, priorities in multiple projects running concurrently can cause exhaustion and, ultimately, attrition, if workflow is managed poorly. As one study noted, "ever increasing market pressures, long and indeterminate hours of work, an almost trademark lack of distinction between work and home life, tight deadlines, budgetary constraints . . . frequently lead to under-staffing and consequently over-working" among software engineers. Although, as Clive Thompson demonstrates, some software engineers are naturally inclined toward that intense coder lifestyle, most experience the same potential for burnout as the rest of us.[48]

Some scholars have noted that workflow can be purposely manipulated to achieve certain goals, whether it is to test an employee's work capabilities or to make a work environment so inhospitable that the employee resigns. It is difficult to perceive a motive for intense work demands other than market pressure or organizational norms, but regardless of intent, the nonstop pace of

work many software engineers face at small, medium, and large technology companies has the effect of marginalizing privacy during design. That is because privacy is often crowded out by other mandates. I attended several meetings that were supposed to discuss privacy issues, including account sign ups, third-party sharing, and the extent of data collection. Though on the agenda, privacy was either last or squeezed out by time constraints in half of those meetings. Team leaders promised to revisit the issue at the next weekly meeting, but one member of that team noted that "that's been on the agenda for the last 4 weeks and we never get to it." Engineers and start-up executives also repeatedly spoke of the need to collect data to optimize user experience as the top priority, with privacy coming far behind: "we looked at data to see what people are interested in, what they're clicking on, and where they're going so we can make the site better. When we had some privacy issue come up, it was added to the engineering queue. But engineers had to prioritize speed, agility, functionality." A computer programmer with experience at start-ups and at larger companies noted that "we would work nonstop. I had a thousand things to do, and this (privacy) was one of them. It wasn't essential to our success, so it didn't get done."

That is not to say that privacy never gets done. It does, but a company that puts privacy on the design team's agenda does not necessarily put it there with any attempt to prioritize it. One way to marginalize it without overtly ignoring it is to inundate design teams with so many demands that only the essential ones get done. This has the effect of both marginalizing privacy in practice and having an expressive effect on privacy's importance in the corporate culture. Indeed, the lack of internal corporate emphasis on privacy suggested to many employees that their companies approached privacy as another form of low-priority corporate social responsibility (CSR) while adopting the rhetoric of consumer privacy and trust. CSR programs are company initiatives that do not necessarily generate revenue but improve social welfare in some way. Companies create them for many reasons, but they sometimes have to fight for attention against core corporate priorities. This is particularly true for privacy. The collection, use, and sale of consumer data are often integral to the information industry's business model: Facebook and Google use personal data to sell targeted advertisements; dating

websites promise compatible romantic matches in exchange for personal information and a monthly membership fee; and most online platforms collect data to optimize site performance and user experiences. Therefore, putting limitations on data collection is thought to be bad for business. Deprioritizing privacy by overworking engineers on other matters is a stealthy way to block privacy's perceived negative impacts on profits.[49]

Restricting the Design Review Process

By 2018 and 2019, some companies represented in my research had adopted a new strategy in the design process – privacy engineering – to great fanfare. Privacy engineering is about integrating privacy into systems requirements and using the tools of software design to shift us from a privacy regime based on corporate promises to one based on features of code, or what Sarah Spiekermann and Lorrie Cranor have called "privacy by policy" to "privacy by architecture."[50]

But that's not what privacy engineering always looks like on the inside. I interviewed three individuals with a "privacy engineer" job title at one large company in the information industry and all of them noted how their employer has changed the "rules of the game" since their hiring. One privacy engineer, a graduate of Columbia University, said that he was hired "to build a new kind of product. That's what we talked about in my multiple rounds of interviews. I met people who were really excited about this." Since he started work, he "hadn't done a single line of coding. I haven't had a single opportunity to be on the inside, from the ground up, actually building things." Instead, his job was as a design "reviewer. I would get reports on designs pretty much after other engineers had done their work. Not saying anything bad about those engineers. It's just that no one gave me a chance to be on those teams."

His colleague, a software engineer who was also offered a job as a privacy engineer at Palantir, echoed some of these concerns, but noted that he was able to have more impact. "I was disappointed," he said, "that the company wasn't actually creating a new type of [platform] like we discussed. Maybe they will in the future. But for now, I'm assigned to some teams and I'm basically their privacy liaison, which is great, right? But I'm more like an

adviser than an engineer." There are benefits to this arrangement. Another engineer can speak the language of engineering, building trust among teams working on products that collect user data. It also creates more privacy expertise. Organizational structures, however, get in the way. The company's privacy engineers, like the frontline privacy lawyers assigned to different products, are not always co-located with the engineering teams to which they are assigned. Nor do they have wide latitude to make changes. Their power is limited to "mak[ing] recommendations." And like the privacy professionals who moderate their advice in order to maintain access, the privacy engineers reviewing designs limit their recommendations to "catch the stupidest stuff because otherwise, we're going to get reprimanded by our bosses and no engineer is going to listen to me again."

Privacy professionals at this company stated that the privacy engineering review process was supposed to happen throughout the design process. But, again, corporate procedures made that difficult. The privacy review process was listed at the end of several internal documents about product development "teamwork," which made engineering teams less likely to seek our privacy engineering advice during their work. The three privacy engineers I interviewed said that was mostly accurate in terms of their experience.

Antiprivacy Performances

Executives silo privacy and isolate workers. They amplify workers' professional biases when those biases foster data-extractive ends. They interpret and recast the law in ways that minimize disruption to corporate surveillance. And they set workers' agendas and strategically allocate assignments to channel employee efforts. When you keep teams separate and uninformed, they can't effectuate change on a broader scale. When you quarantine the very people who may be more capable of spotting privacy issues, you get designs that ignore privacy. When you inculcate workers with the idea that privacy is anathematic to profit, you get antiprivacy corporate cultures. When you mandate that design must always achieve better engagement, you implicitly deprioritize privacy. And when you overwork engineers, you make privacy an inessential component of design work.

These strategies marginalize privacy. With every report or public statement or assignment focused on the value of transparency and notice, the trappings of privacy-as-control are normalized among workers as the ordinary and commonsensical approach to privacy. With every checklist or autofilled compliance report from a vendor or standard privacy impact assessment, symbolic compliance is normalized as actual adherence to the law of privacy. And with every new surveillant design that comes out of the design process, surveillance is normalized as the proper outcome of a regime that really only performed accountability window dressing. As these products become more prevalent in society, everyone becomes inured to corporate tracking, which feeds the perception that people want more surveillance and less privacy. As a result, robust privacy discourses become anathematic in society and within tech companies themselves, making it even easier for the information industry to inculcate corporate-friendly privacy discourses anew.

Our privacy is under attack from a vicious cycle triggered and implemented by coercive bureaucracies in the information industry. In leveraging these tactics, the information industry is exercising power, but one that does not depend on malice or even the awareness and buy-in of its employees. Rather, tech companies have made antiprivacy work entirely ordinary.

5 POWER, PRACTICE, AND PERFORMANCE

Inside the information industry, management leverages the tools of coercive bureaucracies to routinize work that serves data-extractive ends. Corporate bureaucracies work subtly to set privacy discourses among company employees, inculcating corporate-friendly understandings of privacy as frontline workers approach their work. Organizations hobble privacy offices and amplify voices that interpret privacy law in ways that serve corporate interests. Management also constrains designers in the design process, feeding software engineers' ambivalence toward privacy and using organizational structures to make it difficult for anyone to build better privacy protections into the designs of new technologies.

This use of bureaucracy shouldn't be all that surprising. After all, even as he championed the legitimacy of the modern organization, Weber also said its power comes from "the exercise of control over knowledge." Alvin Gouldner said that Weberian bureaucracy was "the best known method of realizing some goal" even as it "was administration based on discipline." Sociologists in the Marxist tradition also saw bureaucracies has inherently coercive, arguing that power asymmetries and divergent economic interests of management and labor inevitably make formalization of work coercive.[1]

But that doesn't explain much about these particular bureaucracies. Nor does it explain why so many privacy professionals, privacy lawyers, and software engineers who see themselves as privacy advocates have embraced their antiprivacy employers or remained blind to the consequences of their actions. Having described the

mechanisms that the information industry uses to routinize antiprivacy practices, this chapter focuses on the workers themselves and how routinization leads to normalization and how normalization leads to performative privacy law. This is the inculcative role of performance, and it explains why privacy professionals, privacy lawyers, and privacy engineers may perceive themselves as privacy advocates even as they do work that undermines consumer privacy and facilitates their employers' data-extractive practices.

Power inside the Information Industry

The information industry relies on a two-step process to entrench its power to design data-extractive technologies despite exogenous privacy law and endogenous privacy advocates. The first step is the use of bureaucracy – reporting structures, budgets, work assignments, team membership, and more – to routinize and habituate corporate-friendly and antiprivacy practices. As they become habits, pro-privacy voices are silenced and work that serves corporate data extraction is normalized as the common sense, customary, and ordinary social practice of privacy discourse, privacy law, and privacy design. The second step flows organically from the first. As the rank and file repeatedly perform those antiprivacy routines, those practices construct what they think privacy law is, making it difficult for anyone to see possible alternatives. In the end, many information industry workers look at the work they do and say, "well, this is what privacy is." Even many of those workers who see themselves as privacy advocates have adopted antiprivacy practices, don't always realize it, and yet think they're just following the law. In truth, their performances are creating a corporate-friendly version of the law that legitimizes and fosters data extraction. Therefore, the story of power inside the information industry is a story of coercion and performance. Coercive bureaucracies create antiprivacy routines, but it is the normalizing effects of repeated performance among the rank and file that really entrenches information industry power. The normalizing effects of those performances are so powerful that almost every new proposal for comprehensive privacy legislation introduced in the U.S. in the last three years integrate the same on-the-ground practices as what privacy law is and should be.

"Deskilling" Frontline Workers

Using bureaucracy to coerce employee output is nothing new; the information industry has successfully adapted an old model to a new context. They feature what organizational sociologists call deskilling approaches to workers on the ground. By deskilling, I don't mean taking away skills. When executives fear that their employees may have dissident views, they adopt a deskilling approach, preferring the output of formal bureaucracies to risking opportunism from below. The sociologists Paul Adler and Bryan Borys identified four features of deskilling in corporate bureaucracies: inability to repair, work opacity, contextual opacity, and inflexibility. All four of these features are present in some information industry bureaucracies.[2]

Inability to repair refers to "separate[ing] routine production tasks from nonroutine repair and improvement tasks and assign [ing] each task to different categories of employees." Adler and Borys were thinking about factories and machining shops, where operators have no access to control panels and have to stop working and call technicians to make changes or repairs. But their insight applies to the information industry. As we saw in Chapter 4, many large tech companies split up software design tasks among many small teams and keep those teams focused on their assignments. Someone on the in-app purchases team would not be able to work on the app's privacy default settings because that work, if assigned at all, was being done by someone else. Privacy professionals who may actually want to improve their employers' privacy work are sidelined when management decides to give that work to IT and cybersecurity folks. Checklists for privacy professionals and software engineers also privilege formalization over worker innovation in ways that silence privacy voices. When privacy leaders translate privacy law's requirements into checkbox compliance for their teams, they are replacing privacy innovation with formal procedures, and weak procedures at that. If those checklists make their way down to engineering teams, they are either ignored, as Adler and Borys would have predicted, or they replace actual engineering thinking about privacy for rote procedure. That creates a situation where one engineering team working on its assignments thinks that some other team is handling privacy, but

the privacy team may just be checking boxes. This division of labor is deskilling rather than efficient: Rather than enabling worker innovation based on their expertise, workers in deskilling bureaucracies are separated because management wants to divide and conquer.[3]

Work opacity involves assigning work without providing employees "with the rationale for the work" or why they're being told to do it in a particular way. Leaders that obscure the rationale for their work also denigrate individual thinking: "we didn't hire you to think, we hired you do." The information industry is rife with this kind of procedural formalism as well. Privacy team leaders build formal structures, check lists, and other procedures for their teams to follow when building paper trails for laws like the GDPR or the CCPA. They share those checklists and pared down versions of PIAs with software engineers without any support – other than lax privacy trainings – to explain what engineers have to do and why they're doing it. This turn toward compliance formalism privileges rote work without much thinking.[4]

Contextual opacity occurs when the "broader system within which [employees] are working" is unintelligible to them, or where employees have no idea how their work fits into the larger corporate project, and it poses an even greater risk for privacy. Adler and Borys give the examples of Bentham's Panopticon – a total-surveillance system where those in power can see everything, but everyone else can see nothing, not even each other – and computer-integrated factories, where supervisors staff a central control room and machine operators only have access to information about the particular machine for which they're responsible. This is a feature, not a bug, of information industry bureaucracies. Software engineers divided into small teams often have no idea what other teams are doing, allowing them to focus on discrete engineering problems on their own turf but making it difficult for them to effectuate change in the product as a whole. Enforcing ignorance between and among teams amplifies engineers' professional and educational biases against privacy, allows them to deflect responsibility by claiming privacy isn't their job, and prevents those assigned elsewhere from having any impact on privacy. We saw this in Chapter 1. Software engineers like Gavin and Peter worked individually or in small teams that focused on discrete parts of a larger product, solving the engineering problems

with which they were tasked. Their role was restricted by team design; they assumed someone else was working on any privacy issues just like they were working on their narrow assignment.[5]

This also sweeps engineers into projects they may find objectionable without them knowing. Bureaucracies put individual workers into roles to enforce order. As Weber wrote, "the individual bureaucrat is chained to his activity in his entire economic and ideological existence." They may be "only a small cog in a ceaselessly moving mechanism which prescribes to [them] an essentially fixed route of march." Ideally, the cog would be situated inside a community with the "common interest" of achieving organizational goals. But if the organization worries that its rank and file do not share the corporation's values – whether because it helped the US government separate undocumented families or assisted municipalities that used racist predictive policing – bureaucracies will try to restrict individual actions and not reveal how they fit into a broader organizational mission. One former Palantir engineer told me that he was "livid" when he realized that an assignment he had been given was part of his employer's work with the US government. He said he had "no idea that this tiny project was part of something bigger." Lawyers are also conscripted into doing research and providing support for antiprivacy arguments in litigation, with several young lawyers noting explicitly that they are rarely, if ever, clued into the larger theory or arguments of the cases to which they're assigned. When they find out that their work has been used to argue that no one has any expectation of privacy anymore, they are often surprised.[6]

Closely related to these coercive features is inflexibility, or internal procedures that "are designed to minimize reliance on users' skill and discretion." In factories or other similar work environments, inflexibility manifests in procedure manuals that detail every single step that workers must follow and organizational rules that require explicit permission from management to skip steps or change procedures. This type of inflexible formalism has echoes in the privacy check lists created by privacy and risk teams. But its strongest manifestation is in the push to outsource privacy compliance to technology vendors. As we've discussed, there are over 300 companies offering software that purports to automate privacy compliance. Some of these vendors offer compliance documents

more than half completed so that companies can check a few boxes and file them away or hand them over to privacy authorities. Outsourcing privacy compliance prioritizes automation – the most formalistic of approaches to compliance – over human-centered decision-making in an area where human thinking about privacy could be helpful. When Kenneth Bamberger and Deirdre Mulligan interviewed privacy professionals, their interviewees used terms like "'values,' 'ethical tone,' 'moral tone,' and 'integrity,' … 'secure, private, reliable,' and 'consistent,' and … 'respect[],' 'responsibility,' 'stewardship,' and … 'trust.'" Software that automates privacy compliance doesn't understand ethics, morality, integrity, trust, or respect. Nor is software a way to achieve those goals.[7]

The Reactions of the Privacy Profession

As they were being deskilled, privacy professionals also moderated their own advice, weakening privacy's place inside their companies. At privacy professional conferences, speakers who work for large, data-extractive companies talk about how much work they're doing inside the information industry to put their employers in compliance with the GDPR, to push privacy issues up to the level of the board of directors, and to systematize privacy work through their ranks. They even talk about how doing privacy well is about more than just compliance, but also about building trust with customers and about integrating robust privacy protections into design. But, as we have seen throughout this book, when many of them are pressed on their commitments and the effect their work has on design, they can't see the downstream consequences, or lack thereof. And when we look under the hood at their institutionalized practices, we see few tangible benefits in terms of designed-in privacy protections on the ground.

"There's only so much I can do," said one privacy leader who told me that "companies hire [her] because they want to do privacy better." She added: "I cannot be there to make the decisions for you. I can help my team build products that put you in the best possible position to protect your privacy. But in the end, it's up to them. It's up to the consumer to be in control of their lives." A chief privacy officer at a large online retailer said that a sector-specific approach to privacy in the United States is the best way to go

because "that gives me the freedom to envision the best possible privacy world at my company, not what a government bureaucrat wants, but what consumers want." A privacy professional in Silicon Valley who called himself an "evangelist for stronger privacy protection" said that "at the end of the day, I'm working my ass off for the customer, to be the guy who is advocating for him to give him what he wants. If that's privacy, I've got his back because I make sure that my guys take privacy seriously and put users in control." To see their work as substantial, yet remain blind to the way the ecosystem of online surveillance weaponizes consent and nudges disclosure is strikingly discordant.

In organization studies, there are two types of workplace identity construction: identity regulation and identity work. Identity regulation reflects Weberian ideas about bureaucracy and Foucauldian ideas about social or disciplinary power. It refers to discourses that define the scripts or roles that connect real workers to an organization. For example, discourses about a role's importance in the organization structure, job descriptions and obligations, responsibilities to go "above and beyond," using the rhetoric of the "family" to describe corporate enterprises, and describing steps up corporate hierarchies as "paying dues" in lower-prestige jobs, among others, enhance workers' sense of their responsibilities to their employers, tacitly constraining actions orthogonal and contradictory to corporate aims. These discourses, though technically worker-generated, actually serve to enhance organizational control because they are "managerially inspired discourses about work." They reduce "'the range of decision' … to alternatives that are compatible with" corporate goals. In Chapter 1, we saw Jamal and Anita make this point obliquely when they acknowledged that part of their job as privacy lawyers is to interpret privacy law in ways that are "doable" for their employer. As Stanley Deetz has noted, "the modern business of management is often managing the 'insides' – the hopes, fears, and aspirations – of workers, rather than their behaviors directly." Privacy professionals recognized this in Chapter 3, highlighting the ways they had to maintain access to their bosses by not being the one to say "no" when everyone else was saying "yes." In Chapter 1, we also saw Janice and other privacy professionals speak of learning how to moderate their advice so as not to lose their jobs, another threat that was front of mind for many privacy professionals I interviewed.[8]

Identity work, on the other hand, captures individuals' attempts to create a coherent sense of self given their responsibilities. These discourses can be appeasing or justificatory – a lawyer who believes in gun safety regulation justifies her representation of a gun manufacturer in court by saying, "I'm not helping them build guns or sell them to children, I'm just representing them in this wrongful termination lawsuit." Lester exemplified this identity work in Chapter 1 when he justified arguing that his company's users have no expectation of privacy as a feature of zealous advocacy and then stormed out. Identity construction, therefore, makes it easier for privacy professionals and privacy lawyers to adopt their employers' positions without denying themselves the identity of privacy advocates.[9]

But trying to maintain one's stated identity with ex ante justifications while working within an organization challenging that identity was just the tip of the iceberg for the privacy profession's complicity in undermining privacy and amplifying information industry power. Many privacy professionals and privacy lawyers saw what they were doing as helping the cause of privacy, both in the sense that they helped their employers do privacy better and helped users realize better privacy protections on the ground. They kept that optimism because they could not see the downstream, surveillant, and power-related consequences of their work. Put another way, they saw the trees, but not the forest.

When information industry employees make decisions, whether to orient privacy law compliance around risks, to improve data use notices in response to privacy scholars, or to design an app that requires users to log in through Google or Facebook, they may understand why they're doing it. They do it to protect their employers, be more transparent, and make the product easier to use. Those may be their intentions. But because of their employers' coercive bureaucracies, which both isolate workers and amplify their anti-privacy biases, these workers did not always see how these decisions served corporate surveillant ends. "How can that be bad," repeated many privacy professionals when they spoke about their work on transparency and notice. It isn't bad on its own. But data use transparency doesn't exist on its own. It exists within a sociolegal context in which industry "takes refuge in consent," in which consent is weaponized against privacy, and in which transparency is part of that weapon.

They saw their small teams as radically efficient, but some didn't realize they are actively being shut out of the product's larger narrative. Instead, software engineers believed that their product managers "were handling it" and that "someone is on that, it's just not me." When I asked if they felt they were being siloed from the rest of the project, two Silicon Valley engineers agreed that they were "not being siloed. We're given a job and we do it." That these engineers professed to care about privacy without realizing that their work assignments made it virtually impossible for them to have any pro-privacy impact on design typified the blindness of many privacy lawyers, professionals, and engineers.

The information industry's coercive bureaucracies dissociate workers' intentions from the consequences of their actions. Foucault famously quipped: "people know what they do; they frequently know why they do ... what they do; but what they don't know is what they do does." More succinctly, Foucault means that we don't always know the full panoply of consequences and effects of our actions. We see the work in front of us and we know that our solutions are meant to have specific and narrow effects on that work. But we don't always see the forest for the trees; we don't always see how our work fits into a wider narrative of a collection of actions. Foucault wasn't writing about workers in the information industry, but he could have been.[10]

Privacy professionals saw new privacy laws requiring PIAs and new record keeping requirements, but they didn't realize how their bosses were marginalizing their contributions by subordinating privacy in the IT or risk management departments. Nor did they see how managerialized privacy compliance had turned into mere symbols and shams. When I asked a privacy team what effect budgetary restrictions and split allocations had on their work, the team members uniformly said that there were no effects. But when I told them that their CTO said that he "replaced having to hire a new employee with two far cheaper vendors," something he boasted about in our interview, one privacy professional said, "well, then he was probably right that we didn't need someone else."

Many privacy folks saw substantial work product coming out of privacy offices, but they didn't see that their work was not being translated into more privacy-protective designs. When I shared the widespread tracking built into an app their employer had just

released on the App Store, the company's most senior privacy professional said, "I don't know what you're showing me. I know the work I do is significant because we talk about it at the highest levels of this company. I don't design these things, but I help those who do." We all want our work to mean something. But all that work privacy professionals are doing is not having much of an impact on the things that really matter for our privacy.

Privacy lawyers and their colleagues saw the work they were doing to make privacy policies more readable, but never realized that they were perpetuating corporate-friendly discourses about privacy self-governance and, therefore, undermining privacy protections for real people. When I asked if more notice and more transparency is going to solve the privacy problem online, one lawyer responded that it wasn't his "responsibility to solve all those problems. If we can be more transparent with our customers, that's a good thing in and of itself." Another attorney working inhouse in New York after several years representing tech companies in private practice added, "nothing we do harms customers. I don't understand how being more transparent could ever be a bad thing." Another privacy lawyer said something similar about his clients' compliance work: "How is it bad in any way for all of us to do impact assessments and develop industry standards? It helps us and it helps" regulators.

The pattern is repeated through all of the procedural tactics described in this book as well. By keeping engineering teams small and separate, focusing A/B testing on engagement, and making it difficult for any one team to see a product's entire picture, a software engineer can go about their work honestly, focusing on the task in front of them and working hard to solve problems all while saying it isn't their job to work on privacy issues. This perpetuates a status quo in which privacy is ignored during design because it is always someone else's problem. Companies can create a complex privacy structure in which privacy experts are assigned to each product or even individual product teams, allowing lawyers and privacy professionals to come to work honestly intending to help their software engineering clients integrate privacy into their designs. But by sequestering, siloing, and stifling that work through reporting structures and organizational hierarchies, companies can marginalize privacy voices effectively. Privacy professionals and privacy lawyers can work within those structures, produce a lot of high-quality work

product, and think they're doing what they can to push the privacy discussion, but end up never changing the corporate ethos, practice, or routine in any material way.

The inability to see how corporate organizations silenced their voices was itself striking. Not surprisingly, many privacy professionals were also blind to their role in fostering data extraction rather than protecting privacy. In particular, some of them could not acknowledge that their work could perpetuate an asymmetrical system that burdens users and protects tech companies. When I asked how their work making data use practices more transparent, enhancing notices, and providing more opportunities for control rights actually protected their customers' privacy when, as we discussed in Chapter 2, those tools presume rationality in an ecosystem designed with dark patterns and other manipulative tricks that rely on and trigger our irrationality, I received almost universal pushback. "Users aren't irrational," one privacy professional told me. Another said that "there's nothing wrong with giving people more choices." A CPO added that "being more transparent about what we do is about building trust with our customers." A privacy lawyer said that "our clients' customers know what they're getting because we tell our clients to up front about their privacy practices."

The following conversation brought this point home. It occurred in a meeting at a large Bay Area technology company with three experienced privacy professionals at the director level and one in-house privacy lawyer.

> "Can you explain precisely how adding more detail to the [product's] privacy policy actually results in stronger privacy protections for users?"
>
> "It gives people a better foundation for making their choices. Do they want to use this feature, or do they not want to use that feature. We're not like some of our competitors who hide the ball. We're on the level and honest with our customers."
>
> "I get how it gives users more information. But ... Let me rephrase my question. Are you familiar with the studies that show notice is ineffective at actually informing people's disclosure decisions online?"

"I am," said the most senior professional in the room. "We all are. We often go to privacy conferences to keep up on the latest work."

"So, you're familiar with the work of Lorrie Cranor, Alessandro Acquisti, Leslie John, and others, yes?"

"Yes, I am familiar with Lorrie and Alessandro. They do amazing work."

"So, among other things, their work shows that people don't read privacy policies and then go make rational decisions by weighing pros and cons and then acting like they added up the pros and added up the cons, right?

"Well, yes," said the lawyer said, "but that doesn't mean we hide what we do."

"Nor was I suggesting that. But you are familiar with the studies that show that quote 'better notice' isn't necessarily going to translate into decisions that better reflect people's actual preferences, right?"

"I don't agree with that," said one of the privacy professionals with 7 years' worth of experience. "It may not lead to the choices you want them to make, but it will help them make their choices."

"Let me be clear. I didn't say that it won't necessarily translate into more pro-privacy decisions. I said decisions that accord with their actual preferences."

"Look," said the lawyer. "I don't know what you're going on about, but transparency isn't a bad thing."

"Okay, I'll start again. Notice-and-consent, consent as a lawful basis under the GDPR, the CCPA's opt-out consent, HIPAA's privacy rule . . . these are all consent-based privacy regimes. And you said earlier that you do a lot of work in your offices enhancing consent and making sure the notices you give your customers and users give them the information they need to make decisions."

"Right," said the senior privacy professional.

"That suggests that the law sees users as rational: making decisions based on the information you present."

"Go on," said the lawyer, "but I'm not saying that's correct."

"Okay. But while the law sees users as rationally making decisions based on your notices, isn't the ecosystem in which we're making those decisions – the internet – designed with the idea that we're not rational?" I then gave several examples from the design of this company's website that we brought up in the room showing dark patterns and other designs that make disclosure more likely.

"There's nothing wrong with that. That's how these things are designed. I don't know that it leads to more disclosure. It just is. It's not manipulative."

"Take the word 'manipulative' out of it," I said, "because I think it's a loaded term. Do you think your privacy policy enhancements help people better realize their privacy preferences if the literature shows that we don't make purely rational decisions online, whether it's because of design or because we're just humans and are imperfect and not perfectly rational?"

"Again, I don't see it. Transparency isn't bad. Transparency is good. It's how we keep our governments honest. It keeps us honest too."

The most senior professional in the room then asked: "So what would you have us do instead of working on being more transparent with our users?"

"What about changing these default settings to something other than most open sharing setting?" I asked, pointing to the disclosure settings on the screen and to access by third parties.

"That's just not how it's done. That would undermine the whole system."

"And besides, that's what the design team does. We focus on the privacy notices and other requirements of compliance with privacy law."

"Do you think that focusing on notice and not a design change that could materially affect people's privacy is the best way to go about this?" I asked.

"I still come back to the same thing: Better transparency is what we should want. We are ahead of the curve. We don't lie. We help people make better decisions and we're proud of that."

The refusal to acknowledge that their work perpetuated an asymmetrical system that favored employers suggests the extent to which some privacy professionals and privacy lawyers have normalized practices that enhance corporate power. They are, after all, professionals who see themselves and their compliance work as synonymous with corporate accountability. The fallback argument – namely, that transparency is always a good thing – is gaslighting. And yet, many of these privacy professionals and lawyers construed themselves as committed to privacy and construed their work as incredibly valuable in support of users. That dissonance – between the actual consequences of their actions and their perceptions of their work – is precisely the goal of the information industry's coercive bureaucracies.[11]

A Mosaic of Coercion and Performance

Deskilling and bureaucratic coercion are only the first stage of the information industry's exercise of power over its rank and file. Executives will deskill if they have to, but they would much rather bring their privacy employees into the fold. Deskilled workers often know they're being deskilled. Machine operators know they are being sidelined when they are denied access to the machine's inner workers or kept ignorant of how their work fits into a larger project. Rather than wholesale replacing the employee with the rote product of formal bureaucracies, the information industry wants its privacy employees to either embrace its agenda or become inured to their data-extractive ends. To do that, industry takes advantage of workplace pressures, organizational barriers, cognitive disconnects, and the inculcative power of performing privacy. The result is, as we have seen, a privacy professional class that neither sees the full mosaic of corporate power nor their role in perpetuating it.

Foucault wrote that power is "a multiplicity of often minor processes, of different origin and scattered location, which overlap, repeat, or imitate one another, support one another, distinguish themselves from one another . . . and gradually produce the blueprint of a general method." The gradual aggregation of small decisions into a coercive bureaucracy describes the pattern discussed throughout this book. Industry representatives shifted the logic of privacy-as-control because it saw markets for data. They managerialized privacy compliance around achieving efficiencies and minimizing corporate risks because they needed to adapt to new legal requirements without making significant, business model–level changes to their companies. They created small engineering teams, made lawyers and privacy professionals wait for engineers to come to them with questions, and put privacy engineers toward the end of design processes all to enhance efficiency. They focused A/B testing on manipulating engagement in order to achieve sales and profit goals. And they overworked their engineers to compete in a fast-moving marketplace. Discursive activities in media and legal arguments about privacy, as well as these more specific organizational procedures, came together into one ecosystem of coercion. They became "connected to one another, attracting and propagating one another, . . . end by forming a comprehensive system: the logic is perfectly clear, the aim decipherable." For the information industry, that aim is to profit off of our data.[12]

Tech companies achieve that goal even though their employees come to work with independent motives that aren't necessarily data extractive. Many of the engineers I interviewed for this project chose their employers and their careers because "this is where the action is" or because a particular company gave them "a chance to do what I've been doing since I was a kid" or, as Clive Thompson has suggested, to put their "engineering pride" to good use, to solve seemingly impossible problems with systems, and to engage the parts of their brains that solve puzzles with precision. Coders don't usually start out intending to manipulate people. Many just love technology and want to "unlock the latent energy" of the world. Privacy professionals and privacy lawyers often go into their fields because they have some concern about or interest in privacy. They want customers to know that someone is protecting them and want customer expectations to guide them. The CPOs who spoke to

Bamberger and Mulligan talked about being stewards of customer data. In my interviews, privacy professionals spoke about the "need," "responsibility," and "expertise" to help companies navigate privacy "because they never cared about it before." There are, of course, people working in the field who fall into their jobs, come to privacy from compliance backgrounds, or just needed a job out of school. And there are lawyers who admit they "don't care about privacy; I just care about protecting my client." But, outside of the amoral folks, few of these words, impressions, or motivations are normally associated with abusive, antiprivacy capitalists.[13]

Instead, many privacy professionals who see themselves as privacy advocates have come on board. This subset of professionals embraces its work on notice-and-consent and symbolic compliance even though it amplifies corporate power. They embrace outsourcing and PIAs, paper trails, and assessments as what the law requires even though it weakens and undermines substantive privacy protections. They embrace the organizational structures that end up keeping privacy out of actual technology designs even though that makes it difficult for users to protect their privacy interests. This dissonance is the result of habituation: Information industry workers repeatedly perform antiprivacy work within constraining organizations such that their repeated performances have normalized them as ordinary, common sense, and the appropriate way to do privacy work.

Performances are actions or behaviors that communicate something to the self and others. Performances can also be performa*tive* – that is, repeated, everyday performances constitute or create reality, including the reality of the economy, of identity, and, I argue, of privacy law. Privacy law performances reflect and impact how we conceptualize, implement, and navigate privacy. Understood in this way, the social practices of privacy law, or the practical, on-the-ground detritus of the law in action, are performed by everyone, including regulators, corporate employees, and individuals like us. And as we perform them as part of a routine, they endogenously create what we think privacy law is and should be.[14]

In other words, the information industry has perfected the use of what Foucault called "techniques of power," or small actions that normalize and inure people to hierarchies of power. Gordon Hull has written about how notice-and-consent is a technique of power that normalizes surveillances and inures users into giving up their

information. Websites and apps deploying notice-and-consent designs "present[] an information environment in which individuals see themselves as functioning autonomously, treating personal information as a low-value, purely personal good they can easily trade for other desired goods and services." But we don't actually control anything; indeed, as Facebook has proven time and time again, clicking buttons and changing privacy preferences sometimes doesn't do anything at all. We take actions like we're in control by clicking "accept" or clicking "agree" or changing certain default sharing functions. And every time we do, we are inculcated with the belief that this is how privacy works. "Characterizing privacy as a question of formal autonomy," Hull continues, "and then offering an endless number of opportunities to enact that characterization," which precisely describes the scaled detritus of privacy-as-control, "is … the process of subjectification." For Foucault, our actions do not just achieve their immediate effects, as in clicking "Agree" does more than just grant access to a platform. It normalizes it, makes it seem like common sense and ordinary. Our actions "establish[] … a moral conduct that commits an individual, not only to other activities always in conformity with values and rules" associated with those actions, "but to a certain mode of being, a mode of being characteristic of the ethical subject." That is, clicking agree, closing a cookie pop up, accepting terms, and leaving defaults in place are repeated actions (choices) that habituate us into thinking that we are autonomously choosing the normal, commonsense thing to do. Each repetition of the performance of privacy further entrenches the performance and its lack of privacy protection as the norm. And by keeping the performance of privacy at a surface level, these seemingly autonomous acts keep hidden what's going on behind the scenes – namely, the asymmetry of the market for data, the vast wealth companies generate, and the risks data processing and transfer pose to our future. This, Hull notes, "is a paradigmatic instance of the operation of power" in the Foucauldian sense: "it is a total structure of actions brought to bear upon possible actions; it incites, it induces, it seduces."[15]

A similar normalization process is happening inside the information industry. By focusing their privacy agendas on the trappings of privacy-as-control – Facebook's report on transparency, for example – tech companies give their workers tasks within a narrow privacy agenda. As workers perform those tasks, they become accustomed

to the idea that privacy is about control, transparency, and choice. Put another way, repeating corporate-friendly privacy work normalizes the idea that privacy work is notice work. "This is what privacy is," said twenty-one different privacy professionals when we were talking about their work on improving notice. Others commented that notice "is what we do" and that "our job is to be transparent." These privacy professionals and lawyers have conceptualized their privacy work as entirely bound up with the discourse of privacy-as-control. They also understand their roles as privacy advocates through the lens of privacy-as-control. "I was hired because [the company] cares about privacy," said one experienced privacy technologist. "I am a privacy advocate, so my job is to have your interests in mind. That's why we work so hard to give you real choice and put you in control." Having performed the work of privacy-as-control for nearly 12 years, this privacy professional has come to identify with it.

Similarly, by tasking their software engineers with making security and encryption fixes after privacy scandals, executives inculcate the idea that privacy is security. And the continued performance of privacy-as-security performatively constructs what these workers think privacy law is. Several interviewees who identified as software engineers not only conceptualized privacy work as "encryption" or making devices "unhackable," but they also saw themselves as part of the move for better privacy: "When I started in coding, I didn't think about privacy at all. But now I realize I can bring my skills to privacy by keeping everyone's data secure." This engineer saw himself as a "privacy engineer" because he was doing most of his work on cryptography and security threat modeling, again showing how the repetition of security-as-privacy work can have an effect on work and identity. "This is what I've done for the last few years, at least. I'm usually one of the guys they ask to rethink privacy when we have a data breach, and there's always going to be a data breach at some point." The slippage from "data breach," which is a breakdown in security, to "privacy" suggests the extent to which privacy-as-security is deeply embedded in some software engineers.

Outsourcing privacy compliance and engaging in ongoing vendor management achieve both specific goals – enhancing efficiency, automating compliance, and reducing compliance costs – and "commits" privacy professionals to "a certain mode of being" – namely, the idea that privacy *should be* outsourced to

technology vendors. This was evident among almost all privacy professionals, many of whom recognized that outsourcing privacy compliance came with a lot of vendor management work, but was overwhelmingly a positive force. As one CPO said, "some privacy compliance is ideal for software because it makes my job so much easier and more efficient. I can realize incredible efficiencies while making it easier for my employer to comply with" privacy law. "It's right there, almost all done for us." It was hard for this CPO to perceive how outsourcing privacy compliance managerializes privacy law by bringing in values like efficiency and productivity where they don't necessarily belong. When I noted that outsourcing privacy could result in narrow approaches that focus only on codable privacy issues, she responded, "I don't see how that would be the case. I am the chief privacy person here. It stops with me. I would never do anything that undermined privacy." Outsourcing privacy had become part of this CPO's identity and part of how she conceptualized privacy work, in general. She had, she admitted, become accustomed to it as the result of how her privacy team was part of her company's compliance and risk management department. "Since long before I got here, the risk management and compliance folks had worked with outside vendors to ensure their work could be done efficiently and well. We were given the opportunity to work with vendors, as well, and that's how we've always done our privacy work."

And talking about privacy in terms of risks to the company as opposed to privacy risks to users normalizes the idea that privacy law is about helping companies avoid responsibility rather than protecting individuals from data-extractive excess. Few privacy professionals saw this as a distortion of privacy law's goals. As one privacy lawyer noted, "Well, of course we're going to assess our products based on risk. We wouldn't want to expose anyone, not the company, not the consumer, to risks associated with poorly designed products." When I noted that focusing on corporate risk in a legal context where enforcement and investigation by the FTC is rare and unlikely means that many risks to consumers are ignored, the lawyer responded that "we don't ignore risks. We make sure we protect privacy by assessing risk." This was another example of how internalizing corporate-friendly approaches to privacy constructed a privacy professional's work in ways that served data-extractive ends.

When tech companies focus solely on engagement and maximizing clicks and then assign teams of software engineers to build interfaces that achieve those goals, dark patterns and manipulation become the norm. We saw that in Chapter 4, where software engineers, so used to using A/B testing to extract data, believe that "that's just how it's done." Privacy professionals in Chapter 3 talked about how common and ordinary it was for privacy budgets to be subordinated to other departments like risk, legal, and IT, and sometimes split among them. In Chapter 2, we saw privacy lawyers justify their antiprivacy legal arguments as part of the ordinary practice of law. Antiprivacy work was, therefore, ordinary and banal throughout the rank and file of the information industry, even as these workers didn't realize the full consequences of their actions and views. They had, in short, become acculturated to serving corporate interests by performing tasks given to them within a constraining organization.

Indeed, every tactic of coercive bureaucracy, in addition to deskilling workers on the surface, does double duty by normalizing corporate-friendly privacy discourses and practices. The more a company says it cares about privacy and, as we saw in Chapters 1 and 2, reminds its employees to tell each other and the public that they care about privacy, the more tech company workers are likely to believe it and likely to commit themselves to believing their work serves the goal of caring about privacy. Every additional motion and brief in which a privacy lawyer argues that users have no privacy rights because they agreed to terms of service or used a platform having clicked "Agree" inculcates the corporate-friendly idea that privacy doesn't exist online. Lawyers then become committed to this idea, justified as zealous advocacy or channeled into a dogmatic belief in the power of consent. And the more a company misdirects the public with performances of accountability, like Facebook's Oversight Board or papers trails and checkbox impact statements, the more the company's employees will perceive that this is what companies are and *should be* doing. With every additional hour spent on notice enhancements and with every additional assignment on better encryption, the rank and file perform management's vision of privacy, normalizing it in their everyday practice. Corporate surveillance becomes the norm. Privacy is erased.[16]

Entrenchment and Resistance

This may sound bleak. It is dangerously insidious that individuals on the ground can engage in privacy performances that actually undermine privacy protections not only without knowing what they're doing but even while they're actively trying to achieve other, contrary goals. It puts the information industry at the center of a system of power that seems difficult to escape. We can't escape it because tech companies have manipulated privacy discourses, law, and design so they can surveil our every move. They have conscripted us into a mass scheme of subordination in which every action we take – where we move our cursors, what shoes we buy, and where we move while a geosocial app is tracking us – helps industry manipulate others. Tech company employees can't escape this because they may not want to, they can't, or they insist nothing is wrong.[17]

But in fact, this scenario also opens windows to resistance. The narrative's strength – routinized performances that create privacy law – also hints at entry points for resistance. We can't escape performance. But we can start to normalize different performances.

Some scholars imbue Foucault with an abject pessimism about our capacity to resist power. The German philosopher and sociologist Jürgen Habermas suggested that Foucault saw "socialized individuals ... as exemplars, as standardized products, of some discourse formation – as individual copies that are mechanically punched out." The political scientist Isaac Balbus argued that "subversive subjectivity cannot be explained within the framework of a discourse for which subjectivity and subjugation are correlative terms," or, put another way, it would seem impossible for anyone constructed by discourses of power to ever resist, counter, or push back against that power. I have even hinted at this point throughout this book: even those privacy professionals, lawyers, and commentators who want to change that status quo are steeped in privacy discourses designed to entrench information industry power, thus making it difficult for those on the ground to step outside their priors.[18]

Difficult, though, is not the same as impossible. Domination, Foucault says, is "when an individual or a social group

manage to block a field of relations of power, to render them impassive and invariable and to prevent all reversibility of movement." I don't think we're there just yet in the world of privacy. Dominant privacy discourses subjugate individuals and tilt the scales of social consciousness against privacy, but counterdiscourses are active too. Managerial approaches to undermining privacy law are common but not universal; there are approaches to law that eschew public-private partnerships and think about regulation in radically different ways. And emerging discourses in engineering ethics and privacy engineering, not to mention egalitarian approaches to organizational structure, suggest that we are not necessarily doomed to live with a technologist class that shirks its privacy responsibilities. Foucault himself does not foreclose the possibility of resistance, either. Discourses are temporary.[19]

The fight for equality is a good example. Marginalized by psychological, religious, and legal discourses that characterized gay people as diseased, sinful, and criminal, respectively, the LGBTQ community fought back: "homosexuality began to speak on its own behalf, to demand that its legitimacy or 'naturality' be acknowledged, often in the same vocabulary, using the same categories by which it was medically disqualified," Foucault wrote. The community created what Foucault called a "reverse discourse" of perversion, much like minority communities today reclaim the language of slurs and epithets and refashion them into discourses of empowerment and repurpose arguments used to justify discrimination in ways that call out the hypocrisies of those in power. What's more, discourse is one piece of a puzzle that depends on the aggregation small, seemingly isolated steps in service of data extraction into strategies to exercise power on society as a whole. That gives us several points of entry for attacking the coercive bureaucracies that perpetuate a vicious cycle undermining our privacy, ranging from the smallest changes to work on the ground to the broadest changes in assumptions, knowledge, and ideas. Foucault may have suggested in much of his work that institutional discourses are likely to reproduce power, but liberation is possible by "giv[ing] one's self the rules of law, the techniques of management, and also the ethics, the ethos, the practice of self, which would allow the game of power to be played with a minimum of domination." So, let's play that game.[20]

6 FIGHTING BACK

We are told that accepting widespread corporate surveillance is a natural progression for human civilization. Peter Schwartz, a senior vice president at Salesforce: "Gradually, we will accept much, much greater surveillance. And in the end we won't be too bothered by it." Thomas Friedman in 2014: "Privacy is over." Mark Zuckerberg in 2010: "The age of privacy is over." Sun Microsystem's former CEO Scott McNealy in 1999: We "have zero privacy anyway. Get over it."[1]

This book has suggested that the erosion of our privacy by corporate titans in the information industry isn't the result of a natural evolution. Nor is it the product of our autonomous will. It is, rather, the end goal of a system purposely designed to inculcate antiprivacy norms, undermine privacy laws, and marginalize privacy in design. Our reaction to the products of that system are anything but natural, autonomous, or free.

If we want to resist the coercive power of the information industry, we can't be content with more of the same. Regulatory paranoia, to use Jodi Short's apt term, pervades privacy law. The statutes we write and the actions administrative agencies take reflect a fear of getting too involved in the marketplace. In the FTC's case, for example, the agency has spent nearly 40 years overreacting to Congress's attempt to rein in its power in the 1980s. The FTC's search for balance has pushed itself dangerously close to shirking its regulatory responsibilities, reflecting just how fully immersed corporate-friendly discourses about government the economist-heavy agency really is. We have allowed our regulatory muscles to

atrophy and have come to assume that little more can be done than lay out industry-influenced "rules of the road" that only hope to soften informational capitalism's worst excesses. Privacy has been marginalized throughout the organizational infrastructure of the information industry, from discourse to law to design, and privacy professionals, the people who are supposed to be our advocates inside tech companies, have facilitated this process. They have embraced form over substance and hitched their professional identities to work that doesn't really translate into real privacy protections for individuals on the ground. Therefore, we have to change how we think about privacy, how we write, implement, and enforce privacy laws, how we organize our technology companies, and how we educate and socialize our software engineers, privacy professionals, and privacy lawyers. We need new privacy performances.[2]

Many companies in the information industry have perfected the art of performing accountability while exercising great power behind the scenes, clearing away the discursive, legal, and procedural obstacles to extracting our data. They inculcate among their workers the values that let them commodify our data for profit and undermine privacy law all while using their privacy professionals, privacy lawyers, and privacy engineers as evidence that things are changing. We need to start thinking about privacy and writing privacy laws differently, with different assumptions and goals.

From a law and political economy perspective, law has a role to play as an explicit counterweight to information industry power. Whereas privacy law has traditionally focused on notice and compliance, we should instead focus on substance, i.e., actual privacy-protective designs and practices. Whereas privacy governance has traditionally been either self-regulatory or collaborative, we should instead seek to make privacy governance democratic, i.e., responsive to our needs and the needs of populations particularly vulnerable to harm in a data-extractive economy. These starting points could help us structure a system of legal accountability that doesn't rely so much on internal privacy advocates who are susceptible to bureaucratic constraint and who are, at best, able to achieve only marginal change and, at worst, complicit in corporate mischief. Although I worry that we have already passed a point no return in corporate domination over our data, we have to start somewhere.

Countering Corporate Power with Discourse

We need to develop and promulgate privacy discourses that are explicit counterweights to information industry power. Talking about privacy law in terms of consent, choice, freedom, control, and even autonomy is incompatible with actually protecting privacy. Undoubtedly, those words don't all mean the same thing. But it is easy to collapse robust conceptions of autonomy into flat or bastardized versions of consent and control. Popular political discourse does this all the time, conflating a weighty and nuanced concept like liberty with the freedom to do anything, say anything, and flout any laws we want. Privacy law has done this too. In civil litigation, courts have confused the choice to share information with friends or a handful of professional colleagues with the choice to share that information with the world. In constitutional litigation, too, many US federal courts still assume that functionally mandatory disclosures to information intermediaries, like internet service providers, wireless phone companies, and banks, among others, is the same as voluntarily consenting to a government search. Autonomy isn't a bad idea, but as we have seen, it's easy to discursively corrupt.[3]

As we saw in Chapter 2, dominant privacy discourses perpetuate and enable corporate power rather than rein it in. And Chapter 3 showed how privacy law today is far more focused on paving the way for corporate data extraction than putting guardrails around it. Privacy law has tried to remain technology-neutral and agnostic about what companies do as long as they follow certain procedures. Such neutrality in the face of corporate dominance isn't just unwise, it can become complicit in entrenching that power. Instead, we need to be focused on countering corporate power.[4]

There is already a robust scholarly research agenda on social approaches to privacy that eschew the individual-focused discourses of control and choice. For example, Daniel Solove has called for nixing the "common denominator" approach to privacy altogether. Relying on the works of Ludwig Wittgenstein and pragmatists like William James and John Dewey, Solove wants us to think of privacy as an "umbrella term that refers to a wide and disparate group of related things, with those particular things varying from context to context." The legal scholar Robert Post has argued that privacy protects social norms of civility, deference, and

demeanor, borrowing the latter two terms from Erving Goffman. Lior Strahilevitz argues that privacy is about the flow of information through and among social networks, concluding that certain information shared within tight networks of friends, loved ones, and others should still be protected as private. Helen Nissenbaum has focused privacy around "context-relative informational norms" that "govern the flow of personal information in distinct social contexts (e.g., education, health care, and politics)." The social norms of those contexts, Nissenbaum writes, prescribe appropriate behavior to particular actors, and violations of those norms are invasions of privacy. Privacy, therefore, in any given situation, should be determined in context, based on "the nature of the situation, … the nature of the information in relation to that context; the roles of agents receiving information; their relationships to information subjects; on what terms the information is shared by the subject; and the terms of further dissemination."[5]

But we need to go further. Although these approaches to privacy are not centered on the individual and, therefore, do not perpetuate the idea that privacy is something we have to govern ourselves, they are still agnostic as to ends. They don't explicitly act as counterweights to corporate power. However, some privacy scholarship is taking this next step. Danielle Citron has called for giving special weight and special protection for sexual privacy, pushing back against corporate surveillance of our sexuality, our bodies, and our intimate selves. Her work elevates sexual privacy as far more worthy of legal protection than the profit-making whims of a company that thinks extracting data from intimate apps and pornography websites is the path to wealth. For sexual privacy, rules of the road aren't enough.[6]

Virginia Eubanks's powerful book, *Automating Inequality*, is another example. Through a series of case studies focused on those on public assistance, child welfare, and the unhoused, Eubanks shows how the use of AI creates a "digital poorhouse" that doesn't just otherwise the poor, but isolates them as well. These AI systems trigger mass data collection and surveillance and capricious rescission of services. They force the poor to disclose information about themselves, all of which is shared with public authorities that track and criminalize them, while discouraging the people who need help from getting any. And the perpetual storage of this information and

its ongoing analysis by AI means that the stigma of poverty, incarceration, homelessness, and illness will always be factored into any algorithmic decision about entitlements. Danielle Citron's research agenda on online harassment and sexual privacy highlights the ways in which surveillance technologies undermine the autonomy, safety, and fundamental rights of women and sexual minorities. Scott Skinner-Thompson's work emphasizes that limited privacy rights make queer people particularly vulnerable. And Khiara Bridges has deftly demonstrated how poor mothers have been systematically deprived of their privacy rights in the United States, contributing to structural inequality that is difficult to escape. We could also think about privacy as a necessary element of human flourishing, or the realization of the whole person, including our physical well-being, happiness, self-determination, and more. For these and other researchers, privacy isn't about individual rights; it is about social justice.[7]

In the context of AI, the law and information scholar Frank Pasquale calls for using law to achieve the democratic goal of building technologies that "complement work" of experts rather than replace them and that do not "counterfeit" humans. The goal of these new principles is to "channel technologies of automation rather than being captured or transformed by them." I would add that this project must also be explicitly liberational and intersectional. These three principles – democracy, equality, and power – should the next wave of privacy discourse.[8]

By democracy, I mean that that the information economy should be accountable "to those who live" within it. That means tearing down barriers that have made it difficult for public law to regulate the information economy and the data-extractive business models on which it depends. There are many such barriers protecting the information industry. Courts have used the First Amendment to limit what government can do to protect privacy. Trade secrecy transforms any algorithmic process into a black box. Section 230 of the Communications Decency Act immunizes industry from all manner of tortious third-party conduct on its platforms, eliminating legal incentives to act against invasions of privacy, cyberharassment, misinformation, and other social harms that flow from data collection and processing. Privacy law should incorporate legal and discursive reform in all of these areas.[9]

The equality principle is the basic notion that information systems should not create or entrench "social subordination." Privacy law follows the equality principle when it centers the experiences of traditionally marginalized groups, including women, BIPOC individuals, the disabled, and members of the queer community, many of whom bear an unequal burden of information age harms. By liberation, I mean that privacy law should strive to free marginalized populations from enduring subjugation at the hands of data-driven technologies by actively focusing on the downstream effects of data extraction on the most vulnerable. That means that the future of privacy law should focus on the ways in which data-extractive capitalism keeps Black men in jail, discriminates against persons of color, silences dissident and women's voices, and stigmatizes minorities by making unreasonable inferences about marginalized groups.[10]

In practice, these principles mean starting from the presumption that public regulation of the information industry is good thing, that regulation should be attuned to structural inequality rather than process, and that marginalized populations need a say in the regulatory process. The political – whether through legislation or the courts – must be part of the social construction of an economic space that has for too long immunized itself from public accountability.

Countering Corporate Power with Law

Privacy law has often been complicit in maintaining traditional power structures; it has also been a privilege of the wealthy and powerful. Chapter 1 showed how privacy-as-control is part of that tradition, functioning mostly to maintain corporate power than unwind it and benefiting only those who have the privilege to make disclosure choices. As such, traditional approaches to privacy law have left a lot of people behind.[11]

Neil Richards and Woodrow Hartzog have leveraged trust-based definitions of privacy to argue that tech companies should be considered fiduciaries of our information and, therefore, subject to similar duties loyalty that characterize our relationships to doctors, lawyers, and trustees. They call for a duty of loyalty on companies who traffic in and profit from our information. Duties of loyalty

mean that a company cannot use our data in ways that would foreseeably cause harm or would be highly offensive to a reasonable user. As Richards and Hartzog explain, a duty of loyalty would also create a rebuttable presumption that certain types of data collection and processing and categories of data-extractive designs are presumptively unlawful, placing the burden on the information industry to justify its designs rather than burdening user with impossible self-governing burdens. This is a good example of explicitly thinking about privacy law as a counterweight to information industry power. But although the indeterminacy of a common law duty of loyalty can be an asset – it can be clarified over time, stay flexible as times change, and respond to changes in technology – the information industry has proven itself remarkably effective at taking advantage of vague laws to suit their interests. As we discussed in Chapter 3, vague laws with procedural escape hatches are hallmarks of legal endogeneity; privacy compliance departments take those vague terms and put their own spins on them. It is unclear to me how duties of loyalty can escape that fate.[12]

If we explicitly construct privacy law as a counterweight to corporate power and build enforcement mechanisms that retained fidelity to that goal, other proposals may have merit as well. Many privacy advocates and pro-privacy policy makers have called for private rights of action to allow individuals to sue tech companies that misuse their data. Although judicial proceedings are not immune to the endogeneity cycle – indeed, as we discussed in Chapter 3, reference, relevance, and deference are judicial contributions to the problem – private rights of action have worked in the past when they part of a larger strategy to rein in corporate excesses. Civil litigation made dangerous machines safer; private lawsuits gave us seatbelts, stronger automobile frames, safer doors, side impact protection, and many other car safety features. Little if any of that would have happened if car safety was the exclusive responsibility of a small, underfunded regulatory agency that has acceded to a self-governing privacy regime.[13]

If we flipped the switch and allowed private rights of action today, they would not be able to bring about real change for privacy on the ground. They would exist in a legal environment actively facilitates corporate power rather than counters it. Corporate-friendly standing requirements mean that a lawsuit,

even if permitted, isn't always an option. Opening the door to impact civil litigation would mean very little without concomitant liberality from judges in recognizing privacy harms. And the right to bring a lawsuit does not change the fact that tech companies can fall back on industry best practices or provide evidence of merely symbolic structures to evade liability. Litigation, in general, also favorably tilts toward wealthy, entrenched interests that have the power, money, and time to litigate not just for individual wins – in which case, settlements may make rational sense – but for structural advantage in precedent, governing law, and legal consciousness. Private rights of action may "catalyz[e] a societal shift toward a thicker notion of industrial responsibility," as it did with mass environmental torts and products liability, but in a world where our courts see themselves as protectors of business rather than protectors of the voiceless, a private right of action is woefully inadequate. That inadequacy proves the need to reorient privacy law in general as a counterweight to corporate power.[14]

In that vein, privacy law should also start becoming more comfortable with two words that are gaining increasing prominence among scholars and advocates: "ban it." Woodrow Hartzog and Evan Sellinger have called for bans on government and private use of facial recognition technology because it is a "perfect tool of oppression." Mary Anne Franks and the Cyber Civil Rights Initiative have worked to criminalize the nonconsensual sharing of identifiable and sexually graphic photos, otherwise known as nonconsensual pornography or "revenge porn." Frank Pasquale has called for a robust "second wave" approach to algorithmic accountability and artificial intelligence that would pause or ban uses of AI that contribute and entrench structural inequality. We should be able to leverage constitutional guarantees like due process and equal protection to challenge any government use of automated systems that make decisions implicating individuals' fundamental rights, with a heavy presumption against use. Privacy law generally can learn from these approaches. We need to consider bans on automated decision-making, not just entitlements to the "logic behind" them. We should consider bans on collecting certain types of information that could harm marginalized populations and not be satisfied with procedural standards when it happens. And we should discuss bans on certain uses of information, from microtargeting on the basis of protected

characteristics or proxies thereof to any use of information processing that has a disparate impact on marginalized populations. All of these options are open if we start thinking about privacy discourse and law as counterweights to corporate power.[15]

Fidelity to this principle also suggests that certain proposals to strengthen privacy law may be insufficient. Scholars have argued that the FTC needs the ability to write rules to clarify its authority. The purpose of agency rulemaking is to specify vague statutory requirements, offering clear notice as to what the law requires, an opportunity to participate in public governance, and a comprehensive resolution of questions facing large numbers of persons and businesses. Today, the FTC is limited by the "procedurally burdensome" process of Magnuson-Moss rulemaking, which requires the FTC to conduct industry-wide investigations, prepare reports, propose rules, engage in a series of public hearings, and consider other alternatives. The process is so difficult that the FTC has not engaged in it in 40 years. This lack of rulemaking authority ensures that, without more, privacy regulation from the FTC will remain vague and technology companies will remain the primary movers in determining what a given legal standard requires. As it is, the only way to discern what the FTC means by a specific term or phrase is to turn to its previous consent decrees, which is what many practitioners do. But the FTC, and the US administrative state as a whole, has been hollowed out by decades of "small government" policies and the same corporate-friendly discourses of privacy and innovation that we discussed in Chapter 2. At most, it averages ten privacy-related settlements per year. Its portfolio extends beyond privacy issues, covering many "unfair and deceptive" practices in commerce. Giving it more power to clarify its corporate-friendly policies won't make much of a difference.[16]

Another proposal to use traditional legal paradigms to invigorate privacy law is to learn from securities law to make FTC assessments more effective, intensive, and independent. In 2002, the Sarbanes-Oxley Act, as clarified by rules promulgated by the Securities and Exchange Commission, requires publicly traded companies to have a completely independent audit committee. The committee serves as a check on nefarious financial reporting and is charged with the "appointment, compensation, and oversight" of the company's independent auditor. The committee must include at

least one financial expert and have a mechanism for anonymously reporting questionable accounting. Sarbanes-Oxley made internal auditing teams cornerstones of business models: long seen as simple cost centers, audit teams are now essential to corporate governance. Sarbanes-Oxley also requires executives to sign financial statements, ensuring greater involvement and establishing a sense of personal responsibility for honesty.[17]

A similar approach may be a step up from the assessments or attestations that we discussed in Chapter 3, but I'm not so sure. Requiring executives to sign off on privacy audits and internal privacy programs, and subjecting them to civil and criminal penalties should they mislead regulators, could have a sufficient motivating effect to take privacy seriously. But auditing-based models like the one in Sarbanes-Oxley are part of the privatization of regulation that we criticized in Chapter 3. And, as Julie Cohen has argued, these audits "sit on the periphery of the regulatory state," having the look and feel of administrative oversight, but with too healthy a dose of private control.[18]

As we saw in Chapter 3, the FTC's requirement that companies operating under its consent orders establish a "comprehensive privacy program" is a perfect opportunity for merely symbolic compliance: the FTC never clarifies what that requirement means, its assessment check-ups are lax, and companies take advantage of that wiggle room to perform accountability in superficial ways. If privacy law was explicitly a counterweight to corporate power, a privacy program would look very different. Companies would put privacy in their missions. Empirical evidence bears this out how effective this can be. Scholars recently showed that a corporate climate dedicated to privacy has a more significant impact on designers than formal policies, legal decisions, or continuing education.[19]

It would mean an end to privacy siloization, which is fatal to the diffusion of pro-privacy norms throughout a company, erode trust and, as a result, prevent the exchange of information. As a result, software engineers are more likely to resist privacy professionals' and privacy lawyer's input, and privacy engineers are less likely to be able to have any impact on the overall designs of new products. Even where privacy professionals staff individual business units or where privacy lawyers were assigned to specific products and teams, reporting structures and organizational

hierarchies limited their ability to have an impact on privacy in design. And, as we have seen, information industry executives have taken steps to marginalize privacy voices, whether through budgetary gimmicks, financial cuts, or reporting hierarchies. They destabilized privacy's position inside the corporation so that privacy professionals would moderate their advice and temper their advocacy in order to protect their jobs.[20]

It isn't enough that privacy professionals and privacy lawyers are integrated into business units. They need to be part of design teams or, at a minimum, given the opportunity to spot privacy issues as they come up. They should not be relegated to waiting for an engineer, an engineering team leader, or a project manager to come to them with privacy questions; few of these workers are trained or qualified to recognize what does or does not raise privacy issues. To alleviate the workplace pressures that cause some privacy professionals to moderate their advice, the law or individual corporate boards could guarantee defined tenures for privacy professionals, elevate the CPO to a board-level position, and make privacy budgets independent, guaranteed, and free from interference from IT, compliance, and legal departments.

A privacy team that is mandated as a counterweight to corporate power would not be subordinated to other departments. Putting privacy under IT prejudices privacy toward the limited world of security and encryption. And giving chief technology officers final say over hiring privacy vendors leaves out important expertise that could ensure that vendors are management thoroughly. Giving privacy responsibilities to a company's risk team is also problematic. As we discussed in Chapter 3, risk framing undermines robust privacy enforcement and giving privacy compliance responsibilities to professionals trained risk brings managerial values to privacy. If data privacy is going to mean anything, it has to be treated like one by corporation.

Even this is not enough. We have to start thinking about privacy law expansively. Future privacy law should give advocacy organizations representing marginalized populations – not corporations – a seat at the table. Groups focused on the cyber civil rights of women, the poor, communities of color, victims of intimate partner violence, sex workers, those living with disabilities, HIV+ individuals, and those who identify as gay, queer, or

transgender, among many others, should be represented in meetings with regulators. As should "gig economy" workers, most of whom lack basic workplace protections and face data-extractive employers actively seeking to disempower them. These are the people who are most likely subordinated by the economic and social systems of data-extractive capitalism and, as such, their voice matters more than those doing the data extraction for profit.[21]

Victims of nonconsensual pornography, most of whom are women, have unique perspectives on the dangers of information sharing. Those seeking public assistance have lived experience with giving up their privacy in humiliating circumstances that could help policy makers write fairer laws. Black men and women, long victims of systemic racism and oversurveillance by police, must be involved in building accountability regimes for the surveillant systems of law enforcement. They must also be involved in the design of those systems from the start. Victims of intimate partner violence know how mobile apps, email, trackers, and other seemingly innocuous tools of social surveillance can be weaponized in a practice of psychological or physical harm. Their experiences should be at the core of how industry designs new technologies and determines what apps will be available on their platforms, in addition to how law holds perpetrators accountable. And transgender individuals, against whom privacy has been weaponized as a pretext for discrimination, can help policy makers understand why disaggregating substantive injustice from procedural law leaves many people behind. Indeed, all of these groups have insights that regulators do not, and yet, so far, it is industry that has holds the levers of power.

One of the results of decentering the needs of industry in privacy law is an emphasis on cyber civil rights. Ohio Senator Sherrod Brown's proposal, the Data Accountability and Transparency Act (DATA) of 2020, comes closest among recent proposals to doing this. Although the draft bill retains some of the rights-compliance framework, it creates a new agency with an office of civil rights that would ensure data collection and use is "fair, equitable, and nondiscriminatory." The proposal would prohibit any data aggregation that results in discrimination in housing, employment, credit, insurance, and public accommodations or has a disparate impact on marginalized populations. It also makes it easier for victims to prove and obtain justice for disparate impact.

As such, DATA nods to the population-level harms that are endemic to business models dependent upon data-driven behavioral targeting. It is worth noting that in drafting his proposal, Senator Brown consulted exclusively with civil society, not with industry. Although marginalized populations were not well represented, Senator Brown's decision to focus on democratic governance rather than what corporations would accept is a welcome model for privacy law's third wave.[22]

Future privacy law should also facilitate critical research on technology. It can do that in two complementary ways. First, by using law to expand independent researchers' access to data and technologies behind the corporate veil, law can democratize technology, take it out of the black box, and enable pro-privacy and pro-social justice movements. Today, however, research about online behavior, AI, and other data-driven technologies is controlled primarily by Big Tech: they not only have the money to fund research, but they control the raw data necessary to conduct it. Therefore, a second, complementary approach to facilitating critical research about data-extractive technologies is the mass unionization of technology researchers employed by industry. Google's summary firing of the AI researcher Timnit Gebru for trying to publish research critical of Google's highly profitable AI systems suggests that corporate-funded information research is not independent. A union could have acted as a check against retaliation and discrimination, or made it more difficult for the company to manipulate its researchers. Organized and empowered employees could push back on corporate development of technologies that harm marginalized populations. Privacy law today implicitly assumes that internal compliance and privacy professionals will play the role of the privacy advocate. That is unlikely, given ordinary workplace pressures facing in-house compliance professionals. A union for tech workers doing important research on information economy harms may help.[23]

Just like the lack of a union creates insecurity and undermines critical research of technology products, our collective incapacity to write robust new environmental laws indirectly enhances corporate power over our data. To process personal data quickly and efficiently, industry builds massive warehouses of servers, computers, and related equipment. The biggest technology companies

have also funded the construction of a maze of undersea cables transferring data all over the world. The former uses an enormous amount of electricity, most of which is powered by coal and other fossil fuels. The latter disrupts ocean wildlife and benefits industry's wealthiest players at the expense of those that cannot afford to build their own cables. Public law aimed at reversing the damages of climate change could put restrictions on emissions, the indirect effect of which would be mass corporate shifts to renewable energy, increased public awareness about the information industry's environmental record, and sand in the gears of Big Tech's data-driven monopolistic practices.[24]

That these ideas – cyber civil rights, data licensing, research funding, unionization, and environmental protection – do not seem to fit within privacy law's traditional purview speaks to the myopia that has characterized privacy law and discourse to date. Privacy law is not merely about data, but also about data's effects on society. The narrowness of today's privacy law has benefited industry at our expense: by focusing primarily on the point of data collection and the process of data management, traditional privacy law was siloed from the social contexts affected by data collection and use.

Countering Corporate Power through Organizations

Civil society organizations should explicitly position themselves as counterweights to corporate power as well. The IAPP, the largest community for privacy professionals today, exists to "help[] practitioners develop and advance their careers" and help "organizations manage and protect their data." As we have seen, this mission translates into publications and programming that is generally corporate-friendly, perpetuating antiprivacy discourses and amplifying the prospect of outsourcing privacy compliance to technology vendors. The IAPP cannot function as a counterweight to the information industry if it and its conferences are funded by that industry. And, as such, privacy professionals are not likely to be exposed to robust privacy discourses and outside-the-box thinking while gathering at IAPP events or working with other IAPP members.[25]

There is an explicitly pro-consumer alternative that could help privacy professionals act as counterweights to management. If

privacy professionals actually saw themselves as privacy advocates, pushing back against corporate bosses that only care about data extraction, then they should start a union of workers that is built around consumer-focused commitments rather than commitments to management. This workers' union could also help privacy professionals advance their careers but do so as it builds a profession that advocates for privacy and justice rather than as tools of management. It could run programming about privacy and bias, algorithmic injustice, dark patterns, and corporate manipulation of consumers, among others, and market their members as privacy leaders who understand how to build privacy-focused organizations. Any company that hires such a privacy professional would immediately signal its commitment to privacy (although such signals are only first steps).

Educational institutions that train privacy professionals, privacy lawyers, and software engineers should also position themselves as counterweights to corporate power. This not only includes stanching the flow of money from tech companies to academics in ways that influence research, publications, and public discourse. It also means building curricula that create socially conscious and privacy conscious future information industry employees.

Currently, many institutions of higher learning fail to adequately train their future software engineers to understand the importance of privacy and the social context in which they work. A LinkedIn search for technology talent currently employed at Google, Facebook, or Apple reveals that nearly 40 percent come from just the top ten engineering and computer science programs in the United States, as rated by *US News and World Report*. With a few important exceptions, those curricula are quite similar in scope and course offerings. Most fail to help their students understand the moral, ethical, and legal contexts in which they do their work. Strikingly few even mention privacy, and when they do, it is often conflated with security. And most classes are taught by faculties with severe gender and racial imbalances. Some universities have introduced "ethics" requirements into their computer science and engineering programs. But although that's a fine start, it isn't enough. An engineering graduate student at Columbia University told me that electives focusing on privacy issues in engineering are "hidden from most students; you can avoid all of it if you want to.

These are things that I am interested in, and, as a result, I've been intentional about accessing them. I can't say the same for my colleagues." A graduate student at the University of Washington's Department of Electrical Engineering noted that she too "had to go out of [her] way" to find classes on policy, ethics, and privacy. An educational system built as a counterweight to corporate power would ensure that ethics, social context, inequality, justice, and equity is built into every single course that students take, not siloed into an elective that's easy to avoid.

The information industry has also been manipulating higher education to amplify its power for decades. Eric Schmidt, the former Google chief executive, has plans to create a technical university to train people interested in technology, cryptography, and security. Google created its own postsecondary certificate program that, the company says, would qualify people for Google jobs even without a college degree. Amazon, Facebook, and Salesforce are expanding their partnerships with colleges to offer credit-based versions of their programs, including certifications in cloud technology, coding, security, and more. Universities have followed along dutifully, building and expanding technical degree programs to attract large donations and meet demand. But these programs are, for the most part, devoid of the social sciences, humanities, and liberal arts courses generally that teach critical thinking skills. That's intentional. A great way to build a compliant workforce that doesn't notice or doesn't care to notice the existence of inculcative and coercive bureaucracies is to eliminate critical thinking and the social sciences from worker education.[26]

***

No single reform will bring about the change we need. It is also possible that these reforms are insufficient and insufficiently imaginative. They, too, are products of current discourses. And the information industry has proved resilient to exogenous and endogenous resistance so far. Resigning ourselves to the status quo, however, is not an option. Nor is timidity; we tried that, and it failed.

Structuring privacy-related discursive, legal, professional, and educational institutions as counterweights to corporate power seems like a self-evident thing to do. It's remarkable,

however, how radical it really is. The FTC "work[s] with industry on self-regulation." It is a facilitator, not a counterweight, in its own words. Even many progressive policy makers use rhetoric that presumes privacy law and innovation are in conflict. And the GDPR lays out "rules of the road" for corporate data collection and processing even though it is framed as an approach based on fundamental human rights. If we stopped and thought about privacy law only in terms of counterweights to corporate power, the problems of informational capitalism, in general, and industry's coercive bureaucracies and pliant work force, in particular, may seem a little less daunting.[27]

CONCLUSION

This book has been about the tools the information industry uses to routinize an antiprivacy ethos and practice through its organizations. Of course, not all tech companies use all of these tactics: some use a few, some use more, some use none. But these strategies are in use, and they have the effect of marginalizing privacy throughout the everyday work of law and design. More than just a collection of strategies, they are features of informational capitalism. They help explain how data-extractive capitalism persists.

At its core, informational capitalism is about the commodification and control not just of our data – our Social Security numbers, our likes and dislikes, our purchase and browsing histories – but of the entire narrative arc of our lives. Data-extractive capitalists operate on the assumption that if they gather enough data, everything can be determined and, therefore, *pre*determined. They can know what cereal we'll buy and what candidate we support, all by turning us into data points and putting those data points through a computer. Although that assumption is wrong – those types of predictive projects are bound to fail or entrench bias, as critical scholarship on AI has already shown – that hasn't stopped an entire economic system from developing around it.

What role has the law played in all of this? As Julie Cohen explains, tech companies are not simply economic actors generating revenue from commodifying data. They also play the law's game and have mobilized legal tools to advance their goals. Law, then, is not an exogenous institution that stood to the side to let the Googles and Facebooks of the world have their run of the place. Those companies

leveraged law to get to where they are today. And our legal institutions were sometimes all too willing to let them.

Given the centrality of data collection and processing in informational capitalism, one would expect privacy to be anathematic to the information industry and the legal institutions that prop it up. And yet, we are told that privacy law is getting stronger and that tech companies are committed to protecting our privacy above and beyond what the law requires. Pushing those companies to do better are thousands of privacy professionals, privacy lawyers, and privacy engineers working on the inside. These professions are relatively new, but some of them are already enshrined in privacy law as the vehicles of privacy protection and legal accountability.

This book has shown that there is reason to believe that this approach is misguided, both inherently and in practice. Today's capitalism is not just an economic system structured to commodify our existence through total surveillance. Nor is it sufficient to add that it has contributed to corporate power. I have argued that informational capitalism survives because of the systematic marginalization of privacy all the way through the ranks of the information industry, and that tech companies use age-old tactics of coercive bureaucracies to do it. They push friendly privacy discourses through their ranks. They reorient privacy law to suit their data-extractive interests. And they constrain designers to make it difficult to integrate privacy into design. This piece of the puzzle is essential.

This subtle, yet powerful antiprivacy entrenchment throughout the ranks of the information industry explains how informational capitalism thrives while thousands of privacy professionals, their bosses, and the emails they send out can say they honestly care about privacy. Tech companies want their workers to care about privacy, but only if privacy means control or encryption. Executives want to comply with new privacy laws, but only to the extent that it looks enough like they're complying to satisfy underfunded regulators. And they want their engineers to integrate privacy into design, but only in performative ways. This performance doesn't flow from the kind of bureaucracies that tech companies tell us they have. Google and Facebook, not to mention many far smaller companies, make much of their generative corporative cultures for technologists: "You have an idea? We want it to hear it!" Industry even gave their engineers time off to work on their own

projects and attracted talent based on promises of a nonhierarchical and innovative workplace. Those promises are empty. If it ever existed, that type of tech company doesn't exist anymore. In its place are coercive bureaucracies that operate so subtly that people on the ground don't event recognize how their work perpetuates a system hostile to privacy. Some refuse to believe it. Others are so steeped in corporate-friendly discourses that they've become true believers. Yet others insist they're doing their best and being on the inside is the best way to make progress.

Regardless of the willingness of privacy professionals, privacy lawyers, software engineers, and others to recognize how their employers use tried and true tactics of coercive bureaucracies to entrench the norm of data extraction throughout the rank and file, the reality is that today's informational capitalism survives because of their work, their performances, and their sometimes-unwitting service in a corporate crusade against privacy.

ACKNOWLEDGMENTS

Writing a book may seem like a solitary affair, but it is, in fact, just the opposite. This book began with the idea that the people interpreting, implementing, and practicing the law sometimes matter more than the law on the books. I wrote this book after several years of mounting questions posed to colleagues, friends, mentors, graduate students, and a gracious partner. I couldn't have done it without them.

There are those who combine brilliant scholarly work with a commitment to supportive mentorship. I am thinking of Danielle Keats Citron, a fierce and generous friend and scholar and winner of a MacArthur Fellowship in 2019, who has a habit of thinking about (and solving) problems ten years before everyone else gets in on the act and uplifting everyone along the way; Julie Cohen, whose book, *Between Truth and Power: The Legal Constructions of Informational Capitalism*, is both a scholarly triumph and a guide to thinking about the information age in which we live; Frank Pasquale, who exemplifies what it means to be a true gentleman and a scholar: a dynamic mind challenging the hierarchical power structures that undermine equality in our society; Neil Richards, legal scholar, avid cyclist, supportive friend, and author of *What Privacy Means*, who graciously welcomed an unknown junior scholar who was doing work on precisely the same topic as he was and who took the time to offer both conceptual critiques and line edits; Woodrow Hartzog, a fantastic friend and interdisciplinary scholar whose great intelligence is matched only by his great generosity and whose book, *Privacy's Blueprint: The Battle to Control the Design of New Technologies*, is not only a canonical piece of privacy scholarship but also a foundational text for my work; Ryan Calo, a brilliant interdisciplinary scholar of law and technology who is

ceaselessly generous with his time, advice, and critiques; Daniel Solove, a leader of the privacy law scholarly community, who read all of my draft papers and gave critical comments to improve my research and arguments; Paul Schwartz, a brilliant scholar and music expert, who invited me to speak with his students, sparked some of the research in this book, and has never ceased to support my career; Joel Reidenberg, whom we sadly lost to cancer in 2020, and who was the center of the privacy law community and my first mentor and volunteered to read anything I wrote even when he wasn't well; and Kathy Strandburg, a privacy and intellectual property scholar at New York University, whose ideas and skill at bringing together smart minds at NYU's Privacy Research Group helped make each of my research projects better.

Of course, there are other friends and mentors without whom this book would never have seen the light of day: Helen Nissenbaum, a towering scholar in information studies, offered important comments on draft papers and read the initial proposal for this book, commending to me work that I had missed in my research to that point; Chris Hoofnagle, a privacy law and information studies expert, helped me crystalize some of my ideas and suggested avenues for research; Pris Regan, a political scientist, opened my ideas to additional literatures I had not considered; Anita Allen, a lawyer and philosopher, inspired me to think critically about my research; Arvind Narayanan, a computer scientist, graciously challenged both my modest and crazier ideas and helped make my arguments more persuasive and nuanced; and Lauren Edelman, a sociolegal scholar, helped guide much thinking in this book.

I would also like to thank my scholarly collaborators, all of whom helped me think about questions from new and exciting perspectives: Karen Levy, an insightful and brilliant sociologist at the nexus of technology and society; Kirsten Martin, an outstanding scholar of human behavior; Jim Mourey, a multitalented academic working in marketing and consumer psychology; Matthew Tokson, a keen mind with an encyclopedic knowledge of Fourth Amendment case law; Mary Anne Franks, the brilliant and fierce feminist scholar; and, of course, my future collaborators – Danielle Citron, Julie Cohen, and those I have yet to meet!

The "thank-you" list also has to include all those, in addition to those above, who asked constructive questions at workshops

and pushed me to be a better scholar. They included, in alphabetical order: Vigjilenca Abazi, Kendra Alpert, B. J. Ard, Jack Balkin, Ann Bartow, Tamara Belinfanti, Philip Bender, Jody Blank, Joseph Calendrino, Celine Castets-Renard, Ignacio Cofone, Rebecca Crootoff, Mary Culnan, evelyn douek, John Duffy, Lauren Edelman, Amit Elazari, Jake Goldenfein, Ashley Gorham, Ben Green, Nikolas Guggenberger, Seda Gurses, Gautam Hans, Joris van Hoboken, Chris J. Hoofnagle, Leslie John, Ariel Fox Johnson, Thomas Kadri, Margot Kaminski, Ian Kerr, Cam Kerry, Anita Krishnakumar, Mike Kwet, Amanda Levendowski, Karen Levy, Asaf Lubin, Mason Marks, Kirsten Martin, Bill McGeveren, Emily McReynolds, James A. Mourey, Frank Munger, Paul Ohm, Peter Omerod, Przemyslaw Palka, Jeremy Paul, Jon Penney, Ed Purcell, Ira Rubinstein, Blaine Saito, Andres Sawicki, Victoria Schwartz, Eli Seims, Andrew Selbst, Jeremy Sheff, Richard Sherwin, Jessica Silbey, Liron Shilo, Priscilla Smith, Luke Stark, Eva Subotnik, Harry Surden, Kara Swanson, Olivier Sylvain, Matthew Tokson, Joseph Turow, Rory Van Loo, Michael Veale, Salome Viljoen, Christopher Wolf, Felix Wu, and Annette Zimmerman. A special additional note of thanks to the tremendous research assistants who worked with me on various parts of this book project: Suzie Allen, Brian Brantley, Lauren Davenport, Felipe Escobedo, Margaret Foster, Maverick James, and Monica Meiterman.

Throughout the course of this research, I delivered works-in-progress talks to distinguished faculty and at various workshops and conferences. Thank you to the faculties of the University of California, Los Angeles School of Law; Georgetown University Law Center; St. John's University School of Law; Hofstra Law School; Northeastern University School of Law; Princeton University; Washington University School of Law; Yale Law School; New York University School of Law; University of California, Berkeley; University of Pennsylvania School of Law; Fordham University School of Law; Columbia University; University of Maryland Carey School of Law; George Washington University School of Law; and New York Law School, among others.

Writing a book also takes a lot of patience: the patience to understand, go with the craziness that can sometimes envelope an academic's life, and read countless drafts of words thrown together. A special thank-you to my partner, Greg Lam, who is

the kindest and most loving person I know. Around him, I can be myself. Around him, I can talk about anything, from Foucault to an episode of *Bob's Burgers*. Greg understood when I had to leave early in the morning or miss a weekend because of a talk or a research trip or stay late on a Tuesday to write 5,000 words. I'm sure I'd be flat on my face without Greg's support. And I mean that literally; I can be very clumsy.

This book is based on approximately four years of field research. Funding for that research was provided by New York Law School and Princeton University. I will note that I run an annual scholarly workshop, the Northeast Privacy Scholars Workshop, that receives funding from Microsoft. That fact has had no impact on my research. The funding was never connected to this work. Nor did Microsoft grant those funds with any strings. For the ability to conduct this research, I am grateful to the administration and faculty of my former institution, New York Law School, including Dean and President Anthony Crowell and Associate Dean Bill LaPiana. Princeton University's Center for Information Technology Policy selected me as the 2019–20 Microsoft Visiting Professor of Information Technology Policy, a position that included a research budget. During this time, I also served as Visiting Professor at the Princeton School of Public and International Affairs. Thank you to Ed Felten, Jonathan Mayer, Matt Salganik, and an inspiring faculty at Princeton University, including Dirk Hartog, Paul Starr, and others, for their generosity and willingness to discuss my work. Additional thanks go to the administration and faculty at my current institution, Northeastern University, including Dean James Hackney of Northeastern University School of Law and Dean Carla Brodley of Khoury College of Computer Sciences. Special thanks to my faculty colleagues for welcoming me into their academic family.

Portions of this book were adapted from several published articles, but the ideas in this book reflect additional research and significantly evolved thinking. These articles include "Designing without Privacy," *Houston Law Review* 55 (2018): 659–727; "Privacy Law's False Promise," *Washington University Law Review* 97 (2019): 773–834; "Cognitive Barriers, Dark Patterns, and the 'Privacy Paradox,'" *Current Opinion in Psychology* 31 (2019): 105–9; "Privacy, Notice, and Design," *Stanford Technology Law Review* 21 (2017): 74–127. Two of these articles –

"Designing without Privacy" and "Privacy Law's False Promise" – won the Best Paper Award at the Privacy Law Scholars Conference in 2017 and 2019, respectively. It is an honor to be the only person who has won the Best Paper Award twice for two single-author papers. Thank you to the Program Committee for the honors.

I am lucky to have earned the trust of so many colleagues. I am lucky to have had the opportunity to spend time working on this research and writing this book. Not everyone has the privilege to make their voice heard, and I write this book and conduct this research conscious of my privilege and dedicated to elevating and empowering those whose voices are traditionally silenced, ignored, and marginalized. Where possible, I have highlighted the work of women, persons of color, queer scholars, and others traditionally underrepresented in the academic community. In all, 58.4 percent of references are from scholars representing marginalized communities. How did I come up with that number? Of course, it is difficult to know how authors identify. Plus, a single person often has intersectional identities. Finding some way to analyze the diversity metrics in my sources was important to me, so I did my best to research if any author of any cited work, including all named authors beyond the primary author, identified as women; Black, Indigenous, or other persons of color; or queer (to roughly capture the full range of people in the LGBTQI community, including myself). I based this on a combination of self-reported gender identities, pronouns, self-reported racial identities, self-reported sexual orientations, and images. I did not simply rely on last names. I recognize that these categories are imperfect, and I am sure my numbers are not completely accurate.

APPENDIX
Research Methods and Limitations

Surveillant technologies are not built by economic systems. They're built by people working together inside organizations. An organization is a network of people with distinct roles, authority, and expertise working together to achieve a series of collective goals. In this context, creating a new piece of technology, whether a mobile game, a social network, an e-commerce platform, or an automated system that surveils street protests, involves – or, at least, *should* involve – many people. There are the software engineers who write the code, the web designers who create user interfaces, and the marketing teams who tell engineers what consumer data they need to collect. Venture capitalists who fund new projects have their own ideas and requirements. And the lawyers and privacy professionals who advise engineers on the constraints on their plans are involved as well. So, too, are the users, beta testers, focus groups, intermediaries, and legal and regulatory institutions outside the organization that may have an impact on what a new technology looks like in the end. Designers also work in teams; they talk to one another to develop new solutions to vexing engineering problems. Executives draft guidelines for frontline workers down the corporate ladder, and employees from different departments work with each other to complete their part of a larger development task. It seems uncontroversial to argue that technologies are the products of social relations, but it is an argument that often gets lost in our drive to understand why our privacy is slipping away and how we can stop – and reverse – our losses. Scholars tend to think about data-extractive political economy, about weak data privacy laws, about culture. These are all important, but they are still just pieces in a puzzle. What technologies look like, how they function, and how they mediate relationships with

and among individuals reflect the social and political dynamics of the people and institutions that create them.[1]

So, that's who I studied. Over the course of several years, I went inside the information industry, following ethnographic fieldwork techniques in the tradition of actor-network theory (ANT) and science and technology studies (STS). That means I studied the development of technology by seeing it as the product of how individuals and groups interact. Like ethnomethodologists, who study how everyday people interact with conversations, gestures, and other forms of communication, ANT researchers treat science as a "cultural practice" based on what scientists actually do. For example, Bruno Latour studied the development of Louis Pasteur's anthrax vaccine, trying to explain how Pasteur's vaccine went from a bunch of chemicals in a lab to an effective and widely available vaccine. Latour found that the vaccine's success depended not on biochemical discovery but on the internal dynamics of the scientists in Pasteur's lab, processes of the French state, a campaign to persuade French farmers, the public hygiene movement, and support from medical professionals and even colonial interests. Without these allied social forces, the anthrax vaccine would have never seen success when it did. Latour and Steve Woolgar studied the "construction" of scientific facts at the Salk Institute by observing the way research scientists worked in a lab. Marianne de Laet and Anna-Marie Mol applied similar methods to their study of the development of water pumps in Zimbabwe. The lesson here is clear: if we want to understand how, if at all, privacy factors into design, we have to look at the people involved, how they work together, and how institutions affect them.[2]

We could do that by studying how software engineers do their work, but their narrative is only one small part of this story. I was mindful that "follow[ing] the actors" with "voluntary blindness" to let them "define themselves," though a well-worn technique of sociological fieldwork, can put too much emphasis on those in power and ignore the impact of structural inequalities that have kept people out of design. By looking at the ways different social groups interpret and construct technologies' roles in society and by focusing on the people and things involved in the creation of knowledge, ANT glosses over variations among those involved and their relative power in the design process. In particular, ANT inadequately

appreciates the role of gender and gender discourses in technology, structural forces that marginalize some people and groups from design, and the oppression of a neutral approach to studying what scientists do. As Judy Wajcman has argued, by focusing on what they saw, ANT researchers ignored what they didn't see: groups excluded from that process for "structural" reasons. "ANT," Wajcman continued, "does not always recognize that the stabilization and standardization of technological systems necessarily involve negating the experience of those who are not standard." Traditional sociology of science never thought to explore the effects that women's or any marginalized group's almost total absence from design had on technology, society, and a technology's place in society. They didn't even think about ways to incorporate marginalized voices into their models; as their focus remained on "relevant social groups," they originally excluded those society pushed out. As a result, Susan Leigh Star has argued that ANT ended up focusing too much on the "heroic" and "entrepreneurial" efforts of (mostly male) designers, or the ones who have the power to position themselves with the right tools, with the right allies, and at the right moment to push their designs to the front.[3]

For Sara Delamont, the sociology of science was too focused on what she called "big science" – high-status men doing exciting things in big research institutions – rather than the "routine" work that is both necessary to make "big science" work and, not surprisingly, done far more often by women. As a result, others' contributions were ignored, missed, or undervalued. Feminist scholars have showed that women helped change the design of many technologies, including the microwave, reproductive technologies, computers, and other household devices. Traditional STS approaches to research miss that. Timing matters too. Latour conducted his research almost entirely within laboratories. For their research on the failure of a proposed state-of-the-art fighter jet for the Royal Air Force, John Law and Michel Callon focused on ministers, engineers, bureaucrats, and shifts in parliamentary majorities. But technological narratives do not involve just a few heroes. Ruth Schwartz Cowan made this explicit in her work. She understood technological development by looking at the "consumption junction," or the place and time at which consumers make choices between competing products. At that point, far more

people – and far more traditionally marginalized populations – are involved in design and development over a longer period of time.[4]

Wajcman noted that the impact of marginalized populations, structural asymmetries, and broader power structures constraining certain people's and groups' contributions becomes clearer "once the lens is widened to include manufacturing operatives, marketing and sales personnel, and the consumers and end-users of technologies," among others. Put another way, to understand why technologies develop the way they do, we need to study who is in the room, who has been kept out, and who draws that line.[5]

That's why I interviewed software engineers, privacy professionals, privacy lawyers (both in-house and at private firms), salespeople, executives, those working in public policy offices, venture capitalists, entrepreneurs, compliance officials, individuals, members of civil society and advocacy groups, and other stakeholders, and collected data not only on what they say but also on who says it, who is missing, and the sources and effects of internal power structures. I wanted to understand the ideas, laws, bureaucracies, and resources involved in designing new technologies and chronicle how people's biases, relationships, and constraints contributed to finished products that perpetuate a system of corporate surveillance for profit. I distributed surveys, reviewed industry literature, and analyzed public and private internal documents, the last of which were often partially redacted. I also had the opportunity to observe design meetings at three companies, each of which was at a different stage of developing three new technology products that collected user data: an app to facilitate photo sharing, a rental listing platform, and a mobile game. I couldn't be present for every meeting over the course of a product's entire development, which can sometimes take years, but my follow-up interviews and observations tried to fill gaps as best as possible.[6]

The methodologies I used for this research included interface ethnography, collecting public records (legal cases and briefs, published articles and blogs, public reports, surveys, and other public data), multilevel analyses of nonpublic documents (internal audit reports, impact assessments, internal policies and organizational protocols), participant observation, systemic interviews, and focused interviews with key figures.[7]

Lifting the veil to see corporate privacy programs in action isn't easy. The anthropologist Laura Nader has noted that "the powerful are out of reach on a number of different planes: they don't want to be studied; it is dangerous to study the powerful; they are busy people; they are not all in one place." In an excellent piece on research methodology, Torin Monahan and Jill Fisher noted that "establishing contacts and gaining permission to conduct ethnographic or qualitative research can be time-consuming" in any field, but "the worlds of technoscientific knowledge production are notoriously difficult to study." Inside the information industry, there are a lot of people who, "for a variety of reasons, would prefer to avoid outside scrutiny." Practitioners are aware that negative portrayals of what they do could provoke backlash; others may be more concerned about trade secrets. Indeed, many companies were at first reticent to subject their internal processes to analysis and critique, even if they were proud of their privacy work. Others were worried about their competitors. This reticence is why it took four years to conduct sufficient research for this project.[8]

To allay some of these concerns, some researchers expose themselves to ethical gray areas and other risks. Some give their subjects preapproval rights over quotes and their manuscripts. Others agree to assist the organization in some way as a condition of access. As Michael Patton has found, this can take many forms, from interning to writing reports to working on projects that are in the organization's interests rather than a core part of the researcher's project. Some academics do "covert research," as where a researcher joins an organization as a volunteer or employee in order to conduct their work without anyone knowing. In some cases, researchers may never be able to obtain access. This requires alternative strategies for obtaining access to the information if formal permission is absent. To address these issues, Monahan and Fisher propose several pathways for obtaining access, many of which I relied on for this project. Following their lead, I attended industry conferences, made cold calls, communicated legitimacy so my research subjects knew about me and my work, reduced the perception of a threat by distinguishing between social science research and "gotcha" journalism, permitted pseudonymization, and mobilized indirect access through other organizations and individuals with experience in the field.[9]

I signed nondisclosure agreements with companies that opened their doors for investigation and interviews. This did not constrain my research because I was never interested in proprietary information. For example, I worked with several companies to study corporate design processes – reporting mechanisms, how day-to-day questions were answered, training protocols, corporate structures, and so forth. None of that touches on the substance of what was being designed during that process. Several major technology companies saw this as an opportunity to share their work, and a number of leading Silicon Valley companies arranged for me to visit, interview some of their employees, observe design meetings, and learn from their experiences. Most of my interviews were conducted outside of official visits, with current and former employees of various companies within the information industry. Both the visits and interviews were conducted independent of company influence. Some company representatives required preapproval of all quotes; others refused to be quoted, even pseudonymously, demanding all comments be on "deep background." I did not accept those terms. Unlike some researchers, I refused to give the companies prepublication review of the draft or their employees' quotes. Facebook refused to participate in this project.[10]

Neither this nor any research project should focus on a single company, especially if that company, for all we know, may not exist in a few years. Instead, I conducted interviews and reviewed documents from current and former Facebook employees through other channels. Nader tried to dismiss the problem of lack of access as one, at least in part, of anthropologist timidity. It is true that social science researchers sometimes hesitate to critique their subjects for fear of losing access. But there are other means available to pierce rarified institutions. There are affinity groups, professional conferences, and those using the same co-working space. No one method is perfect. Nor are ethnographic sample sets ever truly random. But that really isn't the point. My goal is to suggest that there exists a narrative of corporate power based on design, compliance, and discourse, and that if a company wanted to make privacy law meaningless, it could do so by leveraging the tools I discuss throughout the book. That does not happen at every company, but the prevalence of these strategies is unmistakable.[11]

By the end of my research, I had conducted 125 interviews with stakeholders who were either current or former employees of large, medium, and start-up companies in California, New York, Berlin, and London. Ninety-seven of these interviewees reported that they had been involved, in some way or another, with the design or redesign of a technology product or hardware or software that collected user data. They filled positions in a wide variety of departments inside industry, including software engineering, product management, project management, compliance, privacy, legal, executive leadership, web design, data analytics, user experience, marketing, law, compliance, management, public policy, and venture capital investment. I also had the opportunity to observe some part of the design of three technologies – an app to facilitate photo sharing, a rental listing platform, and a mobile game – at three different companies.

To study the design process at major businesses, I started with what sociologists call snowball sampling, a nonprobability sampling technique where existing study subjects recruit additional study subjects from among their friends, acquaintances, and social networks. Snowball sampling can help researchers with limited resources identify and reach hard-to-target populations within a large, diffuse community, i.e., technology workers, and open doors for greater research opportunities down the road. Because network-based sampling techniques like this tend to identify individuals with particularly thick social networks – people who know a lot of other people in the same field – the individuals identified have a high likelihood of being well connected, experienced, and knowledgeable in the research subject. Snowball sampling also has downsides. It tends to identify research targets that are similar to each other. Given that potential for bias, I did not rely solely on snowball sampling for my interviews, which included software engineers, privacy professionals, privacy lawyers, entrepreneurs, product managers, and others. I interviewed many during visits to fourteen different companies during my research. I also attended conferences and approached random attendees, some of whom agreed to short conversations.[12]

I attended privacy industry conferences, including the IAPP national conference, "Privacy. Security. Risk. 2017"; the 2018 and 2019 International Privacy+Security fora and the 2018 Privacy

+Security forum; the Annual Forum of the European School of Management and Technology; and CyberWeek 2018, organized by the University of Tel Aviv. At these conferences, I met and either scheduled or conducted semistructured interviews with privacy professionals in various industries, including high technology, aerospace, retail, finance, and travel. A total of thirty-eight privacy professionals were interviewed. I also spoke with twenty-four in-house counsel and attorneys in private practices whose portfolios included privacy and cyber security, and four middle managers in large technology companies' public policy departments. These interviewees were particularly diverse along gender lines: fourteen of the twenty-four lawyers who agreed to speak with me were women. They earned their degrees at a variety of law schools. All worked for firms with more than fifty employees.[13]

In order to determine how privacy professionals, lawyers, and compliance vendors understood privacy law and how they conceptualized their responsibilities and goals, and to minimize response biases from surveys, I started by interviewing privacy professionals and lawyers who are current or former employees of companies in the information industry. I participated in webinars hosted by tech companies themselves and the IAPP, a trade organization for privacy professionals. I also reviewed internal documents, including PIAs, audit reports, and organizational charts and policies. Some of these documents were redacted or included information that is subject to confidentiality agreements I have on file. I read their and law firm blogs and reviewed articles in industry journals geared toward privacy professionals. Primary source fieldwork also supplemented traditional legal research into privacy statutes, cases, and regulatory orders, both in the United States and in Europe. European privacy law was included because of the outsized impact the GDPR is already having on the information industry worldwide.[14]

To research privacy discourses, I followed critical discourse analysis methodology (CDA). Unlike sociologists in the Goffmanian tradition, who analyze how people use language to frame social encounters, and linguistic anthropologists, who study the transmission of ideas through language over time, CDA studies the social, linguistic, and ideological forces that make it possible for individuals, groups, or institutions to exert power. It is especially interested in uncovering the illegitimate use of discourse to abuse power,

whether through manipulation or what some social theorists would call hegemonic dominance, or persuading the oppressed to accept their oppression as a good thing. Therefore, it has strong descriptive as well as normative components, not just identifying how power is exercised through discursive practice but also showing the negative effects of the status quo and how social movements can push back.[15]

These methods are not perfect. I do not purport to have studied a random sample of the population, even the population of privacy professionals or software engineers. I do not suggest that all companies involved in the design, development, and marketing of digital tools that extract our data manipulate the design process, or do so in same way. Nor am I suggesting that every technology company contorts its compliance obligations and weaponizes the discursive terrain around privacy in disingenuous and manipulative ways. I am showing that a particular type of corporate control over design, compliance, and discourse can undermine privacy. These are corporate tactics of which we have to be aware, and which we need to regulate. They are not necessarily the tactics of every company in information economy, but they are at work.

A final note on quotations used in this book. Many of those I interviewed, particularly software engineers, privacy lawyers, and privacy professionals, were concerned that speaking honestly could jeopardize their positions with their current employers. Some were unwilling to speak freely because of the frequency with which they switch employers, moving from one company to its competitor. To alleviate these concerns, I offered every interviewee the opportunity to discuss their views pseudonymously. I worked with each of them to find a descriptor that made them comfortable. All consented to some mention of the type of company they worked for – "a coder at a large technology company," for example. Lawyers chose this option, as well, opting to be identified only as "a partner at an AmLaw Top 100 law firm," or something similar. Pursuant to confidentiality agreements and Institutional Review Board rules, I respected all of these preferences in order to engage in honest discussions about their privacy-related work. This approach also tried to alleviate the privacy concerns involved in any ethnographic project. Anyone or any company that did not agree to be, at least, pseudonymously quoted was not allowed to participate in this project.[16]

NOTES

Preface

1 **Snapchat lied.** Federal Trade Commission. 2014. Complaint, In the Matter of Snapchat, Inc., FTC File No. 132 3078, Docket No. C-4501 (F.T.C. May 8, 2014).

Pokemon Go forced. Strauss, Valerie. 2016. "Pokémon Go Sparks Concern About Children's Privacy." *Washington Post*, www.washingtonpost.com/news/answer-sheet/wp/2016/07/19/pokemon-go-sparks-concern-about-childrens-privacy/; Hudson, Laura. 2016. "How to Protect Privacy While Using Pokémon Go and Other Apps." *New York Times*, www.nytimes.com/2016/07/14/technology/personaltech/how-to-protect-privacy-while-using-pokemon-go-and-other-apps.html?_r=0.

Zoom's default settings. Cox, Joseph. 2020. "Zoom iOS App Sends Data to Facebook Even if You Don't Have a Facebook Account." *Vice*, www.vice.com/en_us/article/k7e599/zoom-ios-app-sends-data-to-facebook-even-if-you-dont-have-a-facebook-account; Krolik, Aaron and Natasha Singer. 2020. "A Feature on Zoom Secretly Displayed Data from People's LinkedIn Profiles." *New York Times*, www.nytimes.com/2020/04/02/technology/zoom-linkedin-data.html.

Femtech apps extract data. Citron, Danielle K. 2020. "A New Compact for Intimate Information." *William and Mary Law Review* 62.

Uber designed. Electronic Information Privacy Center. 2019. "EPIC Files Complaint with FTC About Zoom." Epic.org, https://epic.org/2019/07/epic-files-complaint-with-ftc-.html; Isaac, Mike. 2017. "Uber's C.E.O. Plays with Fire." *New York Times*, www.nytimes.com/2017/04/23/technology/travis-kalanick-pushes-uber-and-himself-to-the-precipice.html.

listen when they're not supposed to. Geoffrey A. Fowler, *Alexa Has Been Eavesdropping on You This Whole Time*, WASH. POST (May 6, 2019), www.washingtonpost.com/technology/2019/05/06/alexa-has-been-eavesdropping-you-this-whole-time/.

Google G-Suite is so invasive. Brown, Emma. 2016. "UC-Berkeley Students Sue Google, Alleging Their Emails Were Illegally Scanned." *Washington Post*, www.washingtonpost.com/news/grade-point/wp/2016/02/01/uc-berkeley-students-sue-google-alleging-their-emails-were-illegally-scanned/.

2 This meeting was not recorded, and participants were not permitted to quote anyone else by name. Instead, the meeting was conducted pursuant to the Chatham House Rule, in which participants are free to use the information developed during the meeting, but without revealing the identities or affiliations of the participants involved.

3 **Cambridge Analytica.** Chang, Alvin. 2018. "The Facebook and Cambridge Analytica Scandal, Explained With A Simple Diagram." *Vox*, www.vox.com/policy-and-politics/2018/3/23/17151916/facebook-cambridge-analytica-trump-diagram.

4 **informational capitalism.** Cohen, Julie. 2019. *Between Truth and Power: The Legal Constructions of Informational Capitalism*. New York: Oxford University Press (pp. 5–6); Zuboff, Shoshana. 2019. *The Age of Surveillance Capitalism: The Fight for a Human Future at the New Frontier of Power*. New York: Public Affairs.

5 **social practice of privacy.** My focus in this book is on the social practice of privacy law inside corporations in the information industry. A related literature that could fall under the umbrella of the "social practice of privacy" concerns the steps individuals take to protect themselves from corporate and government surveillance. A few examples of outstanding work in that space is as follows: Marwick, Alice. n/d. *Privacy Work: The Labor of Protecting Information in a Networked Age*. Forthcoming. boyd, danah. 2014. *It's Complicated: The Social Lives of Networked Teens*. New Haven, CT: Yale University Press; Marwick, Alice and danah boyd. 2014. "Networked Privacy: How Teenagers Negotiate Context in Social Media." *New Media & Soc.* 16: 1051–1067.

Introduction

1 **General Data Protection Regulation.** Regulation (EU) 2016/679 General Data Protection Regulation, 2016 O.J. (L119).
"comprehensive." McGeveran, William. 2016. "Friending the Privacy Regulators." *Arizona Law Rev.* 58: 959–1025 (p. 963).
"one of the strictest privacy laws in the world." Solove, Daniel. 2017. "Beyond GDPR: The Challenge of Global Privacy Compliance – an Interview with Lothar Determann." TeachPrivacy, https://teachprivacy.com/challenge-of-global-privacy-compliance/.

42 proposals were introduced in 28 states. IAPP. n/d. "State Comprehensive Privacy Law Comparison, Bills Introduced 2018–2020, https://iapp.org/media/pdf/resource_center/State_Comp_Privacy_Law.pdf.

California's Consumer Privacy Act. California Consumer Privacy Act of 2018, Cal. Civ. Code § 1798.100.

limits on the collection, use, and manipulation of personal information. Federal Trade Commission. 2019. FTC Imposes $5 Billion Penalty and Sweeping New Privacy Restrictions on Facebook. Washington, DC: FTC.

requiring warrants for cell-site location data. Carpenter v. United States, 484 U.S. 19 (1987).

challenged the cross-border transfer of European citizens' data. Data Protection Commissioner v. Facebook Ireland and Maximillian Schrems ("Schrems II"), Case C-311/18 (2020), http://curia.europa.eu/juris/document/document.jsf?text=&docid=228677&pageIndex=0&doclang=en&mode=req&dir=&occ=first&part=1&cid=9794635.

2 **Apple markets its iPhones as privacy protective.** Wuerthele, Mike. 2019. "'Privacy. That's iPhone' Ad Campaign Launches, Highlights Apple's Stance on User Protection." *Apple Insider*, https://appleinsider.com/articles/19/03/14/privacy-thats-iphone-ad-campaign-launches-highlights-apples-stance-on-user-protection.

Facebook ... promises. Zuckerberg, Mark. 2019. "A Privacy-Focused Vision for Social Networking." *Facebook*, www.facebook.com/notes/mark-zuckerberg/a-privacy-focused-vision-for-social-networking/10156700570096634/; Wong, Julia Carrie. 2019. "Facebook's Zuckerberg Announces Privacy Overhaul: 'We Don't Have the Strongest Reputation.'" *The Guardian*, www.theguardian.com/technology/2019/apr/30/facebook-f8-conference-privacy-mark-zuckerberg.

"build[s] privacy that works." GoogleSafety Center. n.d. "Your Privacy." Accessed at https://safety.google/privacy/.

spent millions of dollars and hired thousands of privacy professionals. International Association of Privacy Professionals and Ernest & Young. 2019. IAPP-EY Annual Privacy Governance Report 2018, https://iapp.org/resources/article/iapp-ey-annual-governance-report-2019/.

historically not known. Thompson, Clive. 2019. *Coders: The Making of a New Tribe and the Remaking of the World.* New York, NY: Penguin Random House.

3 **face surveillance.** Hill, Kashmir. 2020. "The Secretive Company That Might End Privacy as We Know It." *New York Times*, www.nytimes.com/2020/01/18/technology/clearview-privacy-facial-recognition.html.

DNA testing kits. Garner, Samual and Ji Hyun Kim. 2018. "The Privacy Risks of Direct-to-Consumer Genetic Testing: A Case Study of 23AndMe and Ancestry." *Washington University Law Rev.* 96: 1219–1265.

"smart" devices. There is a growing research agenda on the privacy issues associated with "smart" cities, "smart" appliances, and the so-called Internet of Things, which is an umbrella term for a series of wi-fi enabled consumer devices, from coffee makers and sex toys to entire homes and medical devices. Consider the following small selection: Green, Ben. 2019. *The Smart Enough City: Putting Technology in Its Place to Reclaim our Urban Future*. Cambridge, MA: MIT Press; Crootof, Rebecca. 2019. "The Internet of Torts: Expanding Civil Liability Standards to Address Corporate Remote Interference." *Duke Law Journal* 68: 583–667; Kaminski, Margot et al. (2017). "Averting Robot Eyes." *Maryland Law Review* 76: 983–1025. The breadth of the Internet of Things has also spawned cultural parody. Internet of Shit (@internetofshit), Twitter, https://twitter.com/internetofshit?lang=en.
gratuitous location tracking. Kang, Cecilia. 2013. "Flashlight App Kept Users in the Dark about Sharing Location Data: FTC." *Washington Post*, www.washingtonpost.com/business/technology/flashlight-app-kept-users-in-the-dark-about-sharing-location-data-ftc/2013/12/05/1be26fa6-5dc7-11e3-be07-006c776266ed_story.html.
manipulative "dark patterns." Mathur, Arunesh et al. 2019. "Dark Patterns at Scale: Findings from a Crawl of 11K Shopping Websites." *Proceedings of the. ACM on Human-Computer Interaction*. 3(81): 1–32.
Mozilla's Firefox. The data it collects are minimal, limited to information necessary for us to sync browsing across devices, to report crash reports, to collect usage statistics, and so forth. Firefox deploys what it calls "containers" that isolate cookies so third parties can't track our browsing habits. For example, if we browse Facebook and then open a tab to visit another site, Facebook would normally see what we're doing, collect that information, and integrate it into its targeting algorithms. But Firefox "contains" that information; according to Dave Camp, Mozilla's vice president of engineering, containers "tr[y] to keep separate applications separate so that they can't see each other and prevent Facebook from getting information from that site." Its privacy settings are on by default and its browser-level settings block cross-site tracking cookies and notify users when a website wants access to our computers' microphones or collect more identifiable information, like geolocation. In one week, one researcher found that Firefox blocked 11,189 requests for tracker cookies that Google's Chrome would have allowed. Firefox also offers users a privacy report so we can see who's tracking us, how, and what we can do to opt out. The browser parses cookie requests, keeping those that are necessary for site function and blocking the ones that are just there for surveillance. Smith, Matthew. 2018. "Firefox Is on the Frontline in the Fight to Protect Your Privacy. *Digital Trends*, www.digitaltrends.com/

computing/how-firefox-protects-you-from-intel-cpu-flaws-facebook-leaks-more/; Fowler, Jeffrey. 2010. "Goodbye, Chrome: Google's Web Browser Has Become Spy Software." *Washington Post*, www.washingtonpost.com/technology/2019/06/21/google-chrome-has-become-surveillance-software-its-time-switch/; Colby, Clifford. 2019. "Latest Firefox Browser Shows Who's Tracking You, Because We All Care about Privacy Now." *CNet*, www.cnet.com/how-to/latest-firefox-browser-shows-whos-tracking-you-because-we-all-care-about-privacy-now/; Chen, Brian. 2018. "Firefox Is Back. It's Time to Give It a Try." *New York Times*, www.nytimes.com/2018/06/20/technology/personaltech/firefox-chrome-browser-privacy.html; Wilander, John. 2019. "Intelligent Tracking Protection 2.1." *WebKit*, https://webkit.org/blog/8613/intelligent-tracking-prevention-2–1/.

the Signal messaging app. Signal was designed to offer end-to-end encrypted messaging without data mining for profit. Compared to Facebook's WhatsApp, which also promises encrypted messaging but still allows Facebook to gather metadata for behavioral ad targeting, and Facebook Messenger, which offers little privacy protection, Signal encrypts messaging by default. Signal also hides the metadata about conversations so the only person who can see who sent a message is the message's recipient. These and other design elements put Signal squarely in a camp of platforms that designed with privacy in mind. The platform has used a $50 million investment from WhatsApp founder Brian Acton, to grow its engineering team from three to ten, with a commitment to center its new full-service communications platform. In 2019, for example, Signal added support for ephemeral images and video, which disappear after one viewing, and an experimental method for storing encrypted contacts in the cloud. Grothaus, Michael. 2019. "If You Value Your Privacy, Switch to Signal as Your Messaging App Now." *Fast Company*, www.fastcompany.com/90335034/if-you-value-your-privacy-switch-to-signal-as-your-messaging-app-now; Greenberg, Andy. 2020. "Signal Is Finally Bringing Its Secure Messaging to the Masses." *Wired*, www.wired.com/story/signal-encrypted-messaging-features-mainstream/.

Apple's decision to notify iPhone users when geolocation tracking is on. Haselton, Todd. 2019. "Apple Is Finally Showing You How Often Apps Track Your Location on iPhone." *CNBC*, www.cnbc.com/2019/10/08/apples-new-location-alerts-show-how-often-other-companies-track-you.html.

Our privacy is disappearing. Solove, Daniel. 2004. *The Digital Person: Technology and Privacy in the Information Age*. New York, NY: New York University Press; Pasquale, Frank. 2015. *The Black Box Society: The Secret Algorithms That Control Money and Information*. Cambridge,

MA: Harvard University Press; Citron, Danielle K. 2019. "Sexual Privacy." *Yale Law Journal* 128: 1870–1960; Citron, Danielle K. 2009. "Cyber Civil Rights." *Boston University Law Review* 89(2): 61–125; Citron, Danielle K. and Mary Anne Franks. 2014. "Criminalizing Revenge Porn." *Wake Forest Law Review* 49: 345–391; Hartzog, Woodrow. 2018. *Privacy's Blueprint: The Battle to Control the Design of New Technologies*. Cambridge, MA: Harvard University Press.

4 **Windows 10 gathers information about us.** Warren, Tom. 2017. "Microsoft Finally Reveals What Data Windows 10 Really Collects." *The Verge*, www.theverge.com/2017/4/5/15188636/microsoft-windows-10-data-collection-documents-privacy-concerns.

some have sued Google for surveillance overreach. Brown, Emma. 2016. "UC Berkeley Students Sue Google, Alleging Their Emails Were Illegally Scanned." *Washington Post*, www.washingtonpost.com/news/grade-point/wp/2016/02/01/uc-berkeley-students-sue-google-alleging-their-emails-were-illegally-scanned/.

Facebook ... tracks. Simonite, Tom. 2012. "What Facebook Knows." *MIT Technology Review*, www.technologyreview.com/s/428150/what-facebook-knows/

5 **obscure.** Hartzog, Woodrow and Evan Selinger. 2015. "Surveillance as Loss of Obscurity." *Washington and Lee Law Review* 72: 1343–1387.

intimate. Several scholars have described privacy in terms of intimacy. Danielle Keats Citron. 2019. "Sexual Privacy." *Yale Law Journal* 128: 1870–1960; Skinner-Thompson, Scott. 2018. "Privacy's Double Standards." *Washington Law Review* 93: 2051–2016; Cohen, Jean. 2001. "The Necessity of Privacy." *Social Research* 68: 318–327; Inness, Julie. 1992. *Privacy, Intimacy, and Isolation*. New York: Oxford University Press.

free and autonomous decisions. The scholarly literature conceptualizing privacy is long. For a summary of some of that work, please see the following: Waldman, Ari Ezra. 2018. *Privacy as Trust: Information Privacy for an Information Age*. New York: Cambridge University Press. Some examples of this approach to privacy include, Warren, Samuel and Louis D. Brandeis. 1890. "The Right to Privacy." *Harvard Law Review* 4: 193–220; Cate, Fred. 1997. *Privacy in the Information Age*. Washington, DC: Brookings Institution Press; Fried, Charles. 1968. *Privacy. Yale Law Journal* 77: 475–493.

equality and social justice. For discussions at the intersection of information privacy and equality, please see the following: Citron, Danielle K. 2019. "Sexual Privacy." *Yale Law Journal* 128(7): 1870–1960; Bridges, Khiara. 2017. *The Poverty of Privacy Rights*. Palo Alto, CA: Stanford University Press; Skinner-Thompson, Scott. 2020.

Privacy at the Margins. New York: Cambridge University Press. This literature also includes the expanding scholarship on algorithmic bias and discrimination, which includes, among other sources: Noble, Safiya. 2018. *Algorithms of Oppression: How Search Engines Reinforce Racism*. New York: NYU Press; Benjamin, Ruha. 2019. *Race after Technology: Abolitionist Tools for the New Jim Code*. New York: Polity; Katyal, Sonia. 2019. "Private Accountability in the Age of Artificial Intelligence." *University of California, Los Angeles Law Review* 66: 54–141; Angwin, Julia et al. 2016. "Machine Bias." *ProPublica*, www.propublica.org/article/machine-bias-risk-assessments-in-criminal-sentencing; O'Neil, Cathy. 2016. *Weapons of Math Destruction: How Big Data Increases Inequality and Threatens Democracy*. New York: Crown Books; Madden, Mary, Michele Gilman, Karen Levy, and Alice Marwick. 2017. "Privacy, Poverty, and Big Data: A Matrix of Vulnerabilities for Poor Americans." *Washington University Law Review* 95: 53–125.

6 **Foucauldian discourse theory**. Foucault, Michel. 1978. *The History of Sexuality, Volume 1, An Introduction*. New York: Vintage Books; Foucault, Michael. 1972. "*The Archaeology of Knowledge" and "The Discourse on Language*." New York: Pantheon Books; Foucault, Michel. 1981. "The Order of Discourse." In *Untying the Text: A Post-Structuralist Reader*, edited by Robert Young, 48–79. Boston, MA: Routledge & Kegan Paul.

actor-network theory. Latour, Bruno. 2005. *Reassembling the Social: An Introduction to Actor-Network-Theory*. Oxford: Oxford University Press; Law, John. 2009. "Actor Network Theory and Material Semiotics." in *The New Blackwell Companion to Social Theory*, edited by B. S. Turner. Oxford: Blackwell-Wiley.

science and technology studies. Pinch, Trevor J. and Wiebe E. Bijker. 1984. "The Social Construction of Facts and Artefacts; or How the Sociology of Science and the Sociology of Technology Might Benefit Each Other." *Social Studies of Science* 14:3 399–441, reprinted in Bijker, Thomas P. Hughes and Pinch (eds.) 2012. *The Social Construction of Technological Systems: New Directions in the Sociology and History of Technology*. Cambridge, MA: MIT Press. 17–50; Cockburn, Cynthia and Susan Ormrod. 1993. *Gender and Technology in the Making*. London: Sage; Martin, Michèle. 1991. *Hello Central? Gender, Technology, and Culture in the Formation of Telephone Systems*. London: McGill-Queen's University Press; Bijker, Wiebe E. 1995. *Of Bicycles, Bakelites, and Bulbs: Toward a Theory of Sociotechnical Change*. Cambridge, MA: MIT Press; Douglas, Susan J. 1987. *Inventing American Broadcasting, 1899–1922*. Baltimore, MD: The Johns Hopkins University Press.

performance theory. Goffman, Erving. 1959. *The Presentation of Self in Everyday Life*. New York: Anchor Publishing; Butler, Judith. 1990. *Gender Trouble: Feminism and the Subversion of Identity*. London: Routledge; Callon, Michel. 2007. "What Does It Mean to Say That Economics Is Performative?." In MacKenzie, Donald et al. eds., *Do Economists Make Markets? On the Performativity of Economics*. Princeton, NJ: Princeton University Press, pp. 311–357.
critical studies in STS. Collins, H. M. and Steve Yearly. 1992. "Epistemological Chicken." In *Science as Practice and Culture*, by Andrew Pickering. Chicago: University of Chicago Press; Wajcman, Judy. 2000. "Reflections on Gender and Technology Studies: In What State Is the Art?" *Social Studies of Science*. 30(3): 447–464; Star, Susan L. 1990. "Power, Technology, and the Phenomenon of Conventions: On Being Allergic to Onions." In *Technoscience: The Politics of Interventions*, edited by Kristin Asdal et al. 2007 (pp. 79–109); Star, Susan L. 1990. "Power, Technology, and the Phenomenon of Conventions: On Being Allergic to Onions." *In A Sociology of Monsters: Essays on Power, Technology and Domination*, edited by John Law. 1991. London: Routledge (pp. 26–56); Delamont, Sara. 1987. "Three Blind Spots? A Comment on the Sociology of Science by a Puzzled Outsider." *Social Studies of Science* 17(1): 163–170 (p. 166); Rossiter, Margaret. 1982. *Women Scientists in America: Struggles and Strategies to 1940*. Baltimore, MD: Johns Hopkins University Press; Cowan, Ruth Schwartz. 1987, "The Consumption Junction: A Proposal for Research Strategies in the Sociology of Technology." In *Common Themes in Sociological and Historical Studies of Technology*, edited by Wiebe Bijker et al. Cambridge, MA: MIT Press. 261–281.
critical sociolegal studies. Cohen, Julie. 2019. *Between Truth and Power: The Legal Constructions of Informational Capitalism*. New York: Oxford University Press.

7 **norms and routines are the products of several internal and external influences**. This framework is adapted from work by Ruth Aguilera, a sociologist of business and organizations, to understand why businesses engage in corporate social responsibility programs that are not necessarily profit-oriented. *See* Ruth V. Aguilera et al., *Putting the S Back in Corporate Social Responsibility: A Multilevel Theory of Social Change in Organizations*, 32 *Acad. Mgmt. Rev.* 836, 837 (2007). Although there are differences between encouraging technology companies to embed privacy into design and, say, pushing companies to engage in socially beneficial initiatives, both require changes in organizational norms away from a strict, profit-only perspective. Therefore, organizational learning is important in both scenarios.

behavior of their competitors. DiMaggio, Paul J. and Walter W. Powel. 1983. "The Iron Cage Revisited: Institutional Isomorphism and Collective Rationality in Organizational Fields." *American Sociological Review* 48(2): 147–160.

collection of individuals. Gray, Garry C. and Susan S. Sibey. 2014. "Governing inside the Organization: Interpreting Regulation and Compliance." *American Journal of Sociology* 120(1): 96–145 (p. 97); Inkpen, Andrew C. and Eric W. K. Tsang. 2005. "Social Capital, Networks, and Knowledge Transfer." *Academy of Management Review* 30: 146–165 (p. 148).

embodied experiences. "Embodied" experience, or the idea that humans cannot divorce mental cognition from physical life, emphasizes the practical, behavioral experiences of real people interacting in contextual social situations. Lakoff, George and Mark Johnson. 1999. *Philosophy in the Flesh: The Embodied Mind and Its Challenge to Western Thought.* New York: Basic Books; Merleau-Ponty, Maurice. 1969. *The Essential Writings of Merleau-Ponty*. Edited by Alden L. Fisher. New York: Harcourt, Brace & World (pp. 47–80, 138–181). In this context, this means that engineers, privacy professionals, and privacy lawyers do not exist in vacuums: they approach the world and do their work as fully realized embodied individuals, with unique backgrounds and biases.

8 **discourse.** Julie Cohen has shown that discourses of efficiency, technological agnosticism, entrepreneurial freedom, and even xenophobia work in tandem and alongside narrow definitions of privacy to amplify corporate power and insulate them from accountability. Cohen, *Between Truth and Power.*

9 **collaborative or "new" governance.** Kaminski, Margot. 2019. "Binary Governance: Lessons from the GDPR's Approach to Algorithmic Accountability." *Southern California Law Review* 92: 1529–1616; Lobel, Orly. 2004. "The Renew Deal: The Fall of Regulation and the Rise of Governance in Contemporary Legal Thought." *Minnesota Law Review* 89: 342–470.

a house of cards of compliance. The theoretical foundation of this argument is based on the work of Lauren Edelman. Edelman, Lauren. 2016. *Working Law: Courts, Corporations, and Symbolic Civil Rights.* Chicago, IL: University of Chicago Press. This argument was previewed in the following: Waldman, Ari. 2019. "Privacy Law's False Promise." *Washington University Law Review* 97: 773–834.

managerial lens. Managerial governance is governance that relies on professionals and experts doing their work with "good management" values in mind, such as efficiency, productivity, and low costs. Cohen, *Between Truth and Power*, pp. 144–145.

10 **information industry executives are on record.** Hartlaub, Peter. 2020. "More Surveillance Is Coming. Why That Might Not Be a Bad Thing." *San Francisco Chronicle*, www.sfchronicle.com/culture/article/More-surveillance-is-coming-Why-that-might-not-15481965.php; Friedman, Thomas. 2014. "Four Words Going Bye Bye." *New York Times*, www.nytimes.com/2014/05/21/opinion/friedman-four-words-going-bye-bye.html; Kirkpatrick, Marshall. 2010. "Facebook's Zuckerberg Says the Age of Privacy Is Over." *ReadWrite*, https://readwrite.com/2010/01/09/facebooks_zuckerberg_says_the_age_of_privacy_is_ov/; Springer, Polly. 1999. "Sun on Privacy: Get Over It." *Wired*, www.wired.com/1999/01/sun-on-privacy-get-over-it/.

in the interests of profit. Cook, Tim. 2019. "You Deserve Privacy Online: Here's How You Could Actually Get It." *Time*, https://time.com/collection/davos-2019/5502591/tim-cook-data-privacy/; Hoffman, David. 2014. "Privacy Is a Business Opportunity." *Harvard Business Review*, https://hbr.org/2014/04/privacy-is-a-business-opportunity.

11 **normalizing.** As psychologists Adam Bear and Joshua Knobe have written, when a politician "continues to do things that once would have been regarded as outlandish, [his] actions are not simply coming to be regarded as more typical; they are coming to be seen as more normal. As a result, they will come to be seen as less bad and hence less worthy of outrage." Bear, Adam and Joshua Knobe. 2017. "Normality: Part Descriptive, Part Prescriptive." *Cognition* 167: 25–37.

common sense. Marxist scholars might call this "hegemony." Hegemony is another way of understanding "total domination" of the powerless by the powerful where the dominated actually accept their domination as ordinary, common sense, and normatively good. Hegemony involves "subduing and co-opting dissenting voices through subtle dissemination of the dominant group's perspective as universal and natural, to the point where the dominant beliefs and practices become intractable component of common sense." Litowitz, Douglas. 2000. "Gramsci, Hegemony, and the Law." *Brigham Young University Law Review* 2000: 515–551 (p. 519). It is related to Marx's concept of "false consciousness" among the proletariat, explaining why they perpetuate capitalistic systems that abuse them. Marx was clearest on this point in his essay, "The Eighth Brumaire of Louis Napoleon."

12 **actions and behaviors that communicate something to the self and others.** Goffman, p. 15.

performative. Austin, J. L. 1975. *How to Do Things with Words*. Cambridge, MA: Harvard University Press (pp. 3–7); Butler, *Gender Trouble*, pp. 142–145; Butler, Judith. 1988. "Performative Acts and

Gender Constitution: An Essay in Phenomenology and Feminist Theory." *Theatre Journal* 40(4): 519–531.

13 **law and political economy framework.** Britton-Purdy, Jedediah, David Singh Grewal, Amy Kapczynski, and K. Sabeel Rahman. 2020. "Building a Law-and-Political-Economy Framework: Beyond the Twentieth-Century Synthesis." *Yale Law Journal* 129: 1784–1835.

human flourishing. Human flourishing means living a life that is as fulfilling as possible, not simply as cogs in someone else's wheel. Human flourishing means enhancing the dignity of persons, protecting them from dehumanizing automation, and enabling each person to realize their potential. It means thinking about privacy in terms of its benefits to humanity and to human happiness. This idea isn't new to privacy scholarship, but it certainly would be new to the information industry. Nussbaum, Martha. 1992. "Human Functioning and Social Justice: In Defense of Aristotelian Essentialism." *Political Theory* 20: 202–246; Radin, Margaret Jane. 1996. *Contested Commodities: The Trouble with Trade in Sex, Children, Body Parts, and Other Things*. Cambridge, MA: Harvard University Press.

privacy has long been used a pretext to protect traditional hierarchies of power. MacKinnon, Catharine. 1989. *Toward a Feminist Theory of the State*. Cambridge, MA: Harvard University Press; Allen, Anita. 2011. *Unpopular Privacy: What Must We Hide?* New York, NY: Oxford University Press; McLain, Linda. 1995. "Inviolability and Privacy: The Castle, the Sanctuary, and the Body." *Yale Journal of Law and Humanities* 7: 195–241; MacKinnon, Catharine A. 1991. "Reflections on Sex Equality under Law." *Yale Law Journal* 100: 1281–1328; MacKinnon, Catharine A. 1983. "Feminism, Marxism, Method, and the State: Toward Feminist Jurisprudence." *Signs* 8: 635–658; State v. Rhodes, 61 N.C. 453 (1868).

more of a benefit for the wealthy and privileged. Gilman, Michele Estrin. 2012. "The Class Differential in Privacy Law." *Brooklyn Law Review* 77: 1389–1445.

"rules of the road." Jones, Meg Leta and Margot Kaminski. 2020. "An American's Guide to the GDPR." *Denver Law Review* 98(1): 93–128.

14 **Chapter 2.** The theoretical background to this chapter is Julie Cohen's book, *Between Truth and Power*, which describes, among many other things, how many technological and legal discourses come together to advance corporate goals.

Chapter 3. My research in this space is indebted to the theoretical work of Lauren Edelman, whose book, *Working Law*, explained how companies leverage the tools of compliance to undermine federal

nondiscrimination law. The chapter is based on previously published work: Waldman, Ari Ezra. 2019. "Privacy Law's False Promise." *Washington University Law Review* 97: 773–834.

Chapter 4. This chapter is loosely based on previously published work. Waldman, Ari Ezra. 2017. "Designing without Privacy." *Houston Law Review* 55: 659–727.

Chapter 1

1 What follows is a stylized narrative of some of my research. All of the quotes are real, but the names have been changed to protect everyone's privacy. The events described also did not take place in the course of one single day, but they every conversation did take place at some point during my four years of research.

2 Bill is conceptualizing privacy as encryption. For a detailed discussion of this, please see Chapter 3 and Chapter 5.

3 For more on the role of reporting structures and corporate hierarchies and their effect on privacy, please see Chapter 4 and Chapter 5.

4 The discussion of engagement is in Chapter 5. The primacy of engagement was also a central part of Antonio Garcia Martinez's exploration of the founding of Facebook. Martinez, Antonio Garcia. 2016. *Chaos Monkeys: Obscene Fortune and Random Failure in Silicon Valley*. New York: Harper.

5 For a discussion of what some engineers think about when they think of privacy and the effect those understandings have privacy, please see Chapter 5.

6 For a discussion of the importance of efficiency and its attendant effects on privacy in design, please see Chapter 5.

7 This issue, about shifting responsibilities, and the related issue of protecting one's turf inside a corporate environment, also have effects on integrating privacy into design. Please see Chapter 5 for that discussion.

8 This problem, of policies failing to make their way down the corporate ladder to the engineers doing the coding work, was quite common among my interviewees. This issue is discussed in more detail in Chapter 5.

9 The work lawyers do to interpret privacy law and translate it for their bosses is discussed in more detail in Chapter 4, generally.

10 The role played by privacy professionals is discussed in more detail in Chapter 4, generally.

11 On maintaining access and the effect it has on privacy in design, please see Chapter 4.

12 Access to budgets plays an important role in determining who in an organization has power to make change. This issue is described in more detail in Chapter 4.

13 The Certified Information Privacy Professionals exam is an optional, yet sought-after licensing exam organized by the International Association of Privacy Professionals, a large trade organization for privacy professionals. The IAPP offers several such exams, for a fee. IAPP. n/d. "CIPP Certification." Accessed at https://iapp.org/certify/cipp/.
14 Privacy impact assessments are discussed in Chapter 5.
15 The GDPR, the CCPA, and other privacy laws, and how privacy professionals and privacy lawyers interpret those laws, is discussed in Chapter 4.
16 The discourse of privacy as choice, consent, or control is dominant in the information industry and among legislators, as well. The role of this discourse is discussed at several points in this book, including Chapters 3, 4 and 5.
17 For a more detailed discussion of the role of teams in silencing privacy voices during design, please see Chapter 5.
18 Companies boast about their privacy training programs. A discussion of those in the context of privacy in design is in Chapter 5.
19 Physical separation as a tactic of management power is discussed in Chapter 5.
20 The siloization of privacy is discussed in Chapters 4, 5, and 7.
21 I call this the "codability trap" in Chapter 5.
22 The subtle exercises of power by the public affairs office to integrate friendly academics into their efforts to influence privacy discourse is discussed generally in Chapter 3.
23 Chapter 3 discusses how the information industry inculcates the idea of privacy-as-control and keeps it dominant in the public discourse.
24 Corporate anti-privacy advocacy in legal disputes is discussed in Chapter 3.
25 Companies will often recast the GDPR's approach, which focuses on risks to consumers, as the risks to the company of a lawsuit or an investigation. This tactic of power is discussed in Chapter 4.
26 These structures of compliance can be meaningful or they can be window dressing, standing in for actual adherence to the law. The problem of "merely symbolic" compliance structures is discussed in Chapter 4. The notion of "merely symbolic" compliance programs comes from Lauren Edelman's book, *Working Law*.

Chapter 2

1 **described how these discourses come together.** Cohen, Julie E. 2019. *Between Truth and Power: Legal Constructions of Informational Capitalism*. New York: Oxford University Press.

2 **"bodies of knowledge."** Foucault, Michael. 1972. "*The Archaeology of Knowledge" and "The Discourse on Language.*" New York: Pantheon Books (p. 201); Foucault, Michel. 1978. *The History of Sexuality, Volume 1, An Introduction*. New York: Vintage Books; Foucault, Michel. 1981. "The Order of Discourse." In *Untying the Text: A Post-Structuralist Reader*, edited by Robert Young, 48–79. Boston, MA: Routledge & Kegan Paul (pp. 51–52).

3 **what is up for discussion and what is not.** Turkel, Gerald. 1990. "Michel Foucault: Law, Power, and Knowledge." *Law & Society Review* 17(1): 170–193; Lukes, Steven. 1988. *Power: A Radical View*. New York: Red Globe Press.

4 **normalizing function.** Turkel, "Michael Foucault," pp. 185–186. Foucault showed how same-sex sexual activity came to be understood as "abnormal.' Foucault, *History of Sexuality*, pp. 17–19.
feminist scholars. Siegel, Reva. 1992. "Reasoning from the Body: A Historical Perspective on Abortion Regulation and Questions of Equal Protection." *Stanford Law Review* 44(2): 261–381; Butler, Judith. 1990. *Gender Trouble: Feminism and the Subversion of Identity*. New York: Routledge; MacKinnon, Catharine. 1989. *Toward a Feminist Theory of the State*. Cambridge, MA: Harvard University Press.

5 **as "others" in the collective imagination of society.** Matsuda, Mari. 1993. *Words That Wound: Critical Race Theory, Assaultive Speech and the First Amendment*. Boulder, CO: Westview Press; Williams, Patricia. 1991. *The Alchemy of Race and Rights*. Cambridge, MA: Harvard University Press.
interpellation. Althusser, Louis. 2001. "Ideology and Ideological State Apparatuses (Notes toward an Investigation)." In *Lenin and Philosophy and Other Essays*. New York: Monthly Review Press.
discourses in psychology and criminology. Baxter, Hugh. 1996. "Review Essay: Bringing Foucault into Law and Law into Foucault." *Stanford Law Review* 48: 449–479.
discursive "truth" of political action … automatically excludes women. Jones, Kathleen B. 1987. "On Authority: or, Why Women Are Not Entitled to Speak." *NOMOS* 29: 152–168.

6 **A mobile dating app.** Ghorayshi, Azeen, and Ray, Dri. 2018. "Grindr Is Letting Other Companies See User HIV Status and Location Data." *BuzzFeed*, www.buzzfeednews.com/article/azeenghorayshi/grindr-hiv-status-privacy.

7 **no privacy issues because users chose to share.** There are many cases employing this point of view. For example: Gill v. Hearst Pub. Co., 253 P.2d 441 (Cal. 1953).
HIV status is sensitive. Skinner-Thompson, Scott. 2015. "Outing Privacy." *Northwestern University Law Review* 110(1): 159–222.

nothing went wrong. Solove, Daniel and Danielle Keats Citron. 2017. "Risk and Anxiety: A Theory of Data-Breach Harms." *Texas Law Review* 96(4): 737–786. This cogent article first describes the caselaw in the data breach context where courts have denied standing to victims of data breaches because there was no evident, pecuniary harm and then goes on to critique this approach.

dehumanizing and commodifying. Benn, Stanley I. 1971. "Privacy, Freedom, and Respect for Persons." In *NOMOS XIII: Privacy*, edited by J. Rolland Pennock and John W. Chapman. New York: Atherton Press; Bloustein, Edward J. 1964. "Privacy as an Aspect of Human Dignity: An Answer to Dean Prosser." *New York University Law Review* 39: 962–1007.

8 **right to choose for ourselves what will happen with our data**. There is a robust literature conceptualizing privacy around choice. Among the most prominent examples are as follows: Cohen, Jean. 2001. "The Necessity of Privacy." *Social Research* 68: 318–326 (p. 319); Fried, Charles. 1968. "Privacy." *Yale Law Journal* 77: 475–493 (p. 484); Westin, Alan. 1967. *Privacy and Freedom*. New York: Ig Publishing (p. 7); Inness, Julie. 1992. *Privacy, Intimacy, and Isolation*. New York: Oxford University Press (p. 56); Zittrain, Jonathan. 2000. "What the Publisher Can Teach the Patient: Intellectual Property and Privacy in an Era of Trusted Privication." *Stanford Law Review* 52: 1201–1250 (p. 1203); Matthews, Steve. 2010. "Anonymity and the Social Self." *American Philosophical Quarterly* 47(4): 351–363 (p. 351).

privacy is bound up with trust. Waldman, Ari Ezra. 2018. *Privacy as Trust: Information Privacy for an Information Age*. New York: Cambridge University Press; Richards, Neil and Woodrow Hartzog. 2016. "Taking Trust Seriously in Privacy Law." *Stanford Technology Law Rev.* 19(3): 431–472.

privacy means only sharing information where it is appropriate in context. Helen Nissenbaum has argued that privacy has meaning relative to contextual norms of appropriateness and integrity. Nissenbaum, Helen. 2009. *Privacy in Context: Privacy, Technology, and the Integrity of Social Life*. Cambridge, MA: MIT Press. Daniel Solove previously argued that privacy can reflect a family of values and needs at different times given the circumstances, rather than a single common denominator. Solove, Daniel. 2008. *Understanding Privacy*. Cambridge, MA: Harvard University Press.

with those in our social networks. Strahilevitz, Lior. 2005. "A Social Networks Theory of Privacy." *University of Chicago Law Review* 72: 919–988.

9 **inaccessible APIs, coding to prevent scraping, automatic deletion of data, and blocking cookies**. These designs would shift us from a privacy regime based on corporate promises to one based on features of code, or what Sarah Spiekermann and Lorrie Cranor have called "privacy by architecture" instead of "privacy by policy." Along those lines, Seda Gurses, Carmela Troncoso, and Claudia Diaz have recommended integrating "data minimization" into the design process of every technological artifact. Data minimization is the principle that technological systems should only collect so much data as is absolutely necessary for its function, and no more. It's a legal principle for sure, but also an engineering strategy, an approach that can be designed in. Spiekermann, Sarah and Lorrie Faith Cranor. 2009. "Engineering Privacy." *IEEE Transactions on Software Engineering*. 35(1): 67–82; Gürses, Seda et al. 2011. "Engineering Privacy by Design." In *Computers, Privacy & Data Protection*. Brussels, Belgium: Computers, Privacy & Data Protection Conference. Accessed at https://software.imdea.org/~carmela.troncoso/papers/Gurses-CPDP11.pdf; Gürses, Seda et al. 2015. "Engineering Privacy By Design Reloaded." Accessed at www.carmelatroncoso.com/papers/Gurses-APC15.pdf; Diaz, Claudia et al. 2013. "Hero or Villain: The Data Controller in Privacy Law and Technologies. *Ohio State Law Journal* 74(6): 923–964 (p. 940).
obscurity. Hartzog, Woodrow and Evan Selinger. 2015. "Surveillance as Loss of Obscurity." *Washington and Lee Law Review* 72: 1343–1387.

10 **Control over privacy discourse amplifies power**. Foucault, "Order of Discourse," p. 52.
establish, disseminate, and inculcate discourse can do so to maintain their power. Blommaert, Jan and Chris Bulcaen. 2000. "Critical Discourse Analysis." *Annual Review of Anthropology*. 29: 447–466 (p. 458); Jones, Kathleen B. 1987. "On Authority; or, Why Women Are Not Entitled to Speak." *Nomos* 29: 152–168 (p. 159).

11 **without encountering the discourse of control**. This is true when you study nonexperts as well. At Carnegie Melon University, the "Privacy Illustrated" project asked youths and adults to describe their mental frames about privacy through drawing and art. By November 2019, they had collected a robust sample of 263 images. The sociologist Christine Nippert-Eng also interviewed individuals living in urban environments about how they think about and navigate privacy in densely populated areas. More than 88 percent of the Privacy Illustrated images conceptualized privacy in terms of walls, curtains, separation, and hiding. And many of those and other images pictured showering, nudity, and sexual behaviors to indicate that privacy was bound up with intimacy. Nevertheless, autonomy and choice figured in many of them.

Some participants noted that privacy was about "get[ting] to choose" what they disclose or share. More than half of Nippert-Eng's interviewees defined privacy as either the "ability/power to control access to some thing, place, or piece of information and its dissemination" or "the freedom to make do/live/make decisions," both of which are based on choice. One of those interviewees, who had formerly lived in the southern United States during segregation, talked about how the government's constant surveillance of persons of color imposed restrictions on the choices she made. Another interviewee noted that "privacy is being able to decide what you want to share with the world." And one Privacy Illustrated image showed an individual controlling levers that could pick information to share out of different buckets. Others drew wallets or purses and noted that privacy is the right to control or choose what things in one's wallet to share with others. Oates, Maggie et al. 2018. "Turtles, Locks, and Bathrooms: Understanding Mental Models of Privacy through Illustration." *Proceedings on Privacy Enhancing Technology* 2018(4): 5–32; Nippert-Eng, Christena E. 2010. *Islands of Privacy*. Chicago, IL: University of Chicago Press.

"vague" or in "disarray." Solove, Daniel. 2008. *Understanding Privacy*. Cambridge, MA: Harvard University Press (p. 1).

"retain[] the power" and are "entitled to decide" ... "secures to each individual the right of determining, ordinarily, to what extent his thoughts, sentiments, and emotions shall be communicated to others." Warren and Brandeis, "The Right to Privacy," pp. 196, 198.

"claim of individuals ... to determine for themselves when, how, and to what extent." Westin, Alan. 1967. *Privacy and Freedom*. New York: Ig Publishing (p. 7).

12 **"whether, when, and with whom."** Cohen, Jean. 2001. "The Necessity of Privacy." *Social Research* 68: 318–327 (p. 319).

"having control" ... "decisions about ... access." Inness, Julie. 1992. *Privacy, Intimacy, and Isolation*. New York: Oxford University Press (p. 56).

"control" over information. Zittrrain, Jonathan. 2000. "What the Publisher Can Teach the Patient: Intellectual Property and Privacy in an Era of Trusted Privication." *Stanford Law Review* 52(5): 1201–1250 (p. 1203).

"even between friends the restraints of privacy apply." Fried, Charles. 1968. "Privacy." *Yale Law Journal* 77: 475–493 (p. 484).

"control" and "manage" the boundary. Matthews, Steve. 2010. "Anonymity and the Social Self." *American Philosophical Quarterly* 47 (4): 351–363 (p. 351).

13 **"being protected" from surveillance.** Bok, Sissela. 1983. *Secrets: On the Ethics of Concealment and Revelation*. New York: Vintage.
"secluded" and "separated." Shils, Edward. 1966. "Privacy: Its Constitution and Vicissitudes." *Law and Contemporary Problems*. 31 (2):281–306 (p. 283).
"shields" or protected "spheres." Rosen, Jeffrey. 2001. "Out of Context: The Purposes of Privacy." *Social Research* 68: 209–220 (p. 211).
"sexual privacy." Citron, Danielle K. 2019. "Sexual Privacy." *Yale Law Journal* 128: 1870–1960.
develop new ideas "separate and apart from." Richards, Neil. 2015. *Intellectual Privacy: Rethinking Civil Liberties in the Digital Age*. New York, NY: Oxford University Press.
"obscurity." Selinger, Evan and Woodrow Hartzog. 2016. "Surveillance as a Loss of Obscurity." *Washington and Lee Law Review* 72(3): 1343–1387.
"obfuscation." Brunton, Finn and Helen Nissenbaum. 2015. *Obfuscation: A User's Guide for Privacy and Protest*. Cambridge, MA: The MIT Press.
privacy is a facet of social life that gives people the confidence and moral space to share information with others. Waldman, Ari Ezra. 2018. *Privacy as Trust: Information Privacy for an Information Age*. New York: Cambridge University Press; Richards, Neil and Woodrow Hartzog. 2016. "Taking Trust Seriously in Privacy Law." *Stanford Technology Law Review* 19(3): 431–472.
eschewing definitions that reduce privacy to a single common denominator. Solove, "Conceptualizing Privacy"; Solove, Daniel J. 2008. *Understanding Privacy*. Cambridge, MA: Harvard University Press.
Feminist scholars. MacKinnon, Catharine. 1989. *Toward a Feminist Theory of the State*. Cambridge, MA: Harvard University Press; Allen, Anita. 2011. *Unpopular Privacy: What Must We Hide?* New York, NY: Oxford University Press.
social theorists. Cohen, Julie. 2013. "What Privacy Is For." *Harvard Law Review* 126: 1904–1933; Post, Robert. 1989. "The Social Foundations of Privacy: Community and Self in the Common Law Tort." *California Law Review* 77: 957–1010.

14 **right to access, correct, and have companies delete our information.** These and other rights of control are among the centerpieces of the latest laws and proposals for comprehensive privacy legislation. Regulation (EU) 2016/679 General Data Protection Regulation, 2016 O.J. (L119); International Association of Privacy Professionals. n/d. State

Comprehensive Privacy Law Comparisons: Bills Introduced 2018–2020, https://iapp.org/media/pdf/resource_center/State_Comp_Privacy_Law.pdf.

"involves the various decisions people must make about their privacy." Solove, Daniel J. 2021. "The Myth of the Privacy Paradox." *George Washington Law Review* 89.

"privacy work." Marwick, Alice. n/d. *Privacy Work: The Labor of Protecting Information in a Networked Age*. Forthcoming.

15 **foundation of notice-and-consent.** Notice in privacy law is premised on the idea that full information helps us make informed decisions. Indeed, that premise was at the foundation of the Fair Information Practice Principles (FIPPs), a list of data protection ideals that the United States Department of Housing, Education, and Welfare (HEW) thought should guide data collection and use. US Department of Health, Education, and Welfare. 1973. *Records, Computers, and the Rights of Citizens: Report of the Secretary's Advisory Committee on Automated Personal Data Systems*. Electronic Privacy Information Center, www.epic.org/privacy/hew1973report/. Several years later, the Organization for Economic Cooperation and Development issued similar guidelines, requiring, for example, that data gatherers disclose the purpose and scope of data collection. Organisation for Economic Co-operation and Development. 2001. *OCED Guidelines on the Protection of Privacy and Transborder Flows of Personal Data*. OCED, www.oecd.org/internet/ieconomy/oecdguidelinesontheprotectionofprivacyandtransborderflowsofpersonaldata.htm#top. The FTC joined the chorus in 2000, urging Congress to require commercial websites to provide "notice of their information practices, including what information they collect, how they collect it (e.g., directly or through nonobvious means such as cookies), how they use it, . . . whether they disclose the information collected to other entities, and whether other entities are collecting information through the site." Brill, Julie. 2010. "Privacy 3.0 Panel." Presented at the Conference of Western Attorneys General Meeting, Santa Fe, NM, July 20.

still prominent today. The FTC's privacy jurisprudence over the last two decades has focused on notice, relying on its authority to police "unfair or deceptive acts or practices in or affecting commerce" to investigate companies that lie on their privacy policies. In like In re Eli Lilly & Co., where the company sent out an email to nearly 700 people disclosing personal information about visitors to the website, Prozac.com, or In re Toysmart.com, where the company wanted to sell its customer data to pay off creditors, the FTC settled its claims by, in large part, mandating better notices. In these and many other cases, the FTC said that false

statements in privacy notices made it impossible for individuals to know what would really happen with their data, thus creating information gaps and asymmetries that influenced user choices. In re Eli Lilly & Co., 133 F.T.C. 763 (2002); First Amended Complaint for Permanent Injunction and Other Equitable Relief, FTC v. Toysmart.com, LLC, F.T.C. No. 00–11341-RGS; Complaint for Permanent Injunction and Other Equitable Relief, FTC v. Frostwire, LLC. F.T.C. File No. 1:11-cv-23643 (p. 19); In re Sony BMG Music Entertainment. F.T.C. File No. 062 3019, No. C4195. In 2012, the FTC published what it called a "new" framework for protecting privacy, but nevertheless premised the entire project on "mak[ing] information collection and use practices transparent" so people can "make decisions about their data at a relevant time and context." Federal Trade Commission. 2012. "Protecting Consumer Privacy in an Era of Rapid Change," www.ftc.gov/sites/default/files/documents/reports/federal-trade-commission-report-protecting-consumer-privacy-era-rapid-change-recommendations/120326privacyreport.pdf. The Obama administration's privacy "bill of rights" released that same year called for data use notices to be "presented at times and in ways that enable consumers to make meaningful decisions about personal data collection, use, and disclosure" in order to provide individuals with "clear and simple choices." The White House. 2012. *Consumer Data Privacy in a Networked World: A Framework for Protecting Privacy and Promoting Innovation in the Global Economy*. Washington, DC (p. 47).

information we need to make informed decisions. That isn't unique to privacy. Notice of an activity's dangers helps us decide if we want to step onto a rollercoaster, have surgery, skydive out of a plane, place our belongings in a gym locker, or opt for safer, less risky options. Murphy v. Steeplechase Amusement Co., 166 N.E. 173 (N.Y. 1929). When we are aware of those dangers and voluntarily engage in risky behavior, we assume those risks for the purposes of civil liability and may be responsible for at least some of the injuries we incur. Consider also the void for vagueness doctrine. As the Supreme Court has stated several times, statutes cannot be so broad, unclear, and fuzzy that they "fail[] to give a person of ordinary intelligence fair notice" about what constitutes legal or illegal conduct. By declaring such laws unconstitutional, the doctrine implicitly recognizes that notice helps us make informed decisions. Kolender v. Lawson, 461 U.S. 352 (1983) (p. 357).

244 hours. McDonald, Aleecia M. and Lorrie F. Cranor. 2008. "The Cost of Reading Privacy Policies." *I/S: A Journal of Law and Policy for the Information Society* 4(3): 543–568.

even experts. Reidenberg, Joel R. 2014. "Disagreeable Privacy Policies: Mismatches between Meaning and Users' Understanding." *Berkeley Technology Law Journal* 30(1): 39–88.

"lengthy and growing terms of service and privacy." Hoofnagle, Chris J. and Jan Whittington. 2014. "Free: Accounting for the Internet's Most Popular Price." *UCLA Law Review* 61(606): 608–670 (pp. 640–641),

16 **it doesn't scale.** Solove, Daniel J. 2013. "Privacy Self-Management and the Consent Dilemma." *Harvard Law Review* 126(7): 1880–1903; Richards, Neil and Woodrow Hartzog. 2019. "The Pathologies of Digital Consent." *Washington University Law Review* 96: 1461–1503.

17 **Westin's three categories of consumers.** US House of Representatives, Subcommittee on Commerce, Trade, and Consumer Protection of the House Committee on Energy and Commerce. 2001. *Opinion Surveys: What Consumers Have to Say About Information Privacy.* 107th Cong., 1st sess. H. Hearing Record (prepared statement of Alan F. Westin).

Posner's economic analysis. Posner, Richard. 1978. "The Right of Privacy." *Georgia Law Review* 12(3): 393–422.

bedrock assumption among policy makers as well. Policy makers, lawyers, and regulators presume rational privacy decision-making whenever they suggest that the purpose of more detailed, more conspicuous, and more accurate notices is to help people make better choices. For example, in its report, *Protecting Consumer Privacy in an Era of Rapid Change*, the FTC stated that "privacy statements should contain some standardized elements, such as format and terminology, to allow consumers to compare the privacy practices of different companies" (p. 62). Companies promise to be more transparent so we can engage more deeply and discern what we want to see from what may be misleading us. Zuckerberg, Mark. 2017. "When Someone Buys Political Ads on TV or Other Media, They're Required by Law to Disclose Who Paid for Them. Now We're Bringing Facebook to an Even Higher Standard of Transparency." Facebook, October 27, 2017, www.facebook.com/zuck/posts/10104133053040371. And during Facebook CEO Mark Zuckerberg's testimony before the US Senate in 2018, Iowa Senator Chuck Grassley stated that "consumers must have the transparency necessary to make an informed decision about whether to share their data and how it can be used" and explicitly linked transparency, understanding, and decision-making. US Senate, Committee on Commerce, Science, and Transportation. 2018. *Facebook, Social Media Privacy, and the Use and Abuse of Data.* 115th Cong., 2d sess. S. Hearing Record (oral statement of Senator Grassley).

18 **mental shortcuts and cognitive biases dominate our decision-making processes.** Kahneman, Daniel. 2011. *Thinking, Fast and Slow.*

New York, NY: Farrar, Straus, and Giroux; Kahneman, Daniel, and Amos Tversky. 1982. "Judgments of and By Representativeness." In *Judgment under Uncertainty: Heuristics and Biases* (pp. 84–98). Edited by Daniel Kahneman, Paul Slovic and Amos Tversky. New York: Cambridge University Press; Kahneman, Daniel and Amos Tversky. 1974. "Judgment under Uncertainty: Heuristics and Biases." *Science* 185(4157): 1124–1131.

"choice architecture." Thaler, Richard H. and Cass R. Sunstein. 2008. *Nudge: Improving Decisions about Health, Wealth, and Happiness.* New Haven, CT: Yale University Press.

rely on comparative judgments when making disclosure decisions. Acquisiti, Alessandro, et al. 2012. "The Impact of Relative Standards on the Propensity to Disclose." *Journal of Marketing Research* 49(2): 160–174.

willing to disclose bad behavior on websites that have an unprofessional aesthetic. John, Leslie K. et al. 2011. "Strangers on a Plane: Context-Dependent Willingness to Divulge Sensitive Information." *Journal of Consumer Research* 37(5): 858–873.

our subjective assessment of privacy's importance. Waldman, Ari E. and James A. Mourey. 2020. "Past the Privacy Paradox: The Important of Privacy Changes as a Function of Control and Complexity." *Journal of the Association of Consumer Research* 5(2): 162–180.

"study after study ... choices they're presented." Oremus, Will. 2019. "How Much Is Your Privacy Really Worth? No One Knows. And It Might Be Time to Stop Asking." https://onezero.medium.com/how-much-is-your-privacy-really-worth-421796dd9220.

19 **"the design of the system rigs it in favor of the interests of the company and against the interests of users."** Vaidhyanathan, Siva. 2011. *The Googlization of Everything (and Why We Should Worry).* Berkley and Los Angeles, California: University of California Press (p. 83).

20 **feel resigned to failure.** Marwick, Alice and Eszter Hargittai. 2018. "Nothing to Hide, Nothing to Lose? Incentives and Disincentives to Sharing Information with Institutions Online." *Information, Communication & Society* 22(12): 1697–1713; Hargittai, Eszter and Alice Marwick. 2016. "What Can I Really Do? Explaining the Privacy Paradox with Online Apathy." *International Journal of Communication* 10: 3737–3757.

users feel powerless and helpless. Hoffman, Christian, Cristoph Lutz, and Giulia Ranzini. 2016. "Privacy Cynicism: A New Approach to the Privacy Paradox." *Cyberpsychology: Journal of Psychosocial Research on Cyberspace* 10(4): 7, http://dx.doi.org/10.5817/CP2016-4-7.

"digital resignation." Draper, Nora and Joseph Turow. 2019. "The Corporate Cultivation of Digital Resignation." *New Media & Society* 21(8): 1824–1839.

"managing one's privacy is a vast." Solove, "Myth of the Privacy Paradox."

21 **consent to medical procedures only after full disclosure.** Murray, Brian. 2012. "Informed Consent: What Must a Physician Disclose to a Patient?" *AMA Journal of Ethics* 14(7): 563–566.

law of sexual assault gives us the power to consent. State in Interest of M.T.S., 609 A.2d 1266 (N.J. 1992); United States v. Riley, 183 F.3d 1155 (9th Cir. 1999); United States v. Johnson, 743 F.3d 196 (7th Cir. 2014).

22 **don't read privacy policies.** Milne and Culnan, "Strategies for Reducing Online Privacy Risks."

Nor do we have the cognitive ability to process. Waldman, Ari Ezra. 2019. "Cognitive Biases, Dark Patterns, and the 'Privacy Paradox.'" *Current Opinion in Psychology* 31: 105–109.

Studies by Joe Turow and several colleagues demonstrate. Turow, Joseph et al. 2015. "The Tradeoff Fallacy: How Marketers Are Misrepresenting American Consumers and Opening Them Up to Exploitation." *A Report from the Annenberg Public Policy Center of the University of Pennsylvania*, www.asc.upenn.edu/sites/default/files/TradeoffFallacy_1.pdf; Turow, Joseph et al. 2005. "Open to Exploitation: America's Shoppers Online and Offline." *A Report from the Annenberg Public Policy Center of the University of Pennsylvania*, https://repository.upenn.edu/cgi/viewcontent.cgi?article=1035&context=asc_papers.

23 **emotional manipulation studies in 2014.** Flick, Catherine. 2015. "Informed Consent and the Facebook Emotional Manipulation Study." *Research Ethics* 12(1): 14–28; Talbot, David. 2014. "Facebook's Emotional Manipulation Study Is Just the Latest Effort to Prod Users." *MIT Technology Review*, www.technologyreview.com/2014/07/01/172175/facebooks-emotional-manipulation-study-is-just-the-latest-effort-to-prod-users/.

"users who liked the 'Hello Kitty' brand tended to." Kramer, Adam D. I. et al. 2014. "Experimental Evidence of Massive-Scale Emotional Contagion through Social Networks." *Proceedings of the National Academy of Sciences of the United States of America.* 111(24), 8788–8790.

24 **"take[s] refuge in consent" … "consent legitimizes."** Solove, "Privacy Self-Management," p. 1880.

"we can feel so overwhelmed by the thousands of requests for access." Hartzog, *Privacy's Blueprint*, p. 208.

"predicated on the philosophy." Reidenberg, Joel R. 1999. "Restoring Americans' Privacy in Electronic Commerce." *Berkeley Technology Law Journal* 14: 771–792 (p. 774).

25 **surveillance-innovation complex.** Cohen, *Between Truth and Power*, pp. 89, 96–97, 102–104.

26 **"there is no privacy interest" … "negated any reasonable expectation of privacy."** In re Facebook, Inc. Consumer Privacy User Profile Litigation, No. 18-MD-02843, May 29, 2019. Transcript of Proceedings (p. 7).
"users were told" … "to share it with the world." Ibid. p. 12.
"Facebook does not consider that to be actionable." Ibid. p. 15.
"can control how." Reply in Support of Defendant Facebook, Inc. to Dismiss Plaintiffs' First Amended Consolidated Complaint, In re Facebook, Inc. Consumer Privacy User Profile Litigation, 402 F. Supp 767 (N.D. Cal. 2019).

27 **"consented to the uses of … data."** Campbell v. St. John, No. 17–16873, 4:13-cv-05996-PJH (9th Cir. 2020) (p. 21 n. 9), https://epic.org/amicus/class-action/facebook-campbell/Campbell-v-Facebook-9th-Cir-Opinion.pdf.
"are bound by their consent to those policies." Appellee's Brief, Smith v. Facebook, Inc., No. 17–16206 (9th Cir. 2017) (p. 21), https://epic.org/amicus/facebook/smith/Smith-v-Facebook-9th-Cir-Facebook-Brief.pdf.
"provided their consent to Google … when they sent a GET request … so they could browse websites containing Google ads." Answering Brief of Defendant-Appellee Google Inc., In re Google Inc. Cookie Placement Consumer Privacy Litigation, No. 13–4300, 2014 WL 1413954 (3rd Cir. Apr. 7, 2014) (pp. 36–37).

28 **"plaintiffs knew exactly what data Facebook was collecting, for what purpose, and how to opt out of Tag Suggestions."** Appellant's Brief, Patel v. Facebook, 932 F.3d 1264 (9th Cir. 2019).
users consented to all data collection practices when they signed up for accounts. Facebook, Inc.'s Motion for Summary Judgment, In re Facebook Biometric Information Privacy Litigation, 185 F. Supp. 1115 (N.D. Cal. 2016).
"take steps to keep their browsing histories private." Appellee's Brief, In re Facebook, Inc. Internet Tracking Litigation, 956 F.3d 589 (9th Cir. 2020).

29 **"promise[] to not record the communication."** Defendant Facebook, Inc.'s Reply in Support of Motion to Dismiss Plaintiffs' Second Amendment Consolidated Complaint, In re Facebook, Inc. Internet Tracking Litigation, 263 F. Supp 836 (N.D. Cal. 2017).
"voluntarily disclosed." Defendant Facebook, Inc.'s Motion to Dismiss Plaintiffs' Second Amended Consolidated Complaint, In re Facebook, Inc. Internet Tracking Litigation, 263 F. Supp 836 (N.D. Cal. 2017).

30 **hundreds of motions to dismiss and motions for summary judgment on privacy-related claims.** This is based on Westlaw searches for trial documents as follows: [DT(dismiss! /10 microsoft google apple amazon apple) & TI(microsoft google apple amazon facebook /7 defendant) & consent & privacy data] and [DT(summary +3 judgment) /10 microsoft google apple amazon apple) & TI(microsoft google apple amazon facebook /7 defendant) & consent & privacy data]. This is an imperfect way to search for these arguments, particularly because only a small percentage of trial documents are published on Westlaw.

31 **operating under Federal Trade Commission consent decrees.** In re Google, Inc., FTC File No. 102 3136, No. C-4336 (F.T.C. Oct. 13, 2011), www.ftc.gov/sites/default/files/documents/cases/2011/10/111024googlebuzzdo.pdf; Quinn, Michelle and Tony Romm. 2012. "Google Tells FTC of Privacy Progress." *Politico*, www.politico.com/story/2012/02/google-tells-ftc-of-progress-on-privacy-072731.

compliant with the GDPR. n/d. "Facebook's Commitment to Data Protection and Privacy in Compliance with the GDPR." *Facebook Business*, www.facebook.com/business/news/facebooks-commitment-to-data-protection-and-privacy-in-compliance-with-the-gdpr.

the only way Facebook users could expect privacy. Appellee's Brief, In re Facebook, Inc. Internet Tracking Litigation, 956 F.3d 589 (9th Cir. 2020).

32 **"privacy paradox."** In a now-famous study from 2007, however, Patricia Norberg and her colleagues found that people assert strong interest in privacy while simultaneously disclosing substantial personal information for meager rewards. They gave this inconsistency a name: the "privacy paradox." Norberg, Patricia A. et al. 2007. "The Privacy Paradox: Personal Information Disclosure Intentions versus Behavior." *Journal of Consumer Affairs* 41(1): 100–126. Although this seemed to challenge the rational disclosure model – our disclosure choices didn't match our stated preferences – it is wholly consistent with the logic of self-governance. For one, people could be lying. That is, although people tell researchers they care about their privacy because it seems like the right thing to do or what the researchers want to hear, most would rather sacrifice their privacy for discounts, convenience, efficiency, fun, or any number of other benefits. Holdbrook, Allyson L., Melanie C. Green, and Jon A. Krosnick. "Telephone versus Face-to-Face Interviewing of National Probability Samples With Long Questionnaires." *Public Opinion Quarterly* 67: 79–125 (pp. 86–87). Therefore, the privacy paradox suggests we are acting rationally when we disclose information online, and just fibbing about our preferences when asked. Computer science researchers Bernardo Huberman, Eytan Adar, and Leslie Fine have also argued in favor of the rational model

behind the privacy paradox. They studied the relationship between disclosure and rewards and found that individuals demand a greater price for disclosing stigmatized, less desirable, or embarrassing data, but are quite willing to disclose information they perceive as harmless or innocuous for little to no rewards. The positive correlation between information intimacy and reward demand suggests that people are thinking about the pros and cons of disclosure. Huberman, Bernardo A. 2005. "Valuating Privacy." *IEEE Security & Privacy* 3(5): 22–25.
social desirability bias. The literature on social desirability bias is enormous. For one example, please see the following: DeMaio, Theresa J. 1984. "Social Desirability and Survey Measurement: A Review." In *Surveying Subjective Phenomena*. Edited by Charles F. Turner and Elizabeth Martin, pp. 257–282. New York: Russell Sage Foundation.

33 **industry-backed policy recommendations.** US Senate Committee on Commerce, Science, and Transportation, Subcommittee on Consumer Protection, Product Safety, Insurance, and Data Security. 2019. *Small Business Perspectives on a Federal Data Privacy Framework*. 116th Cong. S. Hearing Record (38:37) (oral testimony of Ryan Weber, President, KC Tech Council).
the company paid teenagers to install a VPN that spied on them. Constine, Josh. 2019. "Facebook Pays Teens to Install VPN That Spies on Them." *TechCrunch*, https://techcrunch.com/2019/01/29/facebook-project-atlas/.

34 **"new oil" ... "convenience over security."** Reid, David. 2017. "Mastercard's Boss Just Told a Saudi Audience That 'Data Is the New Oil.'" *CNBC*, www.cnbc.com/2017/10/24/mastercard-boss-just-said-data-is-the-new-oil.html.
"can improve our lives." Bhageshpur, Kiran. 2019. "Data Is the New Oil – and That's a Good Thing." *Forbes*, www.forbes.com/sites/forbestechcouncil/2019/11/15/data-is-the-new-oil-and-thats-a-good-thing/#3cd0a5fc7304.

35 **sectoral approach to privacy.** Schwartz, Paul M. 2009. "Preemption and Privacy." *Yale Law Journal* 118: 902–947 (pp. 904–905).
opposed state privacy laws. New York Senate Standing Committee on Consumer Protection and Standing Committee on Internet and Technology. 2019. *Joint Public Hearing: To Conduct Discussion on Online Privacy and What Role the State Legislature Should Play in Overseeing It*, www.nysenate.gov/calendar/public-hearings/june-04-2019/joint-public-hearing-conduct-discussion-online-privacy-and.
federal law that boils down to more transparency. Setting an American Framework to Ensure Data Access, Transparency, and Accountability Act. S. ___, 116th Cong. 2nd sess., www.commerce.senate.gov/services/files/BD190421-F67C-4E37-A25E-5D522B1053C7.

data rights, but no enforcement. US Senate, Committee on Commerce, Science, and Transportation. 2019. *Policy Principles for a Federal Data Privacy Framework in the United States.* 116th Cong., 2d sess. S. Hearing Record (statement of Jon Leibowitz).

privacy a fundamental right, but have proposed transparency as the way to protect it. Committee on Commerce, Science, and Transportation. 2018. *Examining Safeguards for Consumer Data Privacy.* 115th Cong. (written testimony of Damien Kieran, Global Data Protection Officer and Associate Legal Director, Twitter, Inc.).

cable industry has said it's different ... but wants to be governed by the same notice-and-consent regime. Committee on Commerce, Science, and Transportation. 2016. *How Will the FCC's Proposed Privacy Regulations Affect Consumers and Competition.* 114th Cong. (written testimony of Dean Garfield, President & CEO, Information Technology Industry Council).

36 **begin with freedom and end with law as antithetical to that freedom.** Cohen, *Between Truth and Power*, pp. 89–92.

37 **innovation is always a normative good.** Ibid. pp. 91–93.

"acquisitions directly facilitate innovation ... [that] yield improvements in features and services of users." US House, Subcommittee on Antitrust, Commercial, and Administrative Law of the Committee on the Judiciary. 2019. *Online Platforms and Market Power Part 2: Innovation and Entrepreneurship.* 116th Cong. 1st sess. (written testimony of Matt Perault).

38 **"right regulation."** Ng, Alfred. 2018. "US Privacy Law is on the Horizon. Here's How Tech Companies Want to Shape It." *CNet*, www.cnet.com/news/us-privacy-law-is-on-the-horizon-heres-how-tech-companies-want-to-shape-it/.

"still allow[s] companies to innovate and develop." Ibid.

"greatest free-market success story in history" ... "return to light-touch regulatory framework." Pai, Ajit. 2017. "The Future of Internet Freedom." Accessed at https://transition.fcc.gov/Daily_Releases/Daily_Business/2017/db0427/DOC-344590A1.pdf.

"impose significant burdens on consumers." US Senate, Committee on Commerce, Science, and Transportation. 2019. *Policy Principles for a Federal Data Privacy Framework in the United States.* 116th Cong. 1st sess. (written testimony of Randall Rothenberg, CEO of the Interactive Advertising Bureau).

39 **"information-sharing significantly enhances economic productivity" and benefits "nonprofit organizations" and "small businesses."** US Senate, Committee on Commerce, Science, and Transportation. 2013. *What Information Do Data Brokers Have on Consumers, and How Do They*

Use It? 113th Cong., 1st sess. S. Hearing Transcript (oral statement of Anthony Hadley, Senior Vice President for Regulatory and Government Affairs, Experian).

"675,000 jobs" and "helps small business" so they "can come in and compete with the big boys." Ibid. (oral statement of Jerry Cerasale, Senior Vice President for Government Affairs, Direct Marketing Association).

"efficiencies" and "resources." US House, Subcommittee on Antitrust, Commercial, and Administrative Law of the Committee on the Judiciary. 2019. *Online Platforms and Market Power Part 2: Innovation and Entrepreneurship*. 116th Cong. 1st sess. (written testimony of Matt Perault).

40 **It sets up a binary choice where no such choice actually exists.** Richards, Neil. 2021. *What Privacy Means*. New York: Oxford University Press.

there is no evidence that privacy law actually stifles innovation. Cohen, Julie E. 2019. "Turning Privacy Inside Out." *Theoretical Inquiries in Law* 20: 1–31 (pp. 29–30); Cohen, "What Privacy Is For," pp. 1919–1920; Strandburg, Katherine J. and Yafit Lev-Aretz. 2020. "Better Together: Privacy Regulation and Innovation Policy."

41 **"thousands of data points" in "intimate profiles of American consumers" ... "right to see these pictures of ourselves."** US Senate, Committee on Commerce, Science, and Transportation. 2013. *What Information Do Data Brokers Have on Consumers, and How Do They Use It?* 113th Cong., 1st sess. S. Hearing Transcript (oral statement of Rockefeller IV, John D.).

"privacy implications" of the data broker industry as "whether consumers are aware ... transparency." US Senate, Committee on Commerce, Science, and Transportation. 2013. *What Information Do Data Brokers Have on Consumers, and How Do They Use It?* 113th Cong., 1st sess. S. Hearing Transcript (oral statement of John Thune).

"transparency," which "allows consumers to make informed decisions about the products and the services that the use." US Senate, Committee on Commerce, Science, and Transportation. 2019. *Policy Principles for a Federal Data Privacy Framework in the United States*. 116th Cong., 1st sess. S. Hearing Record (statement of John Thune).

"transparency" and "access" to data and protecting "sensitive consumer report information." US Senate, Committee on Commerce, Science, and Transportation. 2010. *Protecting Youths in an Online World*. 111th Cong., 2d sess. S. Hearing Record (oral statement of Jessica Rich).

Ron Johnson focused entirely on transparency. US Senate, Committee on Commerce, Science, and Transportation. 2013. *What Information*

Do Data Brokers Have on Consumers, and How Do They Use It? 113th Cong., 1st sess. S. Hearing Transcript (oral statement of Ron Johnson).

42 **privacy law should include some "affirmative obligation ... not to harm you."** US Senate, Committee on Commerce, Science, and Transportation. 2019. *Policy Principles for a Federal Data Privacy Framework in the United States.* 116th Cong., 2d sess. S. Hearing Record (oral statement of Brian Schatz).

asked about rights of access, correction, and deletion. US Senate, Committee on Commerce, Science, and Transportation. 2019. *Policy Principles for a Federal Data Privacy Framework in the United States.* 116th Cong., 2d sess. S. Hearing Record (oral statement of Edward Markey).

inappropriate data transfers and use can also constitute privacy violations. US Senate, Committee on Commerce, Science, and Transportation. 2019. *Policy Principles for a Federal Data Privacy Framework in the United States.* 116th Cong., 2d sess. S. Hearing Record (oral statement of Maria Cantwell).

"tracking devices" ... "simply want[ing] to choose how that information is used or shared." US Senate, Subcommittee on Consumer Protection, Product Safety, Insurance, and Data Security of the Committee on Commerce, Science, and Transportation. 2019. *Small Business Perspectives on a Federal Data Privacy Framework.* 116th Cong., 2d sess. S. Hearing Record (oral statement of Richard Blumenthal).

"knowledge, notice, and 'no.'" US Senate, Committee on Commerce, Science, and Transportation. 2018. *Consumer Data Privacy: Examining Lessons from the European Union's General Data Protection Regulation and the California Consumer Privacy Act.* 115th Cong., 2d sess. S. Hearing Record (oral statement of Edward Markey).

whether "Google's dashboard disclose[s]." US Senate, Committee on Commerce, Science, and Transportation. 2018. *Examining Safeguards for Consumer Data Privacy.* 115th Cong., 2d sess. S. Hearing Record (oral statement of Gary Peters).

43 **telecommunications industry-funded 21st Century Privacy Coalition.** Sasso, Brendan. 2015. "The 'Privacy Coalition' That Wants to Trim Data Regulation for Telecom Giants." *The Atlantic*, www.theatlantic.com/politics/archive/2015/05/the-privacy-coalition-that-wants-to-trim-data-regulations-for-telecom-giants/456477/; Bechman, Katy. 2013. "Telecom Firms Form Privacy Coalition." *AdWeek*, www.adweek.com/digital/telecom-firms-form-privacy-coalition-150783/; Steinbach, David. 2013. "New Privacy Coalition Cashes In on Relationships." *OpenSecrets.org*, www.opensecrets.org/news/2013/06/new-privacy-coalition-cashes-in-on-relationships/.

"framework" for a federal privacy law should ... provide "greater transparency." US Senate, Committee on Commerce, Science, and Transportation. 2019. *Policy Principles for a Federal Data Privacy Framework in the United States.* 116th Cong., 2d sess. S. Hearing Record, at 45:00 (oral testimony of Jon Leibowitz).

"transparency," giving consumers "statutory rights ... for obtaining meaningful consent." US Senate, Committee on Commerce, Science, and Transportation. 2019. *Policy Principles for a Federal Data Privacy Framework in the United States.* 116th Cong., 2d sess. S. Hearing Record (written testimony of Jon Leibowitz, p. 4); ibid. (oral statement of Jon Leibowitz).

Big Tech-funded Internet Association. Internet Association. n.d. https://internetassociation.org/our-members/.

"people should have access and control of their data." US Senate, Committee on Commerce, Science, and Transportation. 2019. *Policy Principles for a Federal Data Privacy Framework in the United States.* 116th Cong., 2d sess. S. Hearing Record, at 47:55 (2019) (oral testimony of Michael Beckerman).

"empower people to better understand and control ... personal information." US Senate, Committee on Commerce, Science, and Transportation. 2019. *Policy Principles for a Federal Data Privacy Framework in the United States.* 116th Cong., 2d sess. S. Hearing Record (written testimony of Michael Beckerman, p. 1).

made similar comments. US Senate, Committee on Commerce, Science, and Transportation. 2018. *Examining Safeguards for Consumer Data Privacy.* 115th Cong. at 55:53 (2018) (oral statement of Bud Tribble); ibid. at 1:00:07 (oral statement of Rachel Welch).

44 **"users a choice of either consuming [content] as a subscription service or using it with ads."** US House, Subcommittee on Antitrust, Commercial, and Administrative Law. 2020. *Online Platforms and Market Power Part 6: Examining the Dominance of Amazon, Apple, Facebook, and Google.* 116th Cong. 2nd sess. (oral statement of Sundar Pinchai, CEO of Alphabet, Inc, at 4:45:50.).

"putting you in control." Ibid. at 37:58 (oral statement of Sundar Pinchai).

"to protect user privacy and give people more control." Ibid. (written testimony of Mark Zuckerberg).

lobbying group funded by Google but claims to be a voice for entrepreneurs. Dayen, David. 2018. "An Advocacy Group for Startups Is Funded by Google and Run by Ex-Googlers." *The Intercept*, https://theintercept.com/2018/05/30/google-engine-advocacy-tech-startups/.

"robust" federal privacy law that "provide[s] transparency and user choice." US Senate, Subcommittee on Consumer Protection, Product

Safety, Insurance, and Data Security of the Committee on Commerce, Science, and Transportation. 2019. *Small Business Perspectives on a Federal Data Privacy Framework*. 116th Cong. 1st sess. (oral testimony of Evan Engstrom, Executive Director of the Engine Advocacy and Research Foundation, at 39:49).

"transparency and consumer choice." Ibid. (oral testimony of Nin Dosanjh, Vice Chair, Technology Policy Committee, National Association of Realtors, at 51:28).

"transparency, control, portability, and security." US Senate, Committee on Commerce, Science, and Transportation. 2018. *Examining Safeguards for Consumer Data Privacy*. 115th Cong. 2nd sess. (oral testimony of Keith Enright).

"should be transparent about, and provide meaningful control." Ibid. (oral testimony of Damien Kieran, Global Data Protection Officer and Associate General Counsel, Twitter, Inc., at 50:45).

45 **defined privacy as "personal control."** Bracy, Jedidiah. 2016. "Public or Private, Celebrities Deserve Control over Their Data, Too." International Association of Privacy Professionals, https://iapp.org/news/a/setting-the-privacy-controls-to-the-heart-of-the-sun/.

"give users more choice about what is collected at all." Therier, Adam. 2015. "CES 2015 Dispatch: Challenges Multiply for Privacy Professionals, Part One." *Privacy Perspectives*, https://iapp.org/news/a/ces-2015-dispatch-challenges-multiply-for-privacy-professionals-part-one/.

46 **framed recommendations around greater choice.** Gray, Stacey. 2016. "How Industry Can Protect Privacy in the Age of Connected Toys." International Association of Privacy Professionals, https://iapp.org/news/a/how-industry-can-protect-privacy-in-the-age-of-connected-toys/.

privacy problems accompanying a WiFi-enabled pacemaker were framed as a lack of choice. Bracy, Jedidiah. 2017. "This Pacemaker Just Incriminated Its Owner." International Association of Privacy Professionals, https://iapp.org/news/a/this-pacemaker-just-incriminated-its-owner/.

defined privacy as providing better notice and choice. Wollen, Chad. 2018. "Opt In, Opt Out – Consent Is What It's All About." International Association of Privacy Professionals, https://iapp.org/news/a/opt-in-opt-out-consent-is-what-its-all-about/.

they talk about trust and power and limitations on data use. Bamberger and Mulligan, *Privacy on the Ground*, pp. 66–68.

"all the information required" and the "choice" to use tools. Kochman, Ben. 2019. "Uber's First Privacy Chief Says She's Looking beyond GDPR." *Law360*, www.law360.com/articles/1121989/uber-s-first-privacy-chief-says-she-s-looking-beyond-gdpr.

"enabling broad participation in privacy self-management" … "are benefited." McCullough, Michael. 2020. "'Trust Arks:' Preparing for the Adtech Privacy Storm." *Privacy Perspectives*, https://iapp.org/news/a/trust-arks-preparing-for-the-adtech-privacy-storm/.

47 **"presenting to customers updated terms."** Hengesbaugh, Brian. 2020. "What Privacy Shield Organizations Should Do in the Wake of 'Schrems II.'" *The Privacy Adviser*, https://iapp.org/news/a/what-privacy-shield-organizations-should-do-in-the-wake-of-schrems-ii/.

"due diligence." Gaudino, Francesca and Michael Egan. 2020. "What 'Schrems II' Means for Controller-to-Processor SCCs." *The Privacy Adviser*, https://iapp.org/news/a/c2p-sccs-are-still-valid-but/.

encourage more companies to transparent. Schwarz, Joel. 2020. "Will Privacy Shield's Demise Usher In Transparency?" *The Privacy Adviser*, https://iapp.org/news/a/will-privacy-shields-demise-usher-in-transparency/.

48 **sociolinguistic functions inside the information industry.** Nelson, Robert and Laura B. Nielsen. 2000. "Cops, Counsel, and Entrepreneurs: Constructing the Role of In-House Counsel in Large Corporations." *Law and Society Review* 34: 457–494.

scholars have suggested that privacy professionals … "company law." Bamberger, Kenneth A., and Deirdre K. Mulligan. 2015. *Privacy on the Ground: Driving Corporate Behavior in the United States and Europe*. Cambridge, MA: The MIT Press.

social practice of privacy law. Balkin, Jack M. and Sanford Levinson. "Law as Performance." In *Law and Literature: Current Legal Issues*, edited by Michael Freeman and Andrew D. E. Lewis. London, UK: Oxford University Press.

49 In the interest of full disclosure, I note that since 2016, I have received an annual grant from Microsoft to host the Joel R. Reidenberg Northeast Privacy Scholars Conference. That money comes with no strings attached and is not related to or has any influence on any academic research I conduct. Nor does that money related to any scholarly work I have published or advocacy work I have done.

threats to withhold investment. Calling the GDPR a "critical" threat to her company, Facebook COO Sheryl Sandberg threatened to withhold investment from Canada and certain EU countries unless they supported Facebook's anti-regulatory positions on issues of jurisdiction and GDPR compliance. The company sought influence with the government of Ireland, a key player in European data protection regulation, through investment and disingenuous social "bond[ing]," a campaign that allegedly resulted in Irish Prime Minister Enda Kenny offering to use his "significant influence" to push Facebook's anti-GDPR position.

Facebook also used Sandberg's controversial feminist memoir, *Lean In*, to try to win support from women in the EU legislature by burnishing the company's feminist bona fides and then painting Facebook's anti-regulatory positions as somehow pro-feminist. Goodwin, Bill et al. 2019. "Facebook Asked George Osborne to Influence EU Data Protection Law." *Computer Weekly*, www.computerweekly.com/news/252458229/Facebook-asked-George-Osborne-to-influence-EU-data-protection-law.

overt push to weaken privacy laws. Cadwalladr, Carole and Duncan Campbell. 2019. "Revealed: Facebook's Global Lobbying against Data Privacy Laws." *Guardian*, www.theguardian.com/technology/2019/mar/02/facebook-global-lobbying-campaign-against-data-privacy-laws-investment.

distribution of company funds to academic centers. Over the past decade, Google has distributed millions of dollars to research organizations and academics that produce scholarship that pushes back against regulation and defends the company's market and legal positions. The *Wall Street Journal* found that Google paid professors to write, publish, and share papers stating that consumer data was an appropriate price to pay for Google's services, that the company didn't engage in anti-competitive behavior, and that minimal privacy regulation was actually a good thing for both the economy and privacy! Although the Journal's investigation also swept in corporate funding for nonacademic-related work, and was, therefore, overbroad, the evidence of a concerted campaign among leading members of the information industry to influence academic output is unmistakable. Mullins, Brody and Jack Nicas. n/d. "Paying Professors: Inside Google's Academic Influence Campaign." *Wall Street Journal*, www.wsj.com/articles/paying-professors-inside-googles-academic-influence-campaign-1499785286. In December 2019, Facebook joined several competitors in the information industry to form an organization called "American Edge" to inculcate the idea that Silicon Valley is "essential to the US economy and the future of free speech." According to sources inside Facebook and American Edge itself, as well as its articles of incorporation on file in Virginia, the organization plans to "fund … studies by academics to make the case for the tech industry." This is on top of the tens of millions Facebook and its corporate allies spend on lobbying every year in Washington, DC. As icing on the cake, American Edge was set up as a nonprofit with an attendant foundation; like the National Rifle Association, American Edge can use this structure to avoid disclosing its donors, raise unlimited amounts of money, and spend lavishly on media and supposedly independent research that touts

its laissez faire policy positions. Romm, Tony. 2020. "Facebook Is Quietly Helping to Set Up a New Pro-Tech Advocacy Group to Battle Washington." *Washington Post*, www.washingtonpost.com/technology/2020/05/12/facebook-lobbying-american-edge/.

normalize privacy governance. Hull, Gordon. 2015. "Successful Failure: What Foucault Can Teach Us about Privacy Self-Management in a World of Facebook and Big Data." *Ethics and Information Technology*. 17(2): 89–101.

50 **Amazon's privacy policy.** Amazon.com Privacy Notice. n.d. www.amazon.com/gp/help/customer/display.html?ie=UTF8&nodeId=468496&ref_=footer_privacy.

"a marketing tool" ... "top level assertion." Turow, Joseph et al. 2007. "The Federal Trade Commission and Consumer Privacy in the Coming Decade." *I/S: A Journal of Law and Policy for the Information Society* 3:723–749 (p. 747).

most individuals think that merely having a privacy policy. Turow, Joseph, Michael Hennessy, and Nora Draper. 2018. "Persistent Misconceptions: Americans' Misplaced Confidence in Privacy Policies, 2003–2015." *Journal of Broadcasting & Electronic Media* 62(3): 461–478.

51 **we come to believe the things we hear often.** This is sometimes called the "repetition-induced truth effect." Unkelback, Christian et al. 2019. "Truth by Repetition: Explanations and Implications." *Current Directions in Psychological Science* 28(3): 247–253. It is related to the "mere exposure" effect. Zajonc, R. B. 1968. "Attitudinal Effects of Mere Exposure." *Journal of Personality and Social Psychology* 9(2): 1–27; Moreland, Richard L. and Scott R. Beach. 1992. "Exposure Effects in the Classroom: The Development of Affinity among Students." *Journal of Experimental Social Psychology* 28(3): 255–276.

52 **"it is not *hard* to get content moderation right at ... scale; it is impossible."** douek, evelyn. 2021. "Governing Online Speech: From 'Posts-as-Trumps' to Proportionality and Probability." *Columbia Law Review* 121(1).

"moderation at the major platforms is as much a problem of logistics as a problem of values." Gillespie, Tarlton. 2018. *Custodians of the Internet: Platforms, Content Moderation, and the Hidden Decisions That Shape Social Media*. New Haven, CT: Yale University Press (p. 116).

53 **testimony before Congress.** US Senate, Committee on Commerce, Science, and Transportation and the Committee on the Judiciary. 2018. *Facebook, Social Media Privacy, and the Use and Abuse of Data*. 115th Cong., 2d sess. S. Hearing Record (oral statement of Mark Zuckerberg).

54 **17 years of this discourse.** Balakrishnan, Anita. 2018. "Mark Zuckerberg Has Been Talking about Privacy for 15 Years – Here's Almost Everything He's Said." *CNBC*, www.cnbc.com/2018/03/21/facebook-ceo-mark-zuckerbergs-statements-on-privacy-2003-2018.html.

55 **what is up for discussion and what isn't.** Turkel, "Michael Foucault," pp. 176–177.

coercive agenda-setting inside organizations. Dutton, Jane. 1986. "Understanding Strategic Agenda Building and Its Implications for Managing Change." *Scandinavian Journal of Management Studies* 3(1): 3–24; Dutton, Jane and W. Penner. 1993. "The Importance of Organizational Identity for Strategic Agenda Building." In *Strategic Thinking: Leadership and the Management of Change*, pp. 89–113. Edited by J. Hendry and J. Newton. New York: John Wiley & Sons. Agenda-setting is also part of the coercive effect of media and advertising. Sutherland, Max and John Galloway. 1981. "Role of Advertising: Persuasion or Agenda-Setting?" *Journal of Advertising Research* 21(5): 25–29; McCombs, Maxwell, 1992. "Explorers and Surveyors: Expanding Strategies for Agenda Setting Research." *Journalism Quarterly* 69: 813–824.

56 **Zuckerberg focused almost exclusively on notice-and-consent.** US Senate, Committee on Commerce, Science, and Transportation and the Committee on the Judiciary. 2018. *Facebook, Social Media Privacy, and the Use and Abuse of Data.* 115th Cong., 2d sess. S. Hearing Record (oral statement of Mark Zuckerberg).

a report on transparency. Egan, Erin. 2020. "Communicating about Privacy: Towards People-Centered and Accountable Design." *Facebook*, https://about.fb.com/wp-content/uploads/2020/07/Privacy-Transparency-White-Paper.pdf.

at Microsoft. n.d. "Security, Privacy, and Cryptography." *Microsoft*, www.microsoft.com/en-us/research/research-area/security-privacy-cryptography.

spyware. Chaterjee, Rahul et al. 2018. "The Spyware Used in Intimate Partner Violence." *IEEE Symposium on Security and Privacy – Oakland 2018*, https://pages.cs.wisc.edu/~chatterjee/papers/IPV_Spyware.pdf.

Apple chooses to focus on app developers' privacy notices. "App Privacy Details on the App Store." *Apple Support*, https://developer.apple.com/support/app-privacy-on-the-app-store/.

57 **he concluded it showed nothing of the sort.** Crain, Matthew. 2018. "The Limits of Transparency: Data Brokers and Commodification." *New Media & Society* 20(1): 88–104.

"political expediency of transparency … to continue or expand their surveillance practices." Ibid., p. 92.

58 **"strategy ... regarding the security of and operations."** Department of Homeland Security. 2010. "Cyberspace Policy Review: Assuring A Trusted and Resilient Information and Communications Infrastructure," www.dhs.gov/sites/default/files/publications/Cyberspace_Policy_Review_final_0.pdf.
"criminality" or "espionage." Coldebella, Gus P. and Brian M. White. 2010. "Foundational Questions Regarding the Federal Role in Cybersecurity." *Journal of National Security Law and Policy* 4: 233–245 (pp. 235–236).
"using computer technology to engage." Brenner, Susan W. 2007. "'At Light Speed': Attribution and Response to Cybercrime/Terrorism/Warfare." *Journal of Criminal Law and Criminology* 97: 379–474 (p. 381). For a critique of these and other definitions of cybersecurity, please see the following: Bambauer, Derek E. 2011. "Conundrum." *Minnesota Law Review* 96: 584– 674 (pp. 591–595).
new "privacy-focused" vision ... proposed changes focused almost entirely on encrypted messaging. Zuckerberg, Mark. 2019. "A Privacy-Focused Vision for Social Networking." *Facebook*, www.facebook.com/notes/mark-zuckerberg/a-privacy-focused-vision-for-social-networking/10156700570096634/

59 **Facebook punished.** Silverman, Craig and Ryan Mac. 2020. "Facebook Fired an Employee Who Collected Evidence of Right-Wing Pages Getting Preferential Treatment." *BuzzFeed News*, www.buzzfeednews.com/article/craigsilverman/facebook-zuckerberg-what-if-trump-disputes-election-results.
Google took the same approach. Scheiber, Noam and Kate Conger. 2020. "The Great Google Revolt." *New York Times*, www.nytimes.com/interactive/2020/02/18/magazine/google-revolt.html.
fired the prominent AI researcher Timnit Gebru. Metz, Cade and Daisuke Wakabayashi. 2020. "Google Researcher Says She Was Fired over Paper Highlighting Bias in A.I." *New York Times*, www.nytimes.com/2020/12/03/technology/google-researcher-timnit-gebru.html.
chilling effect on managers. Gorman, Robert and Matthew Fishkin. 1981. "The Individual and the Requirement of 'Concert' under the National Labor Relations Act." *University of Pennsylvania Law Review* 130: 286–359.

60 **Facebook's Privacy Engineer job postings are now up front about this.** "Privacy Engineer, Technical Audit." *Facebook Careers*, www.facebook.com/careers/jobs/879853205865481/.

61 **canonical ethical duty.** Green, Bruce A. 1991. "Zealous Representation Bound: The Intersection of the Ethical Codes and the Criminal Law." *North Carolina Law Review* 69: 687– 717 (pp. 687–88 nn. 1–2).

"Zealous advocacy" is included in historical ethical canons, including the following: American Bar Association. 2009. Model Rules of Professional Conduct. Preamble ¶ 8, www.abanet.org/cpr/mrpc/preamble.html; American Bar Association. 1908. Canons of Professional Ethics. Canon 15, http://minnesotalegalhistoryproject.org/assets/ABA%20Canons%20(1908).pdf; American Bar Association. 1980. Model Code of Professional Responsibility. Canon 7, https://archive.org/stream/ABAMODELCODEOFPROFESSIONALRESPONSIBILITY/ABA%20MODEL%20CODE%20OF%20PROFESSIONAL%20RESPONSIBILITY_djvu.txt.

"save that client" even if it might cause "the alarm, the torments, [or] the destruction" of others. Luban, David. 1988. *Lawyers and Justice: An Ethical Study*. Princeton, NJ: Princeton University Press (pp. 54–55).

obligation to bracket away personal moral. As Michael Hatfield has noted, law school train students to "accept a division between lawyers' morality and clients' morality." Hatfield, Michael. 2009. "Professionalizing Moral Deference." *Northwestern University Law Review Colloquy* 104: 1–11; Suchman, Mark C. 1998. "Working without a Net: The Sociology of Legal Ethics in Corporate Litigation." *Fordham Law Review* 67: 837–874; Nelson, Robert L. 1988. *Partners with Power: The Social Transformation of the Large Law Firm*. Berkeley, CA: University of California Press (pp. 276–289).

litigators and transactional attorneys. Schaefer, Paula. 2011. "Harming Business Clients With Zealous Advocacy: Rethinking the Attorney Advisor's Touchtone." *Florida State University Law Review* 38: 251–302 (pp. 263–264).

62 **"zones of legal privilege."** Cohen, *Between Truth and Power*, p. 49.

63 **umbrella term often imprecisely used to refer to set of technologies.** Narayanan, Arvind. 2020. "How to Recognize AI Snake Oil." Presentation at the Massachusetts Institute of Technology, www.cs.princeton.edu/~arvindn/talks/MIT-STS-AI-snakeoil.pdf.

"best understood as a set of techniques." Calo, Ryan. 2017. "Artificial Intelligence Policy: A Primer and Roadmap." *University of California, Davis Law Review* 51: 399–435 (p. 403).

problems of bias. Barocas, Solon and Andrew Selbst. 2016. "Big Data's Disparate Impact." *California Law Review* 104: 617–732 (pp. 694–714); Levendowski, "Copyright Law"; Angwin et al., "Machine Bias"; Meyer, David. 2018. "Amazon Reportedly Killed an AI Recruitment System because It Couldn't Stop the Tool from Discriminating against Women." *Fortune*, http://fortune.com/2018/10/10/amazon-ai-recruitment-bias-women-sexist/; Simonite, Tom. 2017. "Machines Taught by Photos Learn a Sexist View of Women." *Wired*,

www.wired.com/story/machines-taught-by-photos-learn-a-sexist-view-of-women/.

lack of accountability. Houston Federation of Teachers, Local 2415 v. Houston Independent School District, 251 F. Supp. 3d 1168 (S.D. Tex. 2017); Citron, Danielle K. and Frank Pasquale. 2017. "The Scored Society: Due Process for Automated Predictions." *Washington Law Review* 89: 1–33 (pp. 8–10).

structural injustice. Eubanks, Virginia. 2018. *Automated Equality: How High Tech Tools Profile, Police, and Punish the Poor*. New York: St. Martin's Press; Taylor, Keeanga-Yamahtta. 2018. "How Real Estate Segregated America." *Dissent Magazine*, www.dissentmagazine.org/article/how-real-estate-segregated-america-fair-housing-act-race; Taylor, Keeanga-Yamahtta. 2019. *Race for Profit: How Banks and the Real Estate Industry Undermined Black Homeownership*. Durham, NC: North Carolina Press; Pasquale, Frank. 2019. "The Second Wave of Algorithmic Accountability." *Law and Political Economy Blog*, https://lpeblog.org/2019/11/25/the-second-wave-of-algorithmic-accountability/.

invasions of privacy. Zuboff, Shoshana. 2019. *The Age of Surveillance Capitalism: The Fight for a Human Future at the New Frontier of Power*. New York: Public Affairs; Zuboff, Shoshana. 2015. "Big Other: Surveillance Capitalism and the Prospects of an Information Civilization." *Journal of Information Technology* 30(1): 75–89 (pp. 84–85); Bellovin, Steven M. et al. 2014. "When Enough Is Enough: Location Tracking, Mosaic Theory, and Machine Learning." *New York University Journal of Law and Liberty* 8: 555–628 (p. 590).

64 **aligned some of its policy recommendations ... with Big Tech's regulatory posture.** Ochigame, Rodrigo. 2019. "The Invention of 'Ethical AI.'" *Intercept*, https://theintercept.com/2019/12/20/mit-ethical-ai-artificial-intelligence/.

65 **Amazon paid scholars.** Streitfeld, David. 2018. "Amazon's Antitrust Antagonist Has a Breakthrough Idea." *New York Times*, www.nytimes.com/2018/09/07/technology/monopoly-antitrust-lina-khan-amazon.html.

66 **the entire competition team at a Google-funded think tank was fired.** Vogel, Kenneth P. 2017. "New America, a Google-Funded Think Tank, Faces Backlash for Firing a Google Critic." *New York Times*, www.nytimes.com/2017/09/01/us/politics/anne-marie-slaughter-new-america-google.html.

67 I experienced some of these tactics myself during my researchers; others are based on interviews with academics and with former members of policy, government affairs, and related departments inside the largest technology companies.

68 **"best way to protect."** Bai, Wei et al. 2017. "Balancing Security and Usability in Encrypted Email." *IEEE Internet Computing* 21(3): 30–38.
feasibility of privacy self-governance. Namara, Moses et al. 2018. "The Potential for User-Tailored Privacy on Facebook." *IEEE Symposium on Privacy-Aware Computing* 2018: 31–42.
willing to trade security for convenience. Bai, Wei. 2016. "An Inconvenient Trust: User Attitudes toward Security and Usability Tradeoffs for Key-Directory Encryption Systems." *Twelfth Symposium on Usable Privacy and Security* 2016: 113–130.
proposing changes that companies can make themselves. Kuppam, Satya. 2019. "Fair Decision Making Using Privacy-Protected Data." *Association for Computing Machinery* 2020: 1–12.

69 **Facebook cited.** Egan, "Communicating about Privacy," pp. 27–29.
Lorrie Cranor, Aleecia McDonald. McDonald, Aleecia and Lorrie Faith Cranor. 2008. "The Cost of Reading Privacy Policies." *I/S: A Journal of Law and Policy for the Information Society* 4: 543–568.
Helen Nissenbaum. Nissenbaum, Helen. 2011. "A Contextual Integrity Approach to Privacy Online." *Daedalus* 140(4): 32–48.
me. Waldman, Ari Ezra. 2018. "Privacy, Notice, and Design." *Stanford Technology Law Review* 21: 74–127.

70 **"designed to express a generic commitment to accountability."** Cohen, *Between Truth and Power*, p. 250.

71 **"a powerful mechanism of control" that has "grown up alongside, and in service to."** Roberts, Sarah. 2019. *Behind the Screen: Content Moderation in the Shadows of Social Media*. New Haven, CT: Yale University Press (p. 14).

72 **in the media.** Paul, Kari and Jim Waterson. 2019. "Facebook Bans Alex Jones, Milo Yiannopoulos and Other Far-Right Figures." *Guardian*, www.theguardian.com/technology/2019/may/02/facebook-ban-alex-jones-milo-yiannopoulos; Dewey, Caitlin. 2015. "Facebook is Embroiled in Yet Another Breastfeeding Photo Controversy." *Washington Post*, www.washingtonpost.com/news/the-intersect/wp/2015/02/26/facebook-is-embroiled-in-yet-another-breastfeeding-photo-controversy/; Sweney, Mark. 2008. "Mums Furious as Facebook Removes Breastfeeding Photos." *Guardian*, www.theguardian.com/media/2008/dec/30/facebook-breastfeeding-ban; Isaac, Mike and Cecilia Kang. 2020. "Facebook Says It Won't Back Down from Allowing Lies in Political Ads." *New York Times*, www.nytimes.com/2020/01/09/technology/facebook-political-ads-lies.html; Mozur, Paul. 2018. "A Genocide Incited on Facebook, with Posts from the Myanmar Military." *New York Times*, www.nytimes.com/2018/10/15/technology/myanmar-facebook-genocide.html; Rosenberg, Eli. 2018. "Facebook Blocked

Many Gay-Themed Ads as Part of Its New Advertising Policy, Angering LGBT Groups, *Washington Post*, www.washingtonpost.com/technology/2018/10/03/facebook-blocked-many-gay-themed-ads-part-its-new-advertising-policy-angering-lgbt-groups/; Trigger, Rebecca. 2017. "Facebook Community Standards under Scrutiny as Out and Proud 'Dykes' Banned." *ABC*, https://mobile.abc.net.au/news/2017-07-06/facebook-banning-algorithims-block-lesbians-from-using-dyke/8676284.

among policy makers. Vaidhyanathan, Siva. 2019. "Why Conservatives Allege Big Tech Is Muzzling Them." *Atlantic*, www.theatlantic.com/ideas/archive/2019/07/conservatives-pretend-big-tech-biased-against-them/594916/; Newton, Casey. 2019. "The Real Bias on Social Networks Isn't against Conservatives." *The Verge*, www.theverge.com/interface/2019/4/11/18305407/social-network-conservative-bias-twitter-facebook-ted-cruz; US Senate Committee on the Judiciary, Subcommittee on the Constitution. 2019. *Stifling Free Speech: Technological Censorship and the Public Discourse*. 116th Cong. S. Hearing Record.

Facebook announced. Rodriguez, Salvador. 2018. "Facebook Says It's Creating an Independent Body to Help It Decide Which Content to Remove." *CNBC*, www.cnbc.com/2018/11/15/facebook-creating-independent-body-for-content-removal-appeals.html.

73 **Princeton University.** CITP Lunch Seminar: Radha Iyengar Plumb – Oversight of Deliberative Decision Making: An Analysis of Public and Private Oversight Models Worldwide, https://citp.princeton.edu/event/plumb/. Facebook refused to allow Princeton to record the talk.

Aspen Institute. "Meet the New Facebook Oversight Board." *Aspen Institute*, www.aspeninstitute.org/events/meet-the-new-facebook-oversight-board/.

74 **"the most challenging content issues for Facebook."** Botero-Marino, Catalina. 2020. "We Are a New Board Overseeing Facebook. Here's What We'll Decide." *New York Times*, www.nytimes.com/2020/05/06/opinion/facebook-oversight-board.html.

"only in the narrowest and most trivial of ways." Vaidhyanathan, Siva. 2020. "Facebook and the Folly of Self-Regulation." *Wired*, www.wired.com/story/facebook-and-the-folly-of-self-regulation/.

75 **only hear appeals.** "Oversight Board Charter." *Facebook Newsroom*, https://fbnewsroomus.files.wordpress.com/2019/09/oversight_board_charter.pdf.

***New York Times* report.** Frenkel, Sheera et al. 2018. "Delay, Deny and Deflect: How Facebook's Leaders Fought through Crisis." *New York Times*, www.nytimes.com/2018/11/14/technology/facebook-data-russia-election-racism.html.

76 **"what really needs to happen."** Wong, Julia Carrie. 2020. "Will Facebook's New Oversight Board Be a Radical Shift or a Reputational Shield?" *Guardian*, www.theguardian.com/technology/2020/may/07/will-facebooks-new-oversight-board-be-a-radical-shift-or-a-reputational-shield.

"a commercial thing of convenience for the company." Ghosh, Dipayan. 2019. "Facebook's Oversight Board Is Not Enough." *Harvard Business Review*, https://hbr.org/2019/10/facebooks-oversight-board-is-not-enough.

77 **many people think a company with a privacy policy is promising to keep our data private.** Turow, Hennessy, and Draper, "Persistent Misconceptions."

78 **advocacy against robust privacy law.** Cadwalladr and Campbell, "Revealed."; Kaye, Kate. 2020. "Amazon Is Quietly Fighting against a Sweeping Facial Recognition Ban in Portland." *OneZero*, https://onezero.medium.com/amazons-quietly-fighting-against-a-groundbreaking-facial-recognition-ban-in-portland-fod1e3c2054; Mehotra, Kartikay, Laura Mahoney and Daniel Stoller. 2019. "Google and Other Tech Firms Seek to Weaken Landmark California Data-Privacy Law." *Los Angeles Times*, www.latimes.com/business/story/2019-09-04/google-and-other-tech-companies-attempt-to-water-down-privacy-law; Oremus, Will. 2018. "Beware of Tech Companies Bearing Privacy Laws." *Slate*, https://slate.com/technology/2018/08/facebook-and-googles-plan-for-a-new-federal-privacy-law-is-really-about-protecting-themselves.html.

Chapter 3

1 **given up on the hope that they can adequately protect their privacy online.** Marwick, Alice and Eszter Hargittai. 2018. "Nothing to Hide, Nothing to Lose? Incentives and Disincentives to Sharing Information with Institutions Online." *Information, Communication & Society* 22(12): 1697–1713; Hargittai, Eszter and Alice Marwick. 2016. "What Can I Really Do? Explaining the Privacy Paradox with Online Apathy." *International Journal of Communication* 10: 3737–3757; Hoffman, Christian, Cristoph Lutz, and Giulia Ranzini. 2016. "Privacy Cynicism: A New Approach to the Privacy Paradox." *Cyberpsychology: Journal of Psychosocial Research on Cyberspace* 10(4): 7, http://dx.doi.org/10.5817/CP2016-4-7; Draper, Nora and Joseph Turow. 2019. "The Corporate Cultivation of Digital Resignation." *New Media & Society* 21(8): 1824–1839.

2 **Federal privacy law is sector specific.** Schwartz, Paul M. 2009. "Preemption and Privacy." *Yale Law Journal* 118: 902–947 (pp. 904–905).
Children's Online Privacy Protection Act. 15 U.S.C. §§ 6501–6506.
Health Insurance Portability and Accountability Act. 42 U.S.C. § 300gg (2012), 29 U.S.C. § 1181, 42 U.S.C. § 1320d.
Gramm-Leach-Bliley. 15 U.S.C. §§ 6801–6809.
primarily pursued companies that break their promises. Solove, Daniel J. and Woodrow Hartzog. 2011. "The FTC and the New Common Law of Privacy." *Columbia Law Review* 114(3): 583–676.
almost universally focuses on ... information asymmetries that undermine markets. Reidenberg, Joel. 2003. "Privacy Wrongs in Search of Remedies." *Hastings Law Journal* 54: 877–898.
zones of immunity. Cohen, Julie. 2019. *Between Truth and Power: The Legal Constructions of Informational Capitalism.* New York: Oxford University Press (p. 90).

3 **companies should regulate themselves.** Federal Trade Commission. 1999. *Self-Regulation and Privacy Online: A Report to Congress.* Washington, DC: Federal Trade Commission (pp. 12–14); US House of Representatives, Subcommittee on Telecommunications, Trade, and Consumer Protection of the House Subcommittee on Commerce. 1998. *Consumer Privacy on the World Wide Web.* 105th Cong., 2d sess. Prepared statement of the Federal Trade Commission by Robert Pitosfky, Chairperson, www.ftc.gov/sites/default/files/documents/public_statements/prepared-statement-federal-trade-commission-consumer-privacy-world-wide-web/privac98.pdf; US Senate, Subcommittee on Communications of the Committee on Commerce, Science, and Transportation. 1999. *Self-Regulation and Privacy Online.* 106th Cong., 1st sess. Prepared statement of the Federal Trade Commission by Robert Pitofsky, Chairperson, www.ftc.gov/sites/default/files/documents/public_statements/prepared-statement-federal-trade-commission-self-regulation-and-privacy-online/privacyonlinetestimony.pdf
broad "common law" of privacy. Solove and Hartzog, "New Common Law."
attorneys-general have grown into their roles as privacy enforcers. Citron, Danielle Keats. 2016. "The Privacy Policymaking of State Attorneys General." *Notre Dame Law Review* 92: 747–814.
privacy professionals are going above and beyond. Bamberger, Kenneth and Deirdre Mulligan. 2015. *Privacy on the Ground: Driving Corporate Behavior in the United States and Europe.* Cambridge, MA: MIT Press; Bamberger, Kenneth and Deirdre Mulligan. 2011. "Privacy on the Books and on the Ground." *Stanford Law Review* 63: 247–315.

4 **GDPR.** Regulation (EU) 2016/679 General Data Protection Regulation, 2016 O.J. (L119).
CCPA. California Civil Code §1798.100.
more than 40 new comprehensive privacy bills. International Association of Privacy Professionals. n/d. State Comprehensive Privacy Law Comparisons: Bills Introduced 2018–2020, https://iapp.org/media/pdf/resource_center/State_Comp_Privacy_Law.pdf.
members of the US Congress introduced 9. Consumer Online Privacy Rights Act of 2019, S. 2968, 116th Cong. (2019); Data Care Act of 2018, S. 2961, 116th Cong. (2019); Mind Your Own Business Act, S. 2637, 116th Cong. (2019); Privacy Bill of Rights Act, S. 1214, 116th Cong. (2019); Setting an American Framework to Ensure Data Access, Transparency, and Accountability Act, S. ___, 116th Cong. (2019); American Data Dissemination Act of 2019, S. 142, 116th Cong. (2019); Online Privacy Act of 2019, H.R. 4978, 116th Cong. (2019); Consumer Data Privacy and Security Act of 2020, S. 3456, 116th Cong. (2020); Data Accountability and Transparency Act of 2020, S. ___, 116th Cong. (2020). There have been many more bills introduced focusing on one aspect of privacy and data protection. For example, Senator Roger Wicker introduced a bill to safeguard personal data during the Covid19 pandemic. COVID-19 Consumer Data Protection Act of 2020, S. 3663, 116th Cong. (2020). Senator Kirsten Gillibrand introduced a bill to create a new data protection agency. Data Protection Act of 2020, S. 3300, 116th Cong. (2020).
"the most significant data privacy reform process in history." Edwards, Lilian. 2019. "Data Protection: Enter the General Data Protection Regulation." In *Law, Policy, and the Internet*. Edited by Lilian Edwards. London, UK: Hart Publishing.
"the most consequential regulatory development ... brings personal data into a complex and protective regulatory regime." Hoofnagle, Chris Jay, Bart van der Sloot, and Frederik Zuiderveen Borgesius. 2018. "The European Union General Data Protection Regulation: What It Is and What It Means." *Information & Communications Technology Law* 28 (1): 65–98 (p. 66).
"protections that follow the data." Kaminski, Margot and Meg Leta Jones. 2020. "An American's Guide to the GDPR." *Denver Law Review* 98(1).
"duties on companies regardless." Ibid.
"strict[]." Solove, Daniel. 2017. "Beyond the GDPR: The Challenge of Global Privacy Compliance – An Interview with Lothar Determann." *Teach Privacy*, https://teachprivacy.com/challenge-of-global-privacy-compliance/.

"far-reaching." Bensinger, Greg. 2020. "So Far, under California's New Privacy Law, Firms Are Disclosing Too Little Data – or Far Too Much." *Washintgon Post*, www.washingtonpost.com/technology/2020/01/21/ccpa-transparency/.

5 **law is also a social practice.** Ewick, Patricia and Susan Silbey. 1998. *The Common Place of Law: Stories from Everyday Life*. Chicago, IL: University of Chicago Press (pp. 15–32); Cotterrell, Roger. 1998. "Why Must Legal Ideas Be Interpreted Sociologically." *Journal of Law and Society* 25: 171–192.

laws are going to be mobilized by the information industry. Cohen, *Between Truth and Power*, pp. 2–9.

6 **legal endogeneity.** Edelman, Lauren. 2016. *Working Law: Courts, Corporations, and Symbolic Civil Rights*. Chicago, IL: University of Chicago Press.

7 **Legal endogeneity describes.** Ibid. pp. 11–14, 22.

8 **Compliance.** Edelman, Lauren B. et al. 1991. "Legal Ambiguity and the Politics of Compliance: Affirmative Action Officers' Dilemma." *Law & Policy* 13(1): 73–97.

develop out of negotiations. Meyer, John W. and Brian Rowan. 1977. "Institutionalized Organizations: Formal Structure as Myth and Ceremony." *American Journal of Sociology* 82(2): 340–363; DiMaggio, Paul J. and Walter W. Powel. 1983. "The Iron Cage Revisited: Institutional Isomorphism and Collective Rationality in Organizational Fields." *American Sociological Review* 48(2): 147–160; March, James G. and Johan P. Olsen. 1989. *Rediscovering Institutions: The Organizational Basis of Politics*. New York: Free Press.

9 **that incorporates social and legal decisions.** Winner, Langdon. 1980. "Do Artifacts Have Politics?" *Daedalus* 109(1): 121–136.

more than 300 companies in the privacy technology vendor market. International Association of Privacy Professionals. 2020. "Privacy Tech Vendor Report." IAPP, https://iapp.org/media/pdf/resource_center/2020TechVendorReport.pdf; Waldman, Ari Ezra. 2021. "Outsourcing Privacy." *Notre Dame Law Review Discourse* 96.

10 **Scholars have recognized the ways compliance can filter and recast the law.** Nelson, Robert and Laura Beth Nielsen. 2000. "Cops, Counsel, and Entrepreneurs: Constructing the Role of In-House Counsel in Large Corporations." *Law and Society Review* 34: 457–494.

11 **levying unprecedented fines.** U.S. v. Facebook, Inc., Case No. 19-cv-2184 (D. D.C. July 24, 2019) (Plaintiff's Consent Motion for Entry of Stipulated Order for Civil Penalty, Monetary Judgment, and Injunctive Relief and Memorandum in Support).

"comprehensive privacy program[s]." In re Google, Inc., FTC File No. 102 3136, No. C-4336 (F.T.C. Oct. 13, 2011), www.ftc.gov/sites/default/files/documents/cases/2011/10/111024googlebuzzdo.pdf.
lead the world in protecting privacy. Bradford, Anu. 2012. "The Brussels Effect." *Northwestern University Law Review*, 107: 1–67.
collaborative governance. Kaminski, Margot. 2019. "Binary Governance: Lessons from the GDPR's Approach to Algorithmic Accountability." *Southern California Law Review* 92: 1529–1616.

12 **right of access.** California Consumer Privacy Act of 2019, Cal. Civ. Code §§ 1798.100(d), 1798.110, 1798.115; Regulation (EU) 2016/679 General Data Protection Regulation, 2016 O.J. (L119), art. 15.
right of data portability. California Consumer Privacy Act of 2019, Cal. Civ. Code §§ 1798.100(d) and 1798.130(a)(2).; Regulation (EU) 2016/679 General Data Protection Regulation, 2016 O.J. (L119), art. 20.
deletion gives. California Consumer Privacy Act of 2019, Cal. Civ. Code § 1798.105; Regulation (EU) 2016/679 General Data Protection Regulation, 2016 O.J. (L119), art. 17.
respond to these requests with specific steps. California Consumer Privacy Act of 2019, Cal. Civ. Code §§ 1798.100(d), 1798.110, 1798.115; Regulation (EU) 2016/679 General Data Protection Regulation, 2016 O.J. (L119), art. 15.
notice requirements. California Consumer Privacy Act of 2019, Cal. Civ. Code §§ 1798.100(a)-(b), 1798.105(b), 1798.110, 1798.115, 1798.120 (b), 1798.130, and 1798.135; Regulation (EU) 2016/679 General Data Protection Regulation, 2016 O.J. (L119), arts. 13–14.
roughly similar … definitions for "personal information." California Consumer Privacy Act of 2019, Cal. Civ. Code §§ 1798.140(o) and 1798.145(c)-(f); Regulation (EU) 2016/679 General Data Protection Regulation, 2016 O.J. (L119), arts. 4(1) and 9(1).

13 **the similarities stop there.** Chander, Anupam, Margot Kaminski, and Bill McGeveran. 2021. "Catalyzing Privacy Law.," https://scholarship.law.georgetown.edu/cgi/viewcontent.cgi?article=3208&context=facpub.
opt-out regime. California Consumer Privacy Act of 2019, Cal. Civ. Code §§ 1798.120 and 1798.135(a)-(b).
right to correct inaccurate data. Regulation (EU) 2016/679 General Data Protection Regulation, 2016 O.J. (L119), art. 16.
right to restrict data processing. Ibid. art. 18.
right to object to data processing. Ibid. art. 21.
right to an explanation of the "logic" behind. Ibid. art. 22.
penalty ceiling is higher. California Consumer Privacy Act of 2019, Cal. Civ. Code § 1798.155; Regulation (EU) 2016/679 General Data Protection Regulation, 2016 O.J. (L119), arts. 83–84.

broader exemption for small businesses. California Consumer Privacy Act of 2019, Cal. Civ. Code § 1798.140(c); Regulation (EU) 2016/679 General Data Protection Regulation, 2016 O.J. (L119), art. 3.

14 **performance of privacy, inculcating the discourse of control with each click.** Hull, Gordon. 2015. "Successful Failure: What Foucault Can Teach Us about Privacy Self-Management in a World of Facebook and Big Data." *Ethics and Information Technology*. 17(2): 89–101.
Creates the impression that our privacy problems have been solved. Butler, Paul. 2013. "Poor People Lose: *Gideon* and the Critique of Rights." *Yale Law Journal* 122: 2176–2204.

15 **describes collaborative governance.** Kaminski, "Binary Governance," pp. 1559–1561, 1564–1565.

16 **accountability.** Ibid. pp. 1564–1569.

17 **insufficient enforcement power.** McGeveran, William. 2016. "Friending the Privacy Regulators." *Arizona Law Review* 58: 959–1025 (p. 963).
"deliberately vague" provisions that become less vague. Kaminski, "Binary Governance," pp. 1587–1588.
codes of conduct. GDPR, arts. 40(2), (5), (9). European Data Protection Board. 2019. "Guidelines 1/2019 on Codes of Conduct and Monitoring Bodies Under Regulation 2016/679, Version 2.0," https://edpb.europa.eu/sites/edpb/files/files/file1/edpb_guidelines_201901_v2.0_codesofconduct_en.pdf.
certification, GDPR, art. 42; European Data Protection Board. 2019. "Guidelines 1/2018 on Certification and Identifying Certification Criteria in Accordance with Articles 42 and 43 of the Regulation, Version 3.0," https://edpb.europa.eu/sites/edpb/files/files/file1/edpb_guidelines_201801_v3.0_certificationcriteria_annex2_en.pdf.
technical standards. GDPR, arts. 21(5), 43(4); Kaminski, "Binary Governance," pp. 1599–1601.

18 **Data Protection Officers.** GDPR, arts. 28, 39(1)(b).
extensive data processing records. GDPR, art. 30.
impact assessments. GDPR, art. 35.
Kaminski suggests that over time, these assessments may affect general compliance. Kaminski, "Binary Governance," pp. 1603–1605.

19 **"common law" of privacy is based almost entirely on … consent decrees.** Solove and Hartzog, "New Common Law," pp. 606–609.
compromises or agreements. United States v. ITT Continental Baking Co., 420 U.S. 223, 238 (1975); United States v. Armour & Co., 402 U.S. 673, 681–682 (1971).
ongoing regulatory partnership between government and industry. Cohen, *Between Truth and Power*, p. 187
NIST. Ibid. p. 103.

20 **lack essential elements.** Kaminski, "Binary Governance," pp. 1599.
the GDPR makes it difficult for civil society. Ibid. pp. 1607–1611.
lack standing to bring cases on behalf of ordinary citizens. Hunt v. Washington Apple Advertising Commission, 432 U.S. 333, 343 (1977); Automobile Workers v. Brock, 477 U.S. 274 (1986).
restrictive rules on standing. Spokeo, Inc. v. Robins, 136 S. Ct. 1540 (2016); Wu, Felix. 2017. "How Privacy Distorted Standing Law." *DePaul Law Review* 66: 439–461.
notorious pro-corporate biases. Constitution Accountability Center. 2010. "Open for Business: The Chamber of Commerce's Supreme Court Success Rate from the Burger Court through the Rehnquist Court and into the Roberts Court," www.theusconstitution.org/wp-content/uploads/2017/12/20101201_Issue_Brief_CAC_Open_for_Business.pdf; Solove, Daniel and Woodrow Hartzog. 2020. "The FTC Zoom Case: Does the FTC Need a New Approach." *LinkedIn*, www.linkedin.com/pulse/ftc-zoom-case-does-need-new-approach-daniel-solove.
courts' long-standing unwillingness to recognize the gravity of privacy-related intangible harms. Solove, Daniel and Danielle Keats Citron. 2017. "Risk and Anxiety: A Theory of Data-Breach Harms." *Texas Law Review* 96(4): 737–786.

21 **most large companies.** Bamberger and Mulligan "Privacy on the Books and on the Ground," p. 260.
"Legal and compliance departments." International Association of Privacy Professionals and Ernst & Young. *IAPP-EY Annual Privacy Governance Report*, www.ey.com/Publication/vwLUAssets/ey-iapp-ey-annual-privacy-gov-report-2018/$File/ey-iapp-ey-annual-privacy-gov-report-2018.pdf (p. xii).
37 percent of CPOs. Ibid. p. xiv.
50,000. 2019. "50K Members: A Landmark for the IAPP and Global Privacy." *The Privacy Adviser*, https://iapp.org/news/a/50k-members-a-landmark-for-iapp-and-global-privacy/.
"sea change" in how privacy is practiced "on the ground." Bamberger and Mulligan, "Privacy on the Books and on the Ground," p. 260.

22 **"allies already."** Hoffmann, Elizabeth A. 2019. "Allies Already Poised to Comply: How Social Proximity Affects Lactation at Work Law Compliance." *Law & Society Review* 53(3): 791–822.
Bamberger and Mulligan suggested. Bamberger and Mulligan, *Privacy on the Ground*, pp. 11–12, 40–43, 59–74.
"a potential cure-all." Heyder, Markus and Sam Grogan. 2018. "The Role of DPAs in Incentivizing Accountability." *Privacy Perspectives*, https://iapp.org/news/a/the-role-of-dpas-in-incentivizing-accountability/.

23 **"substantial."** David, Kevin E. and Florencia Marotta-Wurgler. 2019. "Contracting for Personal Data." *New York University Law Review* 94: 662–705.
"significant." Heiman, Matthew R. A. 2019. "The GDPR and the Consequences of Big Regulation." *Pepperdine Law Review* 47: 945–953.
"worldwide rush of companies to create internal compliance regimes to comply with the GDPR." Kaminski, "Binary Governance," p. 1574.

24 **"regulation as delegation."** Bamberger, Kenneth A. "Regulation as Delegation: Private Firms, Decisionmaking, and Accountability in the Administrative State." *Duke Law Journal* 56: 377–468.
"As industries come together to determine codes of conduct." Kaminski, "Binary Governance," pp. 1609–1610.

25 **do not emerge in a vacuum.** This is one of the core insights of the fields of the sociology of law – namely, that law is a social system made up of people and behaviors and a social institution that has an impact on social life. Sutton, John R. 2000. *Law/Society: Origins, Interactions, and Change.* Thousand Oaks. CA: Pine Forge Press (pp. 8–20).
by the FTC's own count. Solove and Hartzog, "Common Law of Privacy," p. 600.
first mover advantage. The first-mover advantage refers to the benefits that accrue to a company that is first in the market. Agarwal, Rajshree and Michael Gort. 2001. "First Mover Advantage and the Speed of Competitive Entry, 1887–1986." *Journal of Law and Economics* 44(1): 161–177; Robinson, William T. and Sungwook Min. 2002. "Is the First to Market the First to Fail? Empirical Evidence for Industrial Goods Businesses." *Journal of Marketing Research* 39(1): 120–128. In this context, I am arguing that companies have the chance to be first movers when it comes to interpreting what the law means in practice because courts and regulatory agencies can only respond later.
shape the law in ways that … benefit them and their interests. Cohen, *Between Truth and Power*, pp. 139, 186. Here, Cohen describes how patterns of institutional and legal change tilt toward advantages for wealthy corporate interests because, as repeat players in the legal system, they can argue for positive outcomes in any given case or prospective rule changes that work in their favor.

26 **her research suggested.** Edelman, *Working Law*, pp. 6–10, 11, 153–196.

27 **expressive effects.** Citron, Danielle K. 2009. "Law's Expressive Value in Combating Cyber Gender Harassment." *Michigan Law Rev.* 108(3): 373–416; Hellman, Deborah. 2000. "The Expressive Dimension of Equal Protection." *Minnesota Law Rev.* 85(1): 1–70; Sunstein, Cass R. 1996. "On the Expressive Function of Law." *University of Pennsylvania Law Rev.* 144(5): 2021–2053.

28 **legal deference ... was part of the endogenous development of law** (and the paragraph, generally). Edelman, *Working Law*, pp. 21, 170–171. For more on regulatory capture, which has an extensive literature, please see: Freeman Engstrom, David. 2013. "Agencies as Litigation Gatekeepers." *Yale Law J.* 123(3): 616–712; Fang, Lee. 2013. "The Reverse Revolving Door: How Corporate Insiders are Rewarded Upon Leaving Firms for Congress." *The Nation*, www.thenation.com/article/reverse-revolving-door-how-corporate-insiders-are-rewarded-upon-leaving-firms-congres/.

29 **Edelman identified six stages of legal endogeneity**. Edelman, *Working Law*, p. 28.
ambiguous or vague legal requirements. Burstein, Paul. 1998. *Discrimination, Jobs, and Politics: The Struggle for Equal Employment Opportunity in the United States since the New Deal*. Chicago, IL: University of Chicago Press; Nourse, Victoria F. and Jane S. Schacter. 2002. "The Politics of Legislative Drafting: A Congressional Case Study." *New York University Law Review* 77(3): 575–624 (pp. 594–596); Grundfest, Joseph A. and A. C. Pritchard. 2002. "Statutes with Multiple Personality Disorders: The Value of Ambiguity in Statutory Design and Interpretation." *Stanford Law Review* 54(4): 627–736 (pp. 640–641).

30 **vagueness**. Edelman, *Working Law*, pp. 42–55, 72–73.
Meritor Savings Bank v. Vinson. 477 U.S. 57 (1986).
Faragher v. City of Boca Raton. 524 U.S. 775 (1998).
process-oriented escape hatch. Edelman, *Working Law*, pp. 777–778. As Edelman noted, "a defending employer may raise an affirmative defense to liability or damages, subject to proof by a preponderance of the evidence. ... The defense comprises two necessary elements: (a) that the employer exercised reasonable care to prevent and correct promptly any sexually harassing behavior, and (b) that the plaintiff employee unreasonably failed to take advantage of any preventive or corrective opportunities provided by the employer or to avoid harm otherwise."

31 **used the leeway ... to conclude**. Ibid. pp. 30–31.

32 **these systems spread rapidly**. Paul DiMaggio and Walter Power describe how this processes of institutional isomorphism works. DiMaggio, Paul J. and Walter W. Powell. 1983. "The Iron Cage Revisited: Institutional Isomorphism and Collective Rationality in Organizational Fields." *American Sociological Review* 48(2): 147–160.

33 **the law became managerialized**. Edelman, *Working Law*, pp. 33–39.
implementation of legal rules through the guiding prisms of efficiency and innovation. Cohen, *Between Truth and Power*, pp. 143–147. Managerial values are not necessarily neo-liberal values, but there is

substantial overlap. Blalock, Corinne. 2014. "Neoliberalism and the Crisis of Legal Theory." *Law and Contemporary Problems*. 77(4): 71–103.

34 **mobilized these structures to push back when employees tried to vindicate their rights**. Edelman, *Working Law*, pp. 37–38; Bumiller, Kristin. 1992. *The Civil Rights Society: The Social Construction of Victims*. Baltimore, MD: The Johns Hopkins University Press (pp. 25–29, 58–60). Julie Cohen describes the managerialism phenomenon beyond the nondiscrimination context more broadly. Cohen, *Between Truth and Power*, pp. 158–167.

legal consciousness. By "legal consciousness," Edelman was referring to "the set of shared beliefs and ideas that both draw on and constitute the meaning of law." Edelman, *Working Law*, p. 154. Susan Silbey, one of the leading scholars who helped develop the concept, has called it "conceptually tortured" and recommended abandoning it entirely. That said, the idea remains relevant as a path for understanding the connection between, on the one hand, how people tend to experience and understand the law, and how people behave under the law, on the other. Silbey, Susan S. 2005. "After Legal Consciousness." *Annual Review of Law and Social Science* 1: 323–368 (p. 324); Silbey, Susan S. and Patricia Ewick. 1998. *The Common Place of Law: Stories from Everyday Life*. Chicago, IL: University of Chicago Press; Nielsen, Laura Beth. 2004. *License to Harass: Stories from Everyday Life*. Princeton, NJ: Princeton University Press.

35 **final stage of legal endogeneity**. Edelman, *Working Law*, pp. 170–173, 190. Some examples in which this has occurred are: Burlington Industries, Inc. v. Ellerth, 524 U.S. 742, 765 (1998), where the Court an explicit affirmative defense that would allow employers to escape liability if they tried to respond to harassment allegations and had a grievance procedure that the employee declined to pursue) and Meritor Savings Bank v. Vinson, 477 U.S. 57, 72–73 (1986), where the Court said that although the mere presence of a grievance procedure and nondiscrimination did not insulate it from liability, the defendant's argument and position could have benefited from a more specific policy and a more streamlined procedure.

36 **unsure nondiscrimination law can ever recover**. Edelman, *Working Law*, pp. 223–225.

37 **definitions**. There is a rich tradition of scholars exploring the meaning of privacy. Almost all of them recognize its malleability. Arthur Miller said privacy "difficult to define because it is exasperatingly vague and evanescent." Miller, Arthur R. 1972. *The Assault on Privacy: Computers, Data Banks, and Dossiers*. New York: Signet (p. 25). Gerety, Tom. 1977.

"Redefining Privacy." *Harvard Civil Rights-Civil Liberties Law Rev.* 12 (2): 233–296 (pp. 233–234). Robert Post noted that "privacy is a value so complex, so entangled in competing and contradictory dimensions, so engorged with various and distinct meanings" that it is difficult to define it at all. Post, Robert C. 2001. "Three Concepts of Privacy." *The Georgetown Law Journal* 89(6): 2087–2098 (p. 2087). This, of course, has not stopped scholars from trying. Privacy has been defined as a right to be left alone, the capacity to control what others know about us, the ability to protect intimate information, the liberty-affirming need to develop new ideas free of social pressure, controlling the appropriate flow of information, protecting our bodily and sexual integrity, and the negotiation of disclosure in relationships of trust, just to name a few. Inness, Julie. 1992. *Privacy Intimacy and Isolation.* Oxford: Oxford University Press; Nissenbaum, Helen. 2009. *Privacy in Context: Technology, Privacy, and the Integrity of Social Life.* Redwood City: Stanford University Press; Richards, Neil. 2015. *Intellectual Privacy: Rethinking Civil Liberties in the Digital Age.* Oxford: Oxford University Press; Rosen, Jeffrey. 2000. *The Unwanted Gaze: The Destruction of Privacy in America.* New York: Random House; Solove, Daniel. 2004. *The Digital Person: Technology and Privacy in the Information Age.* New York, NY: New York University Press; Westin, Alan F. 1967. *Privacy and Freedom.* New York: Athenum; Citron, Danielle Keats. 2019. "Sexual Privacy." *Yale Law Review* 128(7): 1870–1960; Cohen, Jean L. 2001. "The Necessity of Privacy." *Social Research* 68(1): 318–327; Gerstein, Robert S. 1984. "Intimacy and Privacy." In *Philosophical Dimensions of Privacy*, edited by Ferdinand Shoeman. New York: Cambridge University Press; Fried, Charles. 1968. "Privacy." *Yale Law Journal* 77(3): 475–493; Matthews, Steve. 2010. "Anonymity and the Social Self." *American Philosophical Quarterly* 47(4): 351–363; Richards, Neil M. and Woodrow Hartzog. 2016. "Taking Trust Seriously in Privacy Law." *Stanford Technology Law Review* 19(3): 431–472; Warren, Samuel and Louis D. Brandeis. 1890. "The Right to Privacy." *Harvard Law Review* 4 (5): 193–220; White, Howard B. 1951. "The Right to Privacy." *Social Research* 18(2): 171–202; Zittrain, Jonathan L. 2000. "What the Publisher Can Teach the Patient: Intellectual Property and Privacy in an Era of Trusted Privication." *Stanford Law Rev.* 52(5): 1201–1250; Allen, Anita. 1988. *Uneasy Access: Privacy for Women in a Free Society.* Lanham: Rowman & Littlefield; Cohen, Julie E. 2012. *Configuring the Networked Self: Law, Code, and the Play of Everyday Practice.* New Haven: Yale University Press; Waldman, Ari Ezra. 2018. *Privacy As Trust: Information Privacy for an Information Age.* Cambridge: Cambridge University Press.

standards. There are many scholarly pieces on the relative merits of rules versus flexible standards. The canonical pieces are: Kennedy, Duncan. 1976. "Form and Substance in Private Law Adjudication." *Harvard Law Review* 89(8): 1685–1778; Dworkin, Ronald M. 1967. "The Model of Rules." *University of Chicago Law Review* 35(1): 14–46 (pp. 22–29).

decision-makers on the ground are empowered. Lessig, Lawrence. 1995. "The Path of Cyberlaw." *Yale Law Journal* 104(7): 1743–1755 (pp. 1744–1745).

"staggeringly complex" and "ambiguous." Cool, Alison. 2018. "Europe's Data Protection Law is a Big, Confusing Mess." *The New York Times*, www.nytimes.com/2018/05/15/opinion/gdpr-europe-data-protection.html.

"publish opinion statements or detailed rules." Kaminski, Margot E. 2019. "The Right to Explanation, Explained." *Berkeley Tech Law Journal* 34(1): 189–218.

38 **The Data Protection Board ... was similarly vague.** Article 29 Data Protection Working Party. 2014. "Opinion 06/2014 on the Notion of Legitimate Interests of the Data Controller under Article 7 of Directive 95/46/EC," https://ec.europa.eu/justice/article-29/documentation/opinion-recommendation/files/2014/wp217_en.pdf (pp. 24–25). Since 1997, the Article 29 Working Party, now, with some minor changes, called the European Data Protection Board, has issued more than 250 statements, reports, opinions, and recommendations to help companies comply with European data protection rules. They are available at http://ec.europa.eu/justice/article-29/documentation/opinion-recommendation/index_en.htm.

39 **"find simple ways to tell" individuals the "rationale behind" the decision or the "criteria relied on."** Article 29 Data Protection Working Party. 2018. "Guidelines on Automated Individual Decision-Making and Profiling for the Purposes of Regulation 2016/679," https://ec.europa.eu/newsroom/article29/item-detail.cfm?item_id=612053 (p. 25).

40 **general understanding.** Cavoukian, Ann. 2009. "Privacy by Design: From Rhetoric to Reality." Privacy by Design, www.ipc.on.ca/images/Resources/privacybydesign.pdf; Cavoukian, Ann. 2009. "Privacy by Design: The Seven Foundational Principles." Privacy by Design, www.privacybydesign.ca/content/uploads/2009/08/7foundationalprinciples.pdf. Cavoukian tried to boil down privacy by design into seven principles: Proactive, not reactive; Privacy as the default setting; Privacy embedded into design; Full functionality; End-to-end security; Visibility and transparency; and Respect for user privacy. She has suggested that, in practice, privacy by design can be covered by better processes: more

training, better tracking of data use, enhanced interdepartmental reporting, and regular audits. Cavoukian's seven principles are mantras. They lack administrable specificity, and their resemblance to the Fair Information Practice Principles, the foundation of the privacy regime we have today, suggests they may be little more than a noble effort to repackage a failure. What's more, despite the inclusion of security by design in a recital in the European Union's 1995 Privacy Directive, privacy by design has played little if any role in incentivizing designs without surveillance architecture. And several scholars have argued that Article 25 of the GDPR, which is supposed to finally make privacy by design a legal mandate, is unclear, devoid of meaning, and in need of robust teleological interpretation from the European Court of Justice to give it any weight. Waldman, Ari Ezra. 2020. "Data Protection by Design? A Critique of Article 25 of the GDPR." *Cornell International Law Journal* 53; Bygrave, Lee A. 2017. "Data Protection by Design and by Default: Deciphering the EU's Legislative Requirements." *Oslo Law Review* 4(2): 105–120; Rubinstein, Ira. 2011. "Regulating Privacy by Design." *Berkeley Technology Law Journal* 26: 1409–1426.
translating privacy principles into code. Rubinstein, Ira and Nathan Good. 2013. "Privacy By Design: A Counterfactual Analysis of Google and Facebook Privacy Incidents." *Berkeley Technology Law Journal* 28 (2): 1333–1414 (pp. 1341–1342).
take lessons from the common law of products liability for design defects. Waldman, Ari. 2019. "Privacy's Law of Design." *University of California Irvine Law Review* 9: 1239–1288.
"place privacy and data protection at the forefront of product development." Article 29 Working Party. 2014. Opinion 8/2014 on the Recent Develops on the Internet of Things," http://ec.europa.eu/justice/article-29/documentation/opinion-recommendation/files/2014/wp223_en.pdf. The guidance also said to "apply the principles of Privacy by Design and Privacy by Default," but added little else. (p. 21).

41 **incorporate the many privacy-related FTC consent decrees.** As part of their research on the FTC's privacy jurisprudence, Daniel Solove and Woody Hartzog interviewed leading privacy attorneys, including Chris Wolf, then-director of Hogan Lovells LLP's privacy and information management practice group, who noted that FTC consent decrees are scrutinized by practitioners for insight into the current state of the law. Solove and Hartzog, "Common Law of Privacy," pp. 607, 621. Indeed, the FTC intends for its consent orders to have a norm-setting impact. Ibid. p. 622.

42 **"adequately inform[] consumers that [an Android file sharing] application."** Complaint for Permanent Injunction and Other Equitable

Relief, Fed. Trade Comm'n v. Frostwire, LLC, No. 1:11-cv-23643 (S.D. Fla. Oct. 12, 2011), www.ftc.gov/sites/default/files/documents/cases/2011/10/111011frostwirecmpt.pdf.

"failed to disclose adequately." Complaint for Permanent Injunction and Other Equitable Relief, Fed. Trade Comm'n v. Echometrix, Inc., No. CV10–5516 (E.D.N.Y. Nov. 30, 2010), www.ftc.gov/sites/default/files/documents/cases/2010/11/101130echometrixcmpt.pdf.

"failed to disclose adequately that the software application, when installed." Complaint, In re Sears Holdings Mgmt. Corp., FTC File No. 082 3099, No. C-4264 (F.T.C. Aug. 31, 2009), www.ftc.gov/sites/default/files/documents/cases/2009/09/090604searscmpt.pdf.

don't lie. This is not to say that the FTC only engages in broken promises litigation. However, most scholars agree that broken promises not only constitute the lion's share of FTC actions, but it is also the agency's clearest requirement of industry. Solove and Hartzog, "Common Law of Privacy," pp. 629–638.

43 **"comprehensive privacy program that is reasonably designed to."** Agreement Containing Consent Order at 4, In re Google, Inc., Docket No. C-4336, No. 102 3136 (F.T.C. Oct. 24, 2011), www.ftc.gov/sites/default/files/documents/cases/2011/10/111024googlebuzzdo.pdf (p. 1).

"identify risk, train employees." Solove and Hartzog, "Common Law of Privacy," pp. 617–628.

never explained what a comprehensive privacy program really is, even while it boasts … "protect consumers' privacy and personal information." Federal Trade Commission. 2019. Privacy & Data Security: Update: 2019," www.ftc.gov/system/files/documents/reports/privacy-data-security-update-2019/2019-privacy-data-security-report-508.pdf.

44 **privacy professionals may be able to piece together.** Solove and Hartzog, "Common Law of Privacy," pp. 650, 656, 658–661.

companies that hire … could take advantage of a safe harbor. Lobel, Orly. 2004. "The Renew Deal: The Fall of Regulation and the Rise of Governance in Contemporary Legal Thought." *Minnesota Law Review* 89: 342–470; Kaminski, "Binary Governance," p. 1574.

codes of conduct and industry best practices. Kaminski, "Binary Governance," p. 1574.

industry-wide certification programs. Ibid.

45 **European Court of Justice ruling.** Bundesverband der Verbraucherzentralen und Verbraucherverbände – Verbraucherzentrale Bundesverband eV v. Planet49 GmbH, Case C-673/17, [2019] E.C.J.; Tantleff, Aaron K. 2019. "Top European Court Rules Pre-Checked Cookie Consent Boxes Invalid." *The National Law Rev.* October 11.

46 **limitations of language and the legislative drafting process.** Nourse, Victoria and Jane S. Schacter. 2010. "The Politics of Legislative Drafting: A Congressional Case Study." *New York University Law Review* 77(3): 575–623 (pp. 594–596).

debate over standards and rules is as old as the common law. Kelman, Mark. 1990. *A Guide to Critical Legal Studies*. Cambridge, MA: Harvard University Press (pp. 15–63); Schauer, Frederick. 1991. *Playing by the Rules: A Philosophical Examination of Rule-Based Decision-Making in Law and Life*. New York: Oxford University Press (pp. 149–155); Kennedy, Duncan. 1976. "Form and Substance in Private Law Adjudication." *Harvard Law Review* 89: 1685–1778 (pp. 1689–1690).

47 **makes compliance possible.** Bamberger and Mulligan, "Privacy on the Books," pp. 271, 291.

"make certain laws or norms visible or invisible" … "aesthetic of the law." Edelman, *Working Law*, p. 82.

Human resources professionals and lawyers figure prominently. Ibid. pp. 78–80.

lawyers. In-house counsel operate as the chief filters or "gatekeepers" between the law and corporate organizations. Nelson, Robert L. and Laura Beth Nielsen. 2000. "Cops, Counsel, and Entrepreneurs: Constructing the Role of Inside Counsel in Large Corporations." *Law and Society Review* 34: 457–494 (p. 470). Nelson and Nielsen found that in-house counsel routinely used their legal expertise to advance their employers' financial interests, allowing their companies to make more money, pay fewer taxes, escape liability, and reach new markets. Lawyers also needed to maintain their seat at the table by "mak[ing] their advice more palatable to businesspeople."

consultants. Consultants provide advice and counseling. They can design an internal privacy structure or work with in-house teams to build systems to comply with specific laws. They can also serve as outsourced privacy leads. Protiviti, for example, "designs holistic and comprehensive approaches to GDPR compliance" and helps companies with "regulation interpretation; … compliance solutions – people, process and technology execution for an effective cybersecurity and privacy program; [and] Compliance management – monitoring and maintaining controls going forward." GDPR Is Here – Now What?, www.protiviti.com/US-en/technology-consulting/general-data-protection-regulation. Galexia helps companies "understand their legal, regulatory and best practice requirements," and "develop[s] compliance tools, manage stakeholder consultation and architect solutions." Service, www.galexia.com/public/services/.

laws' underlying purposes. The GDPR's first stated goal is "protection of natural persons with regard to the processing of personal data." Regulation (EU) 2016/679 General Data Protection Regulation, 2016 O.J. (L119), art. 1. The underlying purpose of the CCPA is evident from the legislative findings, which noted that "the unauthorized disclosure of personal information and the loss of privacy can have devastating effects for individuals" and "California consumers should be able to exercise control over their personal information, and they want to be certain that there are safeguards against misuse of their personal information." Assemb. B. 375, 2017–18 Reg. Sess., at § 2.

48 **following a decades-long trend in other industries.** Power, Michael. 2007. *Organized Uncertainty: Designing a World of Risk Management.* New York: Oxford University Press.

gloss over the differences among types of risk and often function as barriers to change. Power, *Organized Uncertainty*, pp. 66–102; Power, Michael. 2009. "The Risk Management of Nothing." *Accounting, Organizations, and Society* 34: 849–855.

undervalues intangible harms … overestimates the present value of compliance. Ackerman, Frank and Lisa Heinzerling. 2004. *Priceless: On Knowing the Price of Everything and the Value of Nothing.* New York: New Press; Heinzerling, Lisa. 2014. "Quality Control: A Reply to Professor Sunstein." *California Law Review* 102(6): 1457–1468. Cohen, *Between Truth and Power*, pp. 183–184.

privacy harms are overwhelmingly intangible. Solove, Daniel and Danielle Keats Citron. 2017. "Risk and Anxiety: A Theory of Data-Breach Harms." *Texas Law Review* 96(4): 737–786.

49 **Privacy Risk Management Framework.** National Institutes of Standards and Technology. n.d. *Risk Management*, https://csrc.nist.gov/Projects/Risk-Management/rmf-overview.

"The Risk-Based Approach to Privacy: Risk or Protection for Business." Coraggio, Giulio and Giulia Zappaterra. 2018. "The Risk-Based Approach to Privacy: Risk or Protection for Business?" *Data Protection and Privacy* 1: 339–344.

practical guidebooks. IT Governance Privacy Team. 2017. *EU General Data Protection Regulation (GDPR): An Implementation and Compliance Guide.* Cambridge, UK: IT Governance Publishing (pp. 14–58); Kolah, Ardi. 2018. *The GDPR Handbook: A Guide to Implementing the EU General Data Protection Regulation.* New York: Kogan Page Limited.

PIAs are supposed to help companies. Bamberger, Kenneth A. and Deirdre K. Mulligan. 2012. "PIA Requirements and Privacy Decision-Making in U.S. Government Agencies." In *Privacy Impact Assessments.*

Edited by David Wright & Paul De Hert. New York: Springer Publishing (p. 228).

PIA as a convenient paper trail. Raphaël Gellert highlighted this problem before. Gellert, Raphaël. 2015. "Data Protection: A Risk Regulation? Between the Risk Management of Everything and the Precautionary Alternative." *International Data Privacy Law* 5: 3–19.

50 **technology vendors.** International Association of Privacy Professionals. 2020. "2020 Privacy Tech Vendor Report V.4.2," https://iapp.org/media/pdf/resource_center/2020TechVendorReport.pdf.

"GDPR-Ready Solutions" as ways to avoid "the risk of unprecedented sanctions." ZLTech. n.d. "GDPR-Ready Solutions" (p. 3).

"the next generation ... data privacy platform that helps brands minimize privacy risks." Clarip. n.d. Clarip, www.clarip.com/business.

"data privacy" and "risk management" together. Ethyca. n.d. "Our Mission," https://ethyca.com/about-ethyca/.

"to save time and money and minimize risk through automating processes." 2BAdvice. n.d. "Leading Data Privacy Provider for 18 Years," www.2b-advice.com/en/.

51 **risk minimization Continuing Legal Education programs.** Perkins Coie. 2018. "Privacy and Data Protection: Managing Your Litigation Risk," https://email.perkinscoie.com/9/765/october-2018/you-re-invited–lessons-learned-from-the-us–privacy-and-data-protection—managing-your-litigation-risk(2).asp.

the IAPP and TrustArc published a study. International Association of Privacy Professionals and TrustArc. 2018. "Getting to GDPR Compliance: Risk Evaluation and Strategies for Mitigation," https://iapp.org/media/pdf/resource_center/GDPR-Risks-and-Strategies-FINAL.pdf.

"legal teams might measure success [in privacy] in terms of regulatory risk reduction." Ensign, Melanie. 2020. "Beyond a Compliance Mindset: How We Communicate About Privacy Impacts Our Influence." *Privacy Perspectives*, https://iapp.org/news/a/beyond-a-compliance-mindset-how-we-communicate-about-privacy-impacts-our-influence.

data minimization as a way of reducing corporate risk. International Association of Privacy Professionals. 2016. "Reducing Risk Through Data Minimization," https://iapp.org/store/webconferences/a0l1a000002hDCIAA2/.

doing what "you can too manage the risk to the company." International Association of Privacy Professionals. 2015. "The Role of Risk Management in Data Protection," https://iapp.org/store/webconferences/a0l1a000000SKCzAAO/.

house their privacy officers within their risk management departments. Bamberger, Kenneth A. and Deirdre K. Mulligan. 2011.

"New Governance, Chief Privacy Officers, and the Corporate Management of Information Privacy in the United States: An Initial Inquiry." *Law and Policy* 33: 477–508 (pp. 488, 493–494).

purpose of the requirement is to reduce privacy risks *to consumers*. Birnhack, Michael, Eran Toch, and Irit Hadar. 2014. "Privacy Mindset, Technological Mindset." *Jurimetrics* 55(1): 55–114. The authors state that "the current GDPR text adopts a risk assessment consideration, namely, that the data controller should apply technological measures that are proportionate to the risk; it requires the data controller and processor to implement 'appropriate and proportionate' technical and organizational measures throughout the entire lifecycle of the system" (p. 65).

"risk to the rights and freedoms." Regulation (EU) 2016/679 General Data Protection Regulation, 2016 O.J. (L119), Recital 75.

52 **risk framing can actually encourage compliance.** Edelman, *Working Law*, p. 98.

seats at the table and the capacity to influence policy. Ibid., p. 97.

53 **obscurity.** Hartzog, Woodrow and Evasn Selinger. 2015. "Surveillance as Loss of Obscurity." *Washington and Lee Law Review* 72: 1343–1387.

trust. Waldman, Ari Ezra. 2018. *Privacy as Trust: Information Privacy for an Information Age*. New York: Cambridge University Press; Richards, Neil and Woodrow Hartzog. 2016. "Taking Trust Seriously in Privacy Law." *Stanford Technology Law Rev.* 19(3): 431–472.

consistent distaste for transfers of data to third parties. Martin, Kirsten and Helen Nissenbaum. 2017. "Privacy Interests in Public Records: An Empirical Investigation." *Harvard Journal of Law and Technology* 31: 112–143 (pp. 131–134).

some privacy professionals see the law's requirements as a floor for their work. Bamberger and Mulligan, *Privacy on the Ground*.

54 **compliance "structure."** Edelman, *Working Law*, p. 101.

GDPR requires the designation of a data protection officer. Regulation (EU) 2016/679 General Data Protection Regulation, 2016 O.J. (L119), arts. 37–39, at 55–56.

right to access their information and erase. Regulation (EU) 2016/679 General Data Protection Regulation, 2016 O.J. (L119), arts. 15, 17, at 43–44.

55 **that many Americans think that they are binding, contractual commitments.** Turow, Joseph, Michael Hennessy, and Nora Draper. 2018. "Persistent Misconceptions: Americans' Misplaced Confidence in Privacy Policies, 2003–2015." *Journal of Broadcasting & Electronic Media* 62(3): 461–478.

56 **nondiscrimination policy, with legal-sounding terms of art, or internal dispute resolution systems.** Edelman, *Working Law*, p. 101. Other examples in the employment discrimination context include formal job descriptions that include language of EEO compliance, salary classification systems, personnel and diversity offices, formal job ladders, performance evaluations, and maternity leave policies.
make their voices heard. Tyler, Tom. R. 2006. *Why People Obey the Law*. Princeton, NJ: Princeton University Press (pp. 96, 116–120, 137–138, 149). Tyler is the founder of and primary contributor to research finding that popular perceptions of the legitimacy of authorities depends, at least in part, on the existence of procedural safeguards and the opportunity to be heard. The effect of fair procedure on legitimacy is more pronounced in contexts where procedure matters more, like a trial.

57 **increasingly complex privacy structures.** Bamberger and Mulligan, *Privacy on the Ground*, pp. 83–86.
privacy policies first developed. Haynes, Allyson W. 2007. "Online Privacy Policies: Contracting Away Control Over Personal Information?" *Penn State University Law Review* 111: 587–624 (p. 593); Hetcher, Steven. 2000. "The FTC as Internet Privacy Norm Entrepreneur." *Vanderbilt Law Review* 53: 2041–2062 (pp. 2046–2047); Reidenberg, Joel R. 2001. "E-Commerce and Trans-Atlantic Privacy." *Houston Law Review* 38: 717–749 (p. 726).
they are now required. Waldman, Ari Ezra. 2018. "Privacy, Notice, and Design." *Stanford Technology Law Review* 21: 74–127 (pp. 90–95).
confusing mess of legal jargon. Joel Reidenberg was leading significant research into the use of ambiguous language in privacy policies before his untimely passing in 2020. He noted that "privacy policies often contain ambiguous language describing website practices for data-processing activities. . . . Ambiguity regarding these practices undermines the purpose and value of a privacy policy for website users." Reidenberg, Joel R. et al. 2016. "Ambiguity in Privacy Policies and the Impact of Regulation." *Journal of Legal Studies* 45: S163-S190 (pp. S163-S164). Elsewhere, he argued that "ambiguous wording in typical privacy policies undermines the ability of privacy policies to effectively convey notice of data practices to the general public." Reidenberg, Joel R. 2014. "Disagreeable Privacy Policies: Mismatches Between Meaning and Users' Understanding." *Berkeley Technology Law Journal* 30(1): 39–88.
designed and presented to us to manipulate our behavior. Waldman, "Privacy, Notice, and Design," pp. 107–117.

58 **"how personally identifiable information is collected, used, shared, and maintained."** Privacy Impact Assessments, www.ftc.gov/site-information/privacy-policy/privacy-impact-assessments.

59 **found similar internal tools at work at other companies.** Bamberger and Mulligan, *Privacy on the Ground*, pp. 83–86.

60 **FTC requires.** In re Google, Inc., FTC File No. 102 3136, No. C-4336 (Oct. 13, 2011), www.ftc.gov/sites/default/files/documents/cases/2011/10/111024googlebuzzdo.pdf; Decision and Order at 4, FTC File No. 092 3093, No. C-4316 (Mar. 2, 2011), www.ftc.gov/sites/default/files/documents/cases/2011/03/110311twitterdo.pdf.

Assessments have to be … certify they are operating effectively. In re Google, Inc., FTC File No. 102 3136, No. C-4336 (Oct. 13, 2011), www.ftc.gov/sites/default/files/documents/cases/2011/10/111024googlebuzzdo.pdf (p. 5).

Facebook. Agreement Containing Consent Order, In re Facebook, Inc., Docket No. C-4365, No. 092 3184, at 5 (F.T.C. Nov. 29, 2011), www.ftc.gov/sites/default/files/documents/cases/2012/08/120810facebookdo.pdf (pp. 6–7).

only real weapons in the FTC arsenal. The FTC's authority to impose administrative fines is severely limited. Hoofnagle, *Federal Trade Commission*, p. 166; Solove and Hartzog, "Common Law of Privacy," p. 605. Companies that violate settlement orders are subject to civil penalties up to $16,000 for each violation. Federal Trade Commission. 2018. "Commission Approves Federal Register Notice Adjusting Civil Penalty Amounts," www.ftc.gov/opa/2008/12/civilpenalty.shtm.

heralded as game changers. Leber, Jessica. 2012. "The FTC's Privacy Cop Cracks Down." *MIT Technology Review*, www.technologyreview.com/s/428342/the-ftcs-privacy-cop-cracks-down/; Hill, Kashmir. 2011. "So What Are These Privacy Audits That Google and Facebook Have To Do For the Next 20 Years?" *Forbes*, www.forbes.com/sites/kashmirhill/2011/11/30/so-what-are-these-privacy-auditsthat-google-and-facebook-have-to-do-for-the-next-20-years/.

61 **Audits are independent third-party analyses.** Macey, Jonathan and Hillary A. Sale. 2003. "Observations on the Role of Commodification, Independence, and Governance in the Accounting Industry." *Villanova Law Review* 48: 1167–1187 (p. 1173); Eisenberg, Melvin A. 1997. "The Board of Directors and Internal Control." *Cardozo Law Review* 19: 237–264 (pp. 254–255).

Assessments are based on assertions from management. Gray, Megan. 2018. "Understanding and Improving Privacy "Audits" Under FTC Orders." *Stanford Law School Center for Internet and Society*, https://cyberlaw.stanford.edu/files/blogs/white%20paper%204.18.18.pdf (p. 6).

FTC wanted an assessment to ensure that Google. Agreement Containing Consent Order at 4, In re Google, Inc., FTC File No. 102

3136, No. C-4336 (F.T.C. Mar. 30, 2011), www.ftc.gov/sites/default/files/documents/cases/2011/03/110330googlebuzzagreeorder.pdf (pp. 5–6).
tracking the language of the FTC order explicitly. Federal Trade Commission. 2012. Initial Report on Google's Privacy Program for the Period Oct. 29, 2011–Apr. 25, 2012, https://epic.org/privacy/ftc/googlebuzz/FTC-Initial-Assessment-09-26-12.pdf (p. 9).
based only on. Ibid., p. 14.

62 **formal and serendipitous interactions at workshops.** Edelman described the impact of professional organizations and information resources in the human resources field. Edelman, *Working Law*, p. 79. The IAPP hosts the largest of the privacy professional conferences, attracting thousands of privacy professionals to several events per year. The Privacy+Security Forum (PSF) runs domestic and international conferences for privacy professionals each year, attracting hundreds of attendees to each event. In Europe, the Française de Correspondants à la Protection des Données à Caractère Personnel and the CPDP conferences in Brussels attract members of the privacy professional class as well. American and European privacy leaders have found these meetings essential to "exchange knowledge[,] … discuss issues and … standards and understandings" and "create[] a network of diverse expertise." Bamberger and Mulligan, *Privacy on the Ground*, p. 99.
isomorphism. DiMaggio, Paul J. and Walter W. Powel. 1983. "The Iron Cage Revisited: Institutional Isomorphism and Collective Rationality in Organizational Fields." *American Sociological Review* 48(2): 147–160 (pp. 147–149, 153).

63 **Edelman discussed the managerialization of antidiscrimination law.** Edelman, *Working Law*, pp. 124–150.
managerial values like efficiency, productivity, and stability. Cohen, *Between Truth and Power*, pp. 143–147.

64 **couch their work in terms of diversity, generally.** Edelman, *Working Law*, pp. 140–142 Edelman found that "diversity rhetoric subtly but dramatically reshaped the focus of civil rights compliance by de-emphasizing the focus on race and sex and replacing it with a broad set of dimensions on which organizations can achieve diversity."
managerial (i.e., profit), rather than social, justifications. Ibid. pp. 142–146.
think about diversity in more nebulous terms. Ibid. pp. 149–150; Edelman, Lauren, Sally Riggs Fuller, and Iona Mara-Drita. 2001. "Diversity Rhetoric and the Managerialization of Law." *American Journal of Sociology* 106: 1589–1641 (pp. 1609–1621). The authors note that "diversity rhetoric subtly alters formal legal ideas of diversity

by advocating diversity on a variety of dimensions that go well beyond those specified by civil rights law." This can have a negative effect on equality and civil rights. As Edelman, Fuller, and Mara-Drita show, managerial models of "diversity" elevate categories of diversity – "geographic location, organizational rank, dress style, communication style, and attitudes" – as equally as important as race and gender, thus de-emphasizing the law's focus on"discrimination, injustice, and historical disenfranchisement." Ibid., p. 1632.

tracks the industry literature. Morey, Timothy, Theodore "Theo" Forbath, and Allison Schoop. 2015. "Customer Data: Designing for Transparency and Trust." *Harvard Business Review*, https://hbr.org/2015/05/customer-data-designing-for-transparency-and-trust.

the value proposition is nevertheless shifted. Edelman discussed this in the area of nondiscrimination law, arguing that managerializing internal dispute resolution tilts the scales away from individuals seeking to effectuate their privacy rights and toward corporate interests of efficiency and eliminating disruptions to innovation. Edelman, *Working Law*, pp. 145.

65 **outsourcing is a cost-saving corporate strategy meant to enhance efficiency.** McIvor, Ronan. 2005. *The Outsourcing Process: Strategies for Evaluation and Management*. New York: Cambridge University Press (pp. 40–59).

AuraPortal. "GDPR: Accelerate Compliance in Record Time," www.auraportal.com/product/gdpr/.

DataFleets. IAPP, "Privacy Tech Vendor Report," p. 58.

MinorEye. Ibid., p. 105.

Poslovna Inteligencija. Ibid., p. 116.

"pre-built templates to assess the validity" … "reduc[e] the burden." "Free Schrems II Templates & Solutions to Operationalize Your Response." Email from OneTrust, dated September 1, 2020, at 11:12 AM.

66 **"can now shop among dozens of vendors to find solutions to challenges created."** International Association of Privacy Professionals. 2018. "2018 Privacy Tech Vendor Report," https://iapp.org/media/pdf/resource_center/2018-Privacy-Tech-Vendor-Report.pdf.

67 **routinizable, irrational, imperfect, or just too human.** Pasquale, Frank. 2019. "A Rule of Persons, Not Machines: The Limits of Legal Automation." *George Washington Law Review* 87: 1–55.

"qualitative evaluation and … humble willingness to recalibrate and risk-adjust quantitative data." Pasquale, Frank. 2019. "Professional Judgment in an Era of Artificial Intelligence and Machine Learning." *Boundary2* 46(1): 73–101.

privacy law is reducible. Breaux, Travis D. et al. 2006. "Towards Regulatory Compliance: Extracting Rights and Obligations to Align Requirements with Regulations." *IEEE International Requirements Engineering Conference* 14. In a study that tried to extract minimal compliance requirements from the Health Insurance Portability and Accountability Act, Breaux and his co-authors conceded that "without further validation, it is premature to automate that which is currently performed manually" (p. 57). The authors also noted that "the role of constraints in identifying conflicts between rights and obligations must still be considered. Herein, we only identify trivial conflicts by observing negation and type-similar values in semantic models" (p. 57). That means that the little the research team was able to automate cannot speak for the ability of automation to adequately and correctly address the many facets of law.

68 **legitimacy.** The connection between due process and the legitimacy of law is a well-worn topic in the legal, political science, and philosophical literatures, including: Rawls, John. 1971. *A Theory of Justice.* Cambridge, MA: Belknap Press; Goldberg v. Kelly, 397 U.S. 254, 270 (1970). In *Goldberg*, the Supreme Court stated that "certain principles have remained relatively immutable in our jurisprudence. One of these is that where governmental action seriously injures an individual, and the reasonableness of the action depends on fact findings, the evidence used to prove the Government's case must be disclosed to the individual so that he has an opportunity to show that it is untrue."

erases these safeguards, leaving consumers unprotected. Citron, Danielle Keats. 2008. "Technological Due Process." *Washington University Law Review* 85(6): 1249–1313.

"black box." Pasquale, Frank. 2015. *The Black Box Society: The Secret Algorithms That Control Money and Information.* Cambridge, MA: Harvard University Press.

69 **Corporate goals ... are often thought to be in tension with the substantive goals.** US House of Representatives, Subcommittee on Commerce, Manufacturing, and Trade of the House Committee on Energy and Commerce. 2012. *Balancing Privacy and Innovation: Does the President's Proposal Tip the Scale?.* 105th Cong., 2d sess. (statement of Rep. Marsha Blackburn, Member, H. Comm. on Energy & Commerce). Then-Representative Blackburn stated her opinion that "what happens when you follow the European privacy model and take information out of the information economy? . . . Revenues fall, innovation stalls, and you lose out to innovators who choose to work elsewhere."). The Federal Trade Commission itself sees privacy and profit in conflict. Federal Trade Commission. 2012. "Protecting

Consumer Privacy in an Era of Rapid Change: Recommendations for Businesses and Policymakers," www.ftc.gov/sites/default/files/documents/reports/federal-trade-commission-report-protecting-consumer-privacy-era-rapid-change-recommendations/120326privacyreport.pdf (pp. 7, 15, 26–28).

scholars have shown. Cohen, Julie. 2019. "Turning Privacy Inside Out." *Theoretical Inquiries in Law* 20: 1–31 (pp. 29–30); Cohen, Julie. 2013. "What Privacy Is For." *Harvard Law Review* 126: 1904–1933 (pp. 1919–1920). Cohen stated that this "simplistic" view of privacy as antithetical to innovation and profit "fails to take into account either the nature of innovative practice or the dynamic function of privacy."

70 **we tend to see merely symbolic structures ... as constituting compliance with the law.** Edelman, *Working Law*, pp. 154–155. Here, Edelman noted that in the employment discrimination context, the managerialization of civil rights law encouraged many social groups – from employees to judges – to perceive the mere presence of an anti-discrimination policy, for example, as proof that the company was following Title VII. The same think is happening in privacy.

hollow shells. John Meyer and Brian Rowan called this the "rationalized myth" of formal structures. Meyer, John W. and Brian Rowan. 1977. "Institutional Organizations: Formal Structure as Myth and Ceremony." *American Journal of Sociology* 83: 340–363 (p. 343).

71 **Paul Butler made a similar argument.** Butler, Paul. 2013. "Poor People Lose: Gideon and the Critique of Rights." *Yale Law Journal* 122: 2176–2204.

Gideon v. Wainwright. 327 U.S. 335 (1963).

"more apparent than real." Butler, "Poor People Lose," pp. 2191–2192.

72 **Joe Turow has shown.** Turow, Hennessy, and Draper, "Persistent Misperceptions," p. 463). The authors found that more than half of Americans surveyed believe that a company with a privacy policy does not share customer information with anyone. Other scholarship noting similar problems include: Smith, Aaron. 2014. "What Internet Users Know About Technology and the Web." *Pew Research Center*, www.pewresearch.org/wp-content/uploads/sites/9/2014/11/PI_Web-IQ_112514_PDF.pdf.

likely to give up on privacy navigation. Draper, Nora and Joseph Turow. 2019. "The Corporate Cultivation of Digital Resignation." *New Media & Society* 21(8): 1824–1839; Marwick, Alice and Eszter Hargittai. 2018. "Nothing to Hide, Nothing to Lose? Incentives and Disincentives to Sharing Information With Institutions Online." *Information, Communication & Society* 22(12): 1697–1713; Hargittai, Eszter and Alice Marwick. 2016. "What Can I Really Do? Explaining

the Privacy Paradox With Online Apathy." *International Journal of Communication* 10: 3737–3757.

nihilistic. Hoffman, Christian, Cristoph Lutz, and Giulia Ranzini. 2016. "Privacy Cynicism: A New Approach to the Privacy Paradox." *Cyberpsychology: Journal of Psychosocial Research on .yberspace* 10 (4): 7, http://dx.doi.org/10.5817/CP2016-4-7.

standing requirements. Spokeo, Inc. v. Robins, 136 S. Ct. 1540 (2016); Wu, Felix. 2017. "How Privacy Distorted Standing Law." *DePaul Law Review* 66: 439–461.

tort law. Dwyer v. Am. Express Co., 652 N.E.2d 1351, 1354 (Ill. App. Ct. 1995). The court rejected an intrusion upon seclusion claim against American Express for renting purchase histories because plaintiffs were "voluntarily, and necessarily, giving information to defendants."

contract law. In re JetBlue Airways Corp. Privacy Litig., 379 F. Supp. 2d 299, 316–318 (E.D.N.Y. 2005).

federal privacy statutes. In re Pharmatrak, Inc. Privacy Litig., 292 F. Supp. 2d 263 (D. Mass. 2003). The court granted summary judgement to the defendant, Pharmatrak, on claims that it violated the Electronic Communications Privacy Act because plaintiffs failed to demonstrate the requisite intent.

the FTC's power … is under attack. LabMD, Inc. v. Fed. Trade Comm'n, No. 16–16270, slip op. at 30–31 (11th Cir. June 6, 2018). The Eleventh Circuit held that a consent order requiring a company to overhaul its security practices to meet a general standard of "reasonableness" is unenforceable for vagueness)

privacy is dead. Hartlaub, Peter. 2020. "More Surveillance is Coming. Why That Might Not Be a Bad Thing." *San Francisco Chronicle*, www.sfchronicle.com/culture/article/More-surveillance-is-coming-Why-that-might-not-15481965.php; Friedman, Thomas. 2014. "Four Words Going Bye Bye." *New York Times*, www.nytimes.com/2014/05/21/opinion/friedman-four-words-going-bye-bye.html; Kirkpatrick, Marshall. 2010. "Facebook's Zuckerberg Says the Age of Privacy is Over." *ReadWrite*, https://readwrite.com/2010/01/09/facebooks_zuckerberg_says_the_age_of_privacy_is_ov/; Springer, Polly. 1999. "Sun on Privacy: Get Over It." *Wired*, www.wired.com/1999/01/sun-on-privacy-get-over-it/.

73 **Information Commissioner's Office.** Information Commissioner's Office. 2018. "Guide to the General Data Protection Regulation," https://iapp.org/media/pdf/resource_center/guide-to-the-general-data-protection-regulation-gdpr-1-0.pdf.

74 **dissuaded from mobilizing their rights and investigative powers in the first place.** Cohen, *Between Truth and Power*, p. 145.

GDPR includes documentation requirements. Regulation (EU) 2016/679 General Data Protection Regulation, 2016 O.J. (L119), art. 30(1).

"reasonable and appropriate" steps. First Amended Complaint for Injunctive and Other Equitable Relief at 10, Fed. Trade Comm'n v. Wyndham Worldwide Corp., No. 2:12-cv-01365-PGR (D. Ariz. filed Aug. 9, 2012), www.ftc.gov/sites/default/files/documents/cases/2012/08/120809wyndhamcmpt.pdf.

75 **merely symbolic structures are leveraged ... as actual evidence.** Edelman, *Working Law*, pp. 168, 171–173.

76 **actually settlement agreements with regulated entities.** Solove and Hartzog, "Common Law of Privacy," p. 606. The authors note that "in nearly all of the FTC's Section 5 cases and complaints alleging violations of COPPA, GLBA, and the Safe Harbor Agreement, the final disposition of the matter is a settlement, default judgment, or abandonment of the action by the FTC in the investigatory stage."

77 **FTC also defers to industry practices.** Ibid., p. 636.

United State v. ValueClick. Complaint for Civil Penalties, Permanent Injunction, and Other Equitable Relief at 11, United States v. ValueClick, Inc., No. CV08–01711MMM(RZx) (C.D. Cal. filed Mar. 13, 2008), www.ftc.gov/sites/default/files/documents/cases/2008/03/080317complaint.pdf.

In re Eli Lilly & Co. In re Eli Lilly & Co., 133 F.T.C. 763 (2002) (No.C-4047).

industry custom has long been a yardstick. Trimarco v. Klein, 436 N.E.2d 502, 505 (N.Y. 1982). The New York Court of Appeals, the highest court in New York, stated in *Trimarco* that "when proof of an accepted practice is accompanied by evidence that the defendant conformed to it, this may establish due care." Similarly, in United States v. Carroll Towing Company, 159 F.2d 169, 179 (2d Cir. 1947), the Second Circuit said that "it may be that the custom" in New York Harbor was to not have bargees aboard their boats and if so, that "custom should control."

78 **FTC v. Toysmart.** First Amended Complaint for Permanent Injunction and Other Equitable Relief, Fed. Trade Comm'n v. Toysmart.com, LLC, No. 00–11341-RGS (D. Mass. July 21, 2000), www.ftc.gov/sites/default/files/documents/cases/toysmartcomplaint.htm/.

79 **Facebook was able to lie routinely to the FTC.** Complaint for Civil Penalties, Injunction, and Other Relief at ¶¶ 12, 124, 181, United States v. Facebook, Inc., Case No. 19-cv-2184 (D.D.C. July 24, 2019), www.ftc.gov/system/files/documents/cases/182_3109_facebook_complaint_filed_7-24-19.pdf.

permits assessments to be based entirely on documents Facebook provides to the assessor. Stipulated Order for Civil Penalty, Monetary

Judgment, and Injunctive Relief, United States v. Facebook, Inc., No. 19-cv-2184 (D.D.C. July 24, 2019), www.ftc.gov/system/files/documents/cases/182_3109_facebook_order_filed_7-24-19.pdf.

assessors never looking under the hood. Cohen, *Between Truth and Power*, p. 191. Cohen notes that standards for what is and what is not acceptable tend to develop among auditors, particularly when their work is based on corporate-defined "best practices," leaving the details undiscovered.

80 **research has shown**. Waldman, Ari Ezra. 2017. "Designing Without Privacy." *Houston Law Review* 55: 659–727.

81 **far less substantive impact than scholars have so far presumed**. Bamberger and Mulligan, *Privacy on the Ground*.

82 **Budgets are moral statements of priorities**. Matthews, Dylan. 2017. "Budgets Are Moral Documents, and Trump's is a Moral Failure." *Vox*, www.vox.com/policy-and-politics/2017/3/16/14943748/trump-budget-outline-moral; Wong, Scott. 2011. "Begich: Budget 'A Moral Document." *Politico*, www.politico.com/story/2011/04/begich-budget-a-moral-document-052947; Schakowsky, Jan. 2011. "A Budget is a Moral Document." *The Hill*, https://thehill.com/blogs/congress-blog/economy-a-budget/155827-a-budget-is-a-moral-document.

83 **surveys of the privacy industry**. International Association of Privacy Professionals. 2014. "Benchmarking Privacy Management and Investments of the Fortune 1000," https://iapp.org/media/pdf/resource_center/2014_Benchmarking_Report.pdf (pp. 5, 23).

84 **noticed both siloed departments and smaller silos within those units**. Inkpen, Andrew C. and Eric W. K. Tsang. 2005. "Social Capital, Networks, and Knowledge Transfer." *Academy of Management Review* 30: 146–165 (pp. 152–154).

85 **some in-house counsel are structurally incapable of constraining corporate actions**. Edelman, Lauren B. et al. 1991. "Legal Ambiguity and the Politics of Compliance: Affirmative Action Officers' Dilemma." *Law & Policy* 13(1): 73–97; Vaughan, Diane. 1983. *Controlling Unlawful Organizational Behavior: Social Structure and Corporate Misconduct*. Chicago, IL: Chicago University Press,

lack sufficient independence. Heinz, John and Edward Laumann. 1982. *Chicago Lawyers: The Social Structure of the Bar*. New York: Russell Sage Foundation and the American Bar Association; Nelson, Robert. 1988. *Partners in Power: The Social Transformation of the Large Law Firm*. Berkeley, CA: University of California Press.

"adviser" that facilitates or a "police[]" person who stops bad behavior. Nelson, Robert and Laura B. Nielsen. 2000. "Cops, Counsel, and

Entrepreneurs: Constructing the Role of In-House Counsel in Large Corporations." *Law and Society Review* 34: 457–494 (p. 458).
job conceptualizations have ... a significant impact. Edelman et al., "Legal Ambiguity."
"advocates" ... "team players" ... "professionals" ... "technicians." Ibid. 79–90.

86 **cops, counsel, and entrepreneurs.** Nelson and Nielsen, "Cops, Counsel, and Entrepreneuers."

87 **study of how in-house counsel construct their roles.** Ibid., pp. 462–473.

88 **"allies already."** Hoffmann, Elizabeth A. 2019. "Allies Already Poised to Comply: How Social Proximity Affects Lactation at Work Law Compliance." *Law & Society Review* 53(3): 791–822.

89 **people behave differently in professional contexts than they do in purely social contexts.** Goffman, Erving. 1959. *Presentation of Self in Everyday Life.* New York: Anchor Publishing.
Employers ... will seek out candidates who exhibit ... agreeability, cooperative capacity, and modesty. Worren, Nicolay and Richard Koestner. 1996. "Seeking Innovating Team Players: Contextual Determinants of Preferred Applicant Attributes." *International Journal of Human Resources Management* 7(2): 521–533.
employees at all stages of their career engage in image management to project these qualities. Singh, Val, Savita Kumra, and Susan Vinnicombe. 2002. "Gender and Impression Management: Playing the Promotion Game." *Journal of Business Ethics* 37: 77–89 (p. 78).
"pragmatic silence." Sobkowiak, Włodzimierz. 1997. "Silence and Markedness Theory." In *Silence: Interdisciplinary Perspectives.* Edited by A. Jaworski. Berlin: Mouton de Gruyter.
don't speak up at one time or another. Pinder, Craig C. and Karen Herlos. 2001. "Employee Silence: Quiescence and Acquiescence as Responses to Perceived Injustice." *Research in Personnel and Human Resources Management* 20: 331–369 (p. 344).

90 **substantial evidence that many people loathe the games they have to play.** Singh, Kumra, and Vinnocombe, "Gender and Impression Management," pp. 78–79.

91 **one-quarter of law schools.** Solove, Daniel J. 2015. "Why All Law Schools Should Teach Privacy Law – and Why Many Don't." *Teach Privacy*, www.teachprivacy.com/law-schools-teach-privacy-law-many-dont/.
privacy casebooks. Solove, Daniel J. and Paul M. Schwartz. 2015. *Information Privacy Law.* New York: Aspen Publishing Co. (pp. 180–188, 318–326, 326–335, 365–410 (5th ed.); McGeveran, William. 2016. *Privacy and Data Protection Law.* New York: Foundation Press.

most students major in nontechnical fields. According to information from the Law School Admissions Council, the ten most common majors among law school applicants in the 2015–2016 academic year were, in order, political science, criminal justice, psychology, English, history, economics, philosophy, arts and humanities, sociology, and communications. Law School Admissions Council. 2016. "Undergraduate Majors of Applicants to ABA-Approved Law Schools," www.lsac.org/docs/default-source/data-(lsac-resources)-docs/2015-16_applicants-major.pdf.

92 **Trust is important among members of teams.** Edmondson, Amy C. 2012. "The Local and Variegated Nature of Learning in Organizations: A Group-Level Perspective." In *Sociology of Organizations: Structures and Relationships*. Edited by Mary Goodwyn and Jody Hoffer Gittel. Washington, DC: Sage Publications, Inc.

93 **"technique of power."** Hull, Gordon. 2015. "Successful Failure: What Foucault Can Teach Us About Privacy Self-Management in A World of Facebook And Big Data." *Ethics and Information Technology*. 17(2): 89–101.

Chapter 4

1 **sociotechnical process by which technologies are instantiated with functionality, meaning, and values.** This definition is based in part on the definition of "design" developed in Hartzog, Woodrow. 2018. *Privacy's Blueprint: The Battle to Control the Design of New Technologies*. Cambridge, MA: Harvard University Press (pp. 11–14).

2 **design translates exogenous requirements ... [into] code.** Broussard, Meredith. 2018. *Artificial Unintelligence: How Computers Misunderstand the World*. Cambridge, MA: MIT Press.
filtering or targeting applicants on the basis of race. Angwin, Julia and Terry Parris. 2016. "Facebook Lets Advertisers Exclude Users by Race." *ProPublica*, www.propublica.org/article/facebook-lets-advertisers-exclude-users-by-race; Lecher, Colin. 2019. "Facebook Drops Targeting Options for Housing, Job, and Credit Ads After Controversity." *The Verge*, www.theverge.com/2019/3/19/18273018/facebook-housing-ads-jobs-discrimination-settlement; States Department of Housing and Urban Development v. Facebook, Inc., FHEO No. 01–18–0323–8 (Mar. 28, 2019), www.hud.gov/sites/dfiles/Main/documents/HUD_v_Facebook.pdf.

3 **"semantic architecture."** Flanagan, Mary and Helen Nissenbaum. 2016. *Values at Play in Digital Games*. Cambridge, MA: MIT Press (p. 33).
expresses values. There is a long literature on technological design, its process, and its social construction. This book's definition of design is

based, in part, on work in privacy by design, human-computer interaction, values in design, and science and technology studies. At the Value Sensitive Design Research Lab, for example, design values work by Batya Friedman, Peter Kahn, and Helen Nissenbaum focuses on how to create computer technologies that consider human rights and needs. "What Is Values in Design?" Values in Design, https://valuesindesign.net/about-2/. The values in design approach recognizes that technologies should not just promote values of efficiency, usability, and reliability, but also "the substantive social, moral, and political values to which societies and their peoples subscribe." Flanagan, Mary et al. 2008. "Embodying Values in Technology: Theory and Practice." In *Information Technology and Moral Philosophy*. Edited by Jeroen van der Hoven and John Weckert. New York: Cambridge University Press. Important works in this field on which this book relies include the following: Hartzog, *Privacy's Blueprint*, pp. 11–14; Friedman, Batya and David G. Hendry. 2019. *Value Sensitive Design: Shaping Technology With Moral Imagination*. Cambridge, MA: MIT Press.

4 **design independent of its coercive capacities and political dynamics.** Winner, Langdon. 1980. "Do Artifacts Have Politics?" *Daedalus* 109(1): 121–136.

Nissenbaum and Batya Friedman. "What Is Values in Design?" Values in Design, https://valuesindesign.net/about-2/.

Julie Cohen. Cohen, Julie. 2007. "Cyberspace As/And Space." *Columbia Law Review* 107: 210–256.

Joel Reidenberg. Reidenberg, Joel. 1997. "Lex Informatica: The Formulation of Information Policy Rules through Technology." *Texas Law Review* 76: 553–593.

Woodrow Hartzog. Hartzog, *Privacy's Blueprint*.

"the realities of technology at scale." Hartzog, Woodrow. 2018. "The Case Against Idealising Control." *European Data Protection Law Rev.* 423(4): 423–432 (p. 426).

"made to happen." Giddens, Anthony. 1979. *Central Problems in Social Theory: Action, Strucure, and Contradiction in Social Analysis*. Berkeley, CA: University of California Press.

5 **Tristan Harris … has likened the power of design to a magician's misdirection.** Harris, Tristan. 2016. "How Technology is Hijacking Your Mind – From a Magician and Google Design Ethicist." *Medium*, https://medium.com/thrive-global/how-technology-hijacks-peoples-minds-from-a-magician-and-google-s-design-ethicist-56d62ef5edf3.

Facebook tells us when our friends have 'liked' a page. Waldman, Ari E. 2019. "Cognitive Bias, Dark Patterns, and the 'Privacy Paradox.'" *Current Opinion in Psychology*. 31:105–109.

"dark patterns." Mathur, Arunesh et al. 2019. "Dark Patterns at Scale: Findings from a Crawl of 11K Shopping Websites." *Proceedings of the. ACM on Human-Computer Interaction.* 3(81): 1–32.

platforms nudge us. Thaler, Richard H. and Cass R. Sunstein. 2008. *Nudge: Improving Decisions About Health, Wealth, and Happiness*. New Haven, CT: Yale University Press.

"among the most quietly influential people on the planet."" Thompson, Clive. 2019. *Coders: The Making of a New Tribe and the Remaking of the World.* New York, NY: Penguin Random House LLC (p. 10).

"the decisions they make guide our behavior." Ibid., p. 11.

6 **education.** Waldman, Ari Ezra. 2017. "Designing Without Privacy." *Houston Law Review* 55: 659–727 (pp. 717–722).

"did not design the product with … foresight." Yuan, Eric S. 2020. "A Message to Our Users." *Zoom Blog*, https://blog.zoom.us/wordpress/2020/04/01/a-message-to-our-users/.

"never considered." Privacy International. 2019. "Nobody's Business But Mine: How Menstruation Apps Are Sharing Your Data." *Privacy International*, www.privacyinternational.org/long-read/3196/no-bodys-business-mine-how-menstruations-apps-are-sharing-your-data; Annex 4. "Response from Grupo Familia." www.privacyinternational.org/sites/default/files/2019-09/Annex%204%20Response%20from%20Mi%20calendario.pdf.

7 **complex mental models**: Kang, Ruogo, Laura Dabbish, Nathaniel Frutcher, and Sara Kissler. 2015. "'My Data Just Goes Everywhere'; User Mental Models of the Internet and Implications for Privacy and Security." *2015 Symposium on Usable Privacy and Security*, www.usenix.org/system/files/conference/soups2015/soups15-paper-kang.pdf.

no normative basis for a right to human decision-making … government decisions by "well-calibrated" machines will improve social welfare. Huq, Aziz. 2019. "A Right to a Human Decision." *Virginia Law Review* 106: 611–688.

problems of rules and standards in the law can be entirely avoided … fuzziness of "reasonableness" with simple "microdirectives." Casey, Anthony J. and Anthony Niblett. 2017. "The Death of Rules and Standards." *Indiana Law Journal* 92(4): 1401–1447.

8 **demonstrated the limits of using computational strategies to protect health care privacy.** Pasquale, Frank. 2019. "A Rule of Persons, Not Machines: The Limits of Legal Automation." *George Washington Law Review* 87: 1–55 (p. 20).

artificial intelligence is still incapable of "rule application and value balancing." Crootof, Rebecca. 2019. "'Cyborg Justice' and the Risk of Technological-Legal Lock-In." *Columbia Law Review Forum* 119: 233–251.

computational thinking. Denning, Peter J. 2017. "Remaining Trouble Spots with Computational Thinking." *Communications of the ACM* 60(6): 33–39, https://cacm.acm.org/magazines/2017/6/217742-remaining-trouble-spots-with-computational-thinking/fulltext.

9 **"encrypted [it] at every point" to allow individuals to talk "privately."** Thompson, Clive. 2019. *Coders: The Making of a New Tribe and the Remaking of the World.* New York: Penguin Press (pp. 229–230).

"privacy hackathons" focus exclusively on encryption and security. Ibid.

"write world-changing software ... by 'encrypting.'" Ibid., pp. 234–235.

Pretty Good Privacy. Ibid. 242.

engineers answered by referring to the level of the tools' security: Kang, "My Data Just Goes Everywhere."

10 **choice is disempowering and narrow.** For this discussion, please see Chapter 3, under the subheading "Privacy-As-Control and Corporate Power."

misinterpret our choice to disclose something. There are many cases employing this point of view. For example: Gill v. Hearst Publishing Company, 253 P.2d 441 (Cal. 1953). Daniel Solove calls this the "secrecy paradigm." Solove, Daniel J. 2004. *The Digital Person: Technology and Privacy in the Information Age.* New York: New York University Press (pp. 42–44).

our choices are subject to manipulation. Calo, Ryan. 2013. "Digital Market Manipulation." *George Washington Law Review* 82(4): 995–1051; Schwartz, Paul. 1999. "Privacy and Democracy in Cyberspace." *Vanderbilt Law Review* 52: 1609–1702; Allen, Anita. 1999. "Coercing Privacy." *William and Mary Law Review* 40: 723–758; Reidenberg, Joel et al. 2015. "Privacy Harms and the Effectiveness of the Notice and Choice Framework." *I/S: Journal of Law and Policy for the Information Society* 11: 485–524.

lays the entire burden of protecting our privacy on us. Solove, Daniel J. 2013. "Privacy Self-Management and the Consent Dilemma." *Harvard Law Review* 126(7): 1880–1903.

the working poor, single parents, and other members of marginalized groups. Allen, Anita. 1988. *Uneasy Access: Privacy for Women in a Free Society.* Totowa, New Jersey: Rowman & Littlefield; Bridges, Khiara. 2017. *The Poverty of Privacy Rights.* Stanford, CA: Stanford University Press.

11 **"from the first moment of undergraduate instruction."** Ohm, Paul and Jonathan Frankle. 2018. "Desirable Inefficiency." *Florida Law Review* 70 (4): 777–838 (pp. 778–779).

one of the most important values in computer science and engineering. Lewis, Harry R. and Christos H. Papadimitriou. 1978. "The Efficiency of Algorithms." *Scientific American* 238(1): 96–109

evaluate programming as "good" or "best" based the codes' efficiency. Thompson, *Coders*.

12 **innate.** Ibid., pp. 20, 35, 79; Perry, Dallis and William Cannon. 1968. "Vocational Interests of Female Computer Programmers." *Journal of Applied Psychology* 52(1): 31–35.

"complete waste of time." Thompson, *Coders*, pp. 80–81.

"speed everything up, remove friction everywhere." Ibid., p. 141.

13 **dubious idea: that more data means better predictions about consumer behavior.** Turow, Joseph. 2013. *The Daily You: How the New Advertising Industry Is Defining Your Identity and Your Worth*. New Haven, CT: Yale University Press; Turow, Joseph. 1998. *Breaking Up America: Advertisers and the New Media World*. Chicago: University of Chicago Press.

many of those algorithms are no better and predicting outcomes than traditional statistical modeling: Salganik, Matthew J. et al. 2020. "Measuring the Predictability of Life Outcomes with a Scientific Mass Collaboration." *Proceedings of the National Academy of Sciences of the United States of America* 117(15): 8398–8403.

14 **bystander effect.** Many may remember the bystander effect from a social psychology class, which may discuss the concept with the example of the horrific rape and murder of Kitty Genovese in 1964. Fischer, Peter et al. 2011. "The Bystander-Effect: A Meta-Analytic Review on Bystander Interventions in Dangerous and Non-Dangerous Emergencies." *Psychological Bulletin* 137(4): 517–537; Latané, Bibb and Steve A. Nida. 1981. "Ten Years of Research on Group Size and Helping." *Psychological Bulletin* 89(2): 308–324.

15 **defaults have both direct and indirect effects.** Shah, Rajiv and Jay P. Kesan. 2007. "How Architecture Regulates." *Journal of Architectural and Planning Research* 24(4): 350–359.

16 **territoriality.** Brown, Graham, Thomas B. Lawrence, and Sandra L. Robinson. 2005. "Territoriality in Organizations." *The Academy of Management Review* 30(30): 577–594 (p. 579).

"valued organizational objects over which members make proprietary claims." Ibid. at 579, 580–583 on some benefits of marking, 587–588 on negatives.

17 **marking.** Ibid., pp. 580–583. The authors discuss the negatives of marking at pp. 587–588.

18 **defending.** Ibid., pp. 583–585.

"arena in which an indeterminate struggle unfolds." Orsato, Renato J., Frank den Hond, and Stewart R. Clagg. 2002. "The Political Ecology of Automobile Recycling in Europe." *Organization Studies* 23(4): 639–665; Bartlett, Dean. 2009. "Embedding corporate responsibility:

the development of a transformational model of organizational innovation." *Corporate Governance* 9(4): 409–414.

19 **"technologies ... will reflect the values of [their] creators."** Crawford, Kate. 2016. "Artificial Intelligence's White Guy Problem." *New York Times*, www.nytimes.com/2016/06/26/opinion/sunday/artificial-intelligences-white-guy-problem.html.

technologies will be tested or trained on incomplete data sets. Levendowski, Amanda. 2018. "How Copyright Law Can Fix Artificial Intelligence's Implicit Bias Problem." *Washington Law Review* 93(2): 579–630.

"comprehensive" health app that ... doesn't allow a woman to track her period. Eveleth, Rose. 20104. "How Self-Tracking Apps Exclude Women." The Atlantic, www.theatlantic.com/technology/archive/2014/12/how-self-tracking-apps-exclude-women/383673/.

Mobile assistants do better at understanding male voices. Adam S. Miner et al. 2016. "Smartphone-Based Conversational Agents and Responses to Questions About Mental Health, Interpersonal Violence, and Physical Health." *JAMA Internal Medicine.* 176(5): 619–625.

20 **women are more concerned than men about being watched.** Friedman, Batya et al. 2006. "Value Sensitive Design and Information Systems." In *Human–Computer Interaction and Management Information Systems: Applications*. Edited by Ping Zhang and Dennis Galletta. 5. New York: M. E. Sharpe. 348–372.

poor pregnant women are sapped of their privacy rights. Bridges, Khiara. 2017. *The Poverty of Privacy Rights*. Stanford, CA: Stanford University Press.

21 **mostly male designers lose sight of how their apps are leveraged by other men to stalk, harass, and harm women.** Freed, Diana et al. 2017. "Digital Technologies and Intimate Partner Violence: A Qualitative Analysis with Multiple Stakeholders." *Proceedings of the ACM on Human-Computer Interaction* 1, CSCW, Article 46: 1–22; Thebault, Reis. 2019. "A Woman's Stalker Used an App that Allowed Him to Stop, Start and Track Her Car." *Washington Post*, www.washingtonpost.com/technology/2019/11/06/womans-stalker-used-an-app-that-allowed-him-stop-start-track-her-car/.

social media are designed with men in mind, not women. Citron, Danielle K. 2009. "Cyber Civil Rights." *Boston University Law Review* 89(2): 61–125; Citron, "Law's Expressive Value."

gendered nature of online platforms' obsession with free speech. Franks, Mary Anne. 2019. *The Cult of the Constitution*. Stanford, CA: Stanford University Press; Franks, Mary Anne. 2012. "Sexual Harassment 2.0." *Maryland Law Rev.* 71(3): 655–704.

13 **engineering pride.** Thompson, Clive. 2019. *Coders: The Making of a New Tribe and the Remaking of the World.* New York, NY: Penguin Random House (p. 7).
seemingly impossible problems. Ibid. p. 16.
solve puzzles with precision. Ibid. p. 30.
"unlock the latent energy." Ibid. p. 57.
stewards of customer data. Bamberger and Mulligan, "Privacy on the Ground," p. 271.
14 **performances are actions and behaviors that communicate.** Goffman, Erving. 1959. *The Presentation of Self in EverydayLife.* New York: Anchor Publishing (p. 15).
constitute or create reality. Callon, Michel. 2007. "What Does It Mean to Say That Economics Is Performative?." In MacKenzie, Donald et al. eds., *Do Economists Make Markets? On the Performativity of Economics.* Princeton, NJ: Princeton University Press, pp. 311–357.
economy. Ibid.
identity. Butler, Judith. 1990. *Gender Trouble: Feminism and the Subversion of Identity.* London: Routledge.
15 **"present[] an information environment in which individuals see themselves as functioning autonomously."** Hull, Gordon. 2015. "Successful Failure: What Foucault Can Teach Us About Privacy Self-Management in A World of Facebook And Big Data." *Ethics and Information Technology.* 17(2): 89–101 (p. 96).
Characterizing privacy as a question of formal autonomy. Ibid., p. 97.
actions "establish[] ... a moral conduct that commits an individual." Foucault, Michel. 1985. *The Use of Pleasure.* Tranlated by Robert Hurley. New York: Vintage Books (p. 28).
"paradigmatic instance of the operation of power." Hull, "Successful Failure," p. 97.
"it is a total structure of actions brought to bear upon possible actions." Foucault, Michel. 1982. "The Subject and Power." In *Michel Foucault: Beyond Structuralism and Hermeneutics* (pp. 108–226). Edited by H. L. Dreyfus and P. Rabinow. Chicago, IL: University of Chicago Press (p. 220).
16 **corporate surveillance becomes the norm.** Marxist scholars would call this "hegemony." Gramsci, Antonio. 1971. *Selections from the Prison Notebooks of Antonio Gramsci.* Edited by Quintin Hoare and Geoffrey Nowell. New York: International Publishers.
17 **mass scheme of subordination.** Viljoen, Salomé. 2021. "Democratic Data: A Relational Theory for Data Governance." Unpublished manuscript.

18 **"socialized individuals ... as exemplars, as standardized products."** Habermas, Jurgen. 1987. *The Philosophic Discourse of Modernity*. Cambridge, MA: MIT Press (p. 293).
"subversive subjectivity cannot be explained within the framework." Balbus, Isaac. 1988. "Disciplining Women." In *After Foucault*. Edited by Jonathan Arac. New Brunswick, NJ: Rutgers University Press (p. 152).

19 **"when individuals or groups manage to block a field of relations of power."** Foucault, Michel. 1988. "The Ethic of Care for the Self as a Practice of Freedom." *The Final Foucault*. Edited by David Rasmussen. Cambridge, MA: MIT Press (p. 3).

20 **"giv[ing] one's self the rules of law, the techniques of management."** Ibid., p. 18.

Chapter 6

1 **"Gradually, we will accept much, much greater surveillance."** Hartlaub, Peter. 2020. "More Surveillance is Coming. Why That Might Not Be a Bad Thing." *San Francisco Chronicle*, www.sfchronicle.com/culture/article/More-surveillance-is-coming-Why-that-might-not-15481965.php
"privacy is over." Friedman, Thomas. 2014. "Four Words Going Bye Bye." *New York Times*, www.nytimes.com/2014/05/21/opinion/friedman-four-words-going-bye-bye.html.
"the age of privacy is over." Kirkpatrick, Marshall. 2010. "Facebook's Zuckerberg Says the Age of Privacy is Over." *ReadWrite*, https://readwrite.com/2010/01/09/facebooks_zuckerberg_says_the_age_of_privacy_is_ov/.
we "have zero privacy anyway. Get over it." Springer, Polly. 1999. "Sun on Privacy: Get Over It." *Wired*, www.wired.com/1999/01/sun-on-privacy-get-over-it/.

2 **Regulatory paranoia.** Short, Jodi. 2012. "The Paranoid Style in Regulatory Reform." *Hastings Law Journal* 63(3): 633–694 (p. 635).
fear of getting too involved in the marketplace. In his comprehensive analysis of the history and development of the FTC, Chris Hoofnagle notes that after several years of rulemaking authority, the Federal Trade Commission Improvement Act of 1980 placed additional procedural hurdles in the FTC's rule-making powers. For example, the Act introduced direct Congressional oversight. And the law explicitly prohibited the FTC from using funds for three years "for the purpose of initiating any new rulemaking proceeding … which prohibits or otherwise regulates any commercial advertising." The Act did much "political and psychological damage to the Agency." Notably, the FTC

does have general rulemaking authority under the Children's Online Privacy Protection Act and the Gramm-Leach-Bliley Act. Hoofnagle, Chris. 2016. *Federal Trade Commission Privacy Law and Policy*. New York: Cambridge University Press.

"rules of the road." Kaminski, Margot and Meg Leta Jones. 2020. "An American's Guide to the GDPR." *Denver Law Review* 98(1).

3 **conflating ... liberty with the freedom to do anything.** Janus v. American Federation of State, City, and Municipal Employees Council 31, 138 S. Ct. 2448 (2018); NeJaime, Douglas and Reva Siegel. 2015. "Conscience Wars: Complicity-Based Conscience Claims in Religion and Politics." *Yale Law Journal* 124: 2516–2591; NeJaime, Douglas. 2012. "Marriage Inequality: Same-Sex Relationships, Religious Exemptions, and the Production of Sexual Orientation Discrimination." *California Law Review* 100: 1169–1238; Liptak, Adam. 2018. "How Conservatives Weaponized the First Amendment." *New York Times*, www.nytimes.com/2018/06/30/us/politics/first-amendment-conservatives-supreme-court.html.

confused the choice to share information with friends. Daniel Solove calls this the "secrecy paradigm." Solove, Daniel J. 2004. *The Digital Person: Technology and Privacy in the Information Age*. New York: New York University Press (pp. 42–44).

is the same as voluntarily consenting to a government search. This is known as the Third-Party Doctrine. Although it has been questioned in limited circumstances by the Supreme Court, the doctrine still holds that, as a matter of Fourth Amendment law, individuals do not have an expectation of privacy in information that is in the hands of third parties. Carpenter v. United States, Smith v. Maryland, 442 U.S. 735 (1979); United States v. Miller, 425 U.S. 435 (1976); Kerr, Orin. 2009. "The Case for the Third-Party Doctrine." *Michigan Law Review* 107: 561–601; Murphy, Erin. 2009. "The Case Against the Case for Third-Party Doctrine: A Response to Professor Epstein and Kerr." *Berkeley Technology Law Journal* 24: 1239–1253.

4 **complicit.** This sentiment is often restated in movements for social justice. For example, Desmond Tutu said, "If you are neutral in situations of injustice, you have chosen the side of the oppressor." Younge, Gary. 2009. "The Secrets of a Peacemaker." *Guardian*, www.theguardian.com/books/2009/may/23/interview-desmond-tutu.

5 **"common denominator" ... "with those particular things varying from context to context."** Solove, Daniel J. 2010. *Understanding Privacy*. Cambridge, MA: Harvard University Press.

civility, deference, and demeanor. Post, Robert. 1989. "The Social Foundations of Privacy: Community and Self in the Common Law Tort." *California Law Review* 77: 957–1010.

Erving Goffman. Goffman, Erving. 1967. *Interaction Ritual.* New York: Anchor House.

flow of information through and among social networks. Strahilevitz, Lior. 2005. "A Social Networks Theory of Privacy." *University of Chicago Law Review* 72: 919–988.

"context-relative informational norms." Nissenbaum, Helen. 2010. *Privacy in Context: Technology, Policy, and the Integrity of Social Life.* Palo Alto, CA: Stanford University Press (p. 141).

"govern the flow of personal information in distinct social contexts." Ibid. p. 3.

6 **special weight and special protection for sexual privacy.** Citron, Danielle Keats. 2019. "Sexual Privacy." *Yale Law Journal* 128: 1870–1960.

7 **"digital poorhouse."** Eubanks, Virginia. 2018. *Automating Inequality: How High Tech Tools Profile, Police, and Punish The Poor.* London, UK: St. Martin's Press.

"sexual privacy." Citron, Danielle Keats. 2019. "Sexual Privacy." *Yale Law Journal* 128: 1870–1960.

queer people particularly vulnerable. Skinner-Thompson, Scott. 2020. *Privacy At the Margins.* New York: Cambridge University Press.

poor mothers have been systematically deprived of their privacy rights. Bridges, Khiara. 2017. *The Poverty of Privacy Rights.* Palo Alto, CA: Stanford University Press.

necessary element of human flourishing. This hasn't been a particularly robust research agenda in privacy and human flourishing, so this is a particularly ripe arena for future study. Substantial work has been done on conceptualizing what human flourishing means, in general: Nussbaum, Martha. 2011. *Creating Capabilities: The Human Development Approach.* Cambridge, MA: Harvard University Press; Sen, Amartya. 1999. *Development as Freedom.* Oxford, UK: Oxford University Press; Sen, Amartya. 2004. "Elements of a Theory of Human Rights." *Philosophy and Public Affairs* 32(4): 315–356.

8 **"complement work" … do not "counterfeit" humans.** Pasquale, Frank. 2020. *New Laws of Robotics: Defending Human Expertise in the Age of AI.* Cambridge, MA: Harvard University Press (pp. 4–9). **"channel technologies of automation."** Ibid., p. 2.

democracy, equality, and power. Britton-Purdy, Jedediah, David Grewal, Amy Kapczynski, and K. Sabeel Rahman. 2020. "Building a Law-and-Political-Economy Framework: Beyond the Twentieth-Century Synthesis." *Yale Law Journal* 129: 1784–1835 (p. 1821, 1824, 1827).

9 **accountable "to those who live" within it.** Ibid., p. 1827. **First Amendment to limit what government can do to protect privacy.** Sorrell v. IMS Health, Inc., 564 U.S. 552 (2011).

trade secrecy transforms. Pasquale, Frank. 2015. *Black Box Society*. Cambridge, MA: Harvard University Press (p. 14). **Section 230 of the Communications Decency Act immunizes.** Citron, Danielle Keats and Benjamin Wittes. 2017. "The Internet Will Not Break: Denying Bad Samaritans §230 Immunity." *Fordham Law Review* 86: 401–423; Sylvain, Olivier. 2018. "Intermediary Design Duties." *Connecticut Law Review* 50: 203–277.

10 **"social subordination."** Britton-Purdy et al., "Building a Law-and-Political-Economy Framework," p. 1824.

11 **complicit in maintaining traditional power structures**. MacKinnon, Catharine. 1989. *Toward a Feminist Theory of the State*. Cambridge, MA: Harvard University Press; Allen, Anita. 2011. *Unpopular Privacy: What Must We Hide?* New York, NY: Oxford University Press; McLain, Linda. 1995. "Inviolability and Privacy: The Castle, The Sanctuary, and The Body." *Yale Journal of Law and Humanities* 7: 195–241; MacKinnon, Catharine A. 1991. "Reflections on Sex Equality Under Law." *Yale Law Journal* 100: 1281–1328; MacKinnon, Catharine A. 1983. "Feminism, Marxism, Method, and the State: Toward Feminist Jurisprudence." *Signs* 8: 635–658; State v. Rhodes, 61 N.C. 453 (1868).

privilege of the wealthy. Gilman, Michele Estrin. 2012. "The Class Differential in Privacy Law." *Brooklyn Law Review* 77: 1389–1445; Barron, James H. 1979; Tokson, Matthew and Ari Ezra Waldman. 2021. "Social Norms and the Fourth Amendment." *Michigan Law Review* 119.

12 **trust-based definitions of privacy**. Waldman, Ari Ezra. 2018. *Privacy as Trust: Information Privacy for an Information Age*. New York: Cambridge University Press; Richards, Neil and Woodrow Hartzog. 2016. "Taking Trust Seriously in Privacy Law." *Stanford Technology Law Rev*. 19(3): 431–472.

data collectors should be treated as fiduciaries of our information. Richards and Hartzog, *A Duty of Loyalty*; Solove, *Digital Person*, p. 102; Citron, Danielle Keats. 2012. "Big Data Brokers as Fiduciaries." *Concurring Opinions*, www.concurringopinions.com/archives/2012/06/big-data-brokers-as-fiduciaries.html; Balkin, Jack M. and Jonathan Zittrain. 2016. "A Grand Bargain to Make Tech Companies Trustworthy. *The Atlantic*, www.theatlantic.com/technology/archive/2016/10/information-fiduciary/502346/. Balkin, Jack M. 2016. "Information Fiduciaries and the First Amendment." *University of California Davis Law Review* 49: 1183–1234 (p. 1186).

duty of loyalty … rebuttable presumption. Richards, Neil and Woodrow Hartzog. n/d. "A Duty of Loyalty for Privacy Law." Unpublished

manuscript, https://papers.ssrn.com/sol3/papers.cfm?abstract_id=3642217.

13 **machines safer.** Grimshaw v. Ford Motor Co., 119 Cal. App. 3d 757, 800–806 (1992) (Ford Pinto case).
seatbelts. AlliedSignal, Inc. v. Moran, 231 S.W.3d 16, 28 (Tex. App. 2007).
stronger automobile frames. Dyson v. Gen. Motors Corp., 298 F. Supp. 1064, 1074 (E.D. Pa. 1969).
safer doors. Seliner v. Ford Motor Co., No. 2002–30454, 2004 WL 5014479 (Tex. Dist. Ct. 2004).
side impact protection. Dawson v. Chrysler Corp., 630 F.2d 950, 958 (3d Cir. 1980).
other car safety features. Am. Ass'n for Justice, Driven to Safety: How Litigation Spurred Auto Safety Innovations 4–11 (2010).

14 **corporate-friendly standing requirements.** Spokeo, Inc. v. Robins, 136 S. Ct. 1540 (2016).
privacy harms. Solove and Citron, "Risk and Anxiety," p. 755.
litigate not just for individual wins ... but for structural advantage. Galanter, Mark. 1974. "Why the 'Have' Come Out Ahead: Speculations on the Limits of Legal Change." *Law and Society Review* 9: 95–160.
"catalyz[e] a societal shift toward a thicker notion of industrial responsibility." Cohen, Julie. 2017. "Information Privacy Litigation as a Bellwether for Institutional Change." *DePaul Law Review* 66: 535–578 (p. 575). As Cohen notes "strictness toward information privacy claims align with the interests of powerful information businesses that are repeat players in the litigation system. But debates about injury-in-fact in the information economy do not simply reflect a banal story of interest group capture. Rather, they hint at a more complex process involving both deep capture and institutional path-dependence. Deep capture – or capture at the level of ideology – proceeds as well-resourced repeat players work to craft compelling narratives about the contours of legal entitlements and the structure of legal institutions" (p. 555).

15 **"perfect tool of oppression."** Hartzog, Woodrow and Evan Selinger. 2018. "Facial Recognition is the Perfect Tool of Oppression." *Medium*, https://medium.com/s/story/facial-recognition-is-the-perfect-tool-for-oppression-bc2a08f0fe66.
criminalize ... nonconsensual pornography or "revenge porn." Citron, Danielle Keats and Mary Anne Franks. 2014. "Criminalizing Revenge Porn." *Wake Forest Law Review* 49: 345–391.
"second wave." Pasquale, Frank. 2019. "The Second Wave of Algorithmic Accountability." *Law and Political Economy*. Accessed

https://lpeblog.org/2019/11/25/the-second-wave-of-algorithmic-accountability/.

uses of AI to replace, rather than support, human work. Pasquale, Frank. 2015. "To Replace or Respect: Futurology as if People Mattered." *Boundary2*, www.boundary2.org/2015/01/to-replace-or-respect-futurology-as-if-people-mattered/.

16 **a new agency tasked specifically with privacy enforcement.** Reidenberg, Joel R. 2003. "Privacy Wrongs in Search of Remedies." *Hastings Law Journal* 54 877–898 (pp. 887–888).

purpose of rulemaking. Jordan III, William S. 2000. "Ossification Revisited: Does Arbitrary and Capricious Review Significantly Interfere with Agency Ability to Achieve Regulatory Goals through Information Rulemaking?" *Northwestern University Law Review* 94: 393–450 (p. 394).

"procedurally burdensome" process of Magnuson-Moss rulemaking. Solove, Daniel J. and Woodrow Hartzog. 2011. "The FTC and the New Common Law of Privacy." *Columbia Law Review* 114(3): 583–676 (p. 620).

40 years. Ibid. p. 620 n. 176.

what many practitioners do. Ibid. p. 585.

ten privacy-related settlements per year. Solove an Hartzog, "The New Common Law," p. 600.

"unfair and deceptive" practices. 15 U.S.C. § 45(a)(4)(B).

17 **requires publicly traded companies to have a completely independent audit committee.** Sarbanes-Oxley Act of 2002 § 301, 15 U.S.C. § 78j-1, Pub. L. 107–204, 116 Stat. 745; SEC Listing Standards Relating to Audit Committees, 17 C.F.R. § 240.10A-3; SEC Standards Relating to Listed Company Auditing Requirements, 68 Fed. Reg. 18788. "Independent" means not being affiliated with the company other than as a director or receiving any compensation other than for serving as a director. Sarbanes-Oxley Act, § 301.

"appointment, compensation, and oversight." Sarbanes-Oxley Act § 301.

mechanism for anonymously reporting questionable accounting. Sarbanes-Oxley Act §§ 301, 407.

sign financial statements. Sarbanes-Oxley Act § 302; 17 C.F.R. § 228.

18 **"sit on the periphery of the regulatory state."** Cohen, Julie. 2019. *Between Truth and Power: The Legal Constructions of Informational Capitalism*. New York: Oxford University Press (pp. 192–193).

19 **corporate climate dedicated to privacy has a more significant impact on designers than formal policies.** Oshrat Ayalon et al., *How Developers Make Design Decisions About Users' Privacy: The Place of Professional*

Communities and Organizational Climate, Companion of the 2017 ACM Conference on Computer Supported Cooperative Work and Social Computing (2017).

20 **erode trust and, as a result, prevent the exchange of information.** Inkpen and Tseng, "Social Capital," pp. 152–154.

21 **Groups focused on the cyber civil rights of.** Consider, for example, the Cyber Civil Rights Initiative, www.cybercivilrights.org, the Detroit Community Technology Project, www.detroitcommunitytech.org/, Data 4 Black Lives, https://d4bl.org/, and the National Network to End Domestic Violence, https://nnedv.org/.
"gig economy" workers. Dubal, V. B. 2017. "Wage Slave or Entrepreneur?: Contesting the Dualism of Legal Worker Identities." *California Law Review* 105: 65–159; Dubal, V. B. 2021. "Invisible Work, Visible Workers: Visibility Regimes in Online Platforms for Domestic Work." In *Beyond the Algorithm: Qualitative Insights for Gig Work Regulation*. Edited by Deepa Das Acevedo. New York: Cambridge University Press.

22 **cyber civil rights.** Danielle Citron proposed a cyber civil rights agenda more than a decade ago. Citron, Danielle Keats. 1009. "Cyber Civil Rights." *Boston University Law Review* 89: 61–125.

23 **firing of the AI researcher Timnit Gebru.** Hao, Karen. 2020. "We Read the Paper that Forced Timnit Gebru Out of Google. Here's What It Says." *MIT Technology Review*, www.technologyreview.com/2020/12/04/1013294/google-ai-ethics-research-paper-forced-out-timnit-gebru/. **ordinary workplace pressures facing in-house compliance professionals.** Edelman, Lauren et al. 1991. "Legal Ambiguity and the Politics of Compliance: Affirmative Action Officers' Dilemma." *Law and Policy* 13: 73–97.

24 **collective incapacity to write robust new environmental laws indirectly enhances corporate power.** Ovide, Shira. 2020. "Big Tech Versus Climate Change." *New York Times*, www.nytimes.com/2020/07/23/technology/big-tech-climate-change.html; Ovide, Shira. 2020. "The Tech Giants' Invisible Helpers."*New York Times*, www.nytimes.com/2020/07/08/technology/internet-infrastructure.html.

25 **"help[] practitioners develop and advance their careers" and help "organizations manage and protect their data."** International Association of Privacy Professionals. n.d. About the IAPP: IAPP Mission and Background, https://iapp.org/about/mission-and-background/.

26 **plans to create a technical university.** Gershgorn, Dave. 2020. "Former Google CEO Wants to Create a Government-Funded University to Train A.I. Coders." *Medium: One Zero*, https://onezero.medium.com/former-google-ceo-wants-to-create-a-government-funded-university-to-train-a-i-coders-9a2df09c5bce.

Google created its own post-secondary certificate program. Fain, Paul. 2019. "Employers as Educators." *Inside Higher Ed*, www.insidehighered.com/digital-learning/article/2019/07/17/amazon-google-and-other-tech-companies-expand-their.
expanding their partnerships with colleges to offer credit-based versions. Ibid.

27 **"work[s] with industry on self-regulation."** Federal Trade Commission. 2012. "Protecting Consumer Privacy in an Era of Rapid Change," www.ftc.gov/sites/default/files/documents/reports/federal-trade-commission-report-protecting-consumer-privacy-era-rapid-change-recommendations/120326privacyreport.pdf.
use rhetoric that presumes privacy law and innovation are in conflict. US Senate, Committee on Commerce, Science, and Transportation. 2019. *Policy Principles for a Federal Data Privacy Framework in the United States*. 116th Cong., 2d sess. S. Hearing Record (oral statement of Maria Cantwell).

Appendix

1 **An organization is a network.** Gray, Garry C. and Susan S. Sibey. 2014. "Governing Inside the Organization: Interpreting Regulation and Compliance." *American Journal of Sociology* 120(1): 96–145.
involves – or, at least, *should* involve – many people. Scholars of the sociology of science have long understood that technology and design are social institutions: they involve people and things, not just code. New technologies are the products of networks of people working together within organizations and under constraint. And they are constructed, or situated and understood in society, by people outside those organizations, all of whom have biases, interests, and prior assumptions that color their approaches to new devices. Bijker, Wiebe E. et al. eds. 2012. *The Social Construction of Technological Systems: New Directions in the Sociology and History of Technology*. Cambridge, MA: MIT Press; Callon, Michel. 1984. "Some Elements of a Sociology of Translation: Domestication of the Scallops and the Fisherman of St. Brieuc Bay." In *Power, Action and Belief: A New Sociology of Knowledge?* edited by John Law, 196–229. London: Routledge & Kegan Paul; Callon, Michel. 1986. "The Sociology of an Actor-Network: The Case of the Electric Vehicle." in *Mapping the Dynamics of Science and Technology* edited by Michel Callon, Arie Rip, and John Law, 19–34. Basingstoke, Hants: Macmillan; Latour, Bruno. 1988. *Science in Action: How to Follow Scientists and Engineers Through Society*. Cambridge, MA: Harvard University Press; Bijker, Wiebe E. 1987. *Technology and Heterogeneous Engineering: The Case of*

Portuguese Expansion. Cambridge, MA: MIT Press. Therefore, if we want to understand the ways privacy is or is not integrated into design, and the ways in which people can influence the design process to suit their own ends, social scientists ask us to engage in on-the-ground fieldwork studying the people involved.

2 **actor-network theory (ANT)**. ANT is more of a research method than a sociological theory. It posits that the development of knowledge should be understood by analyzing how individuals and groups interact because the social and natural world is a "continuously generated effect of the webs of relations." Law, John. 2009. "Actor Network Theory and Material Semiotics." in *The New Blackwell Companion to Social Theory*, edited by B. S. Turner. Oxford: Blackwell-Wiley (p. 141). The canonical literature on ANT includes the following: Callon, Michel. 1984. "Some Elements of a Sociology of Translation: Domestication of the Scallops and the Fisherman of St. Brieuc Bay." In *Power, Action and Belief: A New Sociology of Knowledge?* edited by John Law, 196–229. London: Routledge & Kegan Paul; Callon, Michel. 1986. "The Sociology of an Actor-Network: The Case of the Electric Vehicle." in *Mapping the Dynamics of Science and Technology* edited by Michel Callon, Arie Rip, and John Law, 19–34. Basingstoke, Hants: Macmillan; Latour, Bruno. 1988. *Science in Action: How to Follow Scientists and Engineers Through Society*. Cambridge, MA: Harvard University Press; Bijker, Wiebe E. 1987. *Technology and Heterogeneous Engineering: The Case of Portuguese Expansion*. Cambridge, MA: MIT Press.

"cultural practice." Law, "Actor Network Theory and Material Semiotics," p. 143.

Louis Pasteur's anthrax vaccine. Latour, Bruno. 1993. *The Pasteurization of France*. Cambridge, MA: Harvard University Press.

Latour and Steve Woolgar studied the "construction" of scientific facts. Latour, Bruno and Steve Woolgar. 1979. *Laboratory Life: The Construction of Scientific Facts*. Princeton, NJ: Princeton University Press. They concluded that facts aren't really discovered; it isn't enough to make a biochemical discovery in a petri dish. Rather, what becomes understood as "fact" is a product of scientists following routine lab practices – beta tests, transcription, persuasion, draft paper circulation, among others – while being pressured to publish and under the constraint of limited research funding.

"bush pump." Originally developed for European industry, the first Zimbabwean "bush pump" was designed to bring water to rural communities and build Zimbabwe's farming culture. But the pumps were more than innovations of mechanical engineers. It was a hydraulic device to provide water, a public health device that enhanced community health,

a democratic technology that requires entire communities to maintain and repair, and a nation-building device. It also reflected embedded politics: at first it was a tool to support imperial powers that wanted to extract natural resources from their colonies with brutal efficiency; it then became a tool of the post-colonial government to enhance national public health and industry. de Laet and Mol argue that because the pumps' role in society was socially, rather than purely mechanically, constructed, it would be impossible to reduce its invention to one person or group. It was a product of engineering, manufacturing, narratives about farming and technology, community adaptation, local expertise, and national and international politics. This means that if we want to understand how, if at all, privacy factors into design, we have to look at the people involved, how they work together, and the institutions that support or burden them. Laet, Marianne de, and Annemarie Mol. 2000. "The Zimbabwe Bush Pump: Mechanics of a Fluid Technology." *Social Studies of Science* 30(2): 225–263.

3 **"follow[ing] the actors" with "voluntary blindness."** Latour, Bruno. 2005. *Reassembling the Social: An Introduction to Actor-Network-Theory*. New York, NY: Oxford University Press (p. 57).

"define themselves." Latour, Bruno. 1993. *We Have Never Been Modern*. Cambridge, MA: Harvard University Press (p. 51).

feminist scholars have critiqued ANT. Collins, H. M. and Steve Yearly. 1992. "Epistemological Chicken." In *Science as Practice and Culture*, edited by Andrew Pickering. Chicago: University of Chicago Press

groups excluded from that process for "structural" reasons. Wajcman, Judy. 2000. "Reflections on Gender and Technology Studies: In What State is the Art?" *Social Studies of Science*. 30(3): 447–464 (p. 452).

focusing too much on the "heroic" and "entrepreneurial" efforts of (mostly male) designers. Star, Susan L. 1990. "Power, Technology, and the Phenomenon of Conventions: On Being Allergic to Onions." In *Technoscience: The Politics of Interventions*, edited by Kristin Asdal et al. 2007 (pp. 79–109); Star, Susan L. 1990. "Power, Technology, and the Phenomenon of Conventions: On Being Allergic to Onions." *In A Sociology of Monsters: Essays on Power, Technology and Domination*, edited by John Law. 1991. London: Routledge (pp. 26–56).

4 **"big science."** Delamont, Sara. 1987. "Three Blind Spots? A Comment on the Sociology of Science by a Puzzled Outsider." *Social Studies of Science* 17(1): 163–170 (p. 166); Rossiter, Margaret. 1982. *Women Scientists in America: Struggles and Strategies to 1940*. Baltimore, MD: Johns Hopkins University Press.

women helped change the design of ... the microwave. Cockburn and Ormod, *Gender and Technology in the Making*.

reproductive technologies. Clarke, Adele and Virginia L. Olesen. 1999. *Revisioning Women, Health and Healing: Feminist, Cultural and Technoscience Perspectives.* New York, NY: Routledge.
computers. Turkle, Sherry. 1984. *The Second Self: Computers and the Human Spirit.* New York, NY: Simon & Schuster, Inc.
other household devices. Cowan, Ruth Schwartz. 1983. *More Work for Mother: The Ironies of Household Technology from the Open Hearth to the Microwave.* United States: Basic Books, Inc.; Lerman, Nina et al. 1997. "The Shoulders We Stand on and the View from Here: Historiography and Directions for Research." *Technology and Culture* 38(1): 9–30 (p. 11).
research on the failure of a proposed state-of-the-art fighter jet for the Royal Air Force. Law, John and Michel Callon. 1992. "The Life and Death of an Aircraft: A Network Analysis of Technical Change." In *Shaping Technology/ Building Society: Studies in Sociotechnical Change,* edited by Wiebe E. Bijker and John Law. Cambridge, MA: MIT Press.
"consumption junction." Cowan, Ruth Schwartz. 1987, "The Consumption Junction: A Proposal for Research Strategies in the Sociology of Technology." In *Common Themes in Sociological and Historical Studies of Technology,* edited by Wiebe Bijker et al. Cambridge, MA: MIT Press. 261–281.

5 **"once the lens is widened to … end-users of technologies."** Wajcman, "Reflections on Gender," p. 453.

6 **ideas, laws, bureaucracies, and resources involved.** Scholars have argued that law works alongside code to establish behavioral rules on digital platforms. In a prescient article published in 1997, the law professor and one of the original founders of the field of privacy law, Joel Reidenberg, argued that although "law and government regulation have [historically] established default rules for information policy, including constitutional rules on freedom of expression and statutory rights of ownership of information. … Technological capabilities and system design choices impose rules on participants" in the information economy. Several years later, Lawrence Lessig made roughly the same argument, noting that law, code, norms, and markets work together to regulate human behavior, both online and off. Market forces put pressure on corporate design strategies. Law and norms also do more than coerce behavior; they have expressive effects that remind us what society thinks is appropriate and they set the terms for thinking about what design should and should not do. Reidenberg, Joel R. 1997. "Lex Informatica: The Formulation of Information Policy Rules through Technology." *Texas Law Review* 76 (3): 553–593; Lessig, Lawrence. 2006. *Code: Version 2.0.* New York, NY: Basic Books.

7 **interface ethnography**. Ortner, Sherry. 2010. "Access: Reflections on Studying Up in Hollywood." *Ethnography* 11(2): 211–233. Ortner coined the phrase "interface ethnography" to refer to ethnographic research conducted at events, like up fronts, held and organized by the company and open to the public. These moments are choreographed, but they do offer the opportunity to see how companies are positioning themselves and, in certain situations, ask questions.

8 **"the powerful are out of reach ... not all in one place."** Nader, Laura. 1969/1974. "Up the Anthropologist – Perspectives Gained from Studying Up." In *Reinvesting Anthropology*, edited by Dell Hymes. New York: Vintage Books.

"the worlds of technoscientific knowledge production are notoriously difficult to study." Monahan, Torin and Jill A. Fisher. 2015. "Strategies for Obtaining Access to Secretive or Guarded Organizations." *Journal of Contemporary Ethnography* 44(6): 709–736.

"for a variety of reasons, would prefer to avoid outside scrutiny." Ibid., p. 710.

9 **assist the organization in some way as a condition of access**. Patton, Michael Quinn. 2002. *Qualitative Research and Evaluation Methods*. Thousand Oaks, CA: Sage.

"covert research." Monahan and Fisher, p. 715.

10 **reticent to subject their internal processes to analysis**. This raises the problem of access for sociologists and other social science researchers. For a discussion of this research hurdle and steps to overcome it, please see Ortner, "Access," pp. 219–221.

11 **anthropologist timidity**. Nader, "Up the Anthropologist," p. 302.

12 **snowball sampling**. Goodman, Leo A. 1961. "Snowball Sampling." *The Annals of Mathematical Statistics*. 32(1): 148–170; Coleman, James S. 1958. "Relational Analysis: The Study of Social Organizations with Survey Methods." *Human Organization*. 17(4): 28–29; Welch, Susan. 1975. "Sampling by Referral in a Dispersed Population." *The Public Opinion Quarterly*. 39(2): 237–238; Granovetter, Mark. 1973. "The Strength of Weak Ties." In *American J. of Sociology*. 78(6): 1360–1380. The University of Chicago Press.

13 **attended privacy industry conferences**. I was invited to speak at the IAPP conference, the ESMT Annual Forum, CyberWeek 2018, and the Privacy + Security fora. Funding for travel to the IAPP conference, the ESMT Annual Forum, and CyberWeek 2018 was provided by the organizers of those conferences.

14 **response bias**. Response bias refers to a series of tendencies in which survey respondents do not answer questions honestly. I was particularly concerned with what social scientists call social desirability bias, where

survey respondents answer questions in ways that make them appear more favorable to the experimenter. For additional research and a collection of the seminal literature on response bias, please see Nederhof, Anton J. 1985. "Methods of Coping with Social Desirability Bias: A Review." *European Journal of Social Psychology* 15(3): 263–280.

15 **critical discourse analysis methodology**. Van Dijk, Teun. 1993. "Principles of Critical Discourse Analysis." *Discourse and Society* 2(4): 249–283; Gramsci, Antonio. 1971. *Selections from the Prison Notebooks*. New York: International Publishers Co; Fairclough, Norman. 1992. *Discourse and Social Change*. New York: Cambridge University Press; Chouliaraki, Lilie and Norman Fairclough. 1999. *Discourse in Late Modernity: Rethinking Critical Discourse Analysis*. Edinburgh, UK: Edinburgh University Press.

sociologists in the Goffmanian tradition. Katriel, Tamar and Gerry Philipsen. 1981. "'What We Need is Communication': 'Communication' as a Cultural Category in Some American Speech." *Communication Monographs*. 48(4): 302–317; Blum-Kulka, Shoshana. 1997. *Dinner Talk: Cultural Patterns of Sociability and Socialization in Family Discourse*. New York: Routledge.

linguistic anthropologists. Silverstein, Michael. 1996. "Monoglot 'Standard' in America: Standardization and Metaphors of Linguistic Hegemony." In *The Matrix of Language: Standardization and Metaphors of Linguistic Hegemony*, edited by Ronald Brenneis and K. S. Macauley. New York: Routledge.

Marxist scholars. Some examples include Volosinov, V. N. 1986. *Marxism and the Philosophy of Language*. Cambridge, MA: Harvard University Press; Butler, Judith. 1986. *Gender Trouble: Feminism and the Subversion of Identity*. New York: Routledge; MacKinnon, Catharine. 1989. *Toward a Feminist Theory of the State*. Cambridge, MA: Harvard University Press.

16 **privacy concerns involved in any ethnographic project.** Van Den Hoonaard, Will. 2003. "Is Anonymity an Artifact in Ethnographic Research." *Journal of Academic Ethics* 1: 141–151.

INDEX